Religion Popular and Unpopular
in the Early Christian Centuries

Professor W.H.C. Frend

W. H. C. Frend

Religion Popular and Unpopular in the Early Christian Centuries

VARIORUM REPRINTS
London 1976

ISBN 0 902089 89 7

Published in Great Britain by   *Variorum Reprints*
                                 21a Pembridge Mews London W11 3EQ

Printed in Great Britain by   *Kingprint Limited*
                                 Richmond Surrey

VARIORUM REPRINT CS45

CONTENTS

This volume contains a total of 396 pages

PREFACE

The twenty-five essays brought together in this volume attempt to do two things. They try first to present a picture of some aspects of early Christian civilisation and secondly they represent some of their authors scholarly interests over the past thirty-five years.

My original approach to the history of the early Church was not through Classics or Theology, but as an historian with a keen interest in historical geography and field archaeology. The Romano-Celtic temple at Maiden Castle with Mortimer Wheeler rather than the Theology school at Oxford beckoned. Hence the approach of these essays to their subjects is more non-theological than might be expected. Theological issues, however, are not burked, for only through a study of these can one penetrate into the mind of the early Church and its believers. History and doctrine are inseparable in the study of Christianity.

My main interest in Christianity is as a civilisation. How and when did it emerge from Judaism, how did its mission and its relations with other non-Christian societies in the Ancient World develop? What factors underlay the major schismatic and heretical movements from the 4th to the 7th century? How did the Roman empire appear to the Christians of the time? These are some of the issues I have considered in these essays included in this volume. Finally, the chance I was able to take to work for the Egypt Exploration Society in 1963-1964 (and again in 1972 and 1974) at Q'asr Ibrim in Nubia quickened my interest in the rise, decline and extinction of Christianity in the Nile valley between Azwan and the Ethiopian border.

What to leave out? As the objective was the clear-cut presentation of themes, I have left out all technical archaeological reports and individual discoveries, such as the Sulmenli inscription,[1] or the fine late-Nubian scrolls or Homer papyri from Q'asr Ibrim.[2] I have omitted also accounts of Christianity in Roman Britain for these will be superseded as a result of the sensational find of Roman Christian silver from Water Newton, in Hunts.[3] Modern studies, such as the discussion of the role of the German Foreign

Ministry in the years before World War II,[4] and the interview I had with officials in the German embassy in the Vatican immediately after the anti-Hitler plot (22 July 1944)[5] have suffered the same fate. The one concession I have allowed myself is the Peter Ainslie Memorial Lecture given at Rhodes University in August 1964 where the challenge of multiracial society in South Africa is related to some problems in early Church history. It is hoped that this volume will be of use to students and at the same time give some much needed encouragement to the study of early Christianity in the United Kingdom.

I am grateful to Variorum Reprints for their invitation to publish this collection of essays and to their original publishers for permission to reproduce the articles for which they hold the copyright.

W. H. C. FREND

Glasgow University

1   "A third century inscription relating to *Angariae* in Phrygia". Journal of Roman Studies, XLVI, 1956, pp. 46-56.

2   The scrolls await publication. The Homer papyri are recorded in the Proc. XIV International Congress of Papyrologists, Oxford, 1974 (Egypt Exploration Society, Greco-Roman Memoirs, 61, pp. 103-11).

3   "Religion in Roman Britain during the Fourth Century", *Journal of the British Archaeological Assoc.*, 3rd Ser. XVI, 1955, pp. 1-19, and "The Christianisation of Roman Britain". *Christianity in Britain 300-700* (ed. M.W. Barley and R.P.C. Hanson), Leicester University Press, 1968, pp. 37-51.

4   "Hitler and his Foreign Ministry", *History*, XLII, 1956, pp. 118-129.

5   Published in *Foreign Relations*, Vol. I, pp. 532-537.

I

The Persecutions: some Links between Judaism and the Early Church[1]

Each generation of historiographers has had its own interpretation of the persecutions. In their hour of triumph in the years following the Council of Nicaea, Christians in both halves of the Roman Empire looked back to these events as the heroic age of the Christian faith. The sufferings of the Church were linked to the sufferings of the children of Israel[2] and this time, too, anti-Christ and his abettors, the pagan emperors, their officials and the mobs had been worsted. Like the Egyptians they had perished miserably. But, as so often happens, victory dissolved the common bonds which united the victors. In the next centuries the relations between Church and State in the East and West were to follow different paths. In the East the 'martyrdom in intention'[3] of the monastic life tended to replace the martyrdom in deed in opposition to the emperor. In the West, the martyr tradition was to underline that same opposition. Tertullian, Hilary, Ambrose, Gregory VII, Boniface VIII embody a single trend of ideas extending over a thousand years.

If one seeks to trace back these ideas to their origins, one is at once thrown into the long drawn out debate on the relations between early Christianity and the Roman Empire. 'Coercitio' or 'institutum neroniarum', the protagonists of each have left their mark on three-quarters of a century of historical writing.[4] But the approach is narrow, and it is noticeable that even Grégoire[5] and his pupil Moreau,[6] in two of the latest assessments of the persecutions, have not sought to enlarge it significantly. It is, moreover, difficult to accept, because it appears to isolate one

[1] I would like to acknowledge the advice I have received from G. E. M. de Ste. Croix in preparing this article.

[2] Paulus Orosius, *Historia adversum Paganos*, C.S.E.L., v, vii. 27. Cf. *Liber Genealogus* (*Chronica Minora*, i. 196, ed. Mommsen). Seven persecutions before the coming of Antichrist—a Donatist view.

[3] The phrase is taken from the seventh-century novel, *Barlaam and Joasaph* (ed. Woodward and Mattingley, xii. §103). Monasticism arose 'from men's desire to become martyrs in will that they might not miss the glory of them that were made perfect by blood'.

[4] See the brilliant summary by A. N. Sherwin White, 'The Early Persecutions and Roman Law again', *J.T.S.*, N.S. iii (1952), 199–213.

[5] Henri Grégoire, 'Les Persécutions dans l'Empire romain', in *Mém. de l'Académie royale de Belgique*, Cl. des Lettres, xlvi, fasc. i, 1951.

[6] J. Moreau, *La Persécution du Christianisme dans l'Empire romain*, Mythes et Religions, Paris 1956.

particular aspect of the problem which a militant, apocalyptic and monotheistic religion presented to the Mediterranean world. The initiative was not always on the pagan side. Persecution had its counterpart in martyrdom, and the consideration of the one cannot be divorced from consideration of the other. Without the suffering and the death of the righteous at the hands of earthly rulers the Messianic Age would not dawn nor would the Second Coming take place. In addition, the emphasis on the legal and official aspects of the persecutions tends to ignore the background of long-standing and endemic religious hatred in the cities of the Hellenistic East, which the Christians inherited. As Grégoire points out, up to the time of Origen the Christian mission was essentially Greek, even in the Western provinces of the Empire.[1] If one understands the nature of these hatreds, one may be well on the way towards understanding the relations of the Church and the pagan world in the first two centuries. We will try to show how some of the elements of the crises in which the Church was embroiled during that period were present in the antagonism of Jew and Greek in the previous era. Moreover, part of the confusion over the legal status of Christians may possibly have its origins in the different standing enjoyed by Jews in Rome and in the Hellenistic East respectively. We will try to understand the history of the early Christian mission as a continuation of the great internal problem which confronted the Roman Empire, namely the containment of Judaism.

As Casey has recently stated, in a discussion on the origins of Gnosticism, 'however much philosophy may have softened the blow, conversion to Christianity involved submission to the Jewish way of conceiving the origins of the universe and much of the history of mankind.'[2] This appears to be true in the first two centuries, both as regards the outward organisation and outlook of the Christians,[3] and more important from our point of view, as regards the attitude of the provincials towards them. Though the writer of the *Letter to Diognetus* could claim justifiably that Christians had abandoned the fussiness and ritualism of Jewry,[4] many of those things which interested Christians most could hardly be understood apart from current Jewish usage. Let us take two examples out of many. For instance, it seems evident that as late as A.D. 170 the Christians in the province of Asia continued to observe the Jewish Passover, and that the recently published *Homily on the Passion* of Melito of Sardis is to be regarded as a Paschal Haggadah closely parallel to the type used by Jews to-day.[5]

---

[1] H. Grégoire, op. cit., 18.

[2] R. P. Casey, 'Gnosis, Gnosticism and the New Testament' in *The Background of the New Testament and Eschatology*, ed. W. H. Davies and D. Daube, 1956, 56.

[3] The literature on this subject is very extensive. Here one would direct attention to F. Gavin, *The Jewish Antecedents of the Christian Sacraments*, S.P.C.K., 1928; C. W. Dugmore, *The Influence of the Synagogue upon the Divine Office*, Oxford 1944; T. G. Jalland, *The Origin and Evolution of the Christian Ministry*, London 1948, iv, and the paper by Gerh. Loeschke, *Jüdisches und Heidnisches im Christlichen Kult*, Bonn 1906.

[4] *Ep. ad Diognetum* (ed. Kirsopp Lake), iv. 6.

[5] F. L. Cross in a paper read to the Cambridge Theological Society on 28 February 1957, and summarised in the *Cambridge University Reporter* lxxxvii. No. 45, 1957, p. 1468.

Nearly half a century later the dispute between Callistus and Tertullian on the ability of the Church to forgive deadly sins had an equally syna-gogal background. These sins, idolatry, apostasy and bloodshed are just those which in A.D. 132 Rabbi Akiba had defined as ones to be avoided, if necessary, by martyrdom.[1] That is, they were sins against God for which there could be no earthly forgiveness. The problem in A.D. 220 was whether the Christian Church should continue to maintain the Jewish standpoint or not, and the victory of Callistus was a significant step along the road of full emancipation from Judaism.

Though the authorities had made a clear distinction between Christians and Jews since A.D. 64, that did not prevent them from associating them both as adherents of a single monotheistic creed springing from the same root and potentially hostile to Greco-Roman society.[2] Thus in A.D. 202 Septimius Severus forbade proselytism to Judaism and Christianity alike.[3] Celsus, writing some twenty-five years earlier, assumed that Christians were primarily rebels against Judaism.[4] Galen follows the same line when he brackets 'the followers of Moses and the followers of Christ' as people on whom rational argument was a waste of time.[5] These indications suggest that an effort to consider the general problem of the persecutions within the framework of the relationship between Judaism and the Ancient World has at least the merit of being the way in which its inhabitants were wont to regard Christianity.

This accepted, the story of the persecutions should begin not with Nero but with the Maccabees. The great struggle between the Jews and the Seleucid kings foreshadows the characteristic outlook of the Jews and Christians, on the one hand, and the authorities and their supporters on the other. These outlooks persist to a remarkable degree down to the conversion of Constantine. For, whatever the incidental causes of the conflict,[6] such as the greed of Antiochus IV, his ill-advised interference in a purely internal Jewish quarrel, or his desire to punish specific acts of Jewish disloyalty, the issue came to be dominated by religion. Both the earlier and later Diaspora traditions, represented by II and IV Maccabees respectively, and the Palestinian tradition enshrined in I Maccabees make this quite clear. Antiochus's edict of 168/67 B.C. had as its object 'that they (the Jews) should forget the Law and change the ordinances' (I Macc., i. 49) or 'that they should leave the law of their fathers' (II Macc., vi. 1)

---

[1] L. Finkelstein, *Akiba: Scholar, Saint and Martyr*, New York 1936, 261. The question was a burning one, and Akiba's view was upheld by a majority vote only at the synod of Lydda in 135. *Talmud Babli*, Sanhedrin, ii. 74a (ed. Epstein, London 1935, 502).

[2] For a trace of this view, perhaps taken direct from Tacitus, see Sulpicius Severus, *Chronicon* (ed. Halm, C.S.E.L., i) ii. 30. 7.

[3] Spartian, *Vita Severi*, 17. 1.

[4] Celsus in Origen, *Contra Celsum* (ed. Koetschau, tr. H. Chadwick), ii. 1 and ii. 4.

[5] Galen, *De Differentiis Pulsuum* 3, cited from G. Waltzer, *Galen on Jews and Christians*, Oxford 1949, 37 ff. Cf. Origen, *Contra Celsum*, iv. 23.

[6] For emphasis on the political aspects of Antiochus's measures, see E. Bickermann, *Der Gott der Makkabäer*, Berlin 1937, and a corrective by J. Dancy, *1 Maccabees: a Commentary*, Oxford 1954.

or, in detail, 'that each individual of the nation should taste unclean food through tortures and abjure Judaism' (IV Macc., iv. 26). The penalty for disobedience was death. But in the eyes of the Jew the name of God was being blasphemed (II Macc., viii. 4) and he, like the Christian after him, knew that he must give his life for the sanctification of the Name.[1]

The object of the pagan rulers is portrayed as securing abjurations (ἐξόμνυσθαι τὸν 'Ιουδαισμόν).[2] This would be involved by the public (b'parhesia) transgression of the prohibition of idolatry coupled with the profanation of the divine name. The same means were employed by the Alexandrines against Jewesses in the great pogrom of A.D. 38.[3] The objective was, therefore, identical with that of the magistrates conducting trials of Christians. For a Hierocles in Bithynia during the Great Persecution[4] or for a Carthaginian magistrate in Tertullian's time the moment of triumph was when the Christian recanted.[5] The story of the Maccabees, too, shows that in certain circumstances the profession of Judaism could be a crime. In II Macc., xiv. 38–46 Razis is actually accused of Judaism and prefers to anticipate his fate by committing suicide. The case does not stand alone. In Wisdom, ii. 18–19, there is an interesting passage that can hardly refer to anything else but a trial on the charge of Judaism.[6] Though the identification of the accusing party is uncertain, the words 'Let us examine him with despitefulness and torture . . . let us condemn him with a shameful death' are susceptible of no other meaning. Clearly, in the Hellenistic East the Jewish 'nomen' could be the subject of persecution long before the Romans or Christianity appeared on the scene.

In opposition to this persecuting activity by the Hellenistic rulers one may trace the Jews' glorification of the martyr's lot, and the duty of destroying the symbols of pagan civilisation. This, as recent discoveries at Cyrene have shown, was taken quite literally. In A.D. 115 the great temple of Zeus there was destroyed by the Jewish rebels.[7] The story of the scribe Eleazer as told in II Macc., vi. 24–vii. 42 taught that no deviation from Torah was permitted and, secondly, that the reward for martyrdom was eternal rest with the patriarchs hereafter. The martyr represented Israel. Personally innocent, he expiated the sin of a guilty people. His death hastened the coming of God's mercy. Martyrdom was thus both the means of personal resurrection and an act of atonement on behalf of God's

---

[1] Note for instance, Pesaḥim, 53b (ed. Epstein, London 1935, 261), citing the example of the Three Holy Children. For Christian suffering for the Name, Hermas, Vis., iii. 1. 9 and Simil., ix. 28.

[2] IV Macc., iv. 26 (ed. Hadas, 167–168).

[3] Philo, In Flaccum (ed. Colson), xi. 96.

[4] Lactantius, Div. Inst. (ed. Brandt, C.S.E.L., xxvii. i), v. 11. 15.

[5] Tertullian, Apol., ii. 13.

[6] The expression κρίσιν εἰσενηνεγμένος 'Ιουδαισμοῦ, is strong, suggesting a legal charge, but what the χρόνοις τῆς ἀμιξίας were, which provided the pretext, is uncertain.

[7] R. G. Goodchild, Cyrene p. 71 and P. M. Fraser and S. P. Appelbaum, "Hadrian and Cyrene", Journ. Rom. Studies, XL, 1950, 83 ff.

people as a whole. Both these ideas played their part in Christian martyr-dom.

One need not be surprised, therefore, that martyrdom came to be regarded as a natural and integral part of the Jewish way of life. In the great crises of A.D. 40 and A.D. 66 Josephus describes in detail how thousands of Jews were prepared to die rather than perform an idolatrous act.[1] No friend of extremism himself, he wrote in c. A.D. 95, 'For it becomes natural to all Jews immediately and from their very birth to esteem those books (of the Law) and, if occasion be, willingly to die for them.'[2] Such conduct could be expected from the citizens of 'a theocracy'.[3] Such tendencies were powerfully reinforced by a development to which Fischel has recently drawn attention, namely, for the figure of the prophet to become merged with that of the martyr.[4] The killing of the prophets had become a commonplace in Judaism by the time the Synoptists wrote (Mt., xxiii. 35–37 and Lk., xiii. 34), and the story of the sawing asunder of Isaiah or the murder of Zechariah may be regarded as typical. These facts, coupled with an apocalyptic view of history involving the utter destruction of the Gentiles, complete the background of the tense and horrible situation which developed in the Hellenistic East in the last two centuries B.C.

Two cultures, religious and secular, confronted one another. One must remember, too, that the lines were not static. Jewish proselytism was proverbial (Mt., xxiii. 15), and successful proselytism was destructive alike of the institutions and family life of the classical world.[5] On the other hand, lapses and outright apostasies from Judaism were not infrequent, and these in their turn released fresh waves of hatred.[6] Our sources, pagan and Jewish alike, leave no doubt as to the intensity of ill-feeling which separated Jew and non-Jew in the Greek East throughout the whole period between the Maccabaean wars and Bar Kochba's revolt. There is no need to over-stress the point. Alexandria, Antioch, Damascus, Caesarea, Halicarnassos, Miletus, Ephesus and Laodicea, to mention some examples only, were the scenes of pogroms and acts of repression.[7] Pagan rulers were described as plotting the utter destruction of Jewry in their dominions.[8] One incident out of very many deserves record. In c. A.D. 67 the Jews were massacred at Antioch because they were accused (falsely) of attempting

[1] Particularly, *Antiquities*, xviii. 8 and *Wars*, ii. 10, recording the incidents at Ptolemais and Tiberias in A.D. 40.

[2] Josephus, *Contra Apionem* (ed. Niese, tr. Whiston), i. 8. 42.

[3] Josephus's term: *Contra Apionem*, ii. 16. 165.

[4] H. A. Fischel, 'Prophet and Martyr', *Jewish Quarterly Review*, xxxvii (1946/7), 265 ff. and 363 ff.

[5] The view expressed by Tacitus, *Histories*, v. 5. 2. The Jewish convert 'exuere patriam, parentes, liberos, fratres vilia habere'. For the Christian's similar attitude, Tertullian, *Ad Nationes*, ii. 1 (C.S.E.L., xx. 94 lines 8–12) and *Passio Perpetuae* (ed. Knopf), 3.

[6] See, for instance, III Macc., vii. 10–23 (Hadas, 81).

[7] The situation is described in Philo, *In Flaccum*, iv. 18–xvii. 145 and Josephus, *Antiquities*, xiv. 10 ff., xvi. 2. 3, *Wars*, ii. 18. 1–2 and 7; 20. 2 and vii. 3. 3.

[8] The theme of Esther and III Maccabees.

to set fire to the city—an interesting parallel to the accusation against the Christians in Rome three years earlier. Furthermore, the test applied by the magistrates to identify Jews and proselytes was that of sacrifice.[1] The Jews, it was believed, had forfeited their special status and therefore must sacrifice 'ὥσπερ νόμος ἐστὶ τοῖς ''Ελλησιν'. 'Sacrifice or die'. Here is the situation which was to be all too familiar in pagan-Christian relations. So also were the charges of 'atheism', 'haters of the human race', 'sacrilegious' and 'ritual murderers', hurled against the Jews[2]. It is not difficult to understand how this pattern of embittered relationships could be transferred to a body which popular opinion regarded as a criminal and dangerous off-shoot of Judaism. The same fears and prejudices which produced the pogroms of the period 170 B.C.–A.D. 135 contributed to the anti-Christian outbreaks in the same areas in the second and early third centuries A.D.

So much for the Hellenistic world. In Rome itself, by contrast, the Jews were in an exceptional position. First, they were only one of a large number of foreign cults which the crowds of immigrants from the east had brought with them from the second century B.C. onwards. Secondly, Jews and Romans begin their association as friends and allies against the Seleucids. Indeed, right through the second and first centuries B.C., Rome found the Jews a useful counterpoise in Asia Minor and later in Syria and Egypt against the perpetual grumbling hostility of the Greek autonomous cities. The protection of valuable Jewish privileges in these cities by Julius Caesar and Mark Antony was the result.[3] Hence, in Rome there was the tendency to regard Judaism as a national cult, albeit an unattractive one, and to apply to it the same regulations as governed other foreign cults.[4] From the outset, however, proselytism among Roman citizens was discouraged, if not actually forbidden. The expulsion of the Jews by the Praetor Peregrinus Cornelius Hispalus in 139 B.C. on the ground that they were 'tainting Roman manners with the worship of Jupiter Sabazius'[5], and the affairs of Fulvia in Tiberius's reign[6], and probably also of Pomponia Graecina in A.D. 57, are illustrations.[7] Such recorded instances were few and far between. Relations between Rome and the Jews were on a different and more cordial plane from those of Jews and Greeks in the Hellenistic East, and the fact was acknowledged in the speech which Josephus puts into the mouth of Titus in A.D. 70 (*Jewish War*, vi. 6. 2). No Greek city would have bestowed even-handed justice on Jews and Isis-worshippers alike as did Tiberius in A.D. 19.[8] Where action was taken against the Jews it was on grounds of acts violating the

---

[1] Josephus, *Wars*, vii. 3. 3.

[2] For the catalogue of accusations and reproaches showered on the Jews found in classical authors, J. Juster, *Les Juifs dans l'Empire romain*, Paris 1914, 45. n. 1.

[3] Josephus, *Antiquities*, xiv. 8. 3, and xiv. 10.

[4] On Rome's relations with the Jews, E. G. Hardy, *Christianity and the Roman Government*, 1925 ed., ii, and G. J. Foakes Jackson and Kirsopp Lake, *The Beginnings of Christianity*, i. 163 f.

[5] Valerius Maximus, i. 3. 2.

[6] Josephus, *Antiquities*, xviii. 3. 5.

[7] Tacitus, *Annals*, xiii. 32.

[8] Josephus, *Antiquities*, xviii. 3. 4.

pax deorum, or disturbing the peace,[1] complaints which could be levelled at other cults besides theirs.

In the first decades of the first century A.D. there is some evidence that, quite apart from the mad act of Caligula directed against the Jews in Palestine, the official friendship between Rome and the Jews was breaking down. In the first place, the rebellious tendencies of the Greeks in Asia Minor were lessening. The cult, first of Dea Roma, and then of Augustus, at last provided them with a focus of religious loyalty. Outside of Alexandria, where the *Acts of the Pagan Martyrs* show how the Roman administration continued to be regarded as anti-Hellenic and pro-Jewish until well into the second century A.D.,[2] the Greek became as loyal to the Imperial idea as any other citizen of Augustus's empire. Thus, Rome no longer needed the Jewish counterpoise. Moreover, the establishment of the Imperial cult for the first time linked the fortunes of Rome with those of Hellenism against the Jews. Then came the Alexandrine riots of A.D. 38 and 40. Claudius's solemn warning to the Jewish embassy of A.D. 41 is significant of what was to follow.[3] After confirming Jewish privileges as they stood in the reign of Augustus, he concluded, 'if they continued to introduce or invite Jews who sail down from Syria and Egypt, thus compelling me to conceive greater suspicion, I will by all means take vengeance upon them as fomenting a general plague on the whole world.'[4] The Jewish threat was now seen as world-wide. Would that of the Christians be regarded otherwise? The Christian Church could hardly have entered on the stage of history at a less favourable moment. Within twenty years the charge of moving sedition among all the Jews throughout the world was to be made against them (Acts, xxiv. 5). Rome's position in the East no longer depended on the loyalty of the Jews; it would hardly require concessions to the 'tertium genus'.

But had Rome the means to hand for dealing with a 'world conspiracy'? Much as modern historians may stress the relevance of measures designed to frustrate the effects of astrologers, magicians, Druids, and other violators of the '*pax deorum*',[5] it is questionable whether these provide the full answer. In the East these measures seem to have been combined with the sanctions long adopted in the Greek cities against 'atheism'. This term was not readily naturalised into Latin usage,[6] but as we shall see, was very relevant with regard to Christianity. It may well form the connecting link between the Roman and Hellenistic legal systems in

---

[1] Suetonius, *Claudius*, 25. 4.

[2] Ed. H. A. Musurillo, *The Acts of the Pagan Martyrs*, Oxford 1954. The *Acta Appiani* may relate to events as late as A.D. 190, while the *Acta Hermaisci* must be Trajanic or later. (Musurillo, 211 and 168).

[3] See H. I. Bell, *Jews and Christians in Egypt*, Oxford 1924, 25.   [4] Ibid.

[5] For the importance of these measures in understanding the attitude of the authorities towards the Christians, see H. Last, 'The Study of the "Persecutions"', *J.R.S.*, xxvii (1937) 80–92 and art. 'Christenverfolgung', *Reallexicon für Antike u. Christentum*, ii. 1159 f. and 1208 f.

[6] It is not until Arnobius (*Adv. Gentes*, i. 29) writing at the end of the third century, that the term is used in Latin in the pagan-Christian controversy.

dealing with the early Church. In the mind of Dio Cassius writing in the 220s, magic and atheism were the twin dangers threatening the religious peace and therefore the prosperity of the Empire.[1] Misbelief was such an offence in the Hellenistic rather than the Roman world.[2] The Latin 'sacrilegium' implied more positive action—'deos destruere'.[3] Rome left unchanged so many of the characteristic institutions of the Hellenistic East. Like the *angareia*, was not 'atheism' and the public trial before the authorities on grounds of religion another of the legacies of Hellenism to Rome in the administration of the Empire?

How far then does the history of the early Church's relations with the pagan world in fact continue these same developments? Let us first take the meaning attached to martyrdom in the early Church. Here the *praeparatio evangelica* of Judaism seems obvious enough. Similarities of detail apart, such as those illustrated by Fischel in the Jewish and Christian *Acta Martyrum*,[4] the broad development from the one to the other seems undeniable. Complete obedience to God, where necessary in defiance of the authorities, expiatory sacrifice, self-abnegation on behalf of the People, and the reward of blessed immortality in anticipation of the approaching end of the world, are already firmly established ideas. Perhaps it is no accident that the term μαρτυρεῖν or διαμαρτυρεῖν applied to 'blood witness' first occurs in IV Maccabees.[5] The Jewish martyr bore witness to the Law, the Christian to the New Law. Those things which the Jew resisted to the death, such as idolatry, including the eating of 'impure' meats, and blood-shed, including duty in a pagan army, the Christian was to resist also. Yet martyrdom in Judaism was something of a *Hamlet* without the Prince. However much the Law might be regarded as 'pre-existent from Creation' and the 'breath of the Power of God',[6] the Jews' sufferings were in hope and anticipation only. The Law remained impersonal, and for deep, sensitive minds, such as St. Paul's, an 'occasion for sin' rather than for salvation (Rom., vii. 11). In the last resort the Jew died under the impulse of religious nationalism, as a member of a chosen race.[7] It was left to Christianity to extend this impulse to the individual, regardless of race, and eventually purge religion of the purely national element.

It needed the sacrifice and death of Jesus Christ to give the doctrine of martyrdom a permanent validity. The Christian accepted Jesus as Lord, and as 'the one faithful and true martyr',[8] whose death he should

---

[1] Dio Cassius (ed. Melber), lii. 36, 3 (in the mouth of Maecenas): μήτ' οὖν ἀθέῳ τινὶ μήτε γόητι συγχωρήσῃς εἶναι.

[2] See for instance Josephus, *Contra Apionem*, ii. 38. A. B. Drachmann, *Atheism in Pagan Antiquity*, Gyldendal, 1922.

[3] Cf. Apuleius, *Metamorphoses*, ix. 14, and art. Pfaff, *P.W.*, 'Sacrilegium'.

[4] H. A. Fischel, op. cit., 383 ff.

[5] IV Macc., xii. 16, but in the Alexandrine MS. only (Hadas 208), ἡ διαμαρτυρία occurs, however, at IV Macc., xvi. 16 with the implied meaning of 'bearing witness by death' on behalf of the law.

[6] Wisd., vii. 25 and ix. 9.   [7] See G. F. Moore, *Judaism*, ii. 312.

[8] Eusebius, *H.E.*, v. 2. 3, τῷ πιστῷ καὶ ἀληθινῷ μάρτυρι, citing Rev. i. 5 and iii. 14.

imitate. He believed that by bearing witness of his faith until death, he would also witness His glory.[1]

It has been urged with some justice[2] that the Passion narrative in St. Luke's Gospel is designed to portray the Ideal Martyr. 'St. Luke's portrait in the Passion story is that of the suffering but faithful servant of God, we may even say, the martyr.' His death atoned, however, not only for the sins of Israel, but those of all humanity (Heb., ix. 28). In St. Mark's account of the Passion, too, Christ prophesies a vision of God's power and glory (Mk., xiv. 62), such as may be found in the *Ascension of Isaiah* (v. 7) or in the account of Stephen's martyrdom in Acts (vii. 55). All three Synoptics recount signs and wonders which accompanied Christ's death, and throughout the New Testament suffering has the eschatological significance that it has in late Judaism. Wars, plagues, the persecution of the faithful on earth will precede the coming of the Messiah. The climax of evil was the immediate herald of the destruction of the heathen world by Christ. The sufferings of Christians would hasten the coming of the Messianic Age, and for that reason St. Paul rejoices in his sufferings (Col., i. 24) and hopes to participate in those of his Master (Phil., iii. 10). His message to the Thessalonians (II Thess., i) contains references to persecutions and sufferings which would precede the Parousia.[3] As Irenaeus stated (*Adv. Haer.*, v. 14.1), Christ's death was a recapitulation of (righteous) effusion of blood from the beginning— once again, the theme of human religious history is of righteous suffering and death. These ideas form one of the links between the Old Dispensation and the New.

Indeed, so long as the Second Coming was believed to be at hand, martyrdom and persecution at whomsoever's hands were bound to play a disproportionate part in the life of the Church. It is quite natural that at the end of the first century martyrdom had come to be accepted as the goal of a Christian life. Ignatius of Antioch begged the Roman Christians not to intercede on his behalf.[4] The martyrs of Lyons more than fifty years later defined a true disciple as one who 'follows the Lamb whither-soever He goeth',[5] i.e. to a martyr's death. But not only did martyrdom atone for sin, it had also become a touchstone of catholic orthodoxy. Ignatius uses it as an argument against his Jewish-Docetic opponents,[6] just as Tertullian does against the Gnostics in the next century.[7] In addition, it has become linked to a whole system of penitential disci-pline, particularly in the West. It was the supreme counsel of the Holy

---

[1] See K. Holl, 'Die Vorstellung vom Märtyrer und die Märtyrakte in der geschicht-lichen Entwicklung', *Gesammelte Aufsätze*, ii. 71 ff.

[2] R. H. Lightfoot, *History and Interpretation in the Gospels*, 1934, 176. Also D. W. Riddle, *The Martyrs*, Chicago 1931, ch. viii with reference to St. Mark's Gospel.

[3] On this question, see G. Best, *One Body in Christ*, London 1955, 130–136.

[4] Ignatius, *Ad Romanos*, ii and iv. Cf. Irenaeus, *Adv. Haer.*, v. 28. 4.

[5] Eusebius, *H.E.*, v. 1. 10.

[6] Ignatius, *Ad Smyrn.*, iv. 2 and *Ad Trall.*, ix. 1.

[7] Tertullian, *Scorpiace*, passim. Cf. art. by the writer 'The Gnostic Sects and the Roman Empire', *J.E.H.*, v. 1 (1954) 25–37.

Spirit. Baptism by water merely prepared the way for suffering and the baptism of blood.[1] The intense belief prevalent in North Africa of the supreme value of martyrdom underlay the baptismal issue between Carthage and Rome, and it was to dominate the Donatist controversy.

For the individual, moreover, martyrdom brought immediate benefits, and here also we find that the Church has built on the well-laid foundations of late Judaism. Like the martyr-prophet of that age, the Christian martyr was credited with visions of divine glory,[2] converse with the Lord,[3] prophetic powers,[4] and immediate entry into Paradise where he would judge his enemies.[5] More than that, he and he alone held the 'claves Petri', the power to bind and loose on earth and hereafter.[6] He was already an angel.[7] Above all, Christ speaks and suffers through him, thus manifesting the type of victorious suffering which would precede the Last Days.[8] The persecutors were faced with the hopeless task of fighting against God.[9] Their methods were merely the means to Christian victory. There was every reason for the Christian to defy the authorities.

And so, one notices in the early Church that same aggressive side to martyrdom that one can see from time to time in Judaism. There was a strong element who agreed with the writer of Revelation rather than I Peter. It was difficult to dissociate Rome from idolatry, and the Christian duty of destroying idols could easily take on an anti-Roman bias. In Asia Minor and Africa at the turn of the third century there were plenty of zealous Christians who were prepared to provoke the authorities and rejoiced at the consequences.[10] But the precedent for voluntary martyrdom had already been established by the young men whom Josephus describes, as boasting of cutting down Herod's Golden Eagle over the gateway of the Temple with the express object of being executed, 'for they would enjoy greater happiness after they were dead'.[11] No Montanist or Donatist asked more.

The extraordinary fact is that, granted the state of exaltation among so many of the early Christians and the firm dogmatic basis for their outlook, so few were put to death. Origen, himself no despiser of the martyr's crown, writing just before the Decian persecution, claimed that

---

[1] *Passio Perpetuae*, iii. 3: 'Mihi Spiritus dictavit: Non aliud petendum ab aqua, nisi sufferentiam carnis'.

[2] Acts, vii. 55; *Acta Carpi* (ed. Knopf), 13. 3 and 39.

[3] *Passio Perpetuae*, 4: 'et ego quae me sciebam fabulari cum Domino'. *Mart. Polyc.*, (ed. Knopf), 1. 2 and 2. 2.

[4] *Mart. Polyc.* (ed. Knopf), 5.

[5] *Passio Perpetuae*, 17; Eusebius, *H.E.*, vi. 42. 5; *Mart. Polyc.*, 19. 2. Cf. Wisd., v. 1 and v. 5. For further references Holl, op. cit., 72–73.

[6] Eusebius, *H.E.*, v. 2. 5; cf. Tertullian, *De Pudicitia* (C.S.E.L., xx), 21.

[7] *Mart. Polyc.*, 2. 3.

[8] Eusebius, *H.E.*, v. 1. 23 (the deacon, Sanctus).

[9] *Acta Saturnini*, 6: 'Peccatis, infelices, adversus Deum facitis.' (P.L., viii. 707).

[10] *Acta Carpi*, 42; *Mart. Polyc.*, 4. Tertullian, *Ad Scapulam*, 5. Cf. *Apol.*, 50. 3 and *De Spect.*, 1.

[11] Josephus, *Wars*, i. 33. 3.

one could easily enumerate the number of martyrs to date.[1] The biggest recorded massacre, that of Lyons in 177, seems to have claimed only 48 victims.[2] In the same period, the numbers of Jewish dead by pogrom and persecution must have run into many thousands. Perhaps this is in itself an indication of the relative importance of the Jewish compared with the Christian problem in the Mediterranean world in the first two centuries.

Is it possible to say, before one leaves the Christian side of our problem, whether these parallels between late Judaism and Christianity were conscious or not? Thanks to the excellent work done by Perler[3] and Surkau[4] on IV Maccabees, it seems that the answer is in the affirmative, that is to say, that late Jewish literature provided the literary models as well as the ideas of some of the earliest Christian *Acta Martyrum*. That the Christians of the first generation were well acquainted with the *Assumption of Moses* and the *Ascension of Isaiah* is well known.[5] More recently, however, detailed studies of IV Maccabees have established what would appear to be the direct influence of this work on the letters of Ignatius, the martyrdom of Polycarp and the account of the martyrdoms at Lyons. The borrowings include style and vocabulary as well as general ideas, and even without following Perler into mazes of linguistic analysis, it is perfectly clear, for instance, that the description of Blandina at Lyons is modelled on the mother of the Maccabaean youths, and that bishop Pothinus finds his prototype in the scribe Eleazer. There seems to be little doubt that with IV Maccabees 'the historian is dealing with one of the roots of early Christian enthusiasm for martyrdom and martyr literature'.[6] The continuity between Jewish and early Christian ideas of martyrdom seems remarkably complete, and to deny the fact, as even Delehaye[7] and Campenhausen[8] have sought to do, merely makes unnecessary difficulties.

We can now go on to the second stage of our argument and investigate possible affinities in the treatment of Jews and Christians by the Imperial and local authorities in the Roman Empire. The Jews, we have seen,

[1] Origen, *Contra Celsum*, iii. 8. H. Grégoire, *Les Persécutions*, 12.
[2] H. Quentin, 'La liste des martyrs de Lyon de l'An 177', *Analecta Bollandiana*, xxxix (1921), 113–138.
[3] O. Perler, 'Das vierte Makkabäerbuch, Ignatius von Antiochen und die ältesten Märtyrerberichte', *Riv. di arch. crist.* xxv (1949), 47–72.
[4] H. Surkau, *Martyrien in jüdischer und frühchristlicher Zeit*, Göttingen 1938.
[5] R. H. Charles, *The Ascension of Isaiah*, London 1900, xliv and *Assumption of Moses*, London 1897, lxii.
[6] O. Perler, loc. cit., 64: 'Wir sind an einer Wurzel der altchristlichen Martyrerbegeisterung und Martyrerliteratur'.
[7] H. Delehaye, 'Martyr et Confesseur', *Analecta Bollandiana*, xxxix (1921), 36–64 at pp. 45–46: 'Et pour le dire en passant, nous ne reconnaissons nullement l'influence des idées juives, par l'intermédiaire du livre ii des Macchabées et de certaines légendes des prophètes, sur les Actes historiques des martyrs'.
[8] H. von Campenhausen, *Die Idee des Martyriums in der alten Kirche*, Göttingen 1936, 1: 'Die Idee des Martyriums und die Vorstellung des Märtyrers sind christlichen Ursprungs.'

were the victims of constant strife in the Greek cities but were comparatively free from molestation in Rome itself. How far can the same be said of the Christians? The evidence for the first two centuries preserved by Eusebius suggests that this may also have been the case. The Greek cities were obviously the main centres of anti-Christian agitation. By the end of the second century, however, this had extended to other great cities where there was a large Jewish community, such as Carthage.[1] Melito of Sardis is quoted as referring to Hadrian's instructions to the cities of Larissa, Thessalonica and Athens and 'to all the Greeks' that 'no new measures should be taken against us (Christians)'.[2] Eusebius prefaces the account of the persecution at Lyons, where the Christians also seem to be in the main Greek-speaking Asiatic immigrants[3], with the statement, 'In this time the persecution of us in some parts of the world was rekindled more violently by popular violence in the cities.'[4] In Rome after A.D. 64 we hear of isolated denunciations and individual trials, such as that of Justin in A.D. 163, but on the whole, the Christians there seem to have been left alone. Irenaeus's statement that in Rome the 'faithful from everywhere'[5] met, is confirmed by what is known of the careers of figures such as Marcion, Valentinus and Polycarp. And they met and disputed openly. The Church also accumulated property. If the persecution of A.D. 64 had really had the immediate and decisive importance that is claimed for it, one would expect Rome to have been one of the main centres of anti-Christian repression. This does not seem to have been the case. Eusebius clearly regarded Gnostic heresy as a worse danger to the Church in the second century than persecution.[6] Sporadic pogroms in the Hellenistic cities were the feature of the period and continued to be so up to the very eve of the Decian persecution.[7]

It might perhaps be suggested that the policy of the Roman authorities towards the Church was a patchwork of separate and scarcely coordinated ideas. First, in Rome itself there was concern for the maintenance of the *pax deorum*, and the consequent dread of the violation of the Roman gods by the practice of unholy rites and black magic. Secondly, there was a deep-felt loathing for converts to Judaism—the 'national apostates'[8]—and a tendency where possible to fasten the term borrowed from the Greeks of 'atheist' on to them.[9] Added to this, there was the

---

[1] P. Monceaux, 'Les colonies juives dans l'Afrique romaine', *Rev. des Etudes juives* (1902), 1 ff.

[2] Eusebius, *H.E.*, iv. 26. 10.

[3] See Grégoire, op. cit., 20.

[4] Eusebius, *H.E.*, v. 1. 1.

[5] Irenaeus, *Adv. Haer.*, iii. 3. 2.

[6] Eusebius, *H.E.*, iv. 7. 1.

[7] The last great anti-Christian outbreak was that which took place in Alexandria in A.D. 248. Eusebius, ibid., vi. 41. 1 ff.

[8] Mommsen's phrase, in his famous 'Der Religionsfrevel nach römischen Recht', *Historische Zeitschrift*, lxxv (1890), 389–429 at p. 407. See also, his letter in *Expositor* (1893), 1–7, under the title of 'Christianity in the Roman Empire'.

[9] A. Harnack, 'Der Vorwurf des Atheismus', *Texte u. Untersuchungen*, xii. 4 (1903), and Mommsen, art. cit., 393. For the unpopularity of proselytes, Tacitus, *Histories*, v. 5, Juvenal, *Sat.*, xiv. 96 ff., Origen, *Contra Celsum*, v. 41.

continuous, bitter hostility of the Jews towards the Christians, which ensured that there would lack neither accusers nor mobs to shout 'down with the atheists' at the appropriate moment.

The affair of A.D. 64 is quite clearly the application of the first of these principles to the problem of Christianity. Coupled with reproaches of 'hatred against the human race' applicable to Jews,[1] one can point to the parallel of the Bacchanal conspiracy. With Last[2] and Sherwin-White[3] we can see common ground between the Republican treatment of the Bacchanals, the Claudian treatment of the Druids and Magi and the Neronian persecution of the Christians. Tacitus's description of the searching out of the Christians in Rome involving an 'ingens multitudo' suggests almost word for word Livy's account of the famous days of 186 B.C.[4] Suetonius's language 'nova et malefica superstitio' indicates magic as the underlying fear of the authorities.[5] So far as one can tell, there was no sacrificial test. The victims are said simply to 'have confessed', and no attempt appears to have been made to secure recantations —no more so than with the Bacchanals. But this great round-up remained a unique event. It was designed as an act of reprisal against a conspiracy or a spectacular *alibi* to cover the tracks of Nero himself.[6] If there had been no other factors to influence the relations between Church and Empire, the Church might soon have gained the status of relative respectability obtained by the Druids and Bacchanals after similar acts of repression. But from the end of the first century onwards the centre of anti-Christian action switches to the Hellenistic world,[7] and there, there were plenty of factors which favoured religious strife. It did not need the precedent of the Neronian persecution[8] to stir up an anti-Christian pogrom.

The basic religious problem which Rome inherited from the Hellenistic governments was the containment of Judaism and its ramifications. These, if our thesis is correct, included Christianity and also the extension of Judaism to neighbouring peoples in Palestine, such as the Samaritans. Whatever villainies they might commit, whatever the results of their frustrated universalist ambitions, the Jews remained a 'people' (an ἔθνος) with a right to their own laws and customs established by antiquity.[9]

---

[1] Cf. Tacitus, *Histories*, v. 5. 2. The Jews were characterised as 'apud ipsos fides obstinata, misericordia in promptu, sed adversus omnes alios, hostile odium'.

[2] See H. Last, 'Christenverfolgung', 1208–1228, and 'The Study of the Persecutions', 88 ff.

[3] A. N. Sherwin-White, 'The Early Persecutions and Roman Law', 211.

[4] Tacitus, *Annales*, xv. 44: 'ingens multitudo'. Livy, xxxix. 13: 'multitudinem ingentem, alterum iam populum esse'.

[5] Suetonius, *Vita Neronis*, 16. Cf. also Pliny's views.

[6] Tacitus, though he did not believe that the Christians actually fired Rome, thought them guilty of something. They were 'sontes et novissima exempla meritos'. See, H. Fuchs's scholarly discussion of the problems arising from Tacitus, *Ann.*, xv. 44, in 'Tacitus über die Christen', *Vigiliae Christianae* (1950), 65–93. Also H. Last, art. cit.; 1211.

[7] Cf. Rev., ii. 13 (martyrdom of Antipas).

[8] As suggested by A. N. Sherwin-White, art. cit., 209.

[9] Tacitus, *Histories*, v. 5: 'Hi ritus quoque modo inducti, antiquitate defenduntur.' Also, *Contra Celsum*, v. 25.

The authorities were prepared to uphold these. But this policy did not apply to their converts and imitators,[1] and this was clearly understood by ordinary Greek provincials of the time. One of the first reactions of the people of Thessalonica to St. Paul's missions was that 'these men being Jews' were teaching practices which were illegal for Romans to observe (Acts xvi. 20–21). Forty years later, the cases of Flavius Clemens and Domitilla provided the classic examples of the charge of Atheism (ἀθεότης) being levelled at Roman citizens who 'had lapsed into Jewish customs'.[2] And not only citizens. There is an interesting passage in Origen, *Contra Celsum*, ii. 13 in which Origen, in a somewhat obtuse way, draws attention to the more favourable treatment accorded to Christians in contrast to unauthorised imitators of Judaism. The Samaritans, he points out, who accept Jewish practices 'are put to death on account of circumcision as Sicarii, on the ground that they are mutilating themselves contrary to the established laws and are doing what is permitted to the Jews alone'. Mere evidence of the fact was sufficient warrant for a death sentence. The Christians, however, were given a chance to recant even at the last moment by taking an oath and sacrificing. Small comfort perhaps, but it shows that punishment on religious grounds, where an extension of Judaism was concerned, had its place in third-century Roman practice in the Hellenistic East. Indeed, Roman policy, as illustrated by Antoninus Pius's rescript equating the circumcision of non-Jews with the criminal offence of castration,[3] and that of Septimius Severus[4] aimed against Christian and Jewish proselytism, seems to have been consistent throughout the second century. The background and justification lay in the great revolt of the Dispersion Jews in A.D. 115–117, and the continued disaffection of Jewry in general for a generation after the crushing of Bar-Kochba's rebellion in A.D. 135.[5] In these years 'the King of the Jews' upheld by Zealots and opposed to the authority of the Emperor was no myth.

One can go even further and point to the actual persecution of the Jews by the Romans in moments of crisis during the period A.D. 70–135. Thus, at the end of the desperate Jewish War, Josephus records how in the face of countless tortures the defenders of Masada preferred to be done to death rather than give even the mere appearance of confessing Caesar as lord.[6] The Midrash of the Ten Martyrs referring to the period after the

---

[1] On this subject, J. Juster, *Les Juifs dans l'Empire romain*, i. 232 ff. and G. La Piana, 'Foreign Groups in Rome during the first centuries of the Empire', *Harvard Theol. Review*, xx (1927), 183–403 at 387 ff.

[2] Dio Cassius, 67. 15; cf. E. T. Merrill, *Essays in early Church History*, 1924, vi.

[3] *Digest*, xlviii. 8. 11. 1 (Modestinus), and Paulus, *Sententiae*, v. 22. 3 for the specific prohibition on pain of exile for Roman citizens. Th. Mommsen, 'Der Religionsfrevel', 409.

[4] Spartian, *Vita Severi*, 17. 1.

[5] Ammianus Marcellinus (ed. Rolfe), xxii. 5. 5. Rabbis in the third century A.D. continued to boast that 'Jews are like wild beasts to the heathen and like doves before God'. Juster, op. cit., 220, n. 8; cf. O. Cullmann, *The State in the New Testament* (Eng. tr. 1957), ii.

[6] Josephus, *Wars*, vii. 10. 1.

end of the revolt of Bar-Kochba mentions that Rabbi Ishmael was urged to renounce his faith, but that he refused.[1] Akiba was martyred for teaching Torah when this had been declared illegal.[2] Nathan, the Babylonian Jewish sage, writing of the same period about conditions in Palestine, is reported as saying 'The expression in the Decalogue "Those who love me and and observe my commandments" applies to the people who live in Palestine and give their lives for the Law. "Why art thou being taken to execution?" Because I circumcised my son. "Why art thou being taken to crucifixion?" Because I read the Torah and ate the mazzot. "Why art thou being beaten with a hundred stripes?" Because I took the *lulab*" '.[3] This evidence, taken with Hadrian's other measures[4] against the Jews which precipitated the crisis of A.D. 132 suggests that Rome, when faced by the problems of militant Judaism, reacted in much the same way as had the Seleucid kings three centuries before. Indeed, the continuation in the East of the divine aspects of the Hellenistic monarchs by the Roman Emperors would make this almost inevitable. Religious persecution and trials were not a misfortune reserved for Christians alone.

These facts should put Rome's policy towards the Christians in its right perspective. The 'obstinacy' of the Christians and the fact that they were accused of criminal offences as well, made their case worse. The real complaint against them, however, was membership of an unrecognised Judaistic society engaged in spreading atheism[5] and social disruption.[6] The 'flagitia' alone would not have proved deadly unless linked to more fundamental charges, as the history of the Gnostics in this period shows.[7] More serious was that, while living as members of a community, they deliberately rejected the gods on whom the prosperity of that community rested. In addition, like the extreme Jewish sectaries recorded by Josephus[8], they refused to give even nominal recognition of Caesar as lord by swearing on his genius.

Though Pliny himself shared the views of his Roman upper-class

[1] H. A. Fischel, art. cit., 366.

[2] L. Finkelstein, *Akiba*, 272 ff.

[3] *Mechilta, Jethro Bahodesh*, vi (Winter u. Wünsche, 213). See L. Finkelstein, *Akiba*, 270.

[4] Including, of course, the building of a temple to Jupiter Capitolinus on the site of the Temple of Jerusalem, an act not far removed from Antiochus's 'abomination of desolation'.

[5] This is my interpretation of Origen, *Contra Celsum*, I. 1 and 2, 'societies which are public are allowed by the laws, but secret societies are illegal . . . The doctrine was originally barbarian, obviously meaning (Origen comments) Judaism with which Christianity is connected'. Lucian's description of Peregrinus in his Christian days as a προφήτης καὶ θιασάρχης καὶ ξυναγωγεὺς (*De Morte Peregrini*, 11) suggests a 'Judaistic *collegium*'.

[6] For instance, Origen, *Contra Celsum*, iii. 55 and Min. Felix, *Octavius* 8.

[7] See the present writer's 'The Gnostic Sects and the Roman Empire', 31 ff. For the attribution of *Flagitia* to Gnostics by orthodox Christians, Justin 1 *Apol.*, 26. 7 and Clement, *Stromata*, iii. 10. 1.

[8] Josephus, *Wars*, vii. 10. 1 and ii. 8. 10.

contemporaries, and like Suetonius regarded Christianity as a 'prava superstitio',[1] the imposition of a sacrificial test suggests that atheism also was implicit. As Mommsen pointed out, the Bithynian Christians were executed because they refused to sacrifice.[2] By c. 130, however, the charge of atheism seems to have become general. From Justin one learns that it was among the charges spread by the Jews in Asia Minor against the Christians.[3] It was the cry taken up by the people of Smyrna against Polycarp and his community.[4] It was the first of the three major accusations rebutted by Athenagoras.[5] It is reflected in Lucian's account of the charlatan Alexander of Abonuteichos forbidding access to his shrine in Bithynia to 'Christians' and 'atheists'.[6] It is clear from the forged decree of Antonius Pius to the Council of Asia that the population regarded Christians as atheists.[7] So did the people of Lyons.[8] In Africa the charge figures prominently in Tertullian's *Ad Nationes*.[9] Its existence ensured that pressure against the Church would not be relaxed. It was the atheistic 'nomen' rather than the 'flagitia' that mattered.[10]

But compared with the Jews, the Christians were, in general, peaceable and well-affected citizens. They did not behave like the Sicarii, even though the first reaction of the Roman authorities in Palestine was that they were members of this sect (Acts xxi. 38). Therefore, the authorities were prepared to temper the wind for them. Thus the instruction 'conquirendi non sunt'; thus the acquittals of Christians[11]; and, as Origen makes clear in the passage from *Contra Celsum* already cited, the chance of last-minute recantation. It was an illogical system. Tertullian's legal mind could drive a coach and four through it,[12] but it was the only system that could be evolved, having regard both to the religious history of the Hellenistic East and to the Christians' own impulse towards martyrdom. If there ever was a Neronian edict, there is no evidence that a Proconsul of Asia or Africa ever referred to it. While the magisterial right of *coercitio* may have been invoked, it would be more reassuring if specific evidence existed that it was.

In the last resort, the troubles of the early Church were due as much to the virulence of the Christian-Jewish controversy as to any other cause.[13] The literary warfare which has left its mark on the *Epistle of Barnabas*, and

---

[1] Pliny, *Ep.*, x. 96.

[2] Th. Mommsen, art. cit., 395.

[3] Justin, *Dialogue*, xvii. 1.

[4] Eusebius, *H.E.*, iv. 15. 19. See also ibid., v. 1. 9 (martyrdoms at Lyons in 177).

[5] Athenagoras, *Supplicatio*, 3.

[6] Lucian (ed. Harmon), *Alexander*, 25 and 38.

[7] See A. Harnack, 'Das Decret des Antoninus Pius', *Texte und Untersuchungen*, xiii. 4, 1895.

[8] Eusebius, *H.E.*, v. 1. 9.

[9] Tertullian, *Ad Nationes*, i. 1–3.

[10] Tertullian, *Apol.*, ii. 3: 'confessio nominis, non examinatio criminis'.

[11] See, in particular, Eusebius, *H.E.*, v. 18. 9, and Tertullian, *Ad Scapulam*, 3–5.

[12] Ibid., 1 ff.

[13] For a contrary view, M: Simon, *Verus Israel*, Paris 1948, 144 f. and J. Parkes, *The Conflict of the Church and the Synagogue*, London 1934, 125 ff.

the ideas of Marcion, became warfare indeed. There is strong circumstantial evidence that the Jews shifted the blame for the fire at Rome in A.D. 64 to the Christians, but the charge cannot be proved conclusively.[1] During the period, however, between A.D. 60 and A.D. 90, when Acts and the Gospels were being written, it is clear that Christians were concerned with Jewish rather than official hostility. In Acts the reasonable attitude of the Roman authorities is contrasted with the hatred of the Jews. In the Gospels the authorities are acquitted of condemning Jesus to death, though it would have been easy to have branded the Roman persecutors with that crime also. The conflict, however, at the end of the first century was less with the Roman Empire than with the 'synagogue of Satan'.

In the second and third centuries, Christian writers in both East and West make specific references to Jewish hostility towards the Church. Taken together, Justin, the account of Polycarp's martyrdom, Tertullian and Origen make convincing reading. Cursings,[2] and beatings in the synagogues,[3] the spreading of anti-Christian rumours,[4] active assistance at martyrdoms,[5] alliance with pagans in war against the Church, all this justified the charge that 'the synagogues of the Jews were the fountains of persecution'.[6] The parties were evenly matched, for the Christians, if they won the Hellenistic world, lost Palestine and with it all eastern Judaism. The bitter warfare carried on with such tenacity for so long must have been a powerful factor in maintaining popular hostility against the Church. The Greek cities where Diaspora Jew and Christian lived side by side were the natural centres of this strife.

Once the Christians had failed to make good their claim in the eyes of the majority of the Jews to be the New Israel, and at the same time had abandoned the outward signs of Judaism, their position was bound to be precarious. Their claim to the same privileges as Judaism, e.g. freedom from military service, from performance of sacrifices and public service, in exchange for prayer, could not be entertained.[7] The continued closeness, however, of their religion to that of orthodox Judaism would render them liable to the legal and popular penalties reserved for converts to Judaism. To these were added suspicion of black magic and cannibalism, charges calculated to rouse the anger of the city mob.[8] The result was, as the writer of the *Letter to Diognetus* lamented, 'They (Christians) are warred upon by the Jews as foreigners (ἀλλόφυλοι) and are persecuted by the Greeks, and those who hate them cannot state the cause of their enmity'

---

[1] See L. H. Canfield, 'The Early Persecution of the Christians', *Columbia University Studies in History*, lv (1913) 44 ff.

[2] Justin, *Dialogue*, xvi. 4.

[3] Eusebius, *H.E.*, v. 16. 12.

[4] Justin, *Dialogue*, xvii. 1; Origen, *Contra Celsum*, vi. 27 and *Comment. in Deuteron.* xxxi. 21.

[5] *Mart. Polycarpi*, 13 and 17.

[6] Tertullian, *Scorpiace*, 10 and *Adv. Nationes*, i. 14.

[7] For this claim, Origen, *Contra Celsum*, viii. 73.

[8] As they in fact did at Lyons in A.D. 177; Eusebius, *H.E.*, v. 1. 14.

(v. 17). The general interest of the Roman government of the 'containment of Judaism' led to the firmly-held but illogical legal position against
which the Apologists stormed in vain.

Persecution for religion and martyrdom do not start with Christianity.
The problem of a monotheistic religion, exclusive in its outlook towards
surrounding society and yet universalist in its claims, confronted every
ruler of Asia Minor and the Near East from the second century B.C.
onwards. Culturally and politically Christianity was the more formidable
successor of Judaism. Rome eventually tried to handle the problem on
similar lines to her Hellenistic predecessors. The policy failed. Supported
by the assurance of immortality and revenge which his doctrine of
martyrdom gave him, the Christian like the Jew was proof against both
pogrom and, later, official persecution.[1] Up to the end of the second
century A.D. the Hellenistic world was the battleground. Then, gradually
the emphasis shifts, and one finds that during the fourth century the more
extreme aspects of the martyr's creed have entrenched themselves in the
theology of the West. Petilian of Constantine[2] is the final representative
of the philosophy of history asserted in IV Maccabees. How and why this
took place is beyond the scope of this paper. But there can be no doubt
of the great importance of this development. Conflict has been the mark
of Church-State relations in the West down to the present day. By tracing
the origins back into the pre-Christian past one may gain a clearer insight
into the foundations of the Western standpoint.

[1] On the 'conditioning' of Christians for martyrdom, see Riddle, *The Martyrs*, iii.
[2] Augustine, *Contra Litteras Petiliani*, ii. 92. 202 (P.L., xliii. 322–323).

NOTE: On the legal aspects of the persecutions see G. E. M. de Ste Croix "Why were
the early Christians persecuted?", *Past and Present*, 26, 1963, 6-38 and the discussion
between Sherwin White and Ste Croix on Contumacia in *Past and Present*, 27, 1964, 23-33.

II

The Gnostic Sects and the Roman Empire

Two generations of lawyers and historians of the early Church have worked over the scanty evidence bearing on the legal and political relations between the first Christian communities and the Roman Empire. It is not the intention of the present writer to add to the enormous volume of work on the subject. The results of their battles have been ably summarised by A. N. Sherwin-White, and with his conclusions the legal problem may be allowed to rest until new evidence is forthcoming.[1] The object of this paper is to look at the question from another point of view, and to ask who were the sufferers, and in particular, who were martyred in the period before the first general persecution under Decius. Were Polycarp, Justin, Blandina and the rest chance victims of private denunciation and the fury of the mob, or did they represent a tradition of belief in which martyrdom became the climax of earthly life? And what of those who obeyed the precept to flee during persecution? Was their action due to cowardice, or was it the belief that martyrdom was not the will of God? Can we see in the controversy over martyrdom which engaged so much of Tertullian's energies, one more phase in the strife between the orthodox and gnostic concepts of Christianity, on the outcome of which so much in the future of the Church depended? What, in fact, was the relationship between the Gnostics and the Roman authorities?

Apart from their great courage and steadfastness of purpose, the martyrs impress the reader by their conservative and even Judaistic approach to the new religion. Polycarp, for instance, at the time of his death the surviving link with the apostolic era, was also the spokesman of those who would maintain the association between the Passion and the Passover, and celebrate the former on 14 Nisan irrespective of the day of the week.[2] In this he was at one with Montanist enthusiasts such as Blastus, who seem deliberately to have harked back to the law of Moses.[3] His view too, of a Christian's duties, as set out in the letter to the Philippians hardly deviates from the code of the contemporary Hellenistic synagogue. 'Blameless among the Gentiles' (Chap. x)[4] entailed freedom

---

[1] A. N. Sherwin-White, 'The Early Persecutions and Roman Law Again,' *Journal of Theological Studies*, N.S. iii. 2 (Oct. 1952), 199–213.

[2] Eusebius, *Hist. Ecc.*, iii. 36. 1 and v. 24. 16.

[3] Pseudo-Tertullian, *Adversus omn. haer.* 8. (ed. Kroymann, C.S.E.L. xlvii. p. 225). See B. J. Kidd, *A History of the Church to A.D. 461*, Oxford, 1922, i. 355.

[4] Polycarp, *Ep. ad Philipp.*, x. 2. =I Peter ii. 12.

from their vices—love of money, false witness, slander and evil living (Chs. ii. iv. and v.). These were the traditional reproaches heaped by the Jews on their neighbours. The Pharisee in the Temple claimed to be no less by virtue of his calling (Lk. xviii. 11). The community over which Polycarp presided at Smyrna must have resembled the local synagogue both in its ethic and in its outlook towards the Gentiles, and perhaps this was one of the reasons why the Jews of Smyrna played so prominent a part in his martyrdom.[1] Already by A.D. 100, if not while St. Paul was still alive, Christianity had been denounced by orthodox Jewry as heresy and deserving of death.[2] The conflict with the Roman authorities may well have been the by-product of the first clashes between the Old and New Dispensations.

At Lyons, the disaster which befell a large part of the Christian community there and at Vienne during the summer of 177, also appears to have affected those whose ideas had most in common with Jewry.[3] The principal sufferers were Asiatic immigrants who occupied many of the chief positions in these churches. Marked off both by their language and religion from the rest of the inhabitants, they were as conspicuous in the Gallic capitals as Italian immigrants in London and Colchester had been at the time of Boadicea's rising, and they were equally unpopular. Urban Gaul in the second century, with its enthusiastic acceptance of classical civilisation was not favourable ground for the spread of Christianity. One is left with the impression that at this time the churches in the south Gallic cities were almost closed communities consisting of Asiatics and a few proselytes, much as the Jewish communities in their parent cities in Asia and Phrygia formed their own πολίτευμα of born Jews and a scattering of Greek converts.[4] Theirs was an exotic religion, and their isolation and the difficulty of making contact with the bulk of the inhabitants would only increase the tenacity with which they held to tradition.

This tendency is revealed not only in the quotations from II Macc. vii. 21–3 and vii. 27–9, 41, in which the survivors compare the conduct of the slave Blandina with the heroic martyrdom of the mother of the Maccabees.[5] It is to be found also in less conscious asides. For instance, the slave Biblis poured scorn on the charge that the Christians indulged in

---

[1] Eusebius, *Hist. Ecc.*, iv. 15. 26 and 29.

[2] 'To apostates let there be no hope and the kingdom of pride do thou quickly root out in our days. And let the notzrim (Christians) and minim (heretics) perish in a moment.' Statement by Rabbi Samuel the Small, quoted from Lukyn Williams, *Adversus Judaeos*, Cambridge 1935, 32. See also Acts xxiv. 5.

[3] Text in G. Krüger and R. Knopf, *Ausgewählte Märtyrerakten*, Tübingen 1929, 18–28; and Eusebius, *Hist. Ecc.*, v. 1. The martyrdoms took place at the Festival of the Three Gauls for the worship of Augustus on 1 August. See B. J. Kidd, *History of the Church to A.D. 461*, i. 250.

[4] Paganism was still a living force in Vienne at the end of the fourth century when St. Martin baptised Foedula there. It was predominant in the surrounding countryside up to the end of the fourth century. Irenaeus, *Adv. Haereses* (ed. Harvey) Proemium 3, and iv. 38. 2 indicates the formidable difficulties in the way of proselytising in Gaul. See also, F. Mâle, *La Fin du Paganisme en Gaule*, Paris 1950, 10–35.

[5] Eusebius, *Hist. Ecc.*, v. 1. 55.

incest and cannibalism, with the reply, 'How could such men eat children, seeing that they are not allowed to eat the blood of irrational animals?'[1] As Resch pointed out, this shows that the Christians of Lyons were still observing the Hebraic food laws which had been enjoined on converts by the Apostolic Council.[2] This appears to have been true of other conservatives, the African Christians, though elsewhere vegetarianism had ceased to be part of the Christian practice.[3] At Lyons as well as at Carthage the Millenarist ideals so characteristic of late Jewish thought[4] continued to find acceptance, and it is perhaps hardly surprising that the Montanist prophets who imagined the Millenium to be already at hand should have written to the confessors at Lyons for support.[5]

It appears that even in the last quarter of the second century many Christians continued to be regarded as an extreme sect of Jewry and to use among themselves the terminology derived from the Hellenistic synagogue. Irenaeus, in a curious passage in *Adv. Haereses* (1.24.6), records that 'the followers of Basilides had declared that they had ceased to be Jews but not yet become Christians'.[6] In Rome, Irenaeus's contemporary Galen usually associated 'the followers of Moses and the followers of Christ'[7] with the same approach to religious and ethical problems, and this appears to have been true also of the sources which the *Scriptores Historiae Augustae*, Spartian[8] and Lampridius[9], used to compile their lives of Septimius Severus and Severus Alexander. Irenaeus himself refers to the Church as a 'synagoga Dei', and uses 'god-fearing' as an epithet applicable to church members.[10]

But bishop Pothinos and his fellow martyrs were not the only people at Lyons who sought their salvation through Christ. Others had few scruples about animal food, and their notorious practice of magic and immorality should have roused the mob more effectively than the obstinacy of the Asiatics and their slaves.[11] In addition, they appear to have been busy propagators of their views. Despite all this, neither Marcus nor his fellow Gnostics in Lyons were summoned before the magistrates. They even escaped the net when the governor, yielding to the rage and panic of the populace, ordered a general search to be made for the Christians.[12]

[1] Op. cit., I. 26. Compare Lucian, *De Morte Peregrini*. 16.
[2] G. Resch, 'Das Aposteldecret,' *Texte und Untersuchungen*, N. F. xiii. 2 (1905), 148.
[3] Tertullian, *Apol.* ix: Minucius Felix, *Octavius* (ed. Glover and Rendall), 30. 6.
[4] Irenaeus, *Adv. Haer.* v. 28. 3. For Jewish Millenarist hopes in the first century A.D., see *The Book of the Secrets of Enoch* (ed. Morfill and Charles), c. 33.
[5] Eusebius, *Hist. Ecc.*, v. iii. 4.
[6] Et Judaeos quidem jam non esse dicunt, Christianos autem nondum.
[7] Galen, *De Pulsuum Differentiis* (ed. Kuehn), ii. 4. and iii. 3. See R. Walzer, *Galen on Jews and Christians*, Oxford 1952, 14 and Ch. iii.
[8] Spartian, *Vita Severi*, 17. 1.
[9] Lampridius, *Vita Alexandri Severi*, 22. 4. It is interesting too, to find that the first known Christian church, that at Doura built circa 230, should have been modelled on a synagogue.
[10] Irenaeus, *Adv. Haer.* iii. 6. 1; i. 13. 4: τῶν ἐχουσῶν τὸν φόβον τοῦ θεοῦ.
[11] Irenaeus, *Adv. Haeres.* i. 13. 1 and 7: P.G. vii, 577 and 592.
[12] Eusebius, *Hist. Ecc.*, v. 1. 14: ἐπεὶ δημοσίᾳ ἐκελεύσεν ὁ ἡγεμὼν ἀναζητεῖσθαι, πάντας ἡμᾶς. This of course, was contrary to the general practice ordered by Trajan 'conquirendi non sunt.'

When Irenaeus denounced their activities a few years later, there is nothing to show that these had caused a moment's concern to the authorities.

Lyons was not a special case. The same situation arose in Carthage twenty-five years later. In about A.D. 208 Tertullian wrote his *Scorpiace adversus Gnosticos* during a period of severe local persecution. He describes how in the midst of 'a savage persecution' 'the heretics went about according to their wont',[1] and were able to intercede with pagans on behalf of some of the confessors. These troubles gave the Gnostics a chance of showing their influence at no personal danger to themselves. As Tertullian complains, it is 'then that the Gnostics break out, then the Valentinians creep forth, then all the opponents of martyrdom bubble up.'[2] The inference is that the weight of public hostility was directed only against some members of the Church at Carthage, and that these did not include Tertullian's gnostic opponents.

In Egypt, Syria and Asia Minor a similar state of affairs seems to have prevailed. Ignatius was despatched to the beasts at Rome, and not Satornilus his Docetic opponent. The writer of the Apocalypse contrasts the faithful martyr Antipas with the Nicolaitans and those who were prepared 'to eat things sacrificed to idols'.[3] There is no evidence that the great gnostic leaders in Egypt, Basilides, Valentinus and Heracleon, or their disciples died other than natural deaths. Indeed, the gnostic attitude towards martyrdom, and its practical consequences are summed up by Irenaeus in a well-known passage—*Adv. Haereses*, iv. 33. 9.[4] He says, 'Wherefore the Church does in every place, because of that love which she cherishes towards God, send forward throughout all time a multitude of martyrs to the Father, while all others not only have nothing of the kind to point to among themselves, but even maintain that such witness-bearing is not necessary and that their system of doctrines is the true witness [for Christ]. Except that perhaps one or two of them, during the whole time which has elapsed since the Lord appeared on earth, have occasionally, along with our martyrs, borne the reproach of the name (as if he too had obtained mercy), and have been led forth with them [to death], being as it were a sort of retinue granted unto them.' Irenaeus, writing while the memory of the Lyons persecution was still fresh, may be exaggerating the number of orthodox martyrs, but his word taken with that of Tertullian is convincing. At this period the Gnostics were not generally molested, and the fact was sufficiently apparent to impress itself on contemporary Christians.

What were the reasons for this? To Clement of Alexandria and to Tertullian the Gnostic escaped because he was a coward. He used ʽδειλίας

---

[1] Tertullian, *Scorpiace adversus Gnosticos* 1 (ed. Reifferscheid and Wissowa C.S.E.L. XX). I have used Roberts and Donaldson's translation.

[2] Ibid. 1: tunc Gnostici erumpunt, tunc Valentiniani proserpunt, tunc omnes martyriorum refragatores ebulliunt.

[3] Rev. ii. 13–17.

[4] Quoted from Roberts's translation, *The Writings of Irenaeus*, ii. 11–12.

THE GNOSTIC SECTS AND THE ROMAN EMPIRE

σοφίσματα'[1] to avoid punishment. But this explanation is belied by the complaints of Catholics that the Gnostics were busy proselytisers,[2] and that they flooded the literate world with 'numberless apocryphal and spurious tracts' (ἀμύθητον πλῆθος ἀποκρύφων καὶ νόθων γραφῶν).[3] The writers of these could have had little fear of the consequence of airing their views. Moreover, despite internecine wranglings with their neighbours, most if not all claimed to be the true Christians,[4] and to one of the gnostic leaders in Egypt, Heracleon, the Church owes the earliest commentary on St. John's Gospel.[5] One must conclude that principle rather than fear underlay their attitude.

There were two points on which the Gnostic was able to satisfy the succeptibilities of contemporary society in a way impossible for more rigid Christians. First, though the teaching of his sect might be exclusive in form, often involving secret marks on the person and hidden pass-words,[6] its approach to religion was so similar to that of other mystery cults as to have no difficulty in harmonising with them. His was a school rather than a church, and an independent observer would not have seen much difference between the position occupied by Heracleon and Basilides and that occupied by Posidonius or Plotinus. His message, like that of a priest of Isis or Cybele was one of personal salvation obtained through successive initiations into mysteries, each providing the believer with a knowledge of how to overcome fate and how to outwit the planetary deities who watched over the destiny of each individual. The gnostic Christ and Mithras were both bringers of personal salvation; both were regarded as cosmic saviours descended from the kingdom of light, born once into the world to saves redeem and restore the soul to its due place in light eternal, and in the end, to bring about the new order that would last for ever.[7] The rites and beliefs common to the Gnostics and worshippers of Mithras which impressed contemporary opinion were not fortuitous.[8] Both cults were ultimately part-heirs to the astrological lore of the Chaldaeans.[9] The characteristics of Gnosticism may be traced back to the dawn of known religion.

[1] Clement, *Stromata*, iv. 16.3 (ed. Stählin, ii. 256). Cf. Tertullian, *De Fuga*, 1.

[2] In Rome, Irenaeus, *Adv. Haer.* i. 25. 6 (Carpocratians). In Africa, Tertullian, *De Praescriptione*, 1. In Egypt, see H. Leclercq, 'Gnosticisme', *Dict. d'archéologie chrétienne et de liturgie*, vi. i., col. 1350.

[3] Irenaeus, *Adv. Haer.* i. 20. 1. Hippolytus, *Refutatio* (ed. Wendland), v. 23. 2; cf. Epiphanius, *Panarion*, xxvi. 8. 1.

[4] Note the very interesting remark made by Celsus in his discussion on the Gnostic sects, cited in Origen, *Contra Celsum*, v. 64: πάντων δὲ φησὶν, ἀκούσῃ τῶν ἐπὶ τοσοῦτον διεστηκότων καὶ σφᾶς αὐτοὺς ταῖς ἔρισιν αἴσχιστα διελεγχόντων, λεγόντων τὸ· "Ἐμοὶ κόσμος ἐσταύρωται, κἀγὼ κόσμῳ.

[5] Ed. J. A. Robinson, *Cambridge Texts and Studies*, i. 4, 1891.

[6] Clement, *Eclogae propheticae*, 25. 1 (ed. Stählin, iii. 143) on the Carpocratians sealing their ears. Cf. Celsus in Origen, (ed. Koetschau) *Contra Celsum* v. 64.

[7] A. D. Nock, 'The Genius of Mithraism,' *Journal of Roman Studies*, xxvii. 1. (1937), 108–113.

[8] Justin, *Dialogus* 70. 1. Tertullian, *De Corona* 15 and *De Praescriptione*, 40. Celsus in Origen, *Contra Celsum*, vi. 22.

[9] I am accepting the views of W. Anz in the still valuable study 'Zur Frage nach dem Ursprung des Gnosticismus', *Texte und Untersuchungen*, xv, 1897, 93 f. A close association

Secondly, and as a consequence of this, the Gnostic did not reject all paganism as idolatry. Conversion to the school of Valentinus or to the Ophites did not oblige the believer to put away pagan philosophy and to study only the Bible. The Naassene hymn, for instance, cited by Hippolytus (*Refutatio*, v. 1–11) seems to be a commentary on a hymn to Attis, and the writer ranges in his quotations from the Old Testament and the Gospels to Homer and Empedocles.[1] In this, the attitude of the Gnostic contrasted with that maintained by Catholics such as Cyprian and, more markedly, with extreme seekers after martyrdom in the fourth century such as the Donatist bishop Marculus.[2] It finds, however, an echo in the claim made by the African Manichaean leader, Faustus, that a true altar to God was a mind well cultivated, which included being well-read in classical literature.[3] A further proof of the intimate association of pagan mysticism and Gnosticism has been provided in a startling fashion by the discovery of Hermetic works among the most prized possessions of the Sethite sect whose library was discovered at Nag-Hammadi in 1946.[4] In one of the codices which seems to have been among those most used, the *Acts of Peter* and *Acts of the Twelve Apostles* were found sewn together with the *Logos Authentikos* of Hermes to his son Thoth and the work which has been known hitherto as the *Asclepius*. This discovery confirms the suspicion which had been held by Lagrange that the Gnostics with whom Plotinus and his pupils debated in Rome had links with Hermetism and pagan Gnosticism.[5] For all his show of exclusiveness and mystery-making, the Gnostic shared to the full the religious syncretism of the age. In fact, he is the embodiment of it, and Gnosticism may perhaps be regarded as a rival religion rather than a heretical manifestation of Christianity.

His attitude towards the authorities and towards surrounding society seems to have been conditioned by one object alone, the protection of his mystery. How important this was in the eyes of the sectaries is indicated once again by a passage found in the Sethite Apocalypse of the Great Seth from the library of Nag-Hammadi.[6] Believers are warned that 'these revelations are not to be disclosed to anyone in the flesh. They must only be

between some forms of Gnosticism and Iranian religion is also suggested by the discovery of an Apocalypse of Zostrianus or Zoroaster among the Sethite library from Nag-Hammadi. Mention too, should be made of Kirsopp Lake's note on the Zoroastrian origins of the Gnostic prophets Bar Kabbas and Bar Coph in his ed. of Eusebius *Hist. Ecc.* iv. 7. 7.

[1] C. H. Dodd, *The Interpretation of the Fourth Gospel*, Cambridge 1952, p. 98.
[2] *Passio Marculi* 1 (Migne, P.L. viii, col. 760): mox ubi beatae fidei rudimenta suscepit, statim mundanas litteras respuens, forense exercitium et falsam saecularis scientiae dignitatem suspensa ad coelum mente calcavit. It would be hard to find an allusion to a classical author in Cyprian, rhetorician and lawyer though he was before his conversion. Tertullian's view in his catholic period is shown in *De Praescriptione* 7 and 36.
[3] Augustine, *Contra Faustum* xx. 3 (P.L. xlii, col. 370). Also, *Confessions*, v. 6. 11 and vii. 12.
[4] C. H. Puech, 'Les nouveaux écrits gnostiques découverts en Haute-Egypte,' in *Coptic Studies in Honour of Walter Ewing Crum*, Byzantine Institute, Boston, 1950, 143.
[5] J. M. Lagrange, 'L'Hermetisme', *Revue Biblique*, xxxv (1926), 240-264, at 252.
[6] Cited from C. H. Puech, 'Les nouveaux écrits gnostiques découverts en Haute-Egypte,' 108. Cf. Celsus in Origen, *Contra Celsum*, v. 63.

communicated to the brethren who belong to the generation of life.' This injunction could dissuade an individual from making a public confession of faith, and that this may have been the result in practice is suggested by two statements put into the mouth of the Gnostics by Tertullian. Confession, the Gnostics maintained, was not to be made on earth, but souls would be put upon trial in the several storeys of the heavens.[1] Further on he quotes the teaching of Valentinus and Prodicus that 'one must not confess on earth before men, and must do so the less in truth, that God may not seem to thirst for blood'.[2] Nearly two centuries later one finds the same resolve to protect the mystery from utterance before the uninitiated in the famous lines attributed by Augustine to the Spanish followers of Priscillian: 'Jura, perjura, secretum prodere noli'.[3] Such an outlook would naturally breed a purely defensive attitude towards the civil authorities, for it would be sheer folly to provoke a situation in which one would be confronted with the choices of premature death or denial. In this too, the gnostic viewpoint was fundamentally opposed to the catholic, but was hardly dissimilar from that accepted by the initiates of other extraneous mystery cults.[4]

Once this objective is understood the statements of the gnostic leaders themselves and the accusations of the Catholics may become more intelligible. It may explain for instance, the passage quoted by Eusebius from the lost work of Agrippa Castor against the Gnostics of Asia. 'The followers of Basilides,' he says, maintained that 'there was no harm in eating things offered to idols or in lightheartedly (ἀπαραφυλάκτως) denying the faith in time of persecution'.[5] While this does not appear to have been the view of Basilides himself, who saw in the martyr's death a punishment for sin committed in this or in a previous existence,[6] it corresponds truly enough with the outlook of many Gnostics of which we have evidence. At Carthage and Alexandria they would argue that martyrdom was akin to suicide.[7] It was not the will of God, but the cruel demand of the Demiurge.[8] Christ had suffered and died for mankind in order to free mankind from death. How could God refuse blood sacrifices and then demand the sacrifice of men?[9] It was not the outward confession of the faith but the practice of the faith by word and deed that marked a man out as a Christian.[10] The idea that martyrdom would bring the individual a reward was utterly rejected. True witness to God was the Gnosis imparted to the perfect believer, and this was an inner possession of the heart to be revealed only at the Last Day.

[1] Tertullian, *Scorpiace* 10 (C.S.E.L. xx. 165–6).

[2] Ibid., 15: quod si iam tunc Prodicus et Valentinus adsisteret suggerens non in terris esse confitendum apud homines. (C.S.E.L. xx. 178).

[3] Augustine, *Ep.* 237. 3. (C.S.E.L., lvii. 528).

[4] Apuleius, *Apol.* 55 (ed. Helm, p. 62). See A. D. Nock, *Conversion*, Oxford 1933, 114.

[5] Eusebius, *Hist. Ecc.*, iv. 7. 7.

[6] Clement, *Stromata*, iv. 81. See H. von Campenhausen, *Die Idee des Martyriums in der alten Kirche*, Göttingen 1936, 94.

[7] Tertullian, *Scorpiace* 1: sed vanitas, immo dementia pro deo mori, ut qui me salvum faciat. (C.S.E.L., xx. 145). Clement, *Stromata*, iv. 72. 2.

[8] Tertullian, *Scorpiace*, 5.

[9] Ibid., 1 and 6.

[10] Clement, *Stromata*, iv. 73. 1 (Heracleon's view).

These ideas had their effect on the degree of conformity which the Gnostic could offer to the demands of the City State, and it is here that the most striking contrasts between Gnosticism and orthodox Christianity may be observed. It is well-known that loyalty to the State or City religion did not involve adhesion to a creed or defined set of beliefs. It did involve, however, certain cult acts such as walking in a procession garlanded, sacrifice to the gods, swearing by the Imperial genius, or eating meat which had previously been sacrificed. This last act has an importance in everyday life, for a good deal of the meat on sale in the meat-market would have come from the temples. The orthodox Christian like the orthodox Jew, would refuse to take it and so draw attention to himself. The Gnostic had no such scruples. The evidence on this point is strong. Irenaeus says of Basilides and his followers 'that he attaches no importance to the question regarding meats offered in sacrifice to idols, and thinks of them as of no consequence and makes use of them without any hesitation'.[1] He adds for good measure that, 'these men practise magic, use images, incantations, invocations, and every other kind of curious act, including the "theorems of the mathematics".' Social exclusiveness and religious intolerance is the last thing to be expected of such people. Other Gnostics are described as doing the same, and of 'giving out names plausible and credible to the heathen'.[2] They did this on the logical ground that 'they had in their power all things which were irreligious and impious and were at liberty to practise them, for they maintain that things are good or evil simply in virtue of human opinion'.[3]

In other significant ways, the Gnostic found himself able to conform to pagan society. While the Catholic was warned in the sermon, II Peter ii. 13 to avoid the feastings of guilds (ἑταίρειαι), which were among the characteristic features of local pagan society, Gnostics, such as the Nicolaitans, were prepared to expose themselves to the wrath of John the Elder rather than comply.[4] Nor had they scruples about engaging in trades connected directly with pagan worship. Hermogenes for instance, settled down in Carthage as an idol-painter after emigrating from Asia.[5] The gnostic sect did not constitute a serious danger either to the *pax deorum* or to the City State. It is not surprising to find pre-Constantinian inscriptions in Rome openly avowing gnostic beliefs.[6]

The contrasting views held by the Catholics were also founded on theology, and in particular on beliefs which the Gnostics rejected. First, as Ignatius shows, persecution and martyrdom were in imitation of Christ's Passion and physical suffering. This inspired his devotion and almost pathological craving for martyrdom. 'For if it is merely in semblance that these things were done by our Lord, then I am also a prisoner in semblance.

[1] Irenaeus, *Adv. Haer.*, i. 24. 5.
[2] Ibid., ii. 14.
[3] Ibid., i. 25. 3.
[4] Rev., ii. 20–2. See W. M. Ramsay, *Expositor*, (1904), 59.
[5] Tertullian, *Adversus Hermogenem* i. (ed. Kroymann, C.S.E.L., xlvi. 126).
[6] C. Cechelli, *Monumenti cristiano-heretici di Roma*, Rome 1944, 148.

THE GNOSTIC SECTS AND THE ROMAN EMPIRE

And why have I surrendered myself to death, to fire, to the sword and to wild beasts?'[1] Thus he wrote to the Church at Smyrna. The Gnostic, on the other hand, regarding suffering as a token of sin, was prepared to maintain that if Jesus had suffered in reality, then He had sinned.[2] Secondly, persecution was regarded as the divine means of separating just from unjust in preparation for the end of the existing age.[3] It was therefore a necessity, for it had been the lot of all righteous men to suffer, from the time of the prophets onwards.[4] In the coming Millenium, however, the martyrs would execute judgement over the Gentiles, a belief which the *Passio Perpetuae* shows was quite literally held by those who defied the authorities.[5] The prophetic and Messianic tradition of earliest Christianity was inextricably woven with the strictest Jewish tradition of hostility towards the Greco-Roman world. Tertullian's final chapter in *De Spectaculis* holds out the same prospect as the *Assumption of Moses*.[6] The believer would feast his gaze eternally on the Gentiles writhing in the torments of Hell.

Tertullian's anti-gnostic and anti-pagan polemic pushed this attitude to its logical conclusion of defiance and linked it with the ethical code which he would have the Christian observe. Martyrdom was not merely to be suffered. It was to be acquired. It was the second baptism, the only certain means of removing post-baptismal sin.[7] It was part of the Christian's oath of obedience to God's law. This meant open warfare on pagan society. 'Ye shall utterly destroy all the places wherein the nations which ye shall possess by inheritance, served their gods' (Deut. xii. 2).[8] Tertullian reminds the Gnostics of this command, and of other similar injunctions in the Old Testament. Both the Old Testament as the word of God, and the command of the Spirit were towards the crown of martyrdom.[9] In visions of Paradise only the martyrs could be seen.[10] Conversely, rejection of the Old Testament and distrust of prophecy involved rejection of martyrdom.

As one reads through these texts, it seems clear that whatever had been the policy of the Roman Empire its hand would have been forced by Christians of this tradition. It was the Maccabean conflict over again, only extended to the whole Mediterranean. Tertullian himself recalls an incident which took place in the province of Asia in about 185 and which must have been well known. The proconsul, Arrius Antoninus, was holding a periodic assize in one of the towns of the province. A number of Christians presented themselves before him and demanded martyrdom. The aston-

---

[1] Ignatius, *Ep. ad Smyrnaeos*, 4 (ed. Kirsopp Lake, *Apostolic Fathers*, i. 257).

[2] See J. Lebreton and J. Zeiller, *Histoire de l'Église*, ii. 11.

[3] Tertullian, *De Fuga*, 1.

[4] Tertullian, *Scorpiace*, 8.

[5] Particularly in Saturus's speech in *Passio Perpetuae*, 17 (ed. J. A. Robinson): notate tamen nobis facies diligenter ut recognoscatis nos in die illo (i.e. the Last Day).

[6] Tertullian, *De Spectaculis* 30, *Assumptio Moseos* x. 8–10 (ed. Charles). Cf. T. R. Glover, *Conflict of Religions in the Early Roman Empire*, 171.

[7] Tertullian, *Apol.*, 50.

[8] Tertullian, *Scorpiace* 2 (C.S.E.L., xx. 148).

[9] Tertullian, *De Fuga*, 9.

[10] Tertullian, *De Anima*, 55 (C.S.E.L., xx. 388): Perpetua fortissima martyr sub die passionis in revelatione paradisi solos illic commartyres suos vidit.

ished official ordered a few off to execution, and turned to the rest, 'Unhappy men, if you want to die, you have ropes and precipices'.[1] Two centuries later in Africa he might not have been able to maintain such detachment. Augustine relates how an official would be ambushed by Circumcellions and given the alternatives of making them martyrs or being himself despatched to Hell.[2] The germ of this attitude is to be found in Tertullian, and it is no accident that the Gnostics were his opponents.

Accompanying this theology went an ethic which corresponded in its detail to the 'odium generis humani' which had been applied to the Jews by Greeks and Latins alike.[3] The 'Israel of God' was no less arrogant and exclusive towards those whom it termed 'ἔθνη' or 'nationes' than the Old Dispensation had been. The earlier apologists, Aristides and the writer of *Ad Diognetum*, repeat the favourite arguments against idolatry used by the Hellenistic Jews in the last centuries before Christ.[4] Idolatry was the supreme crime. It is interesting to see how Tertullian, like his Jewish contemporaries, extends the term to cover practically every aspect of daily life and so exclude the Christian from any participation in the government of his city and the normal society of his fellows. The norms of Christian conduct set out in *De Idololatria* bear a curious resemblance to those laid down for Jews in the *'Aboda Zara* which was written at nearly the same time.[5] The spirit behind both suggests a state of embittered political warfare with pagan society. Tertullian's attitude does not seem to have been isolated. It corresponds only too well with the charges made by pagan writers in Asia Minor, such as Aelius Aristides, against the social outlook of the Christians.[6] Perhaps this, rather than abstract ideas about salvation through *gnosis* bestowed on believers by Christ was the main cause of the persecutions. Conduct which, to the outside world, might be summed up as proselytising atheism and misanthropy carried the seeds of endemic hatred. From the official point of view this was aggravated by the Christians' senseless obstinacy (*contumacia*) and a theatrical longing for death.

If we accept the taunts of Irenaeus and Tertullian against the Gnostics our estimate of the persecutions must also be affected. The Gnostics were not isolated and insignificant groups in the second century. At Edessa, and

---

[1] Tertullian, *Ad Scapulam*, 5. See the present writer's *The Donatist Church*, Oxford 1952, 115–6 and 174.

[2] Augustine, *Ep.* 185. 3. 12 (C.S.E.L., lvii. 11).

[3] Detailed in H. Fuchs, 'Tacitus über die Christen,' *Vigiliae Christianae*, iv (1950), 65–93.

[4] Taken from Ps. 115, Wisdom, xiii. 15. See also Book iii of the Jewish Sibyllines (ed. Geffcken, 1902, 78), lines 583–90. There may even have been Jewish and Christian summaries of arguments purporting to show that all that was true in classical philosophy was borrowed from Moses and the remainder was rubbish. See W. L. Knox, *St. Paul and the Church of the Gentiles*, Cambridge 1938, 91, n. 1.

[5] See W. A. L. Elmslie, 'The Jewish Moral Outlook in the first two Centuries A.D.,' *Cambridge Texts and Studies*, viii. 2, 1911.

[6] Aelius Aristides, *Oratio*, 46, (ed. Dindorf, ii. 397): πρὸς Πλάτωνα ὑπὲρ τῶν τεσσάρων. Aristides finds a resemblance between the Christian and Jewish outlooks.

probably in Alexandria and Antioch also, the various sects may have formed a majority of Christians.[1] At Rome, they were a sizeable minority. Their numbers were considerable in the Gallic cities and at Carthage. In the second century as in the fourth many pagans found the way of salvation opened through Christ as cosmic saviour more attractive than a Christianity founded on the prophecies contained in the Septuagint.[2] As Origen plainly indicates, the Gnosticism of this period was partly the result of the effort made by pagans educated in mystery cults to comprehend Christ within their experience.[3] The true name of God, the oracle of Apollo of Claros affirmed was IAO, the god of the Jews, and also the Demiurge of some of the Gnostics.[4] If there had been imperial edicts in existence aimed against Christianity, the effort at syncretism could not have been made on the scale it was. Too many people would have been involved to escape detection. Religion is and has always been a staple topic for discussion in the Middle East, and a man who faced towards the east and crossed himself before eating or entering into a religious debate would not pass unnoticed.[5] Christians did not have to conceal their identity in normal times.

The numbers who died for the Christian faith in the first 250 years A.D. were considered by contemporaries to be small. Origen, writing circa 247, states in two works[6] that persecutions belonged to a past generation, and that the numbers of those who had been martyred could easily be counted up. These statements are interesting, coming from one who knew the Alexandrine Gnostics very well, and who in his youth had scarcely been persuaded not to offer himself for martyrdom.[7] Had any attempt been made by the authorities to root out the schools of Valentinus, Basilides and Heracleon, we might have heard about it from Origen.

One is therefore led to believe that in the first two centuries the persecutions were confined to one type of Christian who might reasonably be called 'the new Israel'. These were men and women who had inherited in full measure the anti-classical traditions of the Septuagint and Hellenistic-Jewish apologies, and who had been schooled to regard persecution either by the synagogues or by the authorities as their lot. Like the Jews of Josephus's day (A.D. 70–90) they attracted into their ranks those to whom the slightest accommodation with Greco-Roman civilisation was treason to

---

[1] I am accepting W. Bauer's theory expressed in *Rechtgläubigkeit und Ketzerei im ältesten Christentum*, Tübingen, 1934, that Gnostics were in a majority in Edessa, and also in Egypt, where the absence of bishops coupled with the abundance of gnostic texts supports this view, but elsewhere I think he over-emphasises the strength of Gnosticism.

[2] This was the experience of Faustus the Manichee (Augustine, *Contra Faustum* iv. 1 and xv. 1) and of Augustine himself for some years.

[3] *Contra Celsum*, iii. 12 (Koetschau, i. 212).

[4] See R. P. Festugière. *La Révélation d'Hermès Trismégiste*, Paris 1944, 13.

[5] As in the story of the debate between Timothy and Aquila. Cited from L. Williams, *Adversus Judaeos*, 52.

[6] Origen, *Contra Celsum*, iii. 8 and *Hom. in Jerem.*, iv. 3 (ed. Klostermann, 1901, 25): also *In Matt. Comment. Sermo*, 39 (Persecutions partial only). See H. Grégoire, *Les Persécutions dans l'Empire romain* (Mémoires de l'académie royale de Belgique, Cl. des Lettres, t. xlvi. fasc. 1), 1951, 12.

[7] Eusebius, *Hist. Ecc.*, vi. 3.

their religion, and they would rather die than accept.[1] Ignatius in his refusal to allow any appeal for clemency to be made on his behalf by the Christians of Rome is characteristic. But whether comparative moderates or fanatics, it seemed as natural to die for Christ as it was to their Jewish contemporaries to die for the Torah. Not unexpectedly, they roused the bitter hostility of both Greeks and orthodox Jews, and in particular the latter, for the advent of Christianity meant that the stream of ardent semi-proselytes who accepted the ethic and practices but not the rites of Judaism began to dry up. With this development disappeared the hope that the conversion of the Gentiles as prophesied in Isaiah would be fulfilled.[2] The Greeks, equally, had real cause for hatred and the early persecutions resemble nothing so much as a continuation of the internecine pograms which took place in Egypt and Asia Minor wherever Jew, native and Greek had rubbed shoulders in unneighbourly proximity. The Jews rejoiced in new-found civic patriotism, and hastened to place the burden of their own unpopularity on the backs of their victorious Christian rivals.[3]

But the future lay with the Church of the Martyrs. The Gnostics, like their Manichaean successors, could make individual converts but they lacked the organisation of the Catholic Church. They spread the name of Christ widely but thinly. They were not, as they put it (Irenaeus, *Adv. Haer.* iii. 15. 2) *ecclesiastici*, and it is interesting that the only group which set out to form a church, the followers of Marcion, were the only Gnostics to claim martyrdoms among their number.[4] What was worse, the other great Christian virtues in the eyes of the people, alms-giving and charity, were, as Ignatius so tellingly pointed out, the fruit of orthodoxy.[5] An inscription on a mosaic at Tipasa shows that these virtues were to be associated with martyrdom as well.[6] It is not only the words of Justin[7] and Tertullian[8] that tell us how great was the impact of the martyr's death on popular imagination. There is also the tribute paid by Galen—'Sometimes they (the Christians) act like genuine philosophers. For that they despise death we can all see with our own eyes, and further that impelled by modesty they shrink from carnal lusts. Some, even in self discipline and self control and by the most ardent longing for excellence, have progressed so far that they are not a whit inferior to true philosophers.'[9] This excellence, however,

---

[1] Josephus, *Antiquities*, xviii. 1. 6: μόνον ἡγεμόνα καὶ δεσπότην τὸν θεόν ὑπειλήφοσιν μηδένα ἄνθρωπον προσαγορεύειν δεσπότην.

[2] Isaiah, xlii. 1–4 and xlix. 6.

[3] The Jews were the first to try to pin a charge of treason on the Christians—Acts, xvii. 7 and Luke xxiii. 2–23. On their systematic propaganda against the Church in the second century see, Justin, *Dial. cum Tryphone*, 17. 4.

[4] Eusebius, *Hist. Ecc.*, iv. 15, and *Acta S. Pionii* (ed. Krüger and Knopf), 21. 5.

[5] Ignatius, *Ep. ad Smyrnaeos*, vi. 2.

[6] *C.I.L.*, viii. 20906. Another inscription from the same site contains the lines 'Aele-mosinam enim facere | Hoc est christianum monstrare.' L. Leschi, *Bull. Archéologique du comité des Travaux historiques*, séance de 27 mai 1940, xvii.

[7] Justin, *Apol.*, ii. 12. 1 (P. G. vi. col. 464).

[8] Tertullian, *Apol.*, 50.

[9] Galen, extract from a lost summary of Plato's *Republic*, written circa 180. Quoted from M. P. Charlesworth, *The Roman Empire*, Home University Library, 1951, 151.

was the result of rigid adherence to the rules of the faith backed by ecclesiastical organisation. The glory of the martyr may not have been completely the glory of the bishop, as Cyprian would have it.[1] It seems likely,
however, that the example of the martyr helped to discredit and to defeat
Gnosticism and thus establish the monarchical episcopate as the sole means
of governing the Church.

So long as the balance was held evenly between Gnostic and Catholic,
the Church was little danger to the Empire. Writing of the second century,
Eusebius could point out that the Devil preferred to use the weapon of heresy
rather than that of persecution as a means of vexing the Church.[2] But the
eclipse of Gnosticism, and indeed of all those Christians, such as the Adop-
tionists, who sought to harmonise the message of the Gospels with the religious experience of their contemporaries brought with it a decisive change.
In the first half of the third century the consolidation of the monarchical
episcopate enabled orthodoxy to be enforced among the Christian communities from one end of the Mediterranean to the other. Only then did
the Church succeed the Jewish Dispersion as the world organisation which
rivalled the organisation of the Roman Empire and showed itself as the
declared enemy of Greco-Roman civilisation. By 250 the issue had
become, for or against paganism. The whole Church was the target. The
sects no longer afforded immunity to their believers.

---

[1] Cyprian, *Ep.* 13. 1 (ed. Hartel, C.S.E.L., iii. 2, 504–5).
[2] Eusebius, *Hist. Ecc.*, iv. 7. 1.

III

THE OLD TESTAMENT IN THE AGE
OF THE GREEK APOLOGISTS A.D. 130-180

FOR or against the Old Testament? Such was one of the main issues that divided developing orthodoxy in the primitive Church from its Gnostic and Marcionite rivals during the second century A.D. Was the Old Testament the work of an inferior god of the Jews to be read perhaps for the sake of the Decalogue and a few striking passages, and the remainder rejected, or did it unfold the gradual story of human salvation, and in the prophetic books, by foretelling the life and death of Christ, assure the Christian of his right to consider himself the Third (and chosen) Race of mankind? Behind this issue lay another equally important, namely the relationship between the Christians as the new Israel and the Old Israel represented by orthodox Judaism, whose role as the light to lighten the Gentiles it was challenging and would eventually take over. If the Old Testament did indeed contain the word of God, to whom did its promises refer, to the Christians or the Jews? Could the Christians claim with success that the prophecies in the Old Testament spoke of Christ and none other? The debate which was to span the second century was carried out in the tradition of the synagogue. At times the Church's essential message of hope and salvation threatened to founder amidst the demands of a new *haggadah* and *halakhah* evolved from the ceaseless challenge of Jewry.

Until comparatively recently the importance of the long-continued debate with the Jews during the second century tended to be underestimated. The moralising and inward-looking character of much of sub-apostolic Christianity had been accepted without attempting to discover the reasons. It had been assumed too readily that there were clear-cut divisions between Christians and Jews that in fact did not exist.[1] The balance has now been redressed by the revival of

---

[1] A landmark in the study of Christian-Jewish relations in the Roman Empire was the appearance of M. Simon's *Verus Israel* (Paris, 1948, 2nd ed. 1964). Since then, for the connexions between Jewish and Christian theology in the first two centuries see J. Daniélou, *Théologie du judéo-christianisme* (Paris, 1958), R. P. C.

studies in the Judaism of the Tannaitic period, while the analysis of the contents of the Gnostic library at Nag Hammadi leaves no doubt as to the extent of Jewish influence on Gnosticism.[1] For their part, contemporaries were struck by the essential similarity of the two cults despite their internecine quarrels. Celsus' unflattering description of the 'race of Jews and Christians' he had encountered, probably in Syria *ca.* 178, as 'clustering bats or ants coming out of a nest, or frogs holding council round a marsh, or worms assembling in some filthy corner, disagreeing with one another about which were the worse sinners', represented a certain consensus of pagan opinion of the day.[2] So, too, did his view that the Christians were in reality apostates from Judaism[3] and that there was no more than 'the shadow of an ass' to choose between their ideas.[4] His introduction of the argumentative Jew in the early part of the *Alethes Logos* to pick holes in Christianity was a clever device designed to demonstrate to his readers the kinship of the two religions, each alien to the cultures and ideals of the Greco-Roman world.

Celsus was correct in his main assumption. In his day the thought-world of Christianity still belonged largely to Judaism. It was the Jewish concept of God, of creation, of history and morality that the Christian accepted on Baptism, and the Jewish arguments against paganism that he adopted in his defence of his new faith. Together with the Jews he opposed the worship of the traditional territorial gods that dominated the life of his pagan contemporaries. There was little to choose between the barriers that Jews and Christians erected against pagan society. The basic identity of outlook, however, masked profound

---

Hanson, *Allegory and Event* (London, 1959), and P. Prigent, *Justin et l'Ancien Testament* (Paris, 1964).

[1] For the ramifications of Gnosticism, see collected studies published as 'The Origins of Gnosticism' in *Studies in the History of Religions* xii (Supplements, to *Numen*), Leiden, 1967, and for Judaism in the Tannaitic period, the successive studies of J. Neusner on the *History of the Jews in Babylon*, (Princeton, 1965) and following. I have also been able to consult a draft English translation of J. Daniélou, *Gospel Message and Hellenistic Culture*, by the courtesy of Messrs Darton, Longman and Todd.

[2] Origen, *Contra Celsum* (ed. and tr. H. Chadwick), iv.23. Compare Lucian of Samosata's use of the terms 'prophet', 'synagogue-leader' and 'first lawgiver' (the Christian equivalent of Moses), in his description of Syrian and Palestinian Christianity in *The Death of Peregrinus*, ch. 13-15.

[3] Origen, op. cit., ii.2 and 4.

[4] Origen, op. cit., iii.1.

rivalry between the two monotheistic religions. Sometimes, as in Smyrna at the time of Polycarp's martyrdom (*cà.* 165-168), this blazed into outright warfare with the Jews siding with the pagans in an effort to rid themselves of their rivals.[1] More often, one may assume there were discussions and debates, such as that between Justin Martyr and Trypho in *ca.* 137 at Ephesus, and recorded at great length by Justin in *ca.* A.D. 160,[2] or between Jason and Papiscus, an Alexandrian, *ca.* 140, or between the Jew and the Christian at Carthage *ca.* 200. The Christian's inept defence of Christianity provoked Tertullian to write his *Adversus Iudaeos.*[3]

These conflicts ranged around the LXX. Did the prophecies contained in the Greek Old Testament refer to Jesus as the Christ and Messiah, or to some other Messiah more in keeping with Jewish hopes for an earthly deliverer? Celsus contemptuously describes the Dialogue between Jason and Papiscus as a work in which a Christian disputes with a Jew out of the Jewish Scriptures, to prove that the predictions regarding the Christ fitted only Jesus.[4] This in fact was to be one of the main tasks of the Apologists. In the debate both sides accepted the Old Testament as the voice of God himself whose will and purposes were unchanging and hence whose message set down in Scripture must be self-consistent.[5] As both believed that a Messiah would come and both accepted identical canons of exegesis there was little room for compromise. Either Jesus did fulfil the prophecies, or he was a deceiver who richly deserved his fate.[6] The argument was concerned with the correct interpretation of specific proof-texts carried out with meticulous attention to detail.[7]

---

[1] Eusebius, *Hist. Eccl.* iv.15.26, 29 and 41.

[2] The date is later than *Apology* written *ca.* 152 to which Justin refers in *Dialogue*, 120.6. That he had been involved in many similar debates is suggested by Trypho (*Dial.* 50.1).

[3] Tertullian, *Adv. Iudaeos,* i.

[4] Origen, *Contra Celsum,* iv.52.

[5] See T. W. Manson, 'The Argument from Prophecy', *J.T.S.* 46, 1945, pp. 129-36.

[6] *Contra Celsum,* i.28 and ii.48. See also Justin, *Dial.* 69.7. Compare the opening scene in the Gnostic *Apocryphon Ioannis* where the Pharisee who encounters John on the steps of the Temple taunts John with believing in a 'Nazarene' and a 'deceiver' (ed. and tr. R. M. Grant, *Gnosticism, an Anthology,* (London, 1961), p. 69).

[7] C. H. Dodd, *According to the Scriptures* (London, 1952), p. 57, lists fifteen Old Testament texts which in his view give us ground 'for believing that New Testament writers were working upon a tradition in which certain passages of the Old Testament were treated as "testimonies" to the Gospel facts'.

By the time the Apologists appear towards the middle of the second century the debate had been continuing for two generations at least. It had constituted the most important single intellectual activity of the primitive Church, the counterpart to the more violent conflicts in the synagogues of the Hellenistic world, and it provides an important link between the ideas of the New Testament writers and those of the sub-apostolic age. When the Synoptists wrote, probably not much later than the fall of Jerusalem in 70, they were conscious of apologetic needs in regard to the orthodox Jews. Luke, though writing for a Hellenistic or Hellenistic-Jewish official, always sought to demonstrate wherever possible that Jesus or John the Baptist as fulfilling Scripture. Thus, John's mission was justified, 'as it is written in the words of Esaias the prophet' (Luke 3.4) and Jesus is recorded as opening his mission at Nazareth with the words, 'This day is Scripture fulfilled in your ears' (Luke 4.16). More than once he warns his hearers to the effect that 'this generation shall not pass away until all be fulfilled' (Luke 16.17). Luke saw Christ fulfilling the prophecies of Scripture and establishing a new covenant for the benefit of all who believed on him. In particular, he was at pains to show that the Passion and Crucifixion were a continuation of the treatment that had been meted out to the prophets and righteous of Israel from the beginning of time.[1] Matthew follows a similar theme only far more intensively. As is well known, almost every significant act performed by Jesus was 'so that the Scripture might be fulfilled'. In this Gospel the reader may feel that the conflict with the 'unbelieving Jews' was among the writer's primary concerns.

The Synoptists were writing at a time of mounting antagonism between Christian and Jew. The common focus and community of outlook derived from loyalty to the Temple cult had been removed for ever by the catastrophe of the Jewish war.[2] The rancours already exhibited in Paul's time were given full rein. There was no place for those who wanted to

[1] Luke 11.49-51. Compare 4.24 and 13.30 both in connexion with prophecy and rejection. Also, Matt. 23.25, and see B. Lindars, *New Testament Apologetic* (London, 1961), p. 20.

[2] But see K. W. Clark, 'Worship in the Jerusalem Temple after A.D. 70', *N.T.S.* 6 (1960), p. 269ff, for the claim that a holy place remained after 70 where propitiation might still be made for divine blessing, and that Heb. 10.11 indicates continued Christian interest.

sit on the fence.[1] Orthodox Jews were ready to put the Christians out of the synagogue whenever opportunity arose. To the Christians orthodox Judaism sometimes represented the 'synagogue of Satan' (Rev. 3.7). The woes called down on the Pharisees (Matt. 23) condemned their hypocrisy and blindness in unmeasured terms. Christians, on the other hand, were put out of synagogues (John 9.22 and 16.2) and harried mercilessly.[2] One notable piece of controversial literature of the sub-apostolic age has survived. This is the *Epistle of Barnabas*, written probably in Alexandria at some date between the two Jewish wars of 70 and 135.[3] It throws light on the intellectual issues which were to be debated with the Jews by the Christian Apologists in the second century and the manner in which each side attempted to establish its case.

The writer of the *Epistle* was a fanatical hater of Judaism though he himself was steeped in the Rabbinic methods of Scriptural interpretation of the day. The Jews indeed are castigated as 'wretched men' (xvi.1-2) who put their hopes in a building, namely the Temple, and Barnabas rejoices in its destruction and that of Jerusalem itself (xvi.5). Jewish fasts and sacrifices are rejected (vii) and circumcision attributed to the machinations of an evil angel (ix.4). The Jews are told that they have failed to understand Scripture, though significant as showing the continuity of traditional methods of exegesis by both Jews and Christians of the time, the writer interprets passages in a way similar to that employed by the Q'mran Covenanters, whereby texts were taken from the prophets and referred to current events. For instance, *Barnabas* xvi.3-4, ' "Lo they who destroyed this temple shall themselves build it" (Isa. 49.17). That is happening now: for owing to the war it was destroyed by the enemy: at present even the servants of the enemy will build it up again.' This can be compared with the Q'mran commentaries on Habakkuk and Nahum,[4] wherein the

---

[1] See Ignatius of Antioch's denunciation of people who evidently wanted to adhere both to Judaism and to Christianity, *Philadelphians*, 6.

[2] Justin, *Dial.* 16.4, 17.1, 47.4 and 110.5.

[3] Probably nearer 135 than 70. See L. W. Barnard's studies on *Barnabas* in his *Studies in the Apostolic Fathers and their Background* (Oxford, 1966), especially pp. 46ff, R. P. C. Hanson, *Allegory and Event* , p. 95, and J. Daniélou, *Théologie du judéo-christianisme*, pp. 43ff.

[4] For instance, the Commentaries on the Book of Nahum and the Book of Habakkuk (ed. and tr. Th. Gaster, *The Scriptures of the Dead Sea Sect* (London, 1957), pp. 231ff).

words of the prophets are made to refer to current political events. The remaining typological interpretations and allegorisations seem also to be Palestinian in character. As L. W. Barnard has shown, the *Epistle* is itself a Talmud, i.e. a *didache* or work of instruction divided into halakhic and haggadic sections, clearly marked at the beginning of ch. xviii (*Metabōmen de kai epi heteran gnōsin kai diathēkēn*).[1] The writer uses the LXX, passages from which are carefully analysed in the Rabbinic method of composing *midrash*. The allegorical and didactic methods of interpretation used by the author are paralleled by what is known of the teaching of the synagogues and at Q'mran. The Two Ways of Life with which he ends his writings also finds parallels at Q'mran[2] and in the Book of the Secrets of Enoch.[3] In the clamour of anti-Jewish controversy Christian virtues of love, forbearance and forgiveness take second place.

More typical perhaps of the Christian approach to the Old Testament at the turn of the second century was *1 Clement*.[4] In this letter from the Roman to the Corinthian community protesting the unjust deposition of presbyters in the latter, the Old Testament is treated simply as Scripture. There are more than a hundred quotations from the LXX and there is the possibility that *Clement's* New Testament consisted simply of *logia* and not of connected Gospels. His outlook was uncomplicated, believing that the New Covenant of Christianity was a continuation of the Old, and that the ethic and organisation of Israel portrayed in the one passed over *en bloc* to the other. Everything in the New Israel could be justified by reference to a counterpart in the Old. The background of his exhortations would be Jewish homiletic, but he is aware also of distinctively Christian usages which were developing at that time. For instance, at the end of a long exhortatory passage regarding faith occupying chs. 10-12, he speaks of Rahab's scarlet thread as a type of the blood of Christ (12.7). The use of this text was to have a long history, through *Barnabas* (xiii.7) to Justin

---

[1] See Barnard, op. cit., p. 49; compare J. Daniélou, *Théologie*, pp. 43-4.
[2] 'All who practise righteousness are under the domination of the Prince of Light and walk in the ways of light: whereas all who practise perversity are under the domination of the Angel of Darkness and walk in the ways of darkness' (*Manual of Discipline*, iii.23-6, tr. Gaster, op. cit., p. 53).
[3] *The Book of the Secrets of Enoch* (ed. Morfill and Charles), 30.15.
[4] On the Jewish-Christian character of *1 Clement*, see Daniélou, op. cit., pp. 53-4.

(*Dial.* 111.4) and Origen. It may even have belonged to a book of *Testimonies* already in use largely for the purpose of combating the Jews when *Clement* was written.[1] Elsewhere one finds a similar specifically Christian application of Old Testament texts. *Clement* is prepared to substitute 'deacons' for 'rulers' in citing Isa. 60.17 in order to support the existence of a hierarchy of 'bishops' and 'deacons' deriving their powers by divine sanction, in the Christian Church (*1 Cl.* 40). His work contains *haggadah* on the effects of jealousy (ch.iv),[2] on the virtues of obedience through Enoch (ix.3), fidelity through Noah (ix.4), faith through Abraham (x.1-7) and hospitality through Lot and Rahab (xi.1-3 and xxi.1-7). All these are based on traditional Jewish interpretations of Scripture.

In their different ways *Clement* and *Barnabas* reflected the outlook of the christianised synagogues of the Greek lands at the beginning of the second century A.D. Christianity was the natural fulfilment and prolongation of the prophetic tradition of Judaism. Jesus was the true 'suffering servant' of Isa. 53.[3] His detractors were the orthodox Jews who had crucified him, to be rebutted by argument and *florilegia* of proof-texts assembled to demonstrate that the suffering and death on the Cross of the Messiah had been foretold and that the ceremonial law which was a stumbling-block to the Gentiles had been abrogated in the new covenant. So long as the intellectual leadership of the Church remained with men such as the writer of the *Epistle of Barnabas*, the Church would not stray far from its Jewish parentage.

The second fall of Jerusalem in 135 was a landmark in the story of Jewish-Christian relations. All hope of a restored Temple and Holy City now faded, and the Jews were thrown on to the defensive. The reference of the prophecies to an earthly restoration of the Jewish kingdom and Messiah in the form of a deliverer from Roman rule clearly had to be abandoned. As the Jews either sought refuge in Gnostic speculation or in the Hebrew Bible and the oral tradition of the Pharisaic schools, the LXX became progressively abandoned to the

---

[1] J. K. Rendel Harris, *Testimonies*, vol. I, p. 2, Cambridge, 1916-1920. Compare B. Lindars, *New Testament Apologetic*, ch. i, and R. P. C. Hanson, *Allegory and Event*, pp. 73-6.
[2] Discussed in detail by K. Beyschlag, *Clemens Romanus und der Frühkatholizismus*, Tübingen, 1966, ch. II.   [3] *1 Clement*, 16.

136

Christians. The latter turned greater attention to the books of the prophets in the interest of establishing the claims of Jesus to be Messiah, while gradually the specifically Christian books in the New Testament assumed equal authority with the Old, thus providing the Church with a testimony to the life and works of Jesus independent of the Jewish Scriptures.

The task of the Apologists in the mid-second century to formulate a distinctively Christian interpretation of the Old Testament was hastened also by the challenge of the Gnostic sects and by Marcion's success in preaching a Christianity which cut itself off decisively from Judaism. The Gnostics could at best take a relative view of the Old Testament, their estimation of it depending on how near or how far they regarded the Creator God, and God of the Old Testament in relation to their conception of God. They 'recklessly twisted the sense of their interpretation and exposition' not only of the Gospels, but also of the Law and the Prophets, complained Irenaeus.[1] In particular they, acknowledged no debt to the Old Testament account of Creation, denied any Divine manifestation before the coming of Jesus.[2] For the first time also in Christian debate, the Old Testament was placed alongside other (pagan) traditions as a source of truth. Thus in the *Gospel of Truth* derived in all probability from the school of Valentinus *ca.* 150, the description of the state of ignorance and incoherent illusion and nightmare whence man is delivered by Gnosis is inspired from the *Iliad*, xxii, lines 199-201.[3] Though the Hebrew Scriptures were granted a higher degree of inspiration than the writings of the Greek philosophers, 'who did not possess the possibility of knowing the cause of existing things',[4] they were no longer regarded as the sole word of God. The most comprehensive statement of this attitude is to be found in the Letter of Ptolemy to Flora written *ca.* 170. Ptolemy was a disciple of Valentinus and one of the targets of Irenaeus' *Against the Heresies*,[5] and hence representative of Gnostic thought of his

---

[1] *Adv. Haereses* 1.3.6.

[2] See Cullen I. K. Story, *The Nature of Truth in 'The Gospel of Truth' and in the Writings of Justin Martyr* (Leiden, 1970), p. 220.

[3] See H. C. Puech, 'The Jung Codex and other Gnostic documents', in *The Jung Codex*, ed. F. L. Cross (London, 1955), p. 32.

[4] *The Treatise on the Three Natures*, cited from Cross, op. cit., p. 59.

[5] *Adv. Haer.* 1.12. Also, especially Preface, para 2, where Irenaeus refers to Ptolemy as a disciple of Valentinus whose views were particularly widespread at this time.

day. The law, Ptolemy says, 'was not ordained by the perfect God the Father, for it is secondary, being imperfect and in need of completion by another, containing (as it does) commandments alien to the nature and thought of such a God'.[1] The Old Testament contained prescriptions such as those concerning marriage and divorce which were contradicted by the law of Christ. The Decalogue itself contained 'pure but imperfect legislation' that required completion by the Saviour. It had its place in Christian ethics, but not the highest. The Old Testament was not indeed the product of the devil, but of an 'Intermediate Being' who was responsible for the creation of the imperfect universe in which mankind dwelt.

Much of what Ptolemy said would be accepted by later generations of Christians. There was a relative value in the Old Testament; the Law of Moses had been necessary because of 'the hardness of heart of the Jews', and the latter by restricting themselves to the literal meaning of the text failed to advance towards the knowledge of God that the Christians possessed. The moral law in the Old Testament was still binding, but the ceremonial and ritual preserved in the Books of Exodus, Numbers and Leviticus were discarded.[2] All this, however, lay in the future. It was from Justin Martyr and Irenaeus that orthodox Christianity derived most of its arguments in support of the acceptance of all Scripture as the word of God.

Meanwhile the value of the Old Testament had been scrutinised and rejected by Marcion (*flor.* 140-160).[3] The latter had not arrived at his conclusions through *a priori* reasoning from the oneness and unapproachability of God, but from a sustained meditation on the meaning of well-known passages of Scripture. Like Ptolemy he was concerned at the contradictions between the Old Law and the New, which he found exemplified in the actual events described in both testaments. There was no possibility of reconciling the Lord's 'Suffer little children to come unto me', with the act of vengeance permitted by Jahweh

[1] Cited from R. M. Grant's *Gnosticism, an Anthology* (London, 1961), pp. 184-190.

[2] See R. M. Grant, 'The Decalogue in Early Christianity', *H.T.R.* xl (1947), pp. 1-17, at p. 13.

[3] See the summary of Marcion's theology in my 'Marcion', *Expository Times*, Vol. LXXX, Aug. 1969, pp. 328-32, and for details E. C. Blackman, *Marcion and his Influence* (London, 1948).

138

when bears were allowed to eat the children who had mocked
Elisha (2 Kings 2.24). Similarly, how could one associate the
command 'Let not the sun go down on thy wrath', with
Jahweh's arrest of the sun so that Joshua could finish slaughter-
ing the Amalekites! Marcion found the answer in the text of
Isaiah (Isa. 45.5-7) where Jahweh describes himself, 'I form the
light and create darkness: I make peace and create evil. I the
Lord do these things.' Marcion shared the current of thought
represented most movingly by Basilides that found it impossible
to accept that pain, suffering, and evil were derived from the
same source that sent Jesus Christ into the world.[1] Hence the
god of the Jews whose acts were recounted in the Old Testament could not be God, and the religious experience of the
Jews themselves as recorded there could have little, if any,
relevance to Christianity. Jesus burst on the historical scene 'in
the fifteenth year of Tiberius' with startling abruptness. God's
gift to humanity in Jesus was to be found only in the New
Testament and in particular in Luke's Gospel and the letters of
Paul his only true Apostle.

This then was the challenge confronting the Apologists. On
the one hand, there were the claims of orthodox Judaism to
exclusive possession of the Old Testament, weakened by events
but still strident and persistent; on the other hand, there were
the many in the Christian camp to whom the Old Testament
was in flat contradiction to the New and possessed little, if any,
religious value. The Apologists rejected both standpoints.
Jews, Gnostics and Marcionites as well as pagans constituted
the opposition, and a Christianity was proclaimed that sought
to harmonise philosophy with the Old Testament without
abandoning traditional canons of scriptural interpretation. The
pattern was set in a passage in the *Letter to Diognetus* (*ca.* 150).
'The fear of the Lord', claims the writer, 'is chanted and the
grace of the prophets is recognised and the faith of the Gospels
is established and the tradition of the apostles is guarded, and
the grace of the Church has free and exulting course. And if you
do not grieve this grace you will understand that the Logos
speaks through whom he pleases and whenever he chooses'
(xi.6). Christianity is thus grounded in the prophetic word of
the Old Testament which formed part of an integrated structure

[1] Basilides, *Exegetica*, xxiii, cited by Clement of Alexandria, *Stromateis*, iv.12.82.2.

of truth through which Christ, identified with the Divine Reason, guides and illumines mankind.

Justin Martyr (*ca.* 100-165) stands in the centre of this development. From the time of his conversion probably at Ephesus *ca.* 130 until his death as a martyr in Rome in 165, he stood for an orthodoxy opposed alike to Gnosticism, Marcionism and Judaism, as well as to the pagan society he had rejected. Despite a purely Hellenistic upbringing, he shows an astonishingly wide knowledge of contemporary Judaism, and his *Dialogue* with Trypho written up perhaps as much as twenty-five years after the event in *ca.* 160 throws light on the intricacies of the struggle which was still being waged with the Jews for possession of the LXX.

Justin's reply to his adversaries moved along two distinct lines, both of which involved acceptance of the Old Testament completely with the Gospels as the word of God. He believed that Christ was the revelation of God in some way analogous to the Stoic concept of the Seminal Word, and that all creation and all mankind through the ages had partaken of the Word. Through Jesus, however, the Word had become fully revealed, and hence the Christians were participants in its revelation to a greater degree than thinkers among either the Greeks or the Hebrews. 'We have been taught', he wrote in a well-known passage, 'that Christ is the first-begotten of God, and we have previously testified that he is the Reason of which every race of man partakes. Those who lived in accordance with Reason are Christians, even though they are called godless, such as among the Greeks, Socrates and Heraclitus and others like them; among the barbarians, Abraham, Ananiah, Azariah, and Misael, and Elijah and many others.'[1] To Justin as to Clement of Alexandria a generation later, Christianity was the supreme wisdom to which all previous teaching and philosophy had been tending. Man was on an upward path towards God; and nothing virtuous in his past, least of all the oracles of God contained in the Old Testament, was to be discarded as irrelevant. This led Justin to his second line of argument in favour of the Old Testament. The prophets, in particular, were the conveyers of divine truths. Inspired by God through the Holy Spirit they taught the same truths as Christ himself

[1] 1 *Apol.* 46.

140

taught. They had proclaimed beforehand all things concerning Jesus, and Jesus had fulfilled their prophecies.[1]

The argument from prophecy was the cornerstone of Justin's defence of Christianity. It had been to the prophets that the old man he had met on the seashore near Ephesus had directed him as 'trustworthy witnesses of the truth which was above all demonstration' (*Dial.* 7.2). He never forgot the encounter.[2] To the middle-class provincials of the Greek cities to whom his ideas in the *First Apology* were probably addressed he repeats the arguments of two centuries of Jewish apologetic in favour of the credibility of the LXX, with an emphasis on the prophets. 'There were among the Jews certain men who were prophets of God through whom the prophetic Spirit announced in advance events that were to occur.[3] Following the *Letter of Aristeas* he describes how the prophecies had been preserved carefully by successive rulers, and Ptolemy of Egypt had had the prophecies translated for the use and guidance of everyone. These prophecies concerned Divine events which had turned out and continued to turn out just as predicted. The Jews, however, had failed to understand the messages concerning Jesus, and, adds Justin, the failure of Bar-Cochba's revolt had brought condign punishment upon them for denying him.[4] The prophets, too, could claim credence on the grounds of great antiquity, and Justin has no hesitation in claiming that Plato plagiarised Moses, 'for Moses was earlier than all the Greek writers'.[5]

While some pagans might have been impressed with the apparent coincidence that 'Zion had become a wilderness' with the second destruction of Jerusalem and the ban on Jews entering the city,[6] few could have bothered themselves with massive quotations and far-fetched interpretations of what in any event was a 'barbarian' book. With Trypho, however, one senses a keener debate between equals whose thought-worlds were strikingly similar. Trypho himself was neither rabbi nor especially trained in philosophy but he represented an educated

[1] 1 *Apol.* 23: compare *Dial.* 7.1.
[2] For the influence of this encounter on Justin's thought see Story, op. cit., pp. 66-7.
[3] 1 *Apol.* 31: compare ibid., 23 and *Dial.* 7.1.
[4] 1 *Apol.* 31: compare ibid., 53. Jews and Samaritans 'did not recognise the Christ when he came'. Also *Dial.* 113.1.
[5] Ibid., 44: compare ibid., 54, 59.1 and 60.1.
[6] 1 *Apol.* 47.

Hellenised Judaism loyal both to the Roman Empire and to its own traditions. Like Justin he was acquainted with Jewish *haggadah*, but his exegesis was confined to the LXX. His indeed was to be almost the last generation of a long tradition of Hellenistic Judaism that had sought both to conquer and to come to terms with the Greco-Roman world. Such people were anathema to the extremists who had risen in Palestine, and the school of Akiba that stood behind them, and Trypho was a refugee in Ephesus.[1] His criticisms of Justin's claims to the Old Testament reflect the criticisms of Jews who had been confronting the Christians for three generations in the cities of Asia Minor.

Trypho demanded more than mere assertion that the prophets had foretold Jesus' coming as Messiah. He and his companions were sceptical about Justin's qualifications to discuss religious questions at all. Justin's Christian teachers 'did not understand the Scriptures'. The Messiah which Justin preached 'was shaped by the Christians themselves'.[2] Even if it were conceded that the prophets told of a Messiah who would suffer, but would also come in glory and be priest and king, how could Justin prove that this was said of Jesus of Nazareth?[3] Like the Platonist Celsus, Trypho found the Incarnation incredible and the Crucifixion an immovable stumbling-block. The idea of a pre-existent Christ who was Jesus was 'not only strange but foolish'.[4] In addition, he considered Christ's moral requirements too high and inconsistent with the willingness of Christians to eat things offered to idols and their failure to separate themselves from the heathen; and he asks whether Christians were allowed to keep the sabbath and be circumcised.[5]

Justin showed himself more qualified to answer convincingly than one would suspect from his description of his upbringing and career. His knowledge of Scripture was confined to the Greek versions of the Old Testament, but he was acquainted with certain Jewish post-biblical practices, beliefs and exegesis. He was also familiar with Jewish sects and with the Jewish

[1] *Dial.* 1.3. (ed. and tr. Lukyn Williams, S.P.C.K., London, 1930).
[2] Ibid., 8.4.   [3] Ibid., 36.1; compare 32.1.   [4] Ibid., 48.1.
[5] Ibid., 47.1. Trypho's objections to Christianity are summarised by L. W. Barnard, *Justin Martyr* (Cambridge, 1967), pp. 41-3. Here Trypho had evidently come into contact with Gnostics.

142

Gnostic syncretistic exegesis of Genesis 1.[1] With a Hellenistic
Jew of Palestinian background, such as Trypho was, he could
give a good account of himself. He could claim, as he did, that
there was a difference between the ceremonial demands of the
Law to which there had always been exceptions, even in the Old
Testament, and its moral demands which were eternally binding. His detailed lines of argument were derived mainly from
themes which had now become traditional, but were applied
with intelligence and debating skill against a background of a
philosophy which accepted salvation for all who participated
in the Logos. His rebuttal, for instance, of Trypho's initial
claim that salvation depended on a minute acceptance of the
Mosaic ceremonial law, follows but goes beyond *Barnabas*. It is
rather more sympathetic towards Judaism, more ready to argue
and understand, if finally to refute. The Law should be understood spiritually, Justin asserted, pointing to the greater honour
given by Jeremiah (9.25-26) to 'circumcision of the heart'
rather than the flesh. All races, claimed Justin, who had
knowledge of God and Christ and carried out the eternal acts
of righteousness were 'circumcised with a fair and profitable
circumcision'.[2] Then, in one of his best passages, he rounds
off his argument with citations from the Old Testament in
the ascending order of importance accepted by the Jews of the
time, namely the Hagiographa, the Prophets and, finally, the
Law. 'You recognise them, Trypho? They are laid up in your
scriptures, or rather not in yours, but in ours, for we obey them,
but you, when you read, do not understand their sense.'[3]

The claim that the Old Testament is 'ours and not yours'
was defended by interpreting events narrated there typologically. As Abraham had obeyed the call to go out from the
land wherein he dwelt, so had Christians obeyed the call of
Christ to abandon their homeland (or 'way of life'=*politeia*)
and inherit the promised land.[4] The Passover lamb was a type
of Christ and the offering of fine flour (Lev. 14.10) on behalf of
the cleansed from leprosy a type of the Eucharistic bread.[5]
The manifold prefiguration of Christ in the Old Testament
could be demonstrated by reference to the appearance of the

[1] Indicated by Barnard, op. cit., pp. 49-50.
[2] *Dial.* 28.8. Compare *Barnabas*, 9.5.
[3] Ibid., 29.2. See Lukyn Williams ' note *Dialogue*, p. 57, n. 6.
[4] Op. cit., 119.5.   [5] Ibid., 40 and 41.1.

angels to Abraham at the oak of Mamre.[1] The pre-existent
Christ, Justin asserted, was 'He who appeared on earth in the
form of a man and appeared to Abraham (as was also the case
with the two angels who came with him); the same was the God
who also existed before the making of the world.'[2] His was the
'hidden hand' that fought against the Amalekites (Ex. 17.16
LXX),[3] or the power of God transferred from Moses to Joshua.[4]
As he explained in support of his application of Prov. 8.22 to
Christ (The Lord created me as the beginning of his ways for
his works), 'God has begotten as a Beginning before all his
creatures a kind of reasonable power from himself, which is
also called by the Holy Spirit the Glory of the Lord, and sometimes Wisdom and sometimes Angel . . . and sometimes he
speaks of himself as Chief Command, when he appeared in the
form of a man to Joshua the son of Nun.[5]' The assimilation
of the Divine Reason, or Logos, with Christ automatically
allowed Justin to attribute these identifications to Jesus and thus
justify the Christian claim to the prophecies in the LXX. The
Psalms also, as Hanson felicitously points out, were regarded
almost as transcripts of conversations between God and Christ.[6]
Ps. 99, for instance, is taken by Justin to represent the Holy
Spirit rebuking the Jews for failing to recognise Jesus as king
and declaring that Samuel, Aaron and Moses did recognise
him.[7]

Similarly, other great events in the New Testament, notably
the Crucifixion, were prophesied in the Old Testament, and
the claim was justified also by means of typological interpretation. Justin cites as symbols of 'proclamations in advance
of everything relating to him' (*Dial.* 131.4)[8] Exod. 17.10-12
(Moses holding up his hands to secure victory over the Amalekites—Jesus was leading God's people against the same enemy)[9],
Deut 33.13-17, which mentions the wild ox (LXX 'unicorn')
whose horns Justin believed resembled the Cross.[10] Num. 21.9

---

[1] Ibid., 56.   [2] Ibid., 56.10.   [3] Ibid., 49.7.
[4] *Dial.* 49.6-7.   [5] *Dial.* 61.1.
[6] Hanson, *Allegory and Event*, p. 105.   [7] *Dial.* 37.1-4.
[8] For this use of the term 'symbol' (*symbolon*) see also *Dial.* 138.3, 'all the
symbols from the time of the Flood'.
[9] *Dial.* 90.4.
[10] Ibid., 91.1-4 and 105.2. See R. P. C. Hanson, *Allegory and Event*, p. 106, on
these examples. Also Hanson's essay in *The Bible and the Early Church* (ed. P. R.
Ackroyd and C. F. Evans, Cambridge, 1970) vol. I, p. 415.

144

recording the lifting up of the Serpent in the wilderness[1] was to be regarded as a 'type or sign of salvation for believers. Similarly the salvation of the Gentiles was foretold in the text 'At the time of Noah's flood I saved thee' (a conflation of the LXX Isa 54.8-9). It was 'by water and faith and wood (i.e. of the Ark) that they that prepare themselves beforehand and repent of their sins should escape the judgment of God that is to come upon them'.[2] The Flood is used here typologically as Judgment, as one finds in Matthew (Matt. 24.37) and in 2 Pet. 3.5, but there is also a new and specifically Christian interpretation, which sees the new Noah and new Flood having actually arrived in Christ (*Dial.* 138). In all this Justin shows the growing flexibility of the orthodox Christian use of the Old Testament and the movement toward the establishment of an allegorical as well as a typological sense in its writings.

Finally, as earlier generations of Christians, Justin conflates and even changes texts to demonstrate a point. Such conflations were not regarded as 'forgery' but as a legitimate means of bringing out the hidden meaning of a text. Justin demonstrates how the Crucifixion was foretold by the Psalmist by conflating Ps. 22.18 and 16 and Ps. 3.5,[3] and the resurrection from three texts from Isaiah, namely 35.3-6, 61.1 and 26.19; that the dead actually rose and walked on earth in Jesus' time was proved 'from the Acts of what took place under Pontius Pilate'.[4] In another interesting passage which contains the first reference to the 'harrowing of hell', Justin relies on a text which he attributes to Jeremiah, but in fact seems to come from an early Jewish-Christian *Testimonium* on the cross.[5]

The whole Old Testament was thus put under contribution to prove that Jesus was Messiah and that he fulfilled to the last detail what had been foretold about the Messiah. Events such as the coming of Elijah, the Virgin Birth, descent of the Holy Spirit at Baptism and Jesus' humiliation, crucifixion and resurrection were all to be found already prefigured in Scripture. Justin indeed was ready to regard 'any passage of the Old

[1] *Dial.* 94.1.   [2] *Dial.* 138.1.
[3] 1 *Apol.* 48. ('They cast lots for my clothing, and pierced my feet and my hands. I lay down and slept and rose up again for the Lord supported me.') See J. Daniélou, *Théologie*, pp. 109-10.
[4] *Ibid.* For another instance of conflation consisting of Matt. 4.10 and 16.23 referring to Christ's Temptation, see *Dial.* 103.6.
[5] *Dial.* 72.4. See Daniélou, op. cit., p. 116.

Testament as spoken in the person of Jesus, or the Jews or the persecuted Christians or the Holy Spirit or God Himself.'[1] As one reads the *Dialogue* one cannot but admire Justin's fervour and persistence, and indeed Trypho's patience. It could not have been easy to have listened to a Gentile telling him that the Jews were ignorant of the meaning of their own Scripture and that 'Christ is hidden from you and when you read you do not understand,'[2] and that this was a divine punishment. As later ages have found, however, analogies might be shown to exist between the hopes of Israel expressed through the prophets and the life of Christ, but it was hazardous to push the analogies to their final conclusion. The two days' debate left neither contestant the victor, and both respectful of each other's prowess.[3]

Justin is a Janus-like figure. On the one hand, his arguments recall attitudes of a generation before, on the other hand, he was preparing the way for the integration of Scripture and philosophy in a single pattern of faith which dominated Christian thought in the Greek east from that time onwards. His younger contemporaries, Melito of Sardis (*flor.* 160-180) and Athenagoras (*flor.* 170-180), represent a further development towards a theology that placed a less tyrannical emphasis on the Old Testament. Melito, however, was a Quartodeciman, accepting 14th Nisan as the date of the Crucifixion, and his Homily on the Passion leant heavily on traditional typology in its attempt to trace analogies between Christ's death and resurrection and the institution of the Passover and the exodus from Egypt in the Old Testament. Christ's suffering was foreshadowed by the suffering of Israel's righteous, Abel, Isaac, Joseph, Moses, and David; while the lamb sacrificed (like Christ) in the land of Egypt smote Egypt and saved Israel through its blood.[4] For Melito, however, the books of the Old Covenant (*ta tēs palaias diathēkēs biblia*) the exact canon of which he had to journey to the 'east' (probably Syria or Palestine) to establish, could be differentiated from those of the New Covenant.[5] Moreover, the Old Testament types were of

---

[1] cf. Hanson, *Allegory and Event*, pp. 104-5.
[2] *Dial.* 113.1. Ignorance as a punishment, ibid., 55.3.   [3] *Dial.* 142.
[4] Ed. Campbell Bonner, *Studies and Documents*, xii (London and Philadelphia, 1940), ch. 59, p. 127. For a similar catena of Israel's Righteous, compare 4 Macc. 18.11ff. and Heb 11.   [5] Eusebius, *Hist. Eccl.* iv.26, 12-1.4.

146

limited value only, like the scale-models which a sculptor uses for patterns by which to work when he is carving the full-scale sculpture. Then the models could be discarded.[1] So, Melito declared both People and Law were held in honour before the Church arose, but 'since the Church arose and the Gospel was shed abroad upon men on earth, the type was void, giving over to the natural truth'. Elsewhere, he writes, 'Old is the Law, new is the Word. The type is transient (*proskairos*), Grace is eternal.'[2]

Here was a significant change in relationship between the New and the Old Testament. Justin had appealed to the New Testament writings as corroborative evidence of prophecy, such as in his discussion of the events in Gethsemane.[3] He had referred to these, however, only as the 'Memoirs of the Apostles' which seem to be identical, though with textual variations, with the Synoptic Gospels; in addition to which he knew some of the Pauline Epistles, but apparently not Acts nor the Pastorals. In the twenty years after his death this situation had changed completely. When Irenaeus wrote *ca.* 185 the canon of the New Testament had assumed something approaching its final form, and had gained thereby an enormously increased authority. Henceforth it was to be the distinctive Christian Book, and, as the Montanist crisis was to show, succession from the Apostles of the New Covenant was of greater importance for the church even than succession from the prophets of the Old.

With Athenagoras, one also senses movement away from reliance on the Old Testament as sole witness to prove the Christian case. In ch. 9 of the *Plea in Defence of the Faith*, written *ca.* 177, Athenagoras puts forward the evidence of 'prophetic voices,' Moses, Isaiah, and Jeremiah, to buttress a claim that God is 'uncreated, impassible and indivisible', and the creator of all things already accepted on the strength of current philosophic argument and natural reason. For the remainder of his Apology, however, references to the Old

---

[1] See G. W. H. Lampe and K. J. Woollcombe, *Essays in Typology* (S.C.M. Press, 1957), p. 71.

[2] Cited from H. Chadwick's reconstruction, 'A Latin epitome of Melitos' Homily on the Pascha', *J.T.S.* N.S. xi (1960), pp. 76-82, at p. 80.

[3] Justin, *Dial.*, 103.7-8, citing Luke 22.44 as contained 'in the Memoirs', in support of the prophecy contained in Ps. 22.14, 'I am poured out like water, and all my bones are out of joint.' Compare ibid., 100.3-4.

Testament are conspicuous by their absence.[1] Within a few years, the emergence of the Catechetical School at Alexandria as the centre of Greek Christian thought was to affect profoundly the attitude of educated Christians towards the Old Testament. The inconsistencies between the Old and the New Testament began to be recognised by the orthodox as well as by Gnostics and Marcionites. In the third century only by the liberal use of free allegorisation inspired largely from Philo's works was it possible to see the whole Bible as word of God. Given this new 'science' of interpretation—even the Decalogue is allegorised by Clement[2]—Origen was able to avoid the pitfalls that Celsus had prepared for the unwary. For him the Law and the Prophets represented a type of things to come. The Old Testament reflected the shadow of the spiritual realities of the New, even as Jewish institutions often prefigured their Christian counterparts.[3] With Christ's coming mankind had moved from the experience of a type or shadow of future blessedness to an apprehension of the image and likeness of God himself through Christ. Some of Origen's disciples, however, were less generous in their views of the Old Testament. Eusebius of Caesarea had to admit that only by allegorisation could the Old Testament be saved from treatment as 'incongruous and incoherent fairy stories.'[4]

Outside the range of the Alexandrian theologians, in Antioch and later throughout the west, the Old Testament would still be regarded with the same profound veneration as a store of divine prophecies and oracles that it had commanded previously. In Antioch this may have been connected with the particularly close relations between Jews and Christians which were to remain exceptional in this regard for another two centuries.[5] Theophilus' three books to *Autolycus*, written *ca.* 180,

---

[1] One notable reference, however, is Athenagoras' reference of Prov. 8.22 to the pre-existent Christ (*Supplicatio* 10.3), thus adding another link in the chain that was to make this text one of the most famous in the Trinitarian debates in the fourth century.

[2] Clement of Alexandria, *Stromateis*, vi 16.133-48. (Ed. Stählin/Früchtel, Berlin, 1960.)

[3] See for instance, Origen, *Comment. in Levit.* 10.1 (*G.C.S.* 6, p. 434), and *Comment. in Ioann.* 10.18 (*G.C.S.* 4, p. 189).   [4] *Demonst Evangelica* ii.3.94.

[5] In Theophilus, for instance, the *sebomenoi* (God-fearers) are 'they who have the Old Testament' (ii.30) 'they who are also called Christians' (iii.4) and 'Jews' (iii.9). He also defends the Jews as well as the Christians against the charge of misanthropy (iii.10.14). For the Jews in Antioch see C. H. Kraeling, *J.B.L.* (1932), pp. 130-60.

148

are a reminder that many Christians, including converts, continued to justify acceptance of Christianity on the ground of Old Testament prophecy, and to interpret the Old Testament itself in the Jewish tradition. For him as for Justin, the prophets play a key role in his vindication of Christianity. They foretell the past as it did take place, the present as it does take place and the future as it will take place. Moses is the 'greatest of the prophets,' and 'our' prophet, Theophilus claims (iii.18). As R. M. Grant points out,[1] Theophilus' exegesis of Genesis which occupies Book ii is derived generally from Jewish or Jewish-Christian teachers. Almost everything he says can be paralleled in haggadic literature. There is a strong note of literalism and a clear reliance on Jewish exegesis, as for instance in ii. 27-29 where the discussion of the nature of Man, the deception of Adam by Eve and the sin of Cain seem to follow directly a Jewish *haggadah* on Adam[2]. The typology which equated carnivorous animals with robbers and murderers and quadrupeds with men who mind earthly things (ii.15) also looks back to earlier strata of Scriptural interpretation and is reminiscent of *Barnabas* or the *Shepherd of Hermas*. Theophilus' work shows how strong were the links in Antioch that bound the two monotheistic religions together through their common claim on the Old Testament. This factor in its turn should be taken into account when weighing the influences which formed the Antiochene attitude towards Trinitarian and Christological Doctrine, as well as the school of Antiochene biblical exegesis.

Fortunately, perhaps, Irenaeus was to be more influential in moulding orthodox opinion. In some ways neither *Against the Heresies* nor the *Demonstration of Apostolic Preaching* deviates far from the exegesis adopted by Justin. The greater part of the *Demonstration* dated perhaps as late as 195 consists of adducing Old Testament texts to prove that every part of the Christian dispensation was predicted there, and one finds Irenaeus appearing to rely on the bizarre interpretations of the Old Testament as found in both *Barnabas* and Justin.[3] Irenaeus, however, cites the New Testament almost as often as he does

[1] R. M. Grant, 'Theophilus of Antioch to Autolycus', *H.T.R.* (1947), pp. 227-257, especially pp. 234-8, and also ibid., xliii, pp. 188-96.
[2] See K. Beyschlag, op. cit., pp. 49-50.
[3] See Hanson, *Allegory and Event*, p. 111.

the Old, and leaves no doubt that the two Testaments were knit together as a single scripture. His theology of Redemption reaching its climax in the process of the Recapitulation, the summing up of all things in Christ and the reversal of the process of the Fall through the life and work of Christ as Second Adam, required this. For him also the successive covenants laid down in the Old Testament were for a limited period only, ending with John the Baptist, and had now been superseded by the new Covenant of Christ.[1] There had been a progressive economy of salvation. Not everything had been revealed at once. Man's way back from the Fall to reconciliation had been painfully slow. Like the old Covenants, however, Judaism had now been set aside. It belonged to the past. God had granted the Jews' inheritance to 'the foolish Gentiles' and they 'needed not the Law for a tutor'.[2] Thus the preaching of the truth and the way of life was proclaimed by the prophets, established by Christ, delivered by the apostles and was handed on by the Church in all parts of the world.[3] Such was the history of human salvation in this unfolding of God's purpose. The Old Testament formed an essential prologue to the New.

The second century had seen the struggle for the Old Testament, first between the Jews and Christians and then among the Christians themselves. Only in the final decades does the smoke of battle clear and a definitive position for the Old Testament is achieved. Much of the credit for this development belongs to the Apologists and in particular to Justin. Laboured and prolix though he is, he was able to demonstrate to his opponents how necessary was the Old Testament to understand the Christian message, and how Creation, the Law, and the Prophecy described in it led up to the Incarnation and the Church, and in his continuous debates and controversies to develop specifically Christian interpretations. Through him and through Irenaeus' refinements this achievement proved to be a permanent legacy for the Church. In the west much of their method and even their interpretations of individual passages survived through the work of Tyconius down to the Middle Ages. Today, while exact parallels between events in the Old

---

[1] *Adv. Haeres.* iv. 38. See also R. M. Grant, 'The Decalogue in Early Christianity', *H.T.R.* (1947), pp. 14-15.

[2] *Demonstratio*, 95-6.

[3] Ibid., 98.

and the New Testament are not sought, the validity of the prophetic message for Christianity is acknowledged. That Christianity did not at an early stage cut itself off from its historic roots in the religious experience of the Jewish people was due in no small measure to Greek Apologists.

IV

A Note on Tertullian and the Jews

The problem of the relations between Jews and Christians in the second
century is a complicated and an important one. The traditional tendency
among historians of the early Church has been to number the Jews among
the persecutors of the Christians, and the evidence of Justin [1], of the writer
of the letter of the Church of Smyrna to that of Philomelium about the death
of Polycarp [2], as well as the reproach against the followers of Montanus
that they did not suffer beatings in the synagogues [3], has tended to
uphold this view, at least so far as the province of Asia is concerned.
In the third century Origen added his testimony on the same side [4].
Recently, however, there has been a reaction [5]. Combined with the silence
of Jewish sources in the Dispersion, and the prescriptions on Jewish
life and conduct contained in the Mishna, scholars have pointed out
that far from being antagonists, Jews and Christians were in reality
allies over a large field of practice and behaviour in face of the hostility of pagan society directed against them both. It is also asserted
that the evidence on which those who would reproach the Jews rely
is either susceptible to other interpretations or is too late in date to be
relevant to the second century.

In this brief study I am taking the situation in Carthage as revealed by
Tertullian at the turn of the third century. We know both from him and
from archaeological evidence that there was a large, active and flourishing

---

[1] For instance, Dialogue with Trypho, 16.4, 17.1, 47.4 (cursing of Christians in the
synagogues of Asia), 122.2 (Jewish proselytes persecuting Christians).

[2] Eusebius, Hist. Eccl., iv. 15, 26 and 29 ('the Jews were extremely zealous as
is their custom in assisting at this', i.e. preparing the stake at which Polycarp was
to be burnt). For the early dating of Eusebius' account of Polycarp's martyrdom,
see H. von Campenhausen, Bearbeitungen und Interpolationen des Polykarpmarty-
riums, Sitzungsberichte der Heidelberger Akad. der Wissenschaften, Phil.-Hist. Kl.,
1957, 8 ff.

[3] Eusebius, Hist. Eccl. v, 16.12.

[4] Contra Celsum, vi. 27.

[5] First represented by J. Parkes, The Conflict of the Church and the Synagogue, London,
1934, 136 and 150; taken up by Y. F. Baer, Israel, the Christian Church and the Roman
Empire, Scripta Hierosolymitana, vii, 1961, 102–104 and by Fergus Millar in Journal of
Roman Studies (= JRS), lvi, 1966, 232–234.

Jewish community in Carthage at this time [1]. Many still used Hebrew[2] and this, together with the tradition of providing the Synagogue with some of its outstanding rabbis, would make Carthaginian Judaism a particularly important field of study[3]. Moreover, at a time when so much Christian activity was concentrated on the cemeteries, it is surely significant to find among the hundreds of Jewish graves cut into the sides of the Jebel Khaoui north of the city some which were recognised by the excavators over seventy years ago as Christian[4]. It would appear that at least some of the recruits to the Church in Carthage came from Judaism and that the links between the two religions were close.

This moreover is what Tertullian would lead us to believe. He betrays the fact for instance, that some Christians still observed the Jewish sabbath[5], and that despite his affirmations to the contrary, they also observed the Jewish prescriptions that no flesh should be eaten from which the blood had not been drawn[6]. Elsewhere we learn that Christian virgins veiled themselves, as did Jewish[7]. In its organisation also the Carthaginian Church for centuries retained the use of *seniores*[8], that is lay-elders charged with administration, as did the synagogues of the west, and its councils numbering even at this period seventy bishops plus one (the bishop of Carthage) may be paralleled to the numbers of the Sanhedrin[9]. Certainly the Old Testament bias of the African concept of the priesthood cannot be ignored. The African Bible even of Tertullian's day seems to have owed something to direct Jewish influence[10]. It would be difficult not to agree with Tertullian when he states that in his day Christianity stood near to the Jewish religion[11], and his

---

[1] On the size and significance of the Jewish cemetery at Gamart, see P. Delattre, Gamart ou la nécropole juive à Carthage, Paris, 1895. For Jewish proselytising at this time, Tertullian, Adversus Judaeos, i.

[2] Tertullian, Apol. 18. *Hebraei retro, qui nunc Iudaei: igitur et litterae hebraeae, et eloquium.* For a Hebrew inscription from Volubilis in Morocco, see Ph. Berger, Bull. Arch. du Comité des travaux historiques, 1892, p. 64. It related to a daughter of a rabbi.

[3] See M. Simon's study, Le Judaïsme berbère dans l'Afrique ancienne, Rev. d'Histoire et de Philosophie religieuse, 1946, 1–145, especially pp. 23–27.

[4] P. Delattre, op. cit., It is interesting too, to find what became the typical Christian invocation *in pace* associated with the seven-branch candlestick, CIL, viii, 14101 and 14104. For the importance of *areae* to the Christians see Tertullian, Ad Scapulam 3.

[5] De Jejunio adversus Psychicos, 14.3 (CSEL, 20, 293).

[6] Apol. 9.13, contrasted with ibid., 21.2.

[7] De Virginibus Velandis, xii, 1, and De Corona, iv, 3. In general, see R. P. C. Hanson, Notes on Tertullian's Interpretation of Scripture, Journal of Theological Studies (= JTS) n. s. xii, 1961, 273–279.

[8] See my note The *Seniores Laici* and the Origins of the Church in North Africa, JTS, n. s. xii, 1961, 280–284.

[9] Derived from Numbers 11[16]. Agrippinus' council which decided *circa* 220 that converted heretics must be baptised anew consisted of seventy bishops together with himself (Augustine, De Unico Baptismo, xiii, 22). In 311 Secundus of Tigisis, Primate of Numidia, was accompanied by the same number of bishops on his journey to Carthage to elect a successor to Mensurius (Augustine, Ad Catholicos Epistola, xviii, 46).

[10] I owe this information to Professor Christine Mohrmann.　　　　[11] Tertullian, Apol. 16.3.

affirmation that Christians were often called by the Jews 'Nazarenes' indicates even a Judaeo-Christian element in the community [1]. The Carthaginian Jews, to judge from the use of this name, regarded the Christians as heretic Jews rather than adherents of a new religion.

Outwardly too, Jews and Christians must have maintained a common front against paganism in so far as both were people of the Book, of the Law, and practised a strictly disciplined way of life dependent on religious precept, whereas the pagans were none of these things. Christian *halacha* was as legalistic as its Jewish rival. But such attitudes would not also preclude fratricidal strife with the Jews as the wealthy, powerful, long-established religion with a traditional place in society using every means to drive its upstart rival from the field [2]. These means included, as in St Paul's, Justin's and Polycarp's day, either direct action against the Christians or indirect by stirring up latent popular fanaticism against them.

Tertullian's attitude illustrates both aspects of Jewish-Christian relations and enables his statements about the persecution of Christians by Jews to be seen in perspective. Though he does not acknowledge the fact, it is evident that many of the regulations through which he sought to insulate the Christian from the surrounding pagan world, discussed in *De Idololatria*, could only be derived from current Jewish practice. Baer has pointed out how the same casuistical problems put forward for discussion by Tertullian are found in current Jewish Baraita [3]. For instance, what was a Christian to do about referring to an idol whose name happened to form part of a place-name? Tertullian is adamant, 'Thou shalt not mention the name of other gods' (Ex. 23 [13]), and his advice was echoed by the Jews in a similar situation [4]. Again, both Tertullian and the Jews would instruct their followers to accept pagan invitations only if there was no mention of any pagan cult act, though Tertullian would be even more restrictive than the Jews [5].

The *De Idololatria*, written perhaps in Tertullian's pre-Montanist period, shows Jews and Christians as co-belligerents against paganism. Both would have agreed that it was better to die than to trifle with idolatry [6]. But Tertullian gives the Jews no credit for their example and more often

---

[1] Adv. Marcionem, iv. 8 (ed. Kroymann, CSEL, 47, 437). *Nos Iudaei Nazarenos appellant.*

[2] That this corresponds to the contemporary picture of Judaism see Origen, Homil. in Canticum Canticorum ii (ed. Baehrens, p. 168), the Jews represented as ὁ πρῶτος λαός or ὁ πάλαι λαός.

[3] Y. F. Baer, op. cit., 88—93.

[4] De Idololatria xx (ed. Reifferscheid-Wissowa, CSEL, 20), 54. Compare Sanhedrin, 63b.

[5] Ibid., xvi, Compare Aboda Zara 1. 3 (ed. Elmslie, Cambridge Texts and Studies viii. 2, ff. 6—7).

[6] Tertullian ibid., xxiv. The Jewish conditions of martyrdom are set out in Jewish Encyclopaedia, art. "Martyrdom, Restriction of".

he sees them as benighted and embittered opponents. The *Adversus Iudaeos* is not one of his more telling scripts, lacking the snap and fire of his work against pagans, Gnostics and doubters, but it shows his willingness to throw himself into an argument and refute the Jews when he felt others were letting the opportunity slip. 'They began the blasphemies against the Christians'[1], and without pity he points to the accuracy of the attribution of the Davidic prophecy referring to the 'destruction of the city' by 'the people of the prince' (Dan. 9[26]) to the destruction of Jerusalem by Titus[2]. Elsewhere, in *De Spectaculis*, whose thesis that Christians should not attend theatres shows Tertullian deriving his arguments apparently directly from rabbinic teaching, he reserves for the Jews the climax of his terrible but majestic description of the Judgement. Pagan magistrates, actors, charioteers, philosophers might be spied 'groaning in the depths of darkness', but 'not even then', says Tertullian, 'would I wish to see them in my desire to turn an insatiable gaze on them who vented their rage and fury on the Lord'[3]. The Jews would have real cause for their traditional lugubriousness on that Day.

Was this intellectual prejudice and propaganda or was it based on deepfelt experience at the hands of the Jews? *De Spectaculis* is one of Tertullian's earlier works, usually dated to around 200, but significantly perhaps, those writings that mark the outset of his career as a Christian provide a clue. The *Adversus Nationes* and *Apologeticum*, both dating to 197, contain an angry description of Jewish tactics against the Christians, and the reason for their hostility. The Jewish community is charged with being the 'seminarium' or seed-plot of every calumny against the Christians[4], and the incident which Tertullian describes as evidence, namely a Jew whom, as a *bestiarius* in the amphitheatre he could characterise as a renegade, carrying about an Onoecetes picture labelled 'the god of the Christians, assbegotten'[5] cannot easily be dismissed. Donkey-worship was attributed to the Jews. It was an obvious point to turn against the Christians. The Alaxamenos inscription in Rome shows that it was. The aim was to excite popular hatred and ridicule against the Christians, and it succeeded. The crowd, Tertullian says, was prepared 'to believe even this wretched Jew[6]. Why not? It was a chance to spread slanders against us.' The fact that this Jew was a renegade was not mentioned by Tertullian in order to acquit the Jews of blame, but to make their action in using such means appear the more despicable. And the reason – as usual Tertullian sums it up in a

---

[1] Adv. Iudaeos (ed. Kroymann, CSEL, 70, 323), 13, *ab illis enim coepit infamia.*
[2] Ibid., 8.
[3] De Spectaculis (ed. Rendall) 30.
[4] Adv. Nationes, i. 14. *Quid enim? Aliud genus* (the Jews) *seminari(um) est infamiae nostrae.*
[5] Apol. 16.12. For the significance of the Onoecetes gibe see J. Préaux, Deus Christianorum Onoeketes, Latomus, 44, 1966, 639–654.
[6] *Et credidit vulgus infami Iudaeo.*

single pithy sentence — 'Count the outsiders and you count its (Christianity's) enemies — the Jews its peculiar enemies from rivalry, the soldiers for blackmail . . .'[1]. The Jews come first on Tertullian's list, for they more than anyone else stood to lose by the spread of Christianity. In this respect Carthage in 197 presented the same picture as that described by Justin in Ephesus sixty years before, or by *I Clement* in his account of the Neronian persecution[2].

Nor was the danger to abate. Fifteen years later about A. D. 212 Tertullian, now a Montanist, wrote a mordant attack on the Gnostics and those Catholics whom he considered their allies, who were advocating that Christians should not voluntarily present themselves for martyrdom. This was *Scorpiace* — *the antidote to the scorpion's bite*, that of 'the little beasts that trouble our sect, that I may effect cures'[3] explains their author. Against these hidden enemies every Christian who confessed Christ's name carried with him the keys of St. Peter[4]. Then Tertullian turns to those who might transport even to the world beyond the 'whole series of means proper to the intimidation of Christians'. First among these once again come the synagogues. 'Will you plant there both synagogues of the Jews — the fountainheads of the persecutions — before which the apostles were scourged, and heathen assemblages with their own circus indeed, where they readily take up the cry, "Death to the third race"[5].' It has recently been urged that the reference to the 'synagogues of the Jews' has no contemporary significance[6] because Tertullian goes on to refer to the scourging of the apostles in them. If one takes the sentence as a whole, however, with its mention of shouts of 'Death to the third race', it must be obvious that Tertullian was thinking of what was happening in Carthage there and then. He was a journalist, not an antiquary, and the reference to the apostles is there for emphasis. He had already cited Jesus' warning (Matt. 10 [16ff.]) that His followers would have to face scourgings in the synagogues (Ch. 9). Now he wants to show that this, together with pagan persecutions, were taking place now, that it was in the divine dispensation, that it would persist to the end of the age and that thence was salvation. The Gnostics and other cowardly Christians must realise the consequences of failure to follow the apostolic example. In the previous decade the *fons* of the persecutions,

---

[1] Apol. 7.3. *Tot hostes eius quot extranei et quidem proprie ex aemulatione Iudaei, ex concussione milites* . . .

[2] I Clement, 5.2 — the deaths of the Apostles διὰ ζῆλον καὶ φθόνον, envy as the mainspring of fratricidal strife within Israel.

[3] Scorpiace, 1 (ed. Reifferscheid and Wissowa, CSEL, 20).

[4] Ibid. 10. For an earlier dating, circa 204, see T. D. Barnes, Scorpiace, JTS, n. s. xx, Oct. 1969.

[5] Ibid., *Illic constitues et synagogas Iudaeorum, fontes persecutionum, apud quas apostoli perpessi sunt, et populos nationum cum suo quidem circo, ubi facile conclamant; usque quo genus tertium?*

[6] See Fergus Millar, loc. cit., 234.

whence they were inspired, had not altered. At the end of the same piece Tertullian returns to his theme. The trials of the Christians of his own day were exactly foreshadowed by the sufferings of the apostles and their followers as set out in Acts. 'The prisons are there and the chains, and the scourges and great stones and the swords and the onsets of the Jews and the assemblies of the heathen and the indictments of the tribunes . . . these need no interpreter'[1]. Carthage at the turn of the third century held the same peril for the Christian as Smyrna in the time of Polycarp. It is not unreasonable to suggest following Tertullian that in both cities 'Jews and pagans were united in common action'[2], for very different motives certainly, but for the Christians it meant a simmering hatred liable to break out on any trivial pretext in savage acts of persecution.

In Carthage Jewish hostility persisted for a long time. A generation later after the Decian persecution, Cyprian was complaining to Pope Cornelius that the Christians in Carthage had been suffering from the threats of the heathen and the Jews as well as treachery in their own ranks[3]. Curiously enough Smyrna again provides a parallel situation with Jews and pagans making common cause against the confessor Pionius[4].

It is true that neither the North African Jews nor indeed those from any part of the Dispersion have left their own record of these events. On that account however there is no reason to call in question the evidence of contemporary Christian writers. The story they tell is a consistent one and inherently probable. The Jews could claim to offer the genuine tradition and true example of opposition to Greco-Roman idolatry. In North Africa they were still characterised as *alienam Romano imperio* in the time of Honorius[5]. At the same time, as we know from Josephus, they held out the prospect of salvation to the pagans on condition that they accepted Judaism[6]. In this dual mission, however, they could brook no rivalry. From the expulsion of Christians from the synagogues to the bitter literary warfare that has left its memorials in the *Letter of Barnabas*, Justin's *Dialogue with Trypho*, and the life and work of Marcion, it was both natural and fatally easy to pass to outright persecution. The means lay ready to hand, for the Jews were but the Christians were not *religio licita*. The pages of Tertullian enlighten both the positive and negative sides of the Jewish-Christian relationship. The latter was hardly, as has been claimed, 'largely irrelevant to the principal conflict between Christianity and its pagan environment'[7]. On the contrary, *synagogae Judaeorum fontes persecutionum* was a fact. It was simply the Carthaginian expression of the *contrarias sibi* aspect of Judaism and Christianity that struck Sulpicius Severus so forcibly even at the end of the fourth century[8].

---

[1] Scorpiace 15, p. 178.
[2] As I have said in Martyrdom and Persecution in the Early Church, 323.
[3] Ep. 59.2 (ed. Hartel, p. 668).   [4] Mart. S. Pionii, (ed. Knopf/Krüger) 4.8.
[5] Cod. Theod., xvi, 8.19.   [6] Josephus, Adv. Apionem, ii, 36.261.
[7] Fergus Millar, loc. cit., 234.   [8] Chronicon (ed. Halm), ii. 30.6.

V

OPEN QUESTIONS CONCERNING THE CHRISTIANS AND THE ROMAN EMPIRE IN THE AGE OF THE SEVERI

THE early years of the third century were a period of great expansion for the Christian Churches. In 180 many provincials in the eastern provinces of the empire would have agreed with Celsus' clever and damaging account of Christianity as a rogue offshoot from Judaism. There were 'Jews and Christians', as he stated,[1] and the Christians were a narrow and introspective clique concerned only with their own righteousness, clannish and credulous, behaving like 'frogs round a marsh', and proclaiming arrogantly that 'the world had been made for them'.[2] Their ideas were based on false, Judaistic concepts of God and man, and only in detail did they differ from their Jewish models. Yet, they were dangerous. They refused military and civic duties, and by avid proselytism among women and children in big establishments they threatened to subvert traditional society.[2] In Celsus' view they deserved the periodic bouts of persecution to which the authorities subjected them.[3]

Twenty years later much of this picture had changed. There were well organized Gentile Christian communities in most of the large cities in the eastern Mediterranean, as well as in Rome and around Carthage. The Phrygian merchant Avircius encountered Christians on his travels all the way from Rome to Nisibis.[4] Moreover, these communities were beginning to impinge seriously on pagan society. In Alexandria Clement, who had settled there *circa* 180, was opening what was probably the first campaign since the time of St. Paul aimed at converting educated provincials by writing and preaching. 'The word of our teacher', he wrote, 'did not stay in Judaea alone, as philosophy stayed in Greece, but was poured out over all the world.'[5] The *Protrepticus*, with its fine

---

[1] Origen, *Contra Celsum* (ed. and Eng. translation by H. Chadwick, Cambridge, 1953), iv. 23.

[2] Ibid. iii. 55, and compare iii. 44 and 52.

[3] Ibid. viii. 69. In general, see the author's *Martyrdom and Persecution in the Early Church* (Oxford, 1965), pp. 279–83.

[4] Text in W. M. Ramsay, *Cities and Bishoprics in Phrygia* (Oxford, 1883), ii. pp. 722–3. See also W. M. Calder, 'The Epitaph of Avircius Marcellus', *Journal of Roman Studies* (= *J.R.S.*) xxix (1939), pp. 1–2 and J. Stevenson, *A New Eusebius* (London, 1957), pp. 143–4.

[5] Clement, *Stromateis* (ed. O. Stählin/L. Früchtel, *GCS*, Berlin, 1960), vi. 18. 167. 3. It 'persuaded Greeks and barbarians alike'.

opening comparison between the music of Amphion and the music of Christ had an avowedly missionary aim,[1] as had the catechetical school which Clement led in Alexandria. Custom, urged Clement, must give way to truth, especially Christian truth.[2] For Rome also, one may perhaps combine evidence for the final Christianization of some of the catacombs towards the end of the second century,[3] with Eusebius' claim that this period saw the conversion of some members of the ruling houses of the city.[4] In Carthage, Tertullian, himself a convert to Christianity, was exultant at the progress his religion was making. 'Day by day', he tells the pagans in Carthage in a well-known passage, 'you groan over the increasing numbers of Christians. Your constant cry is that the state is beset by us, that Christians are in your fields and in your camps and in your blocks of houses (*insulae*). You grieve over it as a calamity, that every age, and in short, every rank of society is passing from you to us.'[5] He made no secret that the religion he had adopted was uncompromisingly opposed to the paganism of the Roman empire.

By A.D. 200 therefore Christianity was rapidly emerging from the shadows and staking its claim to be recognized as a world-religion. The description of its adherents as 'a secret tribe (*latebrosa et lucifuga gens*) that shuns the light'[6] no longer fitted, but amidst the greatly increased prosperity many of the more obvious signs of the Jewish heritage remained. The Christians did not adopt a distinctive garb like the Jews,[7] but they shared with them the same uncompromising abhorrence of idolatry and the corollary of separation from most forms of association with contemporary pagan society.[8] For both the heathen were the 'nations', the *gentes*, the outsiders, the enemies of God and the truth. They shared too, procedures of initiation that emphasized the convert's break from his pagan past. The Christian proselyte like the Jewish was a complete 'convert'. The Christians also followed the Jewish practice of

---

[1] *Protrepticus* (ed. G. W. Butterworth), i. 1.

[2] *Protrepticus*, x. 85 and compare xii. 91.

[3] e.g. the Catacomb of the Caecilii: see G. La Piana, 'The Roman Church at the End of the Second Century', *Harvard Theological Review*, xviii (1925), p. 260.

[4] Eusebius, *Hist. Eccl.* v. 21.

[5] Tertullian, *Ad Nationes*, 1. 14 written in the first half of 197, and compare *Apol.* 37. 2 and *Ad Scapulam*, 2. 10 (ed. V. Buhlart) (written in 212): 'Tanta hominum multitudo pars paene maior civitatis cuiusque.'

[6] Minucius Felix, *Octavius*, 8. 4.

[7] So Tertullian, *Apol.* 42. 1, and compare the second-century tract, the *Letter to Diognetus*, 5.

[8] On this aspect of the Jewish–Christian relationship, see Y. Baer, 'Israel, the Early Church and the Roman Empire', *Scripta Hierosolymitana*, vii (1961), pp. 79 ff.

burying their dead in catacombs. The questions that were interesting their leaders at this time, such as the correct method of calculating Easter with reference, of course, to its connection with the Jewish Passover,[1] and the relationship between the Old Covenant and the New,[2] were questions debated by people at home with Jewish ways of thought. The Jewish heritage was not renounced. The language of Scripture was, on the other hand, repellent to most educated provincials.[3] Origen's picturesque descriptions of Judaism in the 230s as Christianity's 'little sister' or the 'bride's brother' reflect the peculiar surviving intimacy in the relationship between the two monotheist creeds.[4] In time of persecution Judaism sometimes provided a refuge for Christians.[5] For a pagan recording events of the age of the Severi there was nothing incongruous in associating Jews and Christians as members of kindred faiths,[6] evoking similar attitudes on the part of the rulers,[7] even if one was *religio licita* and the other was not.

Eusebius indicates that the reaction of pagans to the advance of Christianity took the form of vicious persecutions, and he records the martyrdom of Apollonius in Rome, *c.* 185, as an instance.[8] At the beginning of Book vi of the *Ecclesiastical History*, however, he states, 'Now when Severus was stirring up persecution against the churches in every place splendid martyrdoms of the champions of piety were accomplished, but with especial frequency in Alexandria' (vi. 1). Thus for him, the initiative for the renewed outbreak of persecution in Severus' reign came from the emperor himself, and the question has been raised, particularly in recent years, how far this can be true.

All historians agree that the middle part of the reign of Septimius Severus (193–211) witnessed more widespread persecutions of the

---

[1] Eusebius, *Hist. Eccl.* v. 23–25.   [2] Irenaeus, *Demonstratio*, 93–6.

[3] For instance, at the end of the third century, Arnobius, *Adv. Gentes* 1. 58 states that the Scriptures were criticized because 'ab indoctis hominibus et rudibus scripta sunt et idcirco non sunt facili auditione credenda'.

[4] Origen, *In Cantic. Canticorum*, Bk. ii (ed. Baehrens, *GCS* 33 = Origenes 8, pp. 168–9). Also, Jerome, *Translatio Homil. Origenis in Cantic. Canticorum* (*P.L.* xxiii. 1187 B): 'Salvator noster sororis ejus est filius, id est synagogae, duo quippe sorores sunt, Ecclesia et Synagoga' (ed. Baehrens, p. 45).

[5] Eusebius, *Hist. Eccl.* vi. 12. 1 (Antioch).

[6] Thus Galen in a lost work *c.* 200, 'If I had in mind people who taught their pupils in the same way as the followers of Moses and Christ teach theirs—for they order them to accept everything on faith—I would not have given you a definition.' Cited from R. Walzer, *Galen on Jews and Christians* (Oxford, 1949), p. 15.

[7] Thus Dio Cassius, writing *c.* 220, seems to make no difference between converts to Judaism and Christianity. Both 'lapsed into Jewish customs': *Epit.* lxvii. 14 concerning the 'Domitianic persecution'.

[8] Eusebius, *Hist. Eccl.* v. 21.

Christians than ever before. The favour towards the Christians alleged by Tertullian, *Ad Scapulam*,[1] would seem to develop in Severus' court towards the end of his reign, when Severus himself was far away from Rome and occupied with his attempt to reconquer the Scottish lowlands. Before that, Christians were subjected to severe attacks by mobs and judicial proceedings by urban magistrates and provincial governors. In Carthage contemporary evidence provided by Tertullian and the writer of the *Passio Perpetuae* shows that the Christians were extremely unpopular throughout the whole decade 196–206,[2] and were subjected to further persecution under the Proconsul Scapula in 212. The events in Carthage in 202–3 have been immortalized by the account of the martyrdom of Perpetua and Felicitas in the amphitheatre on 7 March 203.[3] But there were confessors to be visited in prison in 197 (*Ad Martyras*). In 203, probably the year he wrote *De Baptismo*, Tertullian stressed the sacramental value of martyrdom.[4] In 203 or 204, the most likely date of the *Scorpiace*,[5] he was describing the situation as the 'dog-star of persecution'.[6] The situation was hot for the Christians, and their obvious increase in numbers was among the causes of their unpopularity.[7] In Alexandria, Clement, before he fled the city, probably in 203, wrote of 'roastings, impalings, and beheadings' of Christians there as not uncommon experiences.[8] Under the Prefect of Egypt, Q. Maecius Laetus (201–3), Origen's father Leonides was executed,[9] and Origen had no sooner taken over the headship of the catechetical school after Clement's departure than his friends, contemporaries, and

---

[1] Tertullian, *Ad Scapulam* (ed. V. Buhlart), 4. 6.

[2] Typical examples in *Apologeticum*, 41 and 50. Compare *Passio Perpetuae et Felicitatis* (ed. Knopf/Krueger), 13. 3. The confessor Saturus saw in a dream only martyrs whom he recognized, in Paradise.

[3] *Passio Perpetuae et Felicitatis*. (See T. D. Barnes, 'Pre-Decian Acta Martyrum', *J.T.S.* N.s. xix (1968), pp. 521–3 for its early date.)

[4] *De Baptismo*, 16. Dating see K. H. Schwarte, 'Das angebliche Christengesetz des Septimius Severus', *Historia*, xii (1963), pp. 195–6, following H. Koch, 'Tertullianus', Pauly–Wissowa *RE*, v A. 1, col. 827.

[5] T. D. Barnes's dating is accepted. See the detailed argument in 'Tertullian's *Scorpiace*', *J.T.S.* N.s. xx (1969), pp. 105–31. An additional point in favour of a pre-Montanist date might be that Tertullian's main concern seems to be with Gnostics as in *Adv. Valentinianos*, not with 'Psychics' as in his Montanist period.

[6] *Scorpiace*, 1. 10 'et nunc praesentia rerum est medius ardor ipsa canicula persecutionis ab ipso scilicet cynocephalo'.

[7] *Apol.* 3 and 21. 3 for the contempt in which the convert to Christianity was held in Carthage in 197, 'quanti odium Christianorum'.

[8] Clement, *Stromateis*, ii. 20. 125 (ed. Stählin/Früchtel, *GCS*, Berlin, 1960, pp. 180–1).

[9] Eusebius, *Hist. Eccl.* vi. 2. On Maecius Laetus, see E. Stein, Pauly–Wissowa, art. Maecius, No. 13 (*RE*, xiv. 1, 235 f.).

converts were arrested and some were executed.[1] This second wave of persecution took place under the Prefect Subatianus Aquila who followed Claudius Julianus probably in the autumn of 206 and governed until July 210.[2] Eusebius suggests that the fact of their conversion to Christianity was the immediate cause of the victims' arrest and death.[3] In Rome too, Hippolytus has left vivid descriptions of the mob turning on the Christians. 'Rid the earth of such-like; they are not fit to live', they shouted.[4] For him the persecution presaged the end of the existing age. The blood of the righteous was being shed in town and countryside; Christians were being thrown to the beasts, or killed in the streets, and women and virgins shamefully treated. One Roman confessor of this period was the Monarchian Natalius who eventually made his peace with Pope Zephyrinus.[5] Persecution was real enough. In Corinth also, Hippolytus instances a denunciation of a Christian woman to the magistrates on the grounds that 'she had blasphemed both the times and the emperors and spoken ill of the idols'.[6] *Felicitas Saeculi* of the Severan age did not appeal to everyone. In Cappadocia, Alexander the future bishop of Jerusalem was imprisoned for some years during the reign of Severus,[7] perhaps from 204, and finally, in Antioch there was a persecution during the same period which resulted as already noted in Christians finding refuge with the Jews, and the arrest of the future bishop, Asclepiades.[8]

This is a formidable catalogue of incidents taking place in a relatively short time and over a very wide area. Christians were persecuted not only in the largest centres of population but in sparsely populated areas such as in Cappadocia. Eusebius himself characterizes the situation

[1] Ibid. vi. 3 and 4.
[2] For Aquila's dating see T. D. Barnes, 'Pre-Decian *Acta Martyrum*', *J.T.S.* N.S. xix (1968), pp. 526–7, and for that of Claudius Julianus, J. Rea, 'The date of the prefecture of Claudius Julianus', *La Parola del Passato*, xxii (1967), pp. 48–53.
[3] Eusebius, *Hist. Eccl.* vi. 4. Compare ibid. vi. 3. 6 describing Origen being driven from house to house 'no one receiving him' because of the converts he was making.
[4] Hippolytus, *Commentary on Daniel*, i. 23 (ed. N. Bonwetsch, *GCS*, Leipzig, 1897, p. 35).
[5] Eusebius, *Hist. Eccl.* v. 28. 8–12.
[6] Hippolytus, quoted in Palladius, *Lausiac History*, lxv. For punishment for making rash remarks, see R. Macmullen, 'Social History in Astrology', *Ancient History*, ii (1971), p. 107.
[7] Eusebius, *Hist. Eccl.* vi. 8. 7: 'He played the man during the persecution.' Compare also ibid. 11. 5. For the date, Eusebius, *Chronicon* ad ann. 204 (Helm, p. 212).
[8] *Hist. Eccl.* vi. 11. 4. Eusebius says also of him that 'he was himself distinguished by his confessions in the persecution', as though there was one persecution in Antioch at this period, which was well known.

simply as 'the persecution',[1] as though it was a period that needed no further qualification. Moreover, the attacks were directed mainly against the rank and file of the Christian movement, and in Alexandria and Carthage these included catechumens. Perpetua was baptized in prison[2] and those arrested with her are recorded as 'apprehensi sunt adolescentes catechumini, Revocatus et Felicitas conserva eius',[3] while Perpetua's brother is also mentioned by the writer of the *Passio* as being a catechumen.[3] In Alexandria the roll-call of martyrs among Origen's friends was also made up of those who had been recently baptized or were catechumens.[4] Years later, when he wrote the *Fourth Homily on Jeremiah*, Origen looked back upon those days with pride as a heroic age of Christianity, when 'the catechumens were catechized in the midst of martyrdoms'. Then one really was a believer.[5] All this was going on while the leadership of the churches in the big provincial capitals of the empire was showing a remarkable stability. At Rome Zephyrinus was to be bishop for 18 years (199–217), at Alexandria Demetrius ruled for 43 years (189–232), at Antioch Serapion governed his see for 19 years (190–209), and at Carthage Agrippinus seems to have enjoyed a long and undisturbed reign. All had plenty of time for disciplinary and doctrinal arguments. The situation under Septimius Severus differed therefore from other periods of persecution in the third century when the primary targets for the authorities were the Christian leaders.[6]

Who was responsible for these outbreaks? The immediate pressure came from the mob, probably abetted in Carthage and Rome by the Jews who were bitterly resentful at the advance of a sect which they tended to regard as a noxious heresy.[7] In the *Apologeticum* written towards the end of 197, Tertullian states of the Carthaginian mob that 'none is more apt to demand the death of Christians',[8] and they had the full support of the local magistrates. Hippolytus paints the same picture of the situation in Rome.[9] In Alexandria the prefects Q. Maecius Laetus and Subatianus Aquila who acted so drastically and cruelly against

[1] As in *Hist. Eccl.* vi. 8. 7 and 11. 4. He clearly means the persecution initiated by Severus, with which Eusebius opens the sixth Book of his *Ecclesiastical History*.
[2] *Passio Perpetuae* (ed. Knopf/Krueger), 3. 3.
[3] *Passio Perpetuae*, 2.
[4] Eusebius, *Hist. Eccl.* vi. 4 and 5.
[5] Origen, *Homil. in Jeremiah*, iv. 3 (ed. E. Klostermann *CGS* 6, pp. 25–6).
[6] Compare Eusebius, *Hist. Eccl.* vi. 28.
[7] Thus Tertullian, *Apol.* 7. 2. See the present writer's 'A note on the Jews and Christians in third century North Africa', *J.T.S.* N.S. xxi. 1 (1970), pp. 92–6.
[8] Tertullian, *Apol.* 37. 1–3.
[9] Hippolytus, *In Danielem*, i. 20, compare ibid. iv. 51 (Bonwetsch, pp. 318–20).

V

Christian confessors merely reflected enraged public opinion. There
was also plenty of scope, as Tertullian showed in his address to the Proconsul Scapula, for the whim of ill-disposed governors.[1] The question,
however, arises whether these were the only factors in the situation.
Were the ferocious local persecutions all over the central and eastern
Mediterranean coincidences, dependent, as Hans Lietzmann believed,
on 'local conditions and the character of the governor',[2] or were they at
some point orchestrated by a ruling from the emperor designed to
curb the growth of a cult whose advance was causing disturbance in the
main cities of the empire? Second-century evidence shows that legal
enactments of some sort often lay behind a rash of persecutions. The
'new decrees', probably regulations promulgated by the Proconsul of
Asia, set off the persecutions in that province in the reign of Marcus
Aurelius.[3] When there were disturbances on a scale threatening internal security the emperor himself would be informed, as Marcus
Aurelius had been in 177 when the mob attacked the Christians at
Lyons.[4] In reply, he gave a ruling to the governor concerning his hand-
ling of the Christians. Did a similar chain of events take place in Severus'
reign that resulted in the alleged rescript prohibiting Christian as well as
Jewish proselytism?

Up to a decade ago historians, with the notable exception of Hans
Lietzmann, had been inclined to accept the probability of a persecuting
policy initiated by Severus. Authorities that included Mommsen, J. K.
Neumann, H. Last, Henri Grégoire, and J. Moreau agreed that the
year 201/2 saw a legal measure ordered by Severus that aimed at
restricting the recruitment and propaganda work of Christians,[5] and
that thereby a new era in the history of the Church's relations with
the empire was inaugurated. In 1963, however, K. H. Schwarte in an
important article in *Historia* pointed to the fragility of the evidence.
In particular, the alleged decision to punish converts to Christianity
preserved in Spartian's *Vita Severi* (17. 1) was highly suspect. Not only
was the chronology of the events in which Severus' action was supposed
to have taken place muddled, but the alleged rescript itself was likely to
be the fabrication of the late fourth-century author in pursuance of his
aim to prevent further deterioration of the position of paganism through

---

[1] Tertullian, *Ad Scapulam*, 3.
[2] H. Lietzmann, *Geschichte der Alten Kirche* (Berlin, 1936), ii, p. 164.
[3] On the 'new decrees' as provincial edicts, see G. E. M. de Ste Croix, *J.T.S.*
N.S. xviii (1967), p. 219, whose view I accept.
[4] Eusebius, *Hist. Eccl.* v. 1. 47. Marcus' rescript to the governor of Gallia
Lugdunensis upholding Trajan's ruling.
[5] Authorities listed by K. H. Schwarte, 'Das angebliche Christengesetz des
Septimius Severus', *Historia*, xii (1963), pp. 185-208 on pp. 189-92.

340

conversions to Christianity.[1] Schwarte concluded that there had been no 'Severan persecution', and that Lietzmann's explanation of the persecutions of his reign as local and inspired by individual ill-willed governors was correct.

Schwarte received strong support from T. D. Barnes who drew attention in addition to a fact known but not always appreciated, that there had been an interval of up to four years between Maecius Laetus' persecution of 201/2 and the arrival of Aquila.[2] If Severus' rescript against conversion to Christianity was dated to 202 it could hardly have been enforced only in 206. Eusebius' chronology was confused and his attribution of the persecution in Alexandria to an initiative by the emperor could not be sustained. This view has been accepted in R. M. Grant's recent work. The 'so-called edict of Septimius Severus did not exist'. Persecution 'was due to private and/or local initiative'.[3] This is a question where at the moment there can only be a balance of probabilities. Apart, however, from the rash of persecutions between 201 and 207, there are three independent pieces of evidence that point to some form of imperial intervention in this period.

First, Eusebius, *Hist. Eccl.* vi. 1, already mentioned, and more explicitly in Jerome's edition of the *Chronicle*. Referring to the tenth year of Severus' reign, i.e. either August 201–August 202, or April 202–April 203, the text reads, 'persecutione in christianos facta Leonides, Origenis pater, gloriosa martyrii morte transfertur'.[4] In the *Ecclesiastical History*, Eusebius fills out the details of Leonides' execution and the confiscation of his property, followed by the flight of the leadership of

---

[1] K. H. Schwarte, loc. cit., pp. 205–7.

[2] T. D. Barnes, 'Legislation against the Christians', *J.R.S.* lviii (1968), pp. 32–50 at pp. 40–1. That Subatianus Aquila was in office in 206 had been indicated by J. E. L. Oulton's edition of Eusebius' *Ecclesiastical History* ii (Loeb ed. 1953), p. 16. The difficulty was to harmonize this with Eusebius' statement (*Hist. Eccl.* vi. 3. 3) that Origen 'came to preside over the catechetical school in his eighteenth year', i.e. at latest in 204, and 'at this time (ἐν ᾧ) he came into prominence when the persecutions were going on under Aquila'. Eusebius makes no mention of Maecius Laetus' successor, Claudius Julianus (203 ?–6 ?), and the assumption therefore was that Laetus had been succeeded by Aquila. This is not the only occasion in this part of the *Hist. Eccl.* that Eusebius foreshortens a time span to heighten the effect of his narrative. In vi. 2. 2 referring to Laetus' execution of Origen's father in 202 he states that 'Demetrius had just then (νεωστὶ τότε) received the episcopate of the communities there (in Egypt) in succession to Julian'. In fact, Demetrius had already been bishop twelve or thirteen years! The effect of the rhetorician's training counsels caution in accepting Eusebius as a precise authority, but does not justify dismissing him altogether.

[3] R. M. Grant, *Augustus to Constantine: the thrust of the Christian movement into the Roman World* (New York–London, 1970), p. 100.

[4] Eusebius (Hieronymus, *Chronicon*) *GCS Eusebius Werke*, vii. 1, ed. R. Helm (Leipzig, 1913), p. 212.

the catechetical school, Origen's appointment by Bishop Demetrius as head, his successes, and the renewal of violent persecution directed largely against recent converts and laity. There is no reference, however, to an 'edict of persecution' such as marked the beginning of the Decian persecution,[1] and Bishop Demetrius and his clergy appear to go un-molested.

It might be argued perhaps that Eusebius was attempting to fit the 'persecution of Severus' into a preconceived scheme of persecutions against the Christians. He quotes Tertullian's *Apologeticum* to make the two 'bad emperors', Nero and Domitian, responsible for the first two attacks by the authorities against the Church.[2] He does not, however, continue with this formula. In the second century he blames 'the devil who hates what is good' for persecution and the rise of heresies.[3] The persecutions at Smyrna and Lyons happened in the reign of Marcus Aurelius but the initiative came from the mob and not the emperor.[4] There was no 'persecution of Marcus Aurelius'. That in contrast, Eusebius should place responsibility for the outbreaks in the reign of Severus on the emperor himself might argue for the correctness of his statement. In the *Ecclesiastical History* there is no trace of the number-symbolism attached to persecutions such as was developing in the west.[5] Eusebius' version of events, if foreshortened, reflects what educated Christians in the east at the end of the third century believed to have happened. The situation at Alexandria resembled that at Carthage where, though the writer of the *Passio Perpetuae* does not say that his heroine was arrested *because* she was a catechumen, he emphasizes that she and her companions were so. Again, the clergy do not seem to have been touched unless, like Saturus, they volunteered for martyrdom.

Secondly, Hippolytus' statement in his *Commentary on Daniel*, i. 20. 2–3, 'They (the pagans) seize certain individuals, take them out (of the house of God) and tell them, "Come, agree with us and worship the

---

[1] Eusebius, *Hist. Eccl.* vi. 41. 10, quoting Bishop Dionysius' letter to Bishop Fabius of Antioch: "καὶ δὴ καὶ παρῆν τὸ πρόσταγμα". Dionysius finds it worth mentioning that persecution had just previously broken out 'without an imperial edict' (ibid., vi. 41. 1). Arbitrary acts of persecution on the initiative of officials were apparently not to be expected in Alexandria at this time (A.D. 248).

[2] Eusebius, *Hist. Eccl.* ii. 25. 4 and iii. 20. 7. Compare iii. 17. 1.

[3] Ibid. iv. 7. 1 and 9.

[4] Ibid. v. 1 (Lyons). Regarding Polycarp's martyrdom, Eusebius states simply that it took place in Marcus' reign (ἐν τούτῳ) without attributing responsibility to the emperor; ibid. iv. 15. 1.

[5] For instance, in Sulpicius Severus' *Chronicon*, ii. 29–32. Severus' persecution was listed as 'Sexta deinde Severo imperante Christianorum vexatio fuit' (ii. 32). For a good summary of the evidence, see J. Vogt, 'Die Zählung der Christen-verfolgungen im römischen Reich', *La Parola del Passato*, ix (1954), pp. 5–15.

gods, otherwise we shall testify against you". Those who refuse they take before the tribunal and accuse them as acting against the decree of Caesar (ὡς ἐναντία τοῦ δόγματος Καίσαρος πράσσοντας) and get them condemned to death.' There is nothing to contradict Bonwetsch's view that the *In Danielem* belongs to Hippolytus' earlier works and that it was written after a severe persecution,[1] and at the end of the work Hippolytus returns to the theme of persecution.[2] This, together with the vividness of the narrative, suggests that the events took place as stated and left a deep impression on the writer. This would be the first recorded serious mob outbreak against the Christians since the time of Nero, and the ruthless violence of the crowd causing men 'to be burnt alive and thrown to the dogs', cemeteries robbed, bones of the dead scattered, is consistent with a belief that they were acting in the spirit of an official order which laid the lives and property of the Christians open to coercion and harassment.[3]

Thirdly, there is the most precise yet most controversial piece of evidence, the statement in Spartian's *Vita Severi*, 17. 1, that on his journey through Palestine *en route* to Egypt after his victorious Parthian campaign Severus promulgated a number of decrees. Among these, 'Iudaeos fieri sub gravi poena vetuit. Idem etiam de Christianis sanxit.' Barnes's view that the *Vita Severi* is a '(basically) reliable account' of Severus' life, despite the suspicion that attached to the anecdotes, may be noted here.[4] Certainly, in the passage in which the text comes, there is nothing obviously apocryphal. Spartian has just described (16. 8) how the Senate had decreed a 'Jewish triumph' for Caracalla 'because in Syria also Severus' affairs had prospered' ('cui senatus Iudaicum triumphum decreverat, idcirco quod et in Syria res bene gestae fuerant a Severo'). He had then entered Antioch, conferred the *toga virilis* on Caracalla and designated him consul before moving through Palestine to Egypt where he bestowed the right of having an independent Boulé on the Alexandrines before sightseeing at Memphis (17. 1–4).

---

[1] N. Bonwetsch, *Studien zu den Kommentaren Hippolytus* (1897), pp. 81 f., and *GCS* i, p. xx, 'nicht zu lange nach einer heftigen Verfolgung'. Bonwetsch would also put the emperor's decree to before 201/2 while Severus was sole emperor.   [2] *In Danielem*, iv. 51.

[3] T. D. Barnes's suggestion, 'Legislation against the Christians', pp. 42–3, that the word δόγμα is being used metaphorically seems less likely in view of the indications that severe and calculated acts of persecution had taken place, presumably on the initiative of someone in authority. The comparison of the phraseology of Hippolytus and Acts xvii. 7, though interesting, is not a reason for rejecting the truth of the account.

[4] T. D. Barnes, 'The family and career of Septimius Severus', *Historia*, xvi (1967), pp. 87–107 at pp. 91 and 95.

As with Eusebius' narrative, the chronology is condensed and mistaken.[1] In fact, Severus, having failed to capture the desert stronghold of Hatra by the autumn of 199, spent some time in Syria and Palestine before arriving in Egypt at the turn of the year 199/200. He was in that country during 200–1. He gave Alexandria a constitution of the municipal type and extended these to other Egyptian cities. He sailed from Egypt to Antioch in 201 and there conferred the *toga virilis* and consulship on Caracalla before leaving for the west. So Spartian has put the events in the wrong order and appears to presume a progress through Palestine in 201 which did not take place. On the other hand, he preserves record of trouble in Syria involving the Jews which may be confirmed partially by a passage in the Jewish Eighth Sibylline Oracle. This seems to combine the rise of Severus' rival Niger with the mythical return of Nero as leader of destructive armies from the east and the downfall of the Antonine rulers represented by Severus. The new ruler would storm Rome after it had existed for 948 years (i.e. 195–6).[2] As in other clashes between Rome and Parthia, there were clearly many Syrian Jews who sympathized with the Parthian cause. The reference to the 'Jewish triumph' granted to Caracalla might suggest that military operations against them had been necessary.

Even if this debate could be concluded, the historian would still be confronted by the wider question whether any credence can be attached to Spartian's story. Ever since Hermann Dessau published his classic article in *Hermes* in 1889 suggesting with an impressive variety of evidence that the *Historia Augusta* was the work of a single author writing probably in the reign of Theodosius I and plagiarizing Aurelius Victor and Eutropius in order to give his work the appearance of historical veracity, it has been hazardous to rely on any part of the collection.[3] Moreover, the two most recent authorities on the *Historia*, Syme[4] and Chastagnol,[5] agree with Dessau. To Syme in particular, the

---

[1] T. D. Barnes, 'Legislation against the Christians', p. 41. See S. N. Miller, 'The Personality and Policy of Severus', *Cambridge Ancient History*, xii, pp. 17–19, for the sequence of events.

[2] *Oracula Sibyllina* (ed. J. Geffcken, *GCS* 1902), viii. 138–59. This was not the view of many Palestinian Jews. An inscription from Kasyoun dating to 197 indicates loyalty of the Jewish community to Severus and his family! *Corp. Inscr. Judaicarum*, ii. 972. See R. M. Grant, *Augustus to Constantine*, p. 98.

[3] H. Dessau, 'Über Zeit und Persönlichkeit der *Scriptores Historiae Augustae*', *Hermes*, xxiv (1889), pp. 337–92.

[4] R. Syme, *Ammianus Marcellinus and the Historia Augusta* (Oxford, 1968), and *Emperors and Biography, Studies in the Historia Augusta* (Oxford, 1971). For subsequent discussion, see Alan Cameron in *J.R.S.* lxi (1971), pp. 255–67 and Syme's rejoinder, '*The Historia Augusta*, recent theories', *J.R.S.* lxii (1972), pp. 123–33.

[5] André Chastagnol, *Recherches sur l'Histoire Auguste (Antiquitas*, Reihe 4,

344

Historia is the composition of an impostor who passed himself off as six biographers writing in the age of Diocletian and Constantine, who perpetrated this literary *tour de force* sometime in the last decade of the fourth century.[1]

The situation concerning Spartian's life of Septimius Severus, however, is complicated for, in Syme's view, it belongs to a group of Imperial *Lives* of high historical accuracy compiled by an unknown author (*Ignotus*) perhaps shortly after the death of Caracalla in 217.[2] This would certainly add credence to the entry concerning Severus' treatment of Jews and Christians for, as we have seen, though there is some confusion about the order of the events in 199–201, the events themselves are attested by other evidence.

If one was content with Syme's theory, Spartian could be given a relatively clean bill of health. It would, however, hardly be conceivable to support a hypothesis by an appeal to an unknown author utilized by an unknown impostor. Too many questions crowd in. *Ignotus* himself may have no more reality than the Cheshire Cat's smile, while those who accept the Impostor have still to find a motive for his work. Was it sheer perversity and, if so, how did 'this literary personality, this writer of great skill and versatility, alert and audacious',[3] manage to leave no mark on a period in which collections of *De Viris Illustribus* were so fashionable a literary pursuit? How, too, did he avoid so skilfully the pitfalls which would beset anyone who attempted to write in the idiom of a period two generations before his own?[4] Even where events described seem to refer to actual occurrences in the last years of the fourth century, such as the visit of the Jewish patriarch to Egypt, these can be related with equal probability to an earlier age.[5] Must one postulate the visit of 'the great Gamaliel' to Alexandria in 398 as the inspiration for Vopiscus' portrayal of religion in Egypt, when in Origen's day the Jewish patriarch was also a man of power 'little short of that of royalty' who was used to holding assizes and might be expected to maintain contact with Jewish Diaspora communities of which he was also head?[6]

6, Bonn, 1970). In particular, the 'Quadrigae Tyrannorum' of Vopiscus was 'un exercice plein de fantaisie', compiled by an author in the last few years of the fourth century: ibid., p. 98.

[1] Syme, *Ammianus*, p. 1, and *Emperors and Biography*, p. 283.

[2] Syme, *Emperors and Biography*, Ch. iii, '*Ignotus* ended with Caracalla', p. 51.   [3] Ibid., p. 260.

[4] See A. Momigliano's pertinent comments, *Studies in Historiography* (London, 1966), pp. 152 ff.

[5] Syme, *Emperors and Biography*, Ch. ii, compare *Ammianus*, pp. 61 ff., for his discussion of Vopiscus, *Quadrigae Tyrannorum* 8. 2–4.

[6] Origen, *Ep. ad Africanum* 14. (*P.G.* xi. 84). In the third century it would

The clues whence to substantiate or reject Spartian's account must be sought by different methods. First, one notices that though there is no consistent treatment of the Christians to be observed in the authors, those who refer to Christianity have one point in common.[1] Christianity represented a religion that stood in contrast to the acknowledgement of the Roman gods, but akin to Judaism and even to the cult of the Samaritans. At the same time, it was not a 'superstitio' or a 'prava religio', pejorative descriptions used by Latin authors in the second and early third centuries. Christianity was a 'devotio', different indeed from 'omnia Romanis veneranda', but similar to the 'religiones Iudaeorum et Samaritanorum'.[2] Like Lampridius, Spartian refers to the emperor's attitude towards Jews and Christians in the same sentence,[3] the one favourable to both, the other unfavourable.[4] It is interesting too, that the more cutting references to Christianity are made by authors who place their work before the accession of Constantine. For instance, Flavius Vopiscus' *Vita Aureliani* and the *Quadrigae Tyrannorum*, both of which contain unfriendly references to Christians,[5] purport to be written under Constantius I, while Spartian claims to be writing in the period of Diocletian. The six more favourable references to Christianity come in Lampridius' *Alexander Severus* and *Life* of Heliogabalus, allegedly Constantinian productions.

These may be straws in the wind, because between the formation of the Tetrarchy in 293 and the Council of Nicaea, the fortunes of the Christians went through a kaleidoscopic series of changes. Thus, a court writer writing at any time between 293 and 303 could afford to

be possible also to place the religions of Serapis and Christ on level terms with regard to attractive power, but certainly not in the age of Cyril.

[1] Thus, Alföldi has little on which to base his view that the *HA* was an anti-Christian document, 'that pamphlet against the Christians', *Cambridge Ancient History*, xii, p. 223. One might add, that one does not find anti-Christian sentiments even where one would expect them as in the fragments of the *Valeriani Duo*.

[2] Thus, Lampridius, *Antoninus Heliogabalus*, 3. 4–5 (Hohl, i, p. 225).

[3] Lampridius, *Alexander Severus*, 45. 7 'Christiani et Iudaei', and 51. 7 'sive Iudaeis sive Christianis'.

[4] Thus, Spartian (*Severus*, 17. 1): 'Iudaeos fieri sub gravi poena vetuit. Idem etiam de Christianis sanxit.' Lampridius (*Alexander Severus* 22. 1): 'Iudaeis privilegia reservavit, Christianos esse passus est.'

[5] Thus Flavius Vopiscus, *Aurelianus* (20. 5), Aurelian rebukes the Senate, 'Miror vos, patres sancti, tamdiu de aperiendis Sibyllinis dubitasse libris, proinde quasi in Christianorum ecclesia, non in templo deorum omnium tractaretis.' For Aurelian's reputed hostility towards Christianity see Lactantius, *De Mortibus Persecutorum*, 6, and Eusebius, *Hist. Eccl.* vii. 30. 20. For the mocking reference to Christians and worshippers of Serapis in Alexandria, *Quadrigae Tyrannorum*, 8. 1–4.

346

nudge his patron in a direction unfavourable to Christianity by pointing to a prohibition by Severus against both Jewish and Christian proselytism. Constantius, though better disposed, did not reject his colleagues' edicts of persecution.[1] In Constantine's reign, one should not expect a Latin author writing before the Council of Nicaea in 325 to be more positive towards the Christians than is Lampridius. Outward signs of the emperor's growing conviction that the God of the Christians must become the sole protector of the empire were relatively sparse during the period between the Edict of Milan and the final defeat of Licinius at Chrysopolis in September 324. A coin from the mint of Ticinum showing the Christian monogram on Constantine's helmet dating to 315,[2] a similar short-lived series from the mint of Siscia in 317,[3] and a North African milestone set up in 319 also marked with the monogram,[4] could be explained as signs of a personal commitment to the Christian God without necessarily involving desertion of the traditional gods of the empire, and those of the emperor's own family from whom he had also received great benefits.

Down to the final break with Licinius, the Christian monogram could be regarded as a 'Signum personnel de Constantin'.[5] The interpretation put on the change of official policy towards the Christians since the edict of Milan by some senior officials in the West may be seen in the statement made by the Proconsul of Africa in 314–15, Aelianus.[6] Aelianus was conducting the inquiry at Carthage in February 315 that led to the exoneration of Bishop Felix of Apthungi from the charge of having been a *traditor* during the Great Persecution. Confronted by the miscreant Ingentius who claimed exemption from torture on the grounds that he was a Christian, he replied that the Emperors Constantine and Licinius showed favour (*pietatem*) towards the Christians, because they believed that Christianity upheld the traditional discipline of the state (unlike Diocletian!) and hence they desired to encourage the observance of this

---

[1] Lactantius, *De Mortibus Persecutorum*, 15. 7. A number of scattered martyrdoms are reported in Constantius' dominions in 303–4.

[2] K. Kraft, 'Das Silbermedaillon Constantins des Grossen mit Christo-Monogramm auf dem Helm', *Jahrbuch für Numismatik und Geldgeschichte* (München, 1954–5), pp. 151–78. See also, W. Vogt, art. 'Constantinus der Grosse', *RAC* iii (1955), pp. 318–30.

[3] W. Seston, 'Origines du chrisme constantinien', *Mélanges Franz Cumont* (Bruxelles, 1936), p. 387, and compare A. Alföldi, 'The Helmet of Constantine with the Christian Monogram', *J.R.S.* xxii (1932), pp. 9–23.

[4] P. Salama, 'Le plus ancien chrisme officiel de l'Afrique romaine', *Atti del VI Congresso internaz. di archeologia cristiana*, Ravenna, 1962 (Città del Vaticano, 1967), pp. 537–43.

[5] Ibid., p. 543.

[6] On Aelian, see A. H. M. Jones, J. R. Martindale, and J. Morris, *The Prosopography of the Later Roman Empire*, i (Cambridge, 1971), p. 17.

religion ('ut disciplinam corrumpi nolint, sed potius observari religionem istam et coli velint').[1] This important statement made at this time was in line with the terms of the Edict of Milan. It might be that as Lampridius expressed it, Christianity was a 'devotio' and was permitted, even encouraged by that model predecessor of Constantine, Alexander Severus, but the protector of the Empire remained Sol Invictus, which anyone in the west who used the coinage of the day would recognize as the emperor's *Comes*.

The final point relates to the constant association of the Christians with the Jews of which Spartian's text is one example. Was this part of the author's 'Mystification' or was that relationship conceivable in the early part of the fourth century as it had been a century before? Apart from the continuance of the Jewish apocalyptic tradition in western Christian writers of the time, such as Victorinus of Pettau, and the issue whether Christians should continue to rely on Jewish calendrical decisions for fixing the date of Easter,[2] one strand of evidence suggests that the kinship between Judaism and Christianity was still clearly recognizable. Eusebius of Caesarea, composing his two vast apologetic works round about the time of the Edict of Milan,[3] still found it necessary to explain at great length the relationship between Christianity and Judaism. In the seventh book of the *Preparation of the Gospel* and in the first two books of the *Demonstration of the Gospel*, he claims that the Christians were neither Greeks nor Jews but heirs to a much more venerable pre-Mosaic form of Judaism, whose adherents were called Hebrews. These possessed the purity of Judaism without the accretions of Jewish custom that followed the Covenants of Abraham and Moses. They were pre-Incarnation Christians, and by claiming them as forebears Eusebius was able to claim the whole Old Testament for the Christians.[4] Yet even if the latter were descended from élite Jews, their ancestry remained Jewish. After Nicaea this whole elaborate argument could be dropped as Christianity had become the religion of the empire, but in the interval between the Edict of Milan and that date it served the cause of a rapidly spreading Christianity. Eusebius was not shadowboxing. There were still many, he said, who accused the Christians of

---

[1] *Acta purgationis Felicis*, ed. C. Ziwsa, 'Optatus, De Schismate Donatistarum', *Corp. Script. Eccl. Lat.* 26 (Vienna, 1895), Appendix II, p. 203, lines 5–8. Ingentius' claim to be a Christian was not to save him from judicial torture!

[2] Thus, Constantine, Letter to the Churches, cited by Socrates, *Hist. Eccl.* i. 9: 'It seemed very unsuitable that in the celebration of this sacred feast we should follow the custom of the Jew.'

[3] Dating, see B. Altaner/A. Stuiber, *Patrologie* (7 Aufl.), p. 221.

[4] See J. Parkes, 'Jews and Christians in the Constantinian Empire', *Studies in Church History*, i (1964), pp. 69–79.

apostasizing from ancestral customs 'to become zealous for the foreign myths of the Jews which were of evil report among all men'.[1] Association between the beliefs and outlook of Jews and Christians such as indicated by Lampridius or Vopiscus corresponded therefore to what some educated individuals believed in the early part of the Constantinian era. This, however, would hardly be credible except to hardened anti-Christian propagandists in Julian's reign and unintelligible in that of Theodosius I. The 'Christian texts' in the *HA* thus are consistent with their having been composed by an author or authors writing in the period from 293 to some time shortly after 315, the date of Constantine's first victory over Licinius.[2]

In the circumstances, it may be justified to take Spartian's text as it stands. The first sentence recording Severus' alleged prohibition of conversion to Judaism presents few difficulties. It is simply a reiteration of what since the reign of Antoninus Pius had become the policy of the emperors towards the Jews. Judaism was *religio licita*, but its adherents were to be confined to the narrowest possible racial limits. The circumcision of non-Jews, such as Gentile slaves of Jews, was prohibited under severe penalties.[3] At the end of the third century, an imperial decision preserved in pseudo-Paulus, *Sententiae*, 5. 22. 3, affirmed that 'Roman citizens who allowed themselves or their slaves circumcision by the Jewish rite should be exiled to an island in perpetuity, and that the doctors (who performed the operation) should be executed'.[4] In October

[1] Eusebius, *Praeparatio Evangelica*, 1. 2. (*P.G.* xxi. 28): "οἱ τῶν μὲν πατρίων φυγάδες, τῶν δ' ὀθνείων καὶ παρὰ πᾶσι διαβεβλημένων Ἰουδαϊκῶν μυθολογημάτων γενόμενοι ζηλωταί;"

[2] Attention is drawn to the curious reference to 'Licinius, Severus, Alexander atque Maxentius quorum omnium ius in dicionem tuam venit, sed ita ut nihil eorum virtuti derogetur', *Antoninus Heliogabalus*, 35. 6 (Hohl i. p. 250). Severus was defeated by Maxentius in 307, Alexander who as Maxentius' *praefectus praetorio* in Africa revolted in 308 was overthrown in 311. Maxentius himself fell to Constantine in 312 and Licinius was defeated in Pannonia in 315. It is possible that Constantine's victory in 315 may be intended rather than his final triumph over Licinius in 324. It is hard to imagine the memory of Severus and Alexander being of interest to anyone by the 390s. After 325 it would have sufficed to remind Constantine only of his great triumph over Licinius. At the end of the fourth century what concern would these characters be to the senatorial circle of Symmachus and his friends or, indeed, anyone for whom the 'rogue grammarian' was writing? And who, after Nicaea, would call Diocletian 'aurei parens saeculi' (ibid. 35. 4) and associate him with Constantine? The contrasting reference in this passage to Maximian as '(parens), ut vulgo dicitur, ferrei' can surely be best explained as an implied defence for Constantine's part in getting rid of him in 310.

[3] *Digest*, 48. 8. 11: 'Circumcidere Iudaeis filios suos tantum rescripto divi Pii permittitur: in non eiusdem religionis qui hoc fecerit, castrantis poena irrogatur.'

[4] Pseudo-Paulus, *Sent.* 5. 22. 3: 'Cives Romani, qui se Iudaico ritu vel servos

315 Constantine ordered that any Jews who tried to coerce those 'who fled from their gloomy sect to the worship of God' (i.e. became Christians) or any who joined their evil sect should be burnt alive.[1] Subsequently, the emperor took steps to protect Gentile slaves of Jews, but at the same time confirmed some Jewish traditional privileges and exemptions from the burdens of local government.[2]

Severus' alleged order thus takes its place among a long sequence of rescripts and decrees reiterating the same policy. The addition of the Christians to its provisions might have been a malicious flourish by the author of the *Life*,[3] but given the close relationship that still existed between the two religions this is not a necessary conclusion. Moreover, it reflected the current situation. 'Fiunt, non nascuntur Christiani', as Tertullian told the Carthaginian magistrates in 197.[4] The stream of converts had become too obvious to be overlooked, and in the next few years the full weight of official and popular displeasure fell upon them. While none of the three passages is free from difficulty, taken together they seem to indicate official encouragement of anti-Christian actions by the provincial authorities. The emperor, confronted with a rash of local disturbances caused by popular antagonism to the Christians, moved with the general current of opinion, unlike Hadrian eighty years before when faced with similar anti-Christian mob outbreaks in the province of Asia. A rescript or rescripts was addressed to the provincial authorities most affected and threatened converts to Judaism or Christianity with heavy penalties. Spartian preserves a memory of the text of one of these orders. Eusebius and Hippolytus have left a record of the turbulent events of the period 200–7 that caused its issue and accompanied its reception. All in all, 'the persecution of Septimius Severus', if not resting on the assured foundation as it seemed to the past generation of historians, may still be regarded as an open question, and indeed, if understood as a response to pressure from different parts of the empire a probability.

A final matter concerning Christians in the Severan epoch has been raised recently and related to the victims of the period after the storms of the first decade of the third century had died away. Few, if any,

suos circumcidi patiuntur, bonis ademptis in insulam perpetuo relegantur, medici capite puniuntur. Iudaei si alienae nationis comparatos servos circumciderint, aut deportantur aut capite puniuntur.' Compare K. H. Schwarte, art. cit., p. 188.

[1] *Cod. Theod.* 16. 8. 1, addressed to Evagrius.
[2] *Cod. Theod.* 16. 8. 3, and compare 16. 8. 2 and 4, dating between 321 and 331.
[3] An interpolation, as suggested by A. A. T. Ehrhardt, *Politische Metaphysik von Solon bis Augustin*, ii (Tübingen, 1959), p. 154.
[4] *Apologeticum*, 18. 4.

350

modern historians have accepted literally Sulpicius Severus' claim that a peace lasting thirty-eight years succeeded the persecution of North African Christians by the Proconsul Scapula in 212, and ended with the Decian persecution in 250.[1] For the remainder of the Severan age, i.e. to 235, the Christians reverted to the quasi-toleration they had enjoyed in the reign of Commodus. Christianity and Christian places of worship and burial became part of the scene in some provinces, particularly in the east. Some Christians attained high office in the Imperial household.[2] Even so, there were occasional martyrdoms. Perhaps Pope Callistus was a victim of popular violence in 222.[3] There is, however, no need to suggest that those who suffered in this period have been 'neglected' by historians.[4] As the Christians increased in numbers and became less conspicuous and self-consciously sectarian, some families continued to cherish the stricter traditions of the past. As the present writer has already pointed out, the family of the Decian martyr Celerinus, an African emigrant in Rome, provides 'a pattern of martyrdom running through three generations'.[5] His grandmother, Celerina, had been a confessor while his uncles on both his father's and mother's side had served in the Roman army but eventually had been martyred for their Christian beliefs. Cyprian, our authority for the story, gives no further information,[6] and speculation is useless. From the example of this uncompromising family, we may perhaps glimpse how a pattern was becoming established which would lead after each crisis of persecution to tension and even schism between a majority who wished to work in harmony with the empire and a minority who were determined that the Church should remain free from all contagion with the world. The existence of militants, such as the family of Celerina, indicates the continuance of the martyr-spirit in an age which witnessed the visit of Origen to the Court of the Empress Julia Mammaea (c. 232)[7] and the appointment of Julius Africanus to establish (αὐτὸς ἠρχιτεκτόνησα) the

[1] Sulpicius Severus, Chron. (ed. Halm) ii. 32. 1–3.
[2] Such as Aurelius Prosenes, E. Diehl, ILCV 3332 (A.D. 217). See also G. W. Clarke, 'Two Christians in the Familia Caesaris', Harvard Theological Review, lxiv (1971), pp. 121–4.
[3] For E. Caspar's emphatic refusal to accept the Passio Callisti as anything more than a 'fromme Phantasie', see Geschichte des Papsttums (Tübingen, 1933), i. p. 39. There is nothing to support T. D. Barnes's speculation, Tertullian (Oxford, 1971), p. 59, that Tertullian may have been martyred.
[4] See T. D. Barnes, 'Three Neglected Martyrs', J.T.S. N.S. xxii. 1 (1971), p. 159–61, not a very necessary note.
[5] Martyrdom and Persecution, p. 412.
[6] Cyprian, Ep. 39. 3. 1.
[7] Eusebius, Hist. Eccl. vi. 21. 3. For the suggested date, see K. Bihlmeyer, Die 'Syrischen' Kaiser zu Rom und das Christentum (Rothenburg, 1916), pp. 139–43.

library of Severus Alexander in the Pantheon at Rome.[1] As Lampridius expressed it, the policy of Severus Alexander was that 'Christianos esse passus est';[2] but the martyrs of the period were neither forgotten nor neglected by the Christians of the time, nor, let it be said, by later historians.

---

[1] *Pap. Oxy.* 412, lines 65–8 (ed. Grenfell and Hunt, iii, p. 39), 'Julius arranged the library in the Pantheon for the emperor'.
[2] Lampridius, *Alexander Severus*, 22. 6.

VI

A Note on the Great Persecution in the West

THE Great Persecution in the Western provinces of the Roman Empire was relatively short and sharp. Eusebius in both his *Ecclesiastical History* and the *Martyrs of Palestine* contrasts the eight long years of repression suffered by the East, first under Diocletian and Galerius and then under Maximian, with the persecution of 'scarcely two years' duration' endured by the Western Christians.[1] In the West, indeed, the persecution of Valerian 257-60 seems to have been longer and perhaps more costly in human lives, and that of Decius more dangerous to the Church.

It has even been argued that the Fourth Edict which commanded a general sacrifice and incense-burning by Christians, promulgated in Galerius' dominions in the spring of 304 but probably withheld in Diocletian's until March of the following year, was not enforced in the West at all.[2] The evidence for this view is surprisingly strong and it is the purpose of this note to examine it. It is pointed out that whereas in the East the Councils which met after the Persecution to regulate the position of the penitent lapsed deal only with the crimes of sacrifice to idols or of eating sacrificial meat, similar councils held in Africa are concerned only with the crime of *traditio*, that is, handing over of the Scriptures to the authorities.[3] This fact obviously demands an explanation in view of the amount and variety

---

[1] *Hist. Eccles.* (ed. J. E. L. Oulton), VIII, 6, 10 (severity of persecution in Africa) and VIII, 13, 12 (short duration). *Mart. Palest.* (ed. H. J. Lawlor and J. E. L. Oulton), XIII, 12.

[2] G. E. M. de Ste Croix, 'Aspects of the "Great" Persecution,' *Harvard Theological Review*, XLVII, pt 2 (1954), 74-113, especially 84-6, taking up a suggestion made by C. Bigg, *The Origins of Christianity*, 482-3.

[3] Ste Croix, art. cit. 84-5.

of existing evidence. In the East we have the canonical letter of Peter of Alexandria dating from Easter 306,[1] and the canons of the Council of Ancyra, probably in 314.[2] In the West there are the declarations of the bishops who took part in the consecration of the sub-deacon Silvanus to be bishop of Cirta in March 305,[3] and what would appear to be a synodical letter either by Mensurius of Carthage, or more likely by Donatus, attempting to regulate in detail the situation of various categories of *traditor*. This letter had for long been camouflaged among Pseudo-Cyprianic letters, but since 1899 has been identified as a Donatist document by the great Vatican scholar, Cardinal Mercati.[4] At Arles, too, the Council held in 314 makes no reference to apostasy by sacrifice or incense-burning, only to the *traditores*.[5] Africa, moreover, seems to have had no *libellatici*, whose absence contrasts with the wealth of references to them in the Decian persecution, and the references in Peter of Alexandria's canons to Christians who employed their slaves to sacrifice on their behalf.[6] Finally, the issue is complicated by the fact that the zealous Proconsul of Africa, Anulinus, demanded sacrifice as well as the surrender of Scriptures from the clergy when he promulgated the First Edict in April 303, and his example seems to have been followed by his colleague, Valerius Florus, governor of Numidia.[7] The

[1] M. J. Routh, *Reliquiae Sacrae*, III, 321-49, and see E. Schwartz, 'Zur Geschichte des Athanasius,' *Göttingen Nachrichten*, phil. hist.Kl., 1905, 166-75.

[2] C. J. Hefele-H. Leclercq, *Hist. des Conciles*, I, pt i, 301-26, and Mansi, *Concilia*, II, 513-22.

[3] Ed. C. Ziwsa, CSEL, XXVI, 185-97, and see the author's *The Donatist Church*, Oxford 1952, 11-12.

[4] Pseudo-Cyprian, *Ep.*, 3 (CSEL, III, pt 3, 273-4). This is an extremely interesting document, to which attention was first drawn by G. Mercati in 1899 ('Un falso donatistico nelle opere di S. Cypriano,' in *Rendic. degli Institut. Lombardo di Sci. e Letter.* Ser. ii, 32 (1899), 986-97, and revised by the author in *Studi e Testi*, 77 (1937), 268-78). It is just possible that this encyclical could be the work of Mensurius. The Council was held immediately after the restoration of churches, and the tendency is moderate. *Traditores* would be investigated by category and lay communion would not be denied to penitents. The reference, too, to *antecessores nostri* (p. 274) could indicate Mensurius. At the same time, the appeal to *sententiam fixam sanctis et amicis Dei*, strongly suggests the sentence of the Abitinian confessors towards whom Mensurius had no friendly feelings. He would also have found himself criticised among those who had even pretended to hand over copies of the Scriptures (*qui utique finget tradere supplebit traditionem*). On the whole, one is inclined to suggest an encyclical by Donatus, perhaps as early as summer 313.

[5] Canon 13.

[6] Peter of Alexandria, Canons 5 and 6.

[7] *Gesta Purgationis Felicis* (ed. Ziwsa, 197-204) at 198-9, 'ex jussione proconsulari omnes sacrificarent et si quas scripturas haberent, offerrent secundum sacram legem.' See also, Augustine, *Contra Cresconium*, III, 27, 30 (account of Secundus of Tigisis'

A Note on the Great Persecution in the West

various references, therefore, to members of the African clergy both surrendering Scriptures and sacrificing may record two acts committed at the same time, and not separate acts under the terms of two different edicts.

This evidence suggests that the Great Persecution in the West, and in particular in Africa, differed both from its predecessors under Decius and Valerian and from the repression which was going on in the East. But does the explanation lie in the non-enforcement of the most drastic of all the Tetrarchy's edicts? Let us first go back to Eusebius. His 'scarcely two years' of persecution in the West refers to 'persecution years,' that is, the second Eusebian 'year' ends with the abdication of Diocletian and Maximian on 1 May 305.[1] This estimate, however, squares with Optatus of Milevis' and other contemporary accounts of the persecution in North Africa. These agree that the persecution gradually flagged during the winter of 304-5 and was not continued by Maxentius when the latter seized power in Rome in October 306.[2] By March 305 the Numidian Christians were thinking in terms of new episcopal elections. At the same time, however, Eusebius refers specifically to the sufferings of the Africans, which he compares with those of the Christians in Egypt which he witnessed 310-12.[3] His account of Maximin's persecution in the Thebaid is an horrific document, a tale of torture and massacre matched by an equal degree of fanaticism on the Christian side.[4] Unless there had been some scenes in Africa of sufficient atrocity to be reported to him far away in Caesarea, he could hardly have drawn this comparison. As is known, Eusebius was not usually well informed about conditions in the Christian West.

Another point concerns the victims themselves. Diocletian was a reluctant persecutor. Before signing the first Edict on 23 February 303 he insisted that there should be no bloodshed,[5] and the Edict's

synod at Cirta in 305). On the other hand, the *Acta Saturnini* (PL, 8, 690 and 705) indicate that the edicts of Diocletian and Maximian for 303 ordered only the handing over of the Scriptures and forbade Christian assemblages.

[1] For a study of Eusebius's 'persecution years' see H. J. Lawlor, *Eusebiana*, Oxford 1912, 179-81.

[2] See Optatus of Milevis, *De Schismate Donatistarum* (ed. C. Ziwsa, CSEL, xxvi), 1, 18, 'Maxentio christianis libertas est restituta.'

[3] H.E. VIII, vi, 10: καὶ μάλιστα τῶν (μαρτύρων) κατὰ τὴν Ἀφρικὴν καὶ τὸ Μαύρων ἔθνος Θηβαΐδα τε καὶ κατ' Αἴγυπτον.

[4] Ibid. VIII, 9

[5] Lactantius, *De Mortibus Persecutorum* (ed. J. Moreau, *Sources chrétiennes* 39), 11 and 12.

application was primarily aimed at the clergy. They were called upon to hand over their Scriptures and perform some act of recognition in honour of the 'immortal gods' to whom the Roman world was committed.[1] Laymen suffered only incidentally. They were individuals such as Euethios who tore down the copy of the edict posted in Nicomedia,[2] or Romanus who tried to dissuade the citizens of Antioch from sacrificing,[3] or Agape, Irene, Chione, and their friends who concealed copies of the Scriptures and otherwise defied the authorities.[4]

By the summer and autumn of 304, however, the situation had changed, not least in Africa. There, too, the persecution in 303 had been confined to the clergy. The inquiry carried out by Munatius Felix at Cirta in May of that year had concerned Bishop Paul and his clergy but not his congregation. The *Acta Martyrum* of 303 concern clergy, such as Felix, bishop of Thibuca. Those other Christians who had been arrested, like the confessors of Abitina, had been guilty of disobeying the emperors' orders banning Christian assemblages, or they had deliberately provoked a martyr's end.[5] In 304, however, the surviving *Acta Martyrum* concern simple layfolk, such as Maxima, Secunda, and Donatilla, the only Christians on an imperial estate in the Proconsular Province near Thuburbo Maius (?) who had refused to sacrifice,[6] and on 5 December 304 the wealthy Crispina of Calama was tried before the Proconsul at Theveste for the same offence.[7] In neither case were Scriptures involved. Moreover, the catalogue of martyrs kept in the Catholic church at Carthage records the names of some sixty martyrs who appear to date to the Great Persecution. Inscriptions in honour of about the

---

[1] Eusebius, *Mart. Palest.* Praefatio, 'Presidents of the churches should all everywhere be first committed to prison, and then afterwards compelled by every kind of device to do sacrifice.'

[2] Lactantius, *De Mortibus*, 13, 2. His name, *Syrian Martyrology* (ed. H. Lietzmann, *Kleine Texte* 2, 9).

[3] *Mart. Pal.* 2, 2.

[4] *Mart. Agape, Eirene, Chione* 5 (ed. Knopf and Krüger, *Ausgewählte Märtyrerakten*, 1929, 97-8).

[5] *Acta Saturnini* 2; cf. Augustine, *Breviculus Collationis cum Donatistis* III, 13, 25; PL, 43, 637. See also P. Franchi di Cavalieri, *Studi e Testi*, 65 (1935), 3-5.

[6] Dating: iii Kal. Aug., *Carthage Calendar of Martyrs*, ed. H. Lietzmann, op. cit. 5. Discussed by P. Monceaux, *Histoire littéraire de l'Afrique chrétienne*, III, 148-51. Text: *Analecta Bollandiana*, IX (1890), 110-16.

[7] *Acta Crispinae* (ed. Knopf and Krüger, op. cit. 109-11). P. Monceaux, *Hist. litt.* III, 159-61. For the 'Twenty Martyrs' who also refused to sacrifice, P. Monceaux, op. cit. 153.

A Note on the Great Persecution in the West

same number of laymen are preserved in Numidia,[1] and a fifth-century inscription from a church at Ammaedara gives the names of thirty-four victims, including women who are stated to have 'suffered persecution under the divine laws of Diocletian and Maximian.'[2] Certainly, at this time Numidian folklore recorded a '*dies thurificationis*' as well as a '*dies traditionis*,' and it is difficult to see how the Martyrs of Milevis could have perished otherwise than by disobedience to it.[3]

The governor incriminated for having caused the deaths of the Martyrs of Milevis was the *praeses Numidiae*, Valerius Florus.[4] An objection, however, has for long been urged against the validity of this tradition. Florus is known to have been *praeses* of a province known as Numidia M(ilitana?) in the early part of 303, and the inscriptions which he set up at Timgad in honour of the emperors show him to have been a convinced worshipper of the gods.[5] However, in November 303, he was no longer in charge of southern Numidia, because the *praeses* who commemorated Diocletian's *vicennalia* was Aurelius Quintianus who had previously been *praepositus limes Tripolitanae*.[6] Since 1943 the mystery has, if anything, been deepened by Professor L. Leschi's publication of an important inscription from the frontier fort of Aqua Viva (Mdoukal) in southern Numidia. This showed that in 303 Florus was 'vir perfectissimus praeses provinciae Numidiae,' and not only *praeses* of Numidia M. . . .[7] It may well be that the establishment of a fortified *limes* consisting of a series of massive stone fortresses similar to the Saxon Shore fortresses in Britain involved the appointment of a *praeses* for southern Numidia who possessed

---

[1] See P. Monceaux' list, op. cit. 169-71, supplemented by discoveries up to 1940 in A. Berthier and colleagues, *Les Vestiges du Christianisme antique dans la Numidie centrale*, Algiers 1942, 210.

[2] 'Qui persecutionem Diocletiani et Maximiani divinis legibus passi sunt.' Published in the *Bull. archéologique du Comité des Travaux historiques*, 1934, 68-9, and H. Delehaye, *Analecta Bollandiana*, LIV (1936), 313-16.

[3] CIL, VIII, 6700-19353, 'qui sunt passi sunt sub preside Floro in civitate Milevitana in diebus thurificationis.' See also S. Gsell, *Bull. Arch. du Comité*, 1899, 452-4.

[4] Optatus, op. cit. iii, 8. Under Florus, 'christiani idolorum cogebantur ad templa' (i.e. not *traditio*).

[5] CIL, VIII, 2345-7.

[6] CIL, VIII, 4764-18698 (Macomades). Quintianus is never mentioned as a persecutor.

[7] L. Leschi, 'Le Centenarium d'Aqua Viva,' *Revue Africaine*, LXXXVII (1943), 5-22. The inscription also mentions Valerius Alexander 'agens vices praefectorum praetorio,' who may be the 'Comes Valerius' who judged the confessor Mammarius in May-June 304.

experience of frontier problems. Quintianus who had been commanding the Tripolitanian *limes* which had been reorganised on similar lines for the previous half-century would have been an obvious choice.[1] Florus may have moved to the new civil province of Numidia Cirtensis whose existence is attested by an inscription dated to 306,[2] and therefore would have been responsible for the carrying out of the Fourth Edict there. It must be admitted, however, that more will have to be uncovered before this part of the story becomes clear.

One other factor must be taken into account in considering the difference between the impact made by the persecution on Christians in East and West respectively, namely the difference of theological tradition, and particularly as this affected their outlook towards the Scriptures. The East, it is evident, took sacrifice to the gods far more seriously than the handing over of Scriptures. Thus, Philip, bishop of Heraclea, still remains a hero, having conceded the latter, while refusing to sacrifice.[3] In Africa, on the other hand, the mere rumour that a cleric may have been a *traditor* proved sufficient to damn him in the eyes of Christian enthusiasts.[4] The reason may lie in the relative importance of the Bible in the religion of Greek- and Latin-speaking Christians. To the latter, the Bible was the literal Word of God, the Word of John i, 1, the supreme and only guide of life for a Christian for whose study all other literature must be abandoned.[5] Quite apart from *Acta Martyrum*, the careers of men as different as Cyprian and the Donatist confessor Marculus show this to have been the case. As the imprisoned confessors of Abitina declared from their prison in the winter 303/4, if to change one jot or tittle of the text of Scripture was a crime, then to hand over the Scriptures themselves to be burnt by pagan magistrates was an act of apostacy of unparalleled enormity.[6] No wonder that the confessors asserted that those who maintained communion with *traditores* would not participate

---

[1] See R. G. Goodchild and J. B. Ward Perkins, '*The Limes Tripolitanus* in the light of Recent Discoveries,' *Journ. Roman Studies*, XXXIX (1949), 81–95. A *centenarium* built in the reign of Philip, 91. For Quintianus's career, Pallu de Lessert, *Fastes des provinces africaines*, II, I, 312–14.
[2] CIL, VIII, 5526–18860, 7965.
[3] *Acta Sancti Philippi* (ed. Ruinart), 440–8.
[4] As in the case of Felix of Aptunga.
[5] Pseudo-Cyprian, *Ep.* iii, and note the description of the Donatist martyr Marculus (executed 347) in the *Passio Marculi* as 'statim mundanas litteras respuens' on conversion (PL, 8, 760D).   [6] *Acta Saturnini*, 18 (PL, 8, 701B).

A Note on the Great Persecution in the West

with them in the joys of Paradise.[1] Here was a view of Scripture which allowed no softening of the Divine precepts by way of allegorisation, and for whom the Lord's warning that denial on earth meant denial in Heaven was to be taken literally.

In the East, however, a different view of Scripture had been prevailing for at least a century. Gnostic allegorisation had required Christian allegorisation. Origen and his disciples had been applying the same rules of current literary criticism to the Bible as their contemporaries were applying to the texts of the classics.[2] Thus, in their view, it was the whole Bible interpreted in a spiritual sense that mattered, not this or that incident recorded in the Old or New Testaments. Origen says flatly that the story of Jesus driving out the money changers from the Temple cannot be taken literally, because such acts were uncharacteristic of the Divine Logos.[3] He conceded that taken literally the Synoptists' accounts of a number of incidents in Jesus' ministry contradicted each other.[4] Even Athanasius writes, 'For behold, we take Divine Scripture, and thence discourse with the freedom of religious faith, and set it up as a light upon its candlestick.' But not necessarily literally.[5] So, too, the Lord's commands concerning the abandonment of wealth or the duty of martyrdom could be and were allegorised into meanings which required, not poverty or death for their own sakes, but asceticism and contemplation, enabling the human soul to advance towards communion with the Divine. In the East, idolatry, namely the abandonment of the 'rational' approach to God in favour of a lapse into irrationality and service to demons would be the prime error. The literal text of Scripture could be replaced, but not the baptised Christian's surrender to forces of unreason, the demons.

This difference of theological approach between Greek and Latin at the beginning of the fourth century might therefore account partly for the differences between Eastern and Western views as to what constituted apostasy, and hence the difference of emphasis in the Canons. This seems preferable to the more drastic solution which would deny that the Fourth Edict was ever promulgated in the West. *Prima facie* this would seem unlikely, for Maximian was probably

[1] Ibid. 18 (PL, 8, 701B-C).
[2] See R. M. Grant, *The Earliest Lives of Jesus*, 1961, ch. ii.
[3] Origen, *Comment. in Joann.* 10, 4 (ed. E. Preuschen, Leipzig 1903).
[4] Examples given in Grant, op. cit. 62-4.
[5] Athanasius, *Orat. contra Arianos* 1, 9 (26, 28).

more anti-Christian than Diocletian.[1] There is a legend that the Fourth Edict was initiated by him at the end of April 304 on the occasion of the *ludi saeculares* of Rome and thus promulgated first in the West.[2] If one accepts Grégoire's dating of the Council of Elvira in southern Spain as 15 May 309,[3] then it is quite obvious that there, too, the crime of apostasy was reckoned in terms of sacrifice to the gods and not surrender of Scriptures.[4] For the rest, Africa's overwhelming emphasis on *traditio* may not be typical of the West as a whole. Carthage and Alexandria are revealed by the Great Persecution, as in every crisis in the Church in the third and early fourth centuries, as the homes of rival Biblical theologies whose legacies remain with us even today.

[1] Note for instance, the tradition preserved in the *Passio Tipasii*, 8, 'Maximianus qui persecutionis fuerat princeps' (Text, *Analecta Bollandiana*, IX (1890), 123).

[2] H. M. Gwatkin, *Early Church History A.D. 313*, II, 339.

[3] H. Grégoire, 'Les Persécutions dans l'Empire romain,' *Mém. de l'Académie royale de Belgique*, XLVI, pt i (1951), 128-30.

[4] Canons 1-4.

VII

Some Cultural Links between India and the West in the Early Christian Centuries

The attraction of the religions of India to the Western world has been long-standing. From the moment when the conquests of Alexander the Great brought the Indian sub-continent within the ken of the Greeks as the land of age-old wisdom, trading, artistic and religious contacts developed between the more accessible parts of India and the Mediterranean world. The object of this short note is to describe some of these links with an eye to their importance in the development of early Christianity.

In the first half of the first century A.D. an anonymous merchant from Roman Egypt left an account of voyages down the Red Sea as far as the Somali coast and Zanzibar and then following the monsoon winds round the Arabian peninsular to the mouth of the Indus and thence to the Malabar coast. His *Periplus of the Erythrean Sea* (i.e. the Red Sea and Indian Ocean) not only tells the story of great enterprise by the merchant, but gives a unique account of the well established organization of markets used by western merchants trading with India.[1] One sees a system of exchange through accredited merchants grouped in "factories" not unlike that which grew up in the early days of Portuguese, Dutch, French and British ventures at the end of the sixteenth century. One of these Greco-Roman "free ports", the Podouke of the "Periplus" has been identified by Mortimer Wheeler with some certainty with a site south of Pondicherry.[2]

The exchanges were fruitful. In south India year after year "the beautifully built ships of the Yavana (Westerners) agitating the white foam of the Periyaru" were awaited by the Tamil merchants. They brought gold and returned with spices and pepper.[3] Some members of the crews stayed behind to become celebrated for their strength as palace-guards and their skill as universal handymen.[3]

---

[1] I have followed R. E. M. Wheeler's account in *Rome Beyond the Imperial Frontiers*, London, 1954, 112 ff. Strabo records that using the monsoon nearly 100 ships were trading with Indian ports each year. (*Geogr.* ii, 5, 12.)

[2] R. E. M. Wheeler, op. cit., 123 and 145.

[3] Cited from ibid., 132.

[4] Compare the *Acts of Thomas* (ed. M. R. James), 17 ff., where King Gundaphorus sets "Thomas" to work on building his new palace and

The trade, moreover, led to official contacts, Indian embassies being received at the courts of Augustus, Trajan, Aurelian and Constantine. India was becoming a land of mystery and promise, so that in 116 the aged emperor Trajan standing on the shores of the Persian Gulf and seeing a ship sailing on its way to India is recorded as exclaiming "I would assuredly have crossed over to the Indi if I were still young."[5] Where Alexander the Great had led, his imitators sought to follow. Rome aimed at controlling at least the northern overland route to the Indian market.

The trading contacts both with south India and with the ex-Seleucid kingdom of Bactria on the north-western frontier naturally led to exchanges of ideas as well as goods. The Greco-Roman contribution to the forms in which Indian artists expressed themselves is illustrated by some westernizing tendencies in north Indian Buddhist art. Wheeler cites the schist frieze from the Kumala monastery at Taxila showing vine tendrils and "putti" among other figures, and at the Buddhist site at Hadda in Afghanistan a stucco figure reminiscent of a youthful diety in the Antinous tradition has been found.[6] Indeed, western motifs seem to have been accepted with enthusiasm by artists working in "Mahayana" Buddhist contexts in the first three centuries A.D.

These influences were more than peripheral. Early in the third century readers of Philostratus were startled to hear of Greek gods being worshipped by Indian sages with Greek rites.[7] This is a tantalizing piece of evidence especially as it seems to be corroborated by the presence of western pagan statuettes on Indian sites. Can one go further? Did Buddhism, itself predominant in northern India in the second and third centuries A.D., derive inspiration from the Greco-Roman cults illustrated by the objects traded with the West? Are there any links between the personal cult of the third century emperor and the Buddha of the same period?

The influences of the religious life of India on the West were more tangible. By the middle of the second century, the time when Christianity was beginning to emerge as a missionary movement in the eastern provinces of the empire, the Brahmins had gained a place in popular imagination as examplars of the religious life. Lucian of Samosata, whose satire seems accurately to have reflected literate public opinion in the provinces of Pontus and Asia in

---

"Thomas" claims to be equally at home in making a plough or a ship or a palace.

[5] Dio Cassius, LXVII. 29.
[6] Wheeler, op. cit., 160–161.
[7] Philostratus, *Life of Apollonius of Tyana* (ed. F. C. Conybeare), iii. 14.

160–170 A.D., shows how "the Brahmins" were regarded as people of uncanny wisdom and fortitude, holy men who lived naked, their way of life being directed towards contemplation and bodily abstinence. They were people to seek out whom idealists, or to Lucian pseudo-idealists, would go on pilgrimage to India,[8] though there were plenty of quacks among them, and they had achieved a reputation of converting a wonder-working mysterium into publicity-hunting. Some were ready to "cremate themselves, ascending a very lofty pyre and enduring cremation without any change in their outward appearance or sitting position."[9] Were these travellers' tales or were Indians who claimed to be Brahmins a not unusual sight in Greco-Roman cities, especially on great occasions like the Olympic Games?[10] Half a century later, the work of Philostratus shows how the influence of Indian religion had penetrated some of the more significant cults of the Empire. Philostratus was born in Lemnos in about 172 and migrating to Rome found himself drawn into the salon of the philosophic and religiously-minded empress Julia Domna, the wife of Septimius Severus (193–211). She evidently put into Philostratus' hands some memoirs of Apollonius the wise man of Tyana who after a varied and adventurous life had died in the reign of Nerva (96–98). The "Life" of Apollonius that emerged was in some ways to become the pagan rival to the Gospels. Apollonius was a man of marvellous powers. He was consulted by rulers as a counsellor of virtue. Like Jesus he heals a young woman on point of death, he goes on missionary journeys preaching forgiveness and forbearance, he speaks in parables and he is brought before the judgement seat not merely of a prefect like Pilate, but of the emperor himself. After death he inspires an oracle to refute those who doubted that the soul was immortal.

An essential part of his preparation for his work as a man of religion was a journey to India. Philostratus indeed tells us far more about what the educated Greco-Roman provincial thought about the East than any other writer. First, the Indians were regarded as pre-eminently wise. "We have reached men," Apollonius says, "who are unfeignedly wise, for they seem to have the gift of foreknowledge", and he interviews the Indian in question. ("Life", iii.12). After this he describes in detail customs of a group of

---

[8] Lucian *Toxaris, or Friendship* (ed. A. M. Harmon), 34. "Demetrius left his own 20,000 (drachmae) to his friend and went away to India to join the Brahmins."

[9] Lucian, *The Runaways*, 7.

[10] Lucian, *The Passing of Peregrinus,* 35 and 39.

Indian sages whom he encountered dwelling on a hill-top. "I saw Indian Brahmins living upon the earth and yet not on it, and fortified without fortifications and possessing nothing, yet having the riches of all men". ("Life", iii.5). Acts of levitation were performed "not for the sake of display" but as "an act of homage acceptable to God". They slept on mats on the ground and "grew their hair long on principle"; their garments resembled those of Buddhist monks today, and "Masters" among them had complete command over what they said or did. Some believed themselves to be gods. (iii.18). Philostratus believed that the Pythagoreans of his day owed many of their characteristic attitudes and beliefs to the influence of Brahmins, particularly transmigration of souls and vegetarianism, and he regarded Egypt as the mediator between Greek and Indian religious philosophies (viii.7).

This is indeed what one would expect, granting the importance of Alexandria as the major terminal of the seaborne trade between India and the Mediterranean world. When one asks to what extent religious ideas from India were penetrating Christianity at this period one is confronted with unexpected turns of evidence. The first indication of the existence of Christians in "India" (this might mean in this context the Arabian peninsula or the Persian Gulf) is in the record of Pantaenus the first head of the catechetical school of Alexandria leaving for India circa 190 and finding Christians there using the Gospel of Matthew in Hebrew.[11] This points not to a contact with Hinduism but with Jews, perhaps members of Jewish merchant communities settled in Indian coastal towns. It implies that as elsewhere in the Middle East the Christian missionary effort was at this particular time still directed primarily at the Jews. The "Acts of Thomas" which were probably compiled among the Christians of Edessa in the first decades of the third century also show that the first contact which "Thomas" has on his missionary and trading venture in the land of King Gundaphorus, in all probability in northern India, was a Jewish flute-player who retained her command of Hebrew.[12] Such contact between the Christians in the eastern provinces of the Empire and India would be geographical only. Hebrew-speaking people were unlikely to be cultural mediators with Brahmins, and the Parthian empire stood in the way of frequent day-to-day intercourse.

When one comes to consider the teaching of the Alexandrian theologians, Clement and Origen, one is again disappointed.

---

[11] Eusebius. *Hist. Eccles.*, v. 10.3.
[12] *Acts of Thomas* (ed. M. R. James), 5 and 9.

Clement's theology of the Logos involved conscious imitation of Christ through the exercise of reason by means of study and contemplation. Love towards God was the hall-mark of the "truly reasonable soul". The true Christian lived a perfectly controlled life giving way to no passions or physical emotions, becoming in the process ever more a reflection of the divine. The "perpetual imperturbability" (ataraxia) of the Christian sage was the intellectual basis for the monastic movement of the east. It was not the cavern but the opportunity for contemplation that attracted so many members of wealthy families to accept the monk's habit. Clement knows that some Indians were Buddhists and he mentions Brahmins and another group of ascetics called Sarmani who lived in woods among a catalogue of "barbarian philosophers".[13] He compares the Indians to the Christian Encratites, i.e., they might be worthy but they remained outside the pale of orthodoxy, and on one occasion at least he indicates that the Brahmins were not an example to be followed. In discussing martyrdom he singles them out as exhibitionists who threw their lives away by leaping into the fire.[14] They were not true martyrs. On the contrary. Plato provided the Christian with the true copy (paradeigma) of the heavenly city.

Clement therefore seems simply to reproduce some popular prejudices against Indian religion, and it would be surprising to find any direct and conscious influence on his concept of the ascetic life from that quarter. The evidence, however, suggests that such influences were at work on some of the Hellenistic mystery cults of the day. Of these the Pythagoreans played a part in forming both the vocabulary and ideas of the Christian mysticism of Clement's time, such as the image of "Christus medicus" and the theories found a few years later in Origen of successive rebirths of the human soul on its road to ultimate perfection. It looks as though the legacy of the Buddhists and Hindus on early Christianity may have been to a large extent an individual one. The Parthian empire stood in the way of permanent cultural and religious contacts between the Roman world and India. In the generation, however, in which Clement and Origen lived the policies of the dynasty of Septimius Severus (193–235) reawakened the dream of the conquest of the east by Greco-Roman power, and the work of Philostratus is a monument to those dreams. That Buddhists and Alexandrian

---

[13] *Stromateis,* 1.71.3–b. See A. Dihle, "Indische Philosophen bei Clemens Alexandrinus", *Mullus* (Festschrift Th. Klauser), 1964, 60–71.
[14] Ibid., iv. 17.4.

Christians were in fact thinking in much the same type of religious terms also seems evident. It will be the task of research into the comparative study of early religions to discover whether despite all, some direct links existed between the two. Did the Alexandrian idea of the soul's ultimate absorption into the divine owe anything to nirvana? How far did Clement's "true Gnosis" owe its origins to the "tribe of the Brahmins"? Buddhism and Christianity, whose similarities so fascinated the Persian religious reformer Mani in this period that he tried to conflate the two into a new world religion, still present the same challenge to the inquirer today.

---

[15] Ibid., iv. 26.172.

VIII

THE MISSIONS
OF THE EARLY CHURCH 180-700 A.D.

« Christianity », says Fustel de Coulanges, « was not the domestic religion of any family, the national religion of any race
or community. From its first appearance it called to itself the
whole human race » (¹). Yet we are singularly badly informed
about the organisation and method of missions in the early Church
after the Apostolic Age. Who were the successors of Junius and
Epaphras, men who had either accompanied St. Paul through
the Roman province of Asia or worked on their own among the
towns of the Maeander and Lycos valleys? John of Ephesus,
perhaps ; but the peripatetic « teachers » and « prophets » referred to in the *Didache* probably towards the end of the first century (²) disappear and do not seem to be replaced. As Karl Holl
pointed out in a notable contribution to the theme of the development of the Christian missions, the early Church lacked a specific calling of missionary. « The early Church conducted no obvious or planned propagation of the word » (³).

In the first two centuries our sources leave the impression
of the Christian communities being somewhat inward-looking,
concerned individually like Polycarp's at Smyrna with main-

---

(1) FUSTEL DE COULANGES, *The Ancient City*, trans. W. Small, Boston [Mass.],
1874 and London, 1916, p. 391.

(2) *Didache*, 11 and 13. A date of circa 100 A. D. or perhaps earlier is accepted by the writer. See J. P. AUDET, *La Didache, Instructions des Apôtres*
(*Études bibliques*), Paris, 1958, p. 212-219.

(3) K. HOLL, *Gesammelte Aufsätze zur Kirchengeschichte*, III, Tübingen, 1928,
p. 121 122.

4

taining their « conversation blameless among the Gentiles » (¹)
rather than seeking to convert them, and collectively awaiting
the return of the Lord. To outsiders such as the Platonist
Celsus writing c178, the Christians whom he encountered reminded
him of nothing so much as

> « a cluster of bats, or ants coming out of a nest, or frogs holding
> council round a marsh, or worms assembling in some filthy
> corner, disagreeing with one another which of them was the
> worse sinner » (²).

This is no doubt exaggerated, for elsewhere Celsus has many bitter things to say about Christian proselytising, but it is true
that Christian missionary work among the pagans was to a large
extent unplanned, and that the converts of which we hear most,
such as Justin Martyr and Tertullian came to the Christians impressed by their self-sacrifice and high ethical demands rather
than having been sought by representatives of the Church. Every
confessor and martyr was a missionary for the Church, albeit
an unconscious one (³).

In this situation the Bible did not play so clear-cut a role as
one might have expected. True, the possession by the Christians
after the middle of the second century of a series of writings
that contained their entire law had considerable advantages in
propaganda against the pagans. Justin Martyr writing up his
Dialogue with Trypho in *circa* 160 indicates the powerful effect
which the argument from prophecy used by the old Christian he
met near the sea-shore at Ephesus, had on his conversion (⁴) ;
but he also admits that Trypho's companions when they heard
the story laughed him to scorn. Theophilus of Antioch too,
urged his friend Autolycus « to study the prophetic scriptures »
as the best means of escaping eternal punishments (⁵), and like

(1) POLYCARP, *Letter to the Philippians*, ed. KIRSOPP LAKE, *The Apostolic Fathers*, London, 1912-13, I, p. 282-301. 10.

(2) [ORIGEN], *Contra Celsum*, ed. H. CHADWICK, Cambridge, 1953, IV, 23.

(3) For the sight of martyrdom as the point of decision for both Justin and Tertulian, see JUSTIN, II *Apol.*, 12, and TERTULLIAN, *Apol.*, 50. For exor-cism as a missionary force, see TERTULLIAN, *ibid.*, 46, 5.

(4) *Dialogue with Trypho*, 7.

(5) *Ad Autolycum*, I, 13, P[atrologia] G[raeca], VI, col. 1045B.

Justin before him he claims that encounter with these sacred writings exercised a powerful influence on his own conversion (¹).

The Bible however, also provided ammunition for critics of Christianity. To some it indicated the novelty and hence the undesirability of the new religion (²). Others when they followed Theophilus' advice were repelled by the barbarous and ungrammatical turns of phrase they found there (³).

As A.A.T. Ehrhardt has shown, the Christians in the West in the third century had their own peculiar jargon which he has felicitously christened « Quäker-Latein », practically incomprehensible to anyone who was not a Christian (⁴). Not surprisingly, even at the end of the third century Lactantius commented from his own observations how little acceptance even the most prominent Christian men of letters had found among contemporaries. Cyprian « cannot please those who do not know the mystery », and was ridiculed « by the learned of the world to whom his writings by chance became known » (⁵). Christianity could still be dismissed as « old wives » tales' and for many of its leaders *Matthew* 28¹⁹⁻²⁰ and *Mark* 16²⁰ might never have been written (⁶).

Von Harnack has given a brilliant account of the expansion of the Church from Judaistic sect to world religion, and rightly emphasizes the importance of the first half of the third century as the period of numerous individual conversions (⁷). Up to this time one can detect traces of the propagation of Christianity by three distinct methods. First, there were the missions by in-

---

(1) *Ibid.*

(2) *Ibid.*, III-1, col. 1121 A.

(3) Compare ARNOBIUS, *Adv. Gentes*, I, 58 and 59. Scriptures « ab indoctis hominibus et rudibus scripta sunt et idcirco non sunt facili auditione credenda ». Yet Tertullian, *Apol.*, 46, 1, insisted that « our whole position of proving the Christian case » was « by the evidence and antiquity of the divine books ».

(4) A. A. T. EHRHARDT, *Quäker-Latein*, p. 167-171 of *Existenz und Ordnung, Festschrift Erik Wolf*, Frankfurt, 1962.

(5) LACTANTIUS, *Div. Inst.*, V, 1 ff.

(6) One example of the missionary ideal being maintained is the explicit reference to *Matthew* 28¹⁹ cited by Eusebius in defence of the Creed of Caesarea at Nicaea, SOCRATES, *Eccl. Hist.*, I, 8.

(7) *Die Mission und Ausbreitung des Christentums in den ersten drei Jahrhunderten*, Leipzig, 1902, p. 376-408. See also G. BARDY, *La conversion au Christianisme durant les premiers siècles*, Paris, 1949, ch. VII.

dividuals inspired by the Jewish-Christian legacy and addressed to the Jewish settlements in territories bordering the eastern frontier of the Roman Empire and beyond. J. Neusner, for instance, in suggesting the relative authenticity of the *Chronicle of Arbela* considers that it may record the conversion of a large proportion of the Jewish ruling class of the kingdom of Adiabene following the overthrow of the Jewish dynasty there in the reign of Trajan [1]. The enterprise also of specifically Jewish-oriented Christians towards their fellow Jews beyond the Roman frontier may be instanced by the story told in the *Acts of Thomas* (probably compiled in Edessa in the early third century) that the first convert made by « Thomas » in the kingdom of Gundophorus in north India was a Jewish flute-girl who knew Hebrew [2]. From Clement of Alexandria (c190) one learns that a knowledge of Matthew's Gospel in Hebrew was a prerequisite for the success of Pantaenus' mission to India [3].

These missions may look back to those of the Pharisees recorded in *Matthew* 23[15]. Less organized were the public discussions between Christian and non-Christian such as that recorded by Justin with Trypho at Ephesus c135, or the harangues addressed by preachers to random audiences which made Christians comparable to Cynics in public estimation. In these one might detect a continuation of the Pauline tradition — that of the wandering sophist whose message was, however, Christianity. Justin Martyr, active in Ephesus before establishing himself in Rome in rivalry to local Cynics may represent this development [4]. More significant were the surreptitious conversations with interested pagans, in many cases women and slaves in large private houses. These were the underprivileged of the Greco-Roman world to whom the Christian message of salvation for all without distinction of race, condition, or sex would carry conviction. Celsus describes these propagandists as « wool-workers, cobblers and laun-

---

(1) J. NEUSNER, *Numen*, Leiden, 1966, p. 141-145.

(2) *Acts of Thomas*, ed. M. R. James, Oxford, 1926, p. 367 and 368.

(3) EUSEBIUS, *Hist. Eccl.*, V, 10.

(4) For Paul as a preacher on sophist lines, see E. A. JUDGE, *The Early Christians as a Scholastic Community*, Part II, in *Journal of Religious History*, Vol. I, Sydney, 1961, p. 125-137. See also JUSTIN, *II Apol.*, 3.

dry-workers, the most illiterate of rustic yokels » (¹), and makes their activities part of his case against Christianity as inducing revolution against all forms of the established order. His statement shows the sort of groups in provincial society among whom Christianity was beginning to gain significant ground by the end of the second century.

The third means by which Christianity spread was probably through merchants and travellers. These as is well known, were often accompanied by the gods of their homeland, and where they settled they established their own religious communities (²). Christian merchants from the Greek speaking-parts of the empire seem to have done likewise in the western provinces, and outside Africa these immigrant groups may have been the original means whereby Christianity spread. Apart from Lyons, in the second half of the second century, Aquileia, Salona, Trier and perhaps Nola in South Italy all seem to have owed to such groups the early development of the new religion (³). Between them, these activities may give substance to the elaborate claims made by Irenaeus and Tertullian for the spread of Christianity at the end of the second century. Certainly by 200 some educated Christians were consciously engaged in propagating their faith as a matter of Christian duty. The rise to prominence of the Catechetical School at Alexandria may be associated with this development, for at the beginning of his *Stromateis* its master, Clement, stresses the importance of writing as a means of spreading the word (⁴) :

« The word of our teacher did not stay in Judaea alone as philosophy stayed in Greece, but was poured out over all the world » (⁵).

He who kept the truth to himself and did not try to influence his neighbours was « an unprofitable servant (⁶) », and Clement

---

(1) *Contra Celsum*, III, 55, compare III, 50.
(2) See A. D. Nock, *Conversion*, Oxford, 1933, ch. VI.
(3) See my article *A Note on the Influence of Greek Immigrants on the Spread of Christianity in the West*, in *Festschr. Th. Klauser*, 1964, p. 125-129.
(4) See E. F. Osborn, *Teaching and Writing in the first chapter of the Stromateis of Clement of Alexandria*, in *Journal of Theological Studies*, N. S., vol. X, London, 1958, p. 335-343.
(5) *Stromateis*, VI, 18, 167.
(6) *Ibid.*, I,I, 3. Compare I, I, 12. « Wisdom must be passed on ».

8

reminds his readers that his teacher Pantaenus was a traveller and a missionary (¹).

These efforts combined to make Christianity a formidable power in the Greco-Roman world by A.D.200. In the next fifty years progress through the propagation of the Word was rapid. Origen replying to Celsus' gibe that « if all men wanted to be Christian, the Christians would no longer want them » indignantly urges that anyone could see how « as far as they are able, Christians leave no stone unturned to spread the faith in all parts of the worlds (²) ». The *Contra Celsum*, written c.248, is as much a missionary tract emphasizing the providential nature of Christiannity and its spiritual and moral benefit to the convert as a reply to Celsus' work written seventy years before. It foresaw the possibility of all men being Christian (³). Christ was the universal doctor of mankind, and Origen inspired one of his hearers at least to set to and bring this about. This was his pupil, Gregory the Wonderworker, whom he inspired to one of the few missionary campaigns in the pre-Constantinian era of which record has survived. Gregory's mission in Pontus and Cappadocia lasted nearly thirty years, from 243-272, though interrupted by the Decian persecution of 250 and the Gothic invasions of 255-256. Consecrated bishop of Neo-Caesarea shortly after his return home from Caesarea in Palestine in 243, his missionary tours through his great diocese gradually broke the hold of the traditional priestly families on the religious loyalty of the population. Oracles and cures were revealed as swindles, merely part of the irrational world whence Gregory himself had been rescued by Origen. The festivals in honour of former deities were replaced with those in honour of martyrs, thus paving the way for similar transfers of allegiance in later periods. Even though his success may have been much exaggerated by his biographer, Gregory of Nyssa, a century later, he certainly brought about a significant swing towards Christianity, achieved by methods as intelligent as any

---

(1) *Ibid.*, I, I, 11. Clement himself prays for more writers and preachers of the word. *Ibid.*, I, I, 7.

(2) *Contra Celsum*, III, 9.

(3) *Ibid.*, VII, 41 and 60, VIII, 72.

recorded in the Ancient World (¹). Moreover, it was from Cappadocia that his namesake Gregory the Illuminator set out for Armenia and shares with unknown missionaries working northeastwards from Syria the credit of converting the Armenian royal house and its king Tiridates (274-316) on the eve of the Great Persecution.

By this time Christianity had been successfully spread throughout the Roman Empire and beyond. Of the success of individuals on its behalf there can be no doubt. In North Africa and Egypt and eastern Syria Christianity had become a majority religion of town and countryside alike. Yet the steps by which this was achieved are by no means clear. Curiously enough, we know the names of those rivals to Christianity, the Manichaean missionaries in Roman Egypt, such as Papus and Thomas, (²) but apart from the two Gregorys, we know next to nothing of those responsible for achieving the religious revolution among the people of the Mediterranean world. Constantine's victory at the Milvian Bridge assured its success.

At the Council of Nicaea Christianity assumed the character of the official religion of the Roman Empire. At once the missionary situation changed completely. The faith could now be proclaimed openly, its advance was fostered by the emperor, and individuals in official positions had every inducement to convert (³). Moreover, in the countryside the great success of the monastic movement in Egypt, Syria and later in Asia Minor opened up further opportunities for the conversion of populations that had lain beyond the reach of established Christian communities. From the time of Constantine to the death of Justinian in 565 one can discern four distinct types of missionary endeavour. First, there is that directly prompted by the emperor in which religious and political ends were closely connected ; secondly missions organized under episcopal control partly with the aim of pacifying unruly inhabitants within or on the border of their dioceses ; thirdly,

---

(1) GREGORY OF NYSSA, *Vita Gregorii Thaumaturgi*, *P. G.*, XLVI, especially col. 909c, 945 and 954.

(2) ALEXANDER OF LYCOPOLIS, *De Placitis Manichaeorum*, II, *P. L.*, XVIII, col. 413.

(3) See for instance, EUSEBIUS, *Vita Constantini*, ed. HEIKEL, Leipzig, 1902, III, 54 ff., and SOZOMEN, *Hist. Eccl.*, ed. BIDEZ-HANSEN, Berlin, 1960, II, 5.

proselytism by individuals, often captives among barbarians (¹), and finally, and most effectively of all, the conversion of individuals and communities by monks and ascetics.

A major factor in the years between the Council of Nicaea and the death of Constantine in 337 was the ascendancy of Eusebius of Caesarea over the mind of the emperor. The hitherto indispensible Hosius of Cordova disappeared from the Court scene and the historian who had seen his dreams of a Christian world-empire come true became Constantine's mentor and biographer. To Eusebius and the Origenist bishops whom he represented, Constantine reflected the power of the Divine Logos throughout the world, and was the man who « steers and directs in imitation of his Superior the helm of all the affairs of this world (²). Christ's Kingdom and the Roman Empire were co-extensive. To Constantine himself, the office of « bishop of those outside the Church » implied a duty of proclaiming God's word universally and seeing to it that Christians were protected regardless whether or not they lived within the political boundaries of the empire. These beliefs, accepted almost unanimously in the Christian East, led to an active missionary policy beyond the imperial frontiers by both Constantine and Constantius II, and later, by Justinian. Already in his letter to King Sapor Constantine urged on him the need of being favourable to the Persian Christians « and thus win the favour of the Lord of All » (³)— as Constantine himself had done. Similarly, the conversion of the royal house of the Black Sea kingdom of Iberia through the agency of a captive was followed by an alliance between the two realms based on community of religion (⁴). Constantius II maintained the same policy though with less tact. Ulfilas' consecration by Eusebius of Nicomedia near the beginning of his reign must be seen against the background of his interest in the mission of Theo-

---

(1) See especially, SOZOMEN, *Hist. Eccl.*, II. 6, 2, and II, 7.

(2) EUSEBIUS, *Tricennial Oration*, ed. I. A. HEIKEL, Berlin, 1902, I, 6. Again in *ibid.*, I, 16, Eusebius proclaims the co-extensive nature of Christ's kingdom, universal by definition, and the Roman empire.

(3) Cited from EUSEBIUS, *Vita Constantini*, IV, 13. I accept A. H. M. Jones' view that it is genuine, *Constantine and the Conversion of Europe*, London, 1948, p. 207.

(4) SOCRATES, *Hist. Eccl.*, I, 20.

philus « the Indian » to various eastern countries (¹) ; his embassy to
the Red Sea kingdom of the Himyarites was sent, as Philostorgius
says, « in order to induce them to come over to the true religion » (²), and there was a similar intervention in the affairs of the
kingdom of Axum in 356. There the Alexandrian merchant and
sometime captive, Frumentius, had been astonishingly successful
in converting the royal house to Christianity, and had become a
sort of Viceroy of the kingdom, but he was a supporter of Athanasius and had been consecrated bishop by him (³). Constantius
protested, and prefaced a strong letter to the Princes of Axum
with a statement of a theory of the religious unity of mankind
under the guardianship of the Roman emperor :

> « I think that the whole race of mankind claims from us equal
> regard in this respect, in order that they may pass their lives
> in accordance with their hope, being brought to the same know-
> ledge of God, and having no differences with each other in
> their inquiries about justice and truth » (⁴).

No doubt Constantius was spurred to activity by his feud with
Athanasius but it would be unwise to see in his missionary policy no more than that. We can perhaps, on the contrary, discern here the beginnings of the assertion of sovereignty by the
Byzantine emperors over all Christians whether they lived within the boundaries of the empire or not. The Constantinian dynasty prepared the way for the universalist theories of a world
Christian empire associated with Justinian.

For the time being, however, such ideas died with Constantius in 361. Valentinian (364-375) espoused the cause of religious
toleration for all except Manichees, and Valens (364-378) showed
little desire to see a Christianity which could be at variance with
his own semi-Arian beliefs expanded outside his control beyond
the Roman frontiers (⁵). Philostorgius' account of the conver-

---

(1) PHILOSTORGIUS, *Hist. Eccl.*, II, 6.

(2) *Ibid.*, III, 4. More accurately RUFINUS, *Hist. Eccl.*, I, 9.

(3) SOCRATES, *Hist. Eccl.*, I, 19. and SOZOMEN, *Hist. Eccl.*, II, 7.

(4) ATHANASIUS *Apol. ad Constantium*, tr. J. STEVENSON, *Creeds Councils and Controversies*, London, 1966, p. 34. Text in *P. G.*, XXV, col. 636 ff.

(5) Note the rebuff suffered by Valens', bishop of Alexandria, Lucius, when he sought to baptise the would-be Saracen Christians, reported by SOZOMEN, *Hist. Eccl.*, VI, 38, 6.

12

sion of the Goths to Christianity raises difficulties (¹). There is no reason to disbelieve his statement that the first contact which the Goths had with Christianity was from clergy captured during their great raids through Galatia and Cappadocia in the reign of Valerian, and that despite conversions (²), for a long time after that Christianity remained the religion of a minority. Moreover the immediate cause of Ulfilas' consecration c340 was that he was the leader of a large band of Christian Gothic exiles settled on the south side of the Danube following a persecution (³). It is clear that Christianity penetrated the Gothic tribes beyond the Roman frontier by a variety of means, through Roman traders, Goths returning from service with the Roman armies, as well as Christian captives and ex-captives settled among them. In two important studies of the history of the conversion of the Germanic peoples to Arian Christianity, Professor E.A.Thompson concludes that the success of Christianity among the Goths owed less to Ulfilas than to the disintegrating effect of their migration into Roman territory on traditional beliefs associated with another geographical and cultural pattern (⁴). He points out that apart from the Suevi no Germanic people retained their paganism for more than a generation following their entry into the Roman empire (⁵), and that the real agent of conversion was the social disintegration this vast transfer of life and custom brought about. Religious transformation followed social transformation.

If this is true, however, the question still remains, « Why Arianism (⁶)? » Granted that in the 370s and 380s the emperors had abandoned the forward, missionary policy of their Constantinian

---

(1) PHILOSTORGIUS, *Hist. Eccl.*, II, 5.

(2) PHILOSTORGIUS, *Hist. Eccl.*, II, 5. « These pious captives, by their intercourse with the barbarians brought over a great number of the latter to the true faith ».

(3) The consensus of opinion is to agree with Auxentius, *Epistola de fide, vita et obitu Ulfilae*, that Ulfilas was driven out « cum grandi populo confessorum » : compare JORDANES, *Getica*, 51, 267.

(4) E. A. THOMPSON, *Christianity and the Northern Barbarians*, ch. IV. of *The Conflict between Paganism and Christianity in the Fourth Century*, ed. A. MOMIGLIANO, Oxford, 1963, and *The Visigoths* [*in the time of Ulfila*], Oxford, 1966.

(5) E. A. THOMPSON, *art. cit.*, p. 78.

(6) Pertinently asked by J. H. Wallace-Hadrill in his review of Thompson's *Visigoths*, in the *English Historical Review*, vol. LXXXIII, 1968, p. 146-147.

predecessors, and that as a result of the diplomacy of Theodosius Gothic leaders like Gainas adopted Christianity as a symbol of their new-found allegiance to the empire, one is still confronted with the fact that Arianism even in the Balkans was in
decline in the 380s, when the major Visigothic settlement took
place. It is impossible to regard it as an attractive creed at that
time. This was not the case a generation before when Ulfilas
first arrived. If more were known about early Christianity in
Illyricum and in the fortress settlements along the Danube frontier it would probably be found that the ideas of Valens of Mursa
and Ursacius of Singidunum [Belgrade] were representative also
of the Christianity that filtered continuously day by day across the frontier. One must assume that this struck firmer root
than appears on the surface, assisted perhaps by Eudoxius, Valens' able bishop of Constantinople [1] : Ulfilas' Gothic Bible and
his leadership may have been equally decisive factors in bringing about conversion as migration. In later days the Bible was
a powerful weapon in the hands of the missionary.

For more than a century, however, after the death of Constantius II conversion of barbarians beyond the frontiers ceased to
be a primary concern either of emperors, bishops and even of
most individual Christians. St. Patrick, for instance, has to apo-
logise in his *Confession* [2] for his interest in bringing the divine
Word to the barbarous heathen. At the Byzantine court, Christian princes from client states on the frontiers were sometimes
kept as hostages as a means of maintaining political pressure,
a fact which the *Life* of Peter of Iberia (d. 489) makes clear [3].
Elsewhere Christianisation was also regarded as an insurance a-
gainst the savagery of barbarians. E. A. Thompson again has
discussed the evidence [4], pointing to instances such as the motives behind the work of Nicetas of Remesiana in converting
and pacifying Goths and local brigands in his diocese [5], or Ambrose's reply to Queen Fritigel of the Marcomanni which con-

---

(1) Theodoret, *Hist. Eccl.*, IV, 23.
(2) Ch. XV.
(3) *Life*, written c500, ed. J. Raabe, Leipzig, 1895, p. 24-25. Iberia is described as a country « at all times contended for between Romans and Persians ».
(4) *Art. cit.*, p. 65 ff.
(5) Paulinus of Nola, *Carmen*, xvii, 245 ff.

tained not only religious precepts, but the request « to persuade
her husband to keep peace with the Romans (¹) ». Forty years
later in 417 Paulus Orosius claimed that acceptance even of heretical Christianity made the Visigoths more considerate plunderers of
Rome and kinder neighbours to the subject Gallo-Roman population among which they had settled than any erstwhile pagan
conquerors (²). In the same spirit Paulinus of Nola praised his
correspondent Victricius, bishop of Rouen in c400, for carrying
out -a successful mission along the Channel coast which was « in-
fested with foreign barbarians and native brigands (³) ». The ill-
fated mission of Alexander, Sisinnius and Martyrius in 397, inspired by bishop Vigilius of Trent, into the Alpine valleys surrounding his see was also designed to preach to a barbarian nation where Christian peace was new (⁴).

Paganism and barbarism were closely associated in the minds
of western bishops at the end of the fourth century. Both were
outside the pale and no great effort was made to convert the
barbarians except when their activities were a menace to ordered
civilian life. It is interesting that the writer of the work attributed to Prosper Tiro, significantly called *De vocatione omnium gentium*, mentions the conversion of the barbarians only
towards the end of the second book of a treatise devoted to
refuting Pelagian interpretation of Scripture. The conversion of
barbarians either by captives, or through their service among the
Romans, is used to demonstrate that the grace of Christ extended
everywhere (⁵). Generally speaking, however, the Church was not
represented beyond the Roman frontier in the West. In the early
part of the fifth century similar considerations prevailed. In 429
Germanus' mission to Britain aimed at suppressing Pelagianism
and the baptism of thousands of the inhabitants at the time
of the « Alleluia » victory was regarded as an additional bonus.
In Ireland Palladius was sent by Pope Celestine to minister to

---

(1) Paulinus, *Vita Sancti Ambrosii*, 36.
(2) *Historia adversus Paganos*, VII, 32, 13.
(3) *Ep.* XVIII, 17.
(4) Vigilius, *Ep.* I, 1, *P. L.*, XIII, col. 550D .
(5) *De Vocatione*, II, 33, *P. L.*, LI, col. 717-718 : « Nulla pars mundi ab
Evangelio vacat Christi ». The writer does not suggest any first-hand knowledge of missionary work among the barbarians.

Irish who were already Christians and not necessarily to carry out a mission (¹).

It was perhaps fortunate that these somewhat timorous efforts by some individual bishops were aided powerfully by the monks. The great popular religious movements of the last quarter of the third century and the first half of the fourth resulted in the upsurge of monasticism. This in turn led eventually to the total eclipse of rural paganism throughout the Greco-Roman world. The historian Sozomen gives a clear idea why the monks were so influential (²). In the popular mind they were individuals inspired by the Spirit, prophesying the future (³) and often, as Aba Schenuti, in direct contact with the Lord himself. They fought demons, cured diseases, brought relief to the poor and oppressed, chased away extortionate tax-collectors and acted in a curious yet extremely effective way as the channels whereby popular grievance reached the ears of the emperor. The monk Macedonius the Barley-eater saved Antioch from Theodosius' wrath in 387 (⁴). Three years later there were no monks to help the unfortunate population of Thessalonica! Sozomen narrates how in Palestine his grandfather and his household were among the first Christian converts in the populous village of Bethelea near Gaza in 330. The village had a large and ancient temple, but when Alaphion, a friend of Sozomen's grandfather, became ill nothing that pagans or Jews could do availed. At this moment the monk Hilarion appeared and calling on the name of Christ expelled the demon (⁵). Conversions followed as a matter of course. Similar stories are told by Theodoret bishop of Cyrrhus in north-eastern Syria in the mid-fifth century (⁶). The hermit, Abram, for instance, settled in the village of Libanus, set up as a walnut seller, intervened on behalf of the people against the depredations of the local tax-collectors, and found himself

---

(1) PROSPER TIRO, *Chronica Minora*, I, 473. Palladius was sent by Celestine « ad Scottos in Christum credentes » as their first bishop.

(2) *Hist. Eccl.*, I, 12, and VI, 27, 10 (monastic virtue turns the populace from Apollinarius).

(3) For the monk Isaac foretelling the fate of Valens, *ibid.*, VI, 40.

(4) JOHN CHRYSOSTOM, *Homil. de Statuis*, XVII, and THEODORET, *Hist. Eccl.*, V, 20.

(5) SOZOMEN, *Hist. Eccl.*, V, 15,14.

(6) THEODORET, *Hist. religiosa*, XVII, *P. G.*, LXXXIII, col. 1421-1423.

elected priest — another instance of holy men wresting the leadership of small communities from traditional pagan priests. The
reverse side of the gradual conversion of the masses to Christianity by monks through the destruction of local shrines is
evidenced by Libanius c.390. In a well-known passage he castigates « the men dressed in black who eat more than elephants »
who committed such deeds [1], and his words are echoed by
other pagan authors of the time.

In the West also there were some spectacular missionary enter-
prises inspired by intrepid individuals with an ascetic background.
Sulpicius Severus' *Life* of Martin of Tours shows the saint in the
act of destroying a still flourishing paganism in northern Gaul.
In Normandy he was working where « few if any had previously
received the name of Christ », and he went about his task by simple, direct, and often violent means [2]. The cessation of coin-
series at some temple sites with Magnus Maximus (383-388), an
unusual date in view of the massive output of small copper coins
in the early years of Arcadius and Honorius, suggests that in many
places he succeeded [3]. How far he inspired disciples to undertake
similar missionary work in Britain remains uncertain ; though it
would seem unlikely that the tradition reproduced by Bede and
Ailred of Rievaulx concerning Ninian in south-west Scotland was
completely untrue [4]. Even so, the conversion of Celtic Britain
in the fifth century must in a large measure be attributed to the
Celtic monks whose respective radiuses of action have been so
carefully plotted by Canon Doble [5] and Professor E.G. Bowen [6].

---

(1) LIBANIUS, *Pro Templis*, 8, ed. R. VAN LOY, in *Byzantion*, vol. VIII, 1933,
p. 7-39.

(2) SULPICIUS SEVERUS, *Vita Sancti Martini*, ed. C. HALM, Wien, 1866, 13,
9.

(3) L. DE VESLY, *Les Fana ou les petits temples galloromains de la région
normande*, Rouen, 1909, p. 78.

(4) See N. K. CHADWICK, *St. Ninian : a preliminary study of sources*, in
Trans. of the Dumfrieshire and Galloway Nat. Hist. Soc., 3rd Series, vol. XXVII
for 1948/9 (Dumfries, 1950), p. 9 ff. for a fair summing up of the evidence.

(5) G. H. DOBLE, *Saint Congar*, in *Antiquity*, vol. XIX, 1945, p. 32 ff and
85 ff.

(6) E. G. BOWEN, *The Settlement of the Celtic Saints in South Wales*, in
Antiquity, vol. XIX, 1945, p. 175, and *The Travels of the Celtic Saints, ibid*,
vol. XVIII, 1944, p. 16 ff. Also, R. FAWTIER, *La Vie de Saint Sampson* (*Bibl.
de l'École des Hautes Études*, fasc. cxcvii), Paris, 1912. Sampson had a good

Whether their work ultimately stems from Martin and his disciples is however as yet obscure ([1]). During the sixth century the expansion of Christianity in the East and West took different paths and was inspired by different theological motives. In the East Justinian (527-565) revived the universalist dreams of the Constantinian dynasty, and his missions, as well as those of Theodora were pressed forward by the same mixture of religious and political idealism. In the West, the hitherto prevailing fear and contempt for the Germanic barbarians began to give way to a genuine desire to bring them into God's kingdom. The predominant Augustinian theology that predestined the vast majority of the human race to damnation coupled with deep-felt beliefs in the speedy approach of the Last Judgment inspired bishops and monks alike to attempt some sort of salvage among the multitudes destined to perish. Both aims inspired though they were by such entirely different ideas, brought about major attacks on the remaining strongholds of paganism.

Justinian, like the Constantinian emperors, aimed at extending the bounds of both Christianity and the Empire. He spared no effort. His choice, for instance, of the monk John of Amida who was as much an anti-Chalcedonian as he himself was a Chalcedonian, to undertake the conversion of a vast area of Asia Minor that had somehow missed the main stream of Christian expansion, sheds light on his priorities ([2]). Conversion of heathens took pride of place over what had become subtle technicalities of religious allegiance. The strange story of the separate missions which Justinian and Theodora sponsored to the Nubians in 543 points the same moral ([3]). The temple of Isis at Philae which

deal of missionary work to do even among the local rulers of Armorica, *Vita*, 55-58. See also P. A. WILSON on Welsh Missions, in *Welsh History Review*, vol. III, 1967, p. 5-21.

(1) See A. C. THOMPSON, « *The Evidence from North Britain* ». *Christianity in Britain*, Leicester, 1968, p. 93-120.

(2) JOHN OF EPHESUS, *Hist. Eccl.*, ed. E. W. BROOKS, Paris-Louvain, 1935/6, II, '44. With the ascetic bishop Deuterius he established 99 new churches and 12 monasteries in the course of 35 years' activity.

(3) *Ibid.*, IV, 6. For a useful account of the missions under Justinian, see G. BARDY and L. BRÉHIER, *L'Expansion du Christianisme aux Ve et VIe siècles*, ch. VI of P. DE LABRIOLLE, G. BARDY, L. BRÉHIER and G. DE PLINVAL, *De*

their predecessors had tolerated for nearly a century as a cult centre for the pagan Nobatae [Nubians] had to be destroyed by armed force, and the Nobatae brought into the Christian fold. Theodora's mission was the more successful and thus meant the eventual adherence to Monophysitism of the whole of the Nile valley from Alexandria to Lake Tana.

The main stream of Western thought concerning missions in this period is represented by the correspondence of Pope Gregory. Whatever grain of truth lies behind the *Angli/angeli* story there is little doubt that from the outset of his reign this amazingly busy and active pope placed missions to the heathen among his main objectives. In January 591, following the death of the *nefandissimus Autharith*, king of the Lombards, Gregory ordered his diocesans to vigorous missionary efforts among the Lombards aimed specially at the younger generation. Gregory gave as a reason the plague that threatened all with death (¹). Three years later, in May 594, following an episcopal visitation of the island by his clergy, he wrote to the nobility and landowners of Sardinia urging action to convert the rural population « which was practically entirely given over to idolatry (²) ». At the Last Judgment which was rapidly approaching the landowners would bear part of the responsibility for this situation. The mission to Ethelbert's kingdom of Kent in 597 was to have been prepared by the expedient of buying Anglian slave boys « to be given to God in the monasteries (³) », as well as by the use of Ethelbert's Christian queen, but in 596 Gregory decided to send a mission to the island at once. After a false start, he selected Augustine, who had been *alumnus* to the bishop of Messina, to go with a small mission of monks to Canterbury. The mission was partially successful only (⁴). Bishoprics were est-

---

la Mort de Théodose à l'élection de Grégoire le Grand (Vol. IV of FLICHE and MARTIN, *Histoire de l'Église*), Paris, 1948.

(1) *Ep.* I, 17. ed P. EWALD et M. HARTMANN (*M. G. H.*, *EE.*) Berlin, 1891.

(2) *Ep.* IV, 23. « pene omnes vos rusticos in vestris possessionibus idololatriae deditos habere » ; compare *Ep.* II, 4. In 598 Gregory sent 50 *solidi* to bishop Peter to buy baptismal vestments for pagan converts in Corsica, *Ep.* VIII,. 1.

(3) *Regulae* VI, 10.

(4) The well-known story is told by M. DEANSLEY, *A History of the Medieval Church 590-1500*, 8th. ed., London, 1954, p. 42-46, and L. BRÉHIER and R.

ablished at Canterbury, London, Rochester and York, a monastery
was built also at Canterbury, and 10,000 converts were baptised, but Augustine failed to win the support of the Celtic clergy
in the west, and outside Kent and London a generation passed
before Celtic and Roman missionaries between them began to
make a serious impression on the remaining Anglo-Saxon kingdoms.

The long letter of instructions which Gregory wrote to Augustine in 601 outlining in comprehensive detail how he should organise the new churches (¹) stands in contrast to much of the
haphazard yet equally effective missionary work carried on by
individuals among barbarians at this time. A sort of wander-
lust, taking the form of a missionary pilgrimage (*peregrinatio pro
Christi amore*) (²), seized some enterprising monastic Christians in
the West. The Irish monk Columba (d. 597) crossed the sea to
attempt missionary work amongst the Dal-Réti. He was given
land by the king, built his monastery on Iona in 565 and lived
and worked there for thirty years. Apart from monastic island
sanctuaries round the Scottish coast, many daughter houses to
Iona were founded and became missionary centres (³). Probably
in 590 another Irish monk, Columbanus, crossed from St. Con-
gall's monastery near Bangor in N. Wales to Gaul on a sort of
ecclesiastical tour of Gaul, Switzerland and Italy to establish the
famous communities of Luxeuil and Bobbio (⁴). He thus began
the tradition of missionary enterprise to remote parts by individuals who set out from the British Isles to convert the heathen.
Wilfrid, Willibrord and Boniface were all to some extent his disciples and followers. Almost at the same time, another wandering ascetic, Martin, originally from Pannonia, established himself
at Braga in Galicia in north-western Spain and completed the
conversion of the Suevi as well as many of the native inhabi-

---

AIGRAIN, *Grégoire le Grand, les états barbares et la conquête arabe, 590-797*
(Vol. V. of FLICHE and MARTIN, *Histoire de l'Église*, Paris, 1947), p. 277-289.

(1) GREGORY, *Ep.* XI, 56.

(2) Columba left Ireland, « pro cristo perigrinari volens » *Vita*, Preface II.

(3) See BEDE, *Historia Ecclesiastica*, III, 3.4 and 4.2 and N. K. CHADWICK,
op, cit., p. 79.

(4) See P. A. WILSON, *art. cit.*, p. 20 for dating.

tants (¹). Finally, in 628 a noble from Aquitaine named Amandus set out for the north-eastern borders of the Frankish kingdom and helped to re-establish Christianity on monastic lines in the area which now forms part of Belgium (²).

In the east, the Christianisation of the Byzantine empire had practically been completed by the death of Justinian. Subsequently, first the long Persian wars and then the Arab conquests put an end to imperially inspired missions beyond the Roman frontiers. Even within the frontiers the newly-arrived Slavonic immigrants in the Balkans were converted by Roman missionaries on the Emperor Heraclius' request from 640 onwards (³). As in the case of the Visigoths, Christianisation seems, however, to have been piecemeal. The twin influences of the see of Thessalonica and enrolment in the Byzantine Empire may have been important in the ultimate conversion of the South Slavs (⁴).

One great and lasting enterprise, however, remained, namely the Nestorian missions from Persia eastwards and north-eastwards along the silk route to China. Here scholarship is greatly indebted to the work of A. Mingana (⁵) and more lately to B. Spuler (⁶), the first for his translations of Nestorian texts and the second for his wide-ranging account of eastern Christianity under the Moslems. About 550 the Nestorian Catholicos, Aba I of Ctesiphon, consecrated a bishop for the Huns of Bactria on the borders of Persia and India. The Syriac record says that the request came through an embassy to the Persian king

(1) MARTIN OF BRAGA, Works, ed by C. W. BARLOW, New Haven [Conn.], 1950, especially De Correctione rusticorum, P. L., LXXII, col. 17-52, and C. P. CASPARI, Martin von Braccaras Schrift « De Correctione Rusticorum », Christiana, 1883. For possible connections between Ireland and Galicia at this time, N. K. CHADWICK, op. cit., 58-59.

(2) See E. DE MOREAU, Saint Amand (Museum Lessianum, Section missiologique, VII), Bruges, 1929.

(3) BRÉHIER and AIGRAIN, op. cit., p. 149-150.

(4) For the mystique exercised by Thessalonica on the Slavs, see Sti Demetrii Miracula, 166-167 (P. G., CXVI, col. 1333).

(5) A. MINGANA, The Early Spread of Christianity in Central Asia and the Far East, in Bulletin of John Rylands Library, vol. IX-2, 1925, p. 297-371, and, with Rendel HARRIS, in Woodbrooke Studies, editions and translations of Christian documents in Syriac and Garshuni, Cambridge, 1927-1934.

(6) B. SPULER, Die morgenländischen Kirche, (Handbuch fur Orientalistik, IV), Leiden, 1964.

« who was amazed at the power of Jesus and that even the Christian Huns acknowledged the Catholicos as their Head » (¹).

The Nestorian monks followed the Manichees into Central Asia and China, only more successfully. The great inscription found in 1625 at Sinanfu shows that by 635 missionaries had arrived at the Chinese capital where the Scriptures were translated, and the missionaries received permission both to propagate their faith and to build a monastery to house 21 monks (²). Thereafter Christianity was a tolerated religion in China for nearly 200 years and as an inscription dating 781 shows, held annual synods under the patronage of the Chinese Emperor. Linking these Chinese Christians with those in Persia was a chain of scattered communities extending from the River Oxus to the Chinese frontier (³).

The correspondence of the great Catholicos, Timotheus I, (780-823) sheds much light on the missionary strategy of the Nestorians (⁴). The married monk (marriage being allowed since 486) was a great asset, for often he could establish himself and his family as traders as well as missionaries much as his Moslem counterparts were doing. Such men were also amazingly mobile, reaching Panjab, Sokotra, the Yemen and southern India. As the Catholicos himself wrote, « many crossed the seas towards India and China carrying only a stick and a bag (⁵) ». Missionary successes were immediately followed by the establishment of a hierarchy designed to give the new congregation a firm episcopal government. Timotheus himself saw the creation of six new metropolitans in India and Central Asia and 80 new bishoprics.

The difficulty was to sustain these new sees. Too much depended on the action of individuals. The Nestorians were never more than a tolerated minority in Persia. They lacked the mi-

---

(1) *Life of Mar Aba*, ed. P. BEDJAN, *Acta Martyrum et Sanctorum*, Paris 1890-91, p. 266-269.

(2) P. Y. SAEKI, *The Nestorian Monument in China*, London, 1916 : also E. TISSERANT, *Nestorienne (Église)*, in *Dict. Theol. Cath.*, XI, col. 199-207.

(3) See the useful summary in J. FOSTER, *Beginning at Jerusalem* (*World Christian Books*, 10), London, 1956, p. 48. 49.

(4) Letters edited by O. BRAUN, *Timothei Patriarchae I, Epistulae* (*Corpus Script, christ, orient, Scriptores Syri*, Ser. II, vol. LXVII), Rome, 1914-15.

(5) BRAUN, *op. cit.*, p. 70 of translation. For Nestorian missions to South India, see J. N. FARQUHAR, in *Bulletin of John Rylands Library*, vol. XI, 1927, p. 20-50.

litary power and prestige of Islam and thus were at the mercy of unsympathetic rulers. In China, for example, local and sporadic persecutions in the ninth century thinned their congregations, and after 900 little more is heard of them until the time of Marco Polo. The epic of their missionary endeavour has remained, however, for all time.

In the west the story was different. There were no great steppes to cross and no victorious Moslem power to outwit, but the Germanic and Slavonic tribes who inhabited central and eastern Europe were only gradually converted. When however they were, Christianity made the permanent gain of whole peoples and territories. By the year 650 nearly all the old lands of the western provinces of the Roman empire had been re-christianised. In Anglo-Saxon England there was still the fierce pagan reaction of Penda of Mercia (died 655), but in the royal courts Christianity was recognised as the religion of the future, as Coifi the high priest of the Northumbrians had so poignantly realised (¹). Perhaps in one kingdom, that of the East Anglians, the Sutton Hoo ship-burial with its strange implications of a heathen past and Christian present in the dead ruler's mind may mark a point of transition from the old faith to the new at some moment near the middle of the seventh century (²). In 653 the first native Englishman was made archbishop of Canterbury, and in the next year Cedd, the Northumbrian from Lindisfarne, began his mission to the East Angles. A generation later, bishop Wilfrid of York, shipwrecked on the Frisian coast on his way to Rome, spent the winter preaching to the heathen and set the example of the return of the Anglo-Saxon missions to convert their still heathen kinsmen on the Continent. Meantime, within the former boundaries of the Roman empire the spread of Benedictine monasticism to out of the way parts finally brought Christianity to those among whom the town-based secular clergy had no permanent influence. The missions of Boniface and his companions in the following century to the Germanic and Slav peoples were based on firmly Christianised homelands (³).

(1) BEDE, *Hist. Eccl.*, II, 13.
(2) See the account in *Antiquity*, vol. XIV, 1940, p. 1 ff.
(3) W. LEVISON, *England and the Continent in the eighth century*, Oxford, 1946, is still the standard work. For the missions to the Avars and Slavs in

The story of the conversion first of the Mediterranean world, and then of the Germanic tribes to Christianity remains a fruitful field for research. The general lines of development are well known, thanks to the work of von Harnack, Bardy, Thompson and others, but the many fascinating details of how individual communities were converted still largely escape us. Many questions require answering. What attracted the rural populations of the Roman empire and the Germanic tribes to Christianity? What about the missions of the lesser non-orthodox Churches, such as the Marcionites, or the rivalry between Christian and Manichee in rural Egypt and Syria, or the follow-up of the Church in the wake of the successful missionary ascetic? How were the newly converted congregations organised? How far were Constantinople and Alexandria rivals as missionary centres for the conversion of the Nubians, Himyarites and Ethiopians? No detailed survey of the conversion of the Greco-Roman world in the fourth and subsequent centuries has yet been attempted. It is time it was.

the 8 th. century, see W. H. Fritze, *Slaven and Avaren in Angelsachsischen Missionsprogramm*, in *Zeitschr. für slavische Philologie*, vol. XXXI, Leipzig, 1964, p. 316-338, and subsequent articles in the same periodical.

IX

THE ROMAN EMPIRE IN EASTERN AND WESTERN HISTORIOGRAPHY

'All history is contemporary history.' The statement is true in so far as the questions which each successive generation puts to its past throw light on its own dominant ideas. Today the great compendia of the 'Life and Times' of famous men, so common fifty years ago, are as out of place as contributions to the study of history as *a priori* works of Hegelian or Marxist inspiration. In the study of Classics we have moved on in a single generation, from almost exclusive concern for the literary heritage of aristocratic writers writing for an élite, to a survey in depth of the whole complex of civilizations that composed the Ancient World, in which the classical authors take their place among the inscriptions, papyri and the whole paraphernalia of archaeological evidence that serve to establish how people of all classes and races lived and thought some two thousand years ago. The Classics have become part of the general study of Man, and similarly, works of early Christian writers have taken on a new and less specialized importance. They can be recognized as the products of a provincial middle-class whose members had a detached and critical view of the Roman Empire. Like the New Testament books themselves, they express the outlook of people who were in the Empire but not especially of it. Luke/Acts may now be regarded as one of the best commentaries on Roman provincial rule in the East in the Julio-Claudian period, while Revelation like the Jewish *Sibyllines* is seen to reflect the intensity of articulate protest against that rule in the province of Asia.[1]

To the still pagan aristocracy of the fourth century the Christians remained revolutionaries, and Constantine, as the first Christian emperor, an innovator and the prime disturber of the established order.[2] For a long time the Christians themselves acknowledged their barbarian (i.e. Jewish) origins, and though they might claim the Hebrew patriarchs as their ancestors none paid the same compliment to Romulus. The Church triumphed from below, by making its influence felt first among the lower and middle classes of the Mediterranean lands before penetrating effectively the property-owners who ruled the cities. The fifth-century historian Sozomen gives an interesting example of this. In 362, while the city council of Cyzicus sent an embassy to Julian demanding the restoration of the temples and pagan worship, the artisans engaged in the mint and military clothing manufacture threatened a riot if this were carried out, and Julian, it seems, respected their views.[3] Africa and Egypt, too, provide a number of examples, such as Ptolemais and Timgad, of the ruling bodies of citizens remaining pagan long after the lower classes had become devotedly Christian. We should hardly be mistaken if we accepted the emperor Julian's view that the Christians' ideal of social service and mutual aid was a powerful force in making Christianity the massive movement that it became in the fourth and fifth centuries.[4]

---

[1] See on this theme H. Fuchs, *Der geistige Widerstand gegen Rom* (Leipzig, 1938).
[2] Ammianus Marcellinus XXI. 10. 8. [3] Sozomen, *Hist. Eccles.* (ed. Bidez/Hansen), v. 15. 4 ff.
[4] Julian, Letter to Arsacius, High Priest of Galatia = *Ep.* 22 and Sozomen, *Hist. Eccl.* v. 16. 5–15.

It would be surprising, then, if the Christian view of their times had coincided with that of the Classical historians of pagan antiquity. These aimed at recording accurately events for the sake of posterity, so that the heroic deeds performed in moments of crisis like the Persian wars or the great war between Athens and Sparta might not be forgotten.[1] Theirs was the spirit which inspired countless more humble individuals who have left their life-stories and sometimes also an account of their professional acumen on their tombstones.[2] This was 'memoria', the sole guarantee to personal survival beyond the grave. Then, as Rome grew in power, the scope of the historian was enlarged. Polybius writes to a clearly-defined theme, the conquest of the world by Rome, and he seeks an explanation how this came about through the continuity of her institutions and devotion to the national religion. Livy enlarges the canvas further into a magnificent descriptive narrative of how Rome came to be the mistress of the world. But seldom only does he seek to explain the events, pausing now and then to warn his readers what happened when omens were not heeded and *externa superstitio* preferred to the religion of the gods of Rome. His history too, like that of Thucydides and Polybius, was local, concerned with one state and one set of events. It was not a history of mankind.

To the Christian, however, anything else would be irrelevant, and indeed idolatrous. In the first two centuries A.D., though he might 'render unto Caesar the things that were Caesar's', and be a law-abiding member of society, he would as often as not be echoing the reply of the Scillitan confessor Speratus to the Proconsul of Africa in 180, 'I do not recognize the empire of this world: but rather do I serve that God whom no man sees nor can see with human eyes'.[3] In the world he was a permanent foreigner or sojourner 'confined in the world as in a prison', as the writer of the letter to Diognetus stated.[4] Thus his ideas would tend to be universalist and his interpretation of history conditioned by his theology of the Fall and his expectation of the Coming. He would judge the Roman Empire from the point of view of an outsider, at best as a step forward in the long history of mankind towards an ultimate return to a natural union with God which had been lost by Adam's fall, or less hopefully as the prime example of Babylon, the earthly city to be contrasted at all points with the heavenly state whose citizenship the Christian enjoyed, and which would soon be vindicated even on earth. But in either case neither Rome, nor any other earthly state, could form the central theme in an unfolding history of human salvation.

Two other factors contributed to the formulation of the Christian's attitude towards the Greco-Roman world. First, he had often been drawn to his faith through the inadequacy of current philosophical explanations of the universe or, more potently, by disgust at the cruel attitude of the populace and the authorities towards individual

---

[1] The classic statements of Greek historiography are to be found in Herodotus, Prologue, 9–10, and Thucydides 1. 22. In general R. G. Collingwood, *The Idea of History* (Oxford, 1940), ch. 1.

[2] For instance, the well-known third-century A.D. inscription from Mactar in Tunisia, *CIL* VIII. 11824, *CIL* VI. 3. 17985 *a* from Rome, and the Igel Säule from near Trier.

[3] *Passio Sanctorum Scillitanorum* (ed. Knopf/Krüger), p. 6. 'Speratus dixit: Ego imperium huius mundi non cognosco: sed magis illi Deo servio, quem nemo hominum vidit, nec videre his oculis potest.'

[4] *Ep. ad Diognetum* 6. 7.

Christians. The experience of Justin Martyr c. 130 represents both motives.[1] His outlook tended therefore to be critical of his surroundings. In the *Acta Martyrum* one can sometimes detect how Christian confessors combined political as well as religious attitudes in their 'obstinacy'. Some allegedly inveighed against 'the happy times', or compared the Severan age not to that of gold but to that of iron,[2] and looked forward to the speedy destruction of the world by fire. Origen in his *De Principiis* c. 225 says that it was the zealots (ζηλωταί) who abandoned parental customs and established gods in Greek and barbarian lands to become either Jews or Christians.[3] Not for nothing were Christians in the late second and early third centuries compared with the traditional grumblers against society, the Cynics. Such a movement could be expected to take comfort from 'opposition' interpretations of events, such as the oracle literature which Justin[4] and Lactantius[5] quote, that foretold the destruction of Rome after a definite number of years by powers from the East. 'Nero redivivus' had his place in Christian as well as in Jewish saga.

More important, however, was the legacy of Jewish historiography. Just as the Christian apologists of the second and third centuries defended their faith with arguments drawn from the stock of current Jewish apologetic themes, so did the Christian historians. Indeed, it could hardly be otherwise, and even as the Christian mission was taking shape in the Greco-Roman world in the latter part of the first century A.D., Jewish writers were perfecting theories of history with which the Christians were to equip themselves for the long drawn out process of coming to terms with the world.

Jewish historiography was based on the belief in Jahwe's activity in the affairs of mankind, 'God's providential care for all mankind' as Philo stated.[6] It was therefore universal, embracing all peoples and all times. History started with Adam and would end with the promised end of the Age. It was divided into strict chronological periods, as Jahwe's successive covenants had been. Men and events were judged not in relation to their earthly prosperity but to the degree in which they kept these covenants. Saul, David and Solomon all finally fell from grace on this count, and it served for nothing that King Manasseh reigned for fifty-five years if he did also 'that which is evil in the sight of the Lord, after the abominations of the heathen' (II Kings xxi. 2). Classical historians might stress that he who angered the gods, like the 'atheists' Diagoras and Protagoras, came to unhappy ends, but there is nothing in the history of the Ancient World quite the equivalent of the Jewish writer's emphasis on the role of divine retribution. The fate of Pharaoh's army, vividly depicted on the walls of the third century A.D. synagogue at Dura, was also suffered by other oppressors of the Jews. Antiochus IV, for whom Polybius records a peaceful end,[7] is gleefully described by the writer of II Maccabees as perishing through the attentions of worms.[8] A similar fate was reserved for Rome's ally Herod,[9] and by Luke for

---

[1] As he tells in *Dialogue with Trypho* 2 and *II Apol.* 12.
[2] Hippolytus, cited in Palladius' *Lausiac History*, 62.
[3] *De Principiis* IV. I. I from the Greek (translated in *A.N.C.L.* x, 276).
[4] Justin, *I Apol.* 44.   [5] Lactantius, *Institutes* VII. 15. 11 and 18. 1.
[6] Philo, *Legatio ad Gaium* (ed. E. M. Smallwood), 3.
[7] Polybius XXX. 11.   [8] II Macc. ix. 4–9.   [9] Josephus, *Antiquities* XVII. 6. 5.

Herod Agrippa as a persecutor of the Christians,[1] and by Lactantius, at the end of the Great Persecution, for Galerius.[2] Divine anger was a moving force in the history of men. Linked to this was the vindication of the righteous. At the beginning of the Christian era, pious Jews might look back through the long history of their race's relationship with God and record how the righteous had always suffered, and out of suffering had come victory. In IV Maccabees one reads in the final speech by the mother of the youths who had defied king Antiochus how 'The boys' father had read to us of Abel who was slain by Cain and of Isaac who was offered as a burnt offering and of Joseph in the prison. And he spake to us of Phineas, the zealous priest, and he taught you the song of Ananias, Azarias and Misael in the fire: and he glorified also Daniel in the den of lions...'[3] The *Haggada* on the Sons of Adam embedded in *I Clement* tells a similar story of righteous suffering from one end of creation to the other.[4] Many were the afflictions of the Just. It was a theme that appealed to the early Church.

Within this framework however of providential history that sustained the embattled minority that composed the Jewish people in the Greco-Roman world, it is possible to see the development of two diverging tendencies which were to leave their mark on Christian thought. In Palestine down to 70 and perhaps beyond, the Jew continued to regard himself as the successor of the heroes of the prophetic age of Israel, the Remnant awaiting the coming of a messianic deliverer, and his successful struggle against the Seleucids prompted him to hope for similar victory over Rome.[5] The crisis of the Seleucid wars had produced the *Book of Daniel* in which the seer's symbolic vision of a periodized world-history divided between the hegemony of four successive world-empires to be succeeded on the overthrow of the last and worst by a messianic age of the saints, exactly interpreted his hopes. In the Dispersion, however, attitudes towards secular authorities were less sharply defined. In the Jewish *Sibyllines* and the apocalyptic writings of IV Ezra and II Baruch the historical process is seen as leading to the violent overthrow of the idolatrous Roman power, but this attitude was becoming less typical as time went on. The all-pervading influence of Greek philosophy, coupled with education in the Greek language and respect for the comparative peace and order associated even with pagan city government, tended towards a more sympathetic view of the pagans especially among educated Jews. Philo, for instance, might stress at the outset of the *Legatio ad Gaium* that the Jews were a 'truly reasonable people', who 'saw God' and whose relationship with God was a special one,[6] but he also was aware of the value of the *Pax Augusta* to his nation, and not beyond viewing the reign of Augustus as something akin to the 'godly monarchy' which he believed would interpret ultimately the rule of Providence to all mankind. In an interesting passage in the *Legatio* Philo interprets the victory of Augustus at Actium

---

[1] Acts xii. 23.

[2] Lactantius, *De Mortibus Persecutorum* 33. Also, Orosius VIII. 28. 13.

[3] IV Macc. xviii. 11–18.

[4] *I Clement* iv. For this identification, K. Beyschlag, *Clemens Romanus und der Frühkatholizismus* (Tübingen, 1966), p. 131.

[5] For messianic hopes in the mid-second century, Celsus in Origen, *Contra Celsum* II. 29.

[6] *Legatio ad Gaium* 3–5.

in the sense that by putting an end to the state of war and chaos in the world that was threatening the very existence of humanity, the emperor opened a new era for mankind.

European and Asian nations from the ends of the earth had risen up and were engaged in grim warfare, fighting with armies and fleets on every land and sea, so that almost the whole human race might have been destroyed in internecine conflicts and disappeared completely, had it not been for one man, one *Princeps*, Augustus, who deserves the title of 'Averter of Evil'.[1]

Here indeed was a direct anticipation of the arguments of Origen and Eusebius who were to seek to demonstrate the providential nature of Jesus' birth by reference to the peace and unity brought to the world by Augustus. In this argument Philo implies that toleration accorded the Jews by Augustus and even by Tiberius was in some way associated with their own prosperity and the prosperity of their empire. The same argument was to serve the Greek Christian Apologists well.

Christian writers therefore found themselves the heirs to two diverging approaches to the problems of history bequeathed to them by their Jewish forerunners. Granted that all history was providential history, the working out of God's purposes for man, one could still take two different views of the Greco-Roman world in which the Church had established itself. On the one hand, one could follow the prophetic and apocalyptic view, and interpret events in the context of an eternal contest between the Church representing Israel or Jerusalem and the various forces of pagan society and the provincial administrations representing 'the world' or Babylon. 'Rome drunk with the blood of saints and the blood of the martyrs of Jesus', as described in immortal words by the writer of Revelation (Rev. xvii. 5–6) was one alternative. On the other hand, there was a more hopeful view. Christians, like the Alexandrian or Antiochene Jews before them, who were acquainted with Greek philosophical ideas, could regard all the world as God's world, forming part of a *kosmos* or ordered creation in which all had some part to play. Man's history might then be seen as one of progressive development, from the disaster of the Fall rising gradually but equally through the Jewish Covenants and Greek philosophical teaching to a point where the Incarnation had become possible and the Church, representing the new race of Christians, could come into being. Some divine truths and some insights had already been anticipated by pagans and Jews alike.[2] In this interpretation Church and Empire ultimately would become partners in the work of promulgating God's word to mankind. Their common enemy were the demonic forces of unreason that sought to keep mankind in the thraldom of ignorance of divine truth.

For reasons which are not wholly understood the West tended to adopt the first standpoint and the East the second. To a large extent also differences in historiography reflected differences of emphasis in doctrine which emerged the moment Christianity took root in the Latin-speaking provinces of the Empire. The West long retained its original character of a small 'gathered Church' directed by the Holy

---

[1] *Ibid.* 144.
[2] Cf. the view of Justin, *I Apol.* 46 and *II Apol.* 12–13 and Clement of Alexandria, *Stromateis* I. 5. 28.

24

Spirit, with a strong feeling that the duty of the baptized Christian was to imitate the life and death of Christ to the point of offering himself for martyrdom, and that in the process he must deny the world and its teaching. The Bible was to be his sole guide and he must regard himself as a member of an elect band of saints predestined to reign with Christ for ever. This theology which placed its emphasis on the role and character of the Church and of man's relation to God was summed up by Tertullian in a series of memorable antitheses—'What has Athens to do with Jerusalem, the Academy with the Church', the 'camp of light with the camp of darkness?' 'No man can serve two masters, Christ and Caesar.'[1] It could only lead to a hostile interpretation of Roman history, a hostility which was as much in evidence in the fifth century as in the third.

Yet the basis of this hostility was religious rather than political. Antichrist or Satan was the enemy, Rome only indirectly so as the representative of Satan's kingdom. Thus, for Tertullian, though the world might have been made by God, all that was worldly belonged to Satan.[2] He was no systematic historian, yet where he mentions the Roman Empire, his theology leads him to deny that its prosperity was due to any virtues of paganism. Rome was not great because she was religious. She spread her dominion 'through irreligious war' and her victims were 'not without religions when their kingdoms were melted down to make the sum total of the Roman Empire'.[3] But all empires including Rome's derived their power from God and would last so long and only so long as he willed. Rigorously logical, he saw that a Christian empire was a contradiction in terms: 'the Caesars too', he states,[4] 'would have believed in Christ, either if the Caesars had not been necessary to the world or if Christians could have been Caesars'. 'Legitimus Christianus esse non poteris',[5] he cried. Yet he was not a political revolutionary. For all his hostility to the empire and its institutions he feared the chaos that might result from their extinction.[6] Even so, on individual Roman governors who persecuted he had no mercy. God's justice on them was sudden, deadly and eternal—but it was God's vengeance, not man's.

Tertullian's view of world history depended on a profound doctrine of the Holy Spirit. The latter was continuously at work 'convicting the world of sin' and inspiring the Christian towards martyrdom at the hands of the authorities. Conflict between God's ways and man's throughout history was inevitable, and the Christian gave thanks for the judge's sentence of execution.[7] In Rome, however, the equally vindictive hostility of Tertullian's contemporaries Minucius Felix and Hippolytus rested more on a faithful reproduction of Jewish examples of suffering and perhaps a concept of history derived from oppositional currents of opinion that sought to belittle Rome's achievement and deny her uniqueness. Thus Minucius Felix writes, 'After all, under God's dispensation before the Romans existed, Medes, Persians, Greeks too, and Egyptians ruled great empires although they had no Pontiffs, no Arval brothers, no Salii, Vestals or augurs, no cooped chickens to rule the destinies of state by their

---

[1] Tertullian, De Praescriptione 7, De Corona Militari 11 and De Idololatria 18.
[2] De Spectaculis 5: 'saeculum Dei est, saecularia autem diaboli'.
[3] Apol. 25. 12–17.   [4] Ibid. 21. 24.
[5] Ad Nationes 1. 7.   [6] Apol. 32. 1.   [7] Ibid. 50. 16.

appetite or distaste for food'.[1] Rome would be brought low like her predecessors, and he echoes Tertullian in his claim 'all that the Romans hold, occupy and possess is the spoil of outrage. Their temples are full of loot drawn from the ruin of cities, the plunder of gods and the slaughter of priests.'[2] This, one feels, is lawyers' stuff, part and parcel of an oppositional outlook to which a Christian slant has been added.

Hippolytus was even more abrasive. In his writings one glimpses the intensity of the opposition that existed beneath the outward splendour of the Severan age. Significantly, the two works in which he discusses the Roman Empire were his *Commentary on Daniel* and *Concerning Antichrist*. In the former he interprets the last of the four beasts spoken of in Daniel vii as the Roman Empire. This differs, he points out, from the first three empires of Babylonians, Persians and Macedonians in that whereas each of the three, horrible though they were, had developed from single kingdoms, this last had prospered at the expense of every other nation on earth which it now subdued with feet of iron.[3] Yet like Nebuchadnezzar's statue the Roman Empire had its weaknesses. 'The toes are meant to represent the democracies which are to come and which will be separate one from another like the ten fingers of the statue on which iron will be mingled with clay.'[4] The empire would fall and its place would be taken by the liberated peoples. He half anticipates what actually happened two centuries later, with the new age belonging to them and the people of 'the new name', the Christians. Hippolytus was not unaware of the coincidence of the birth of Christ and the reign of Augustus, but in contrast to every other Christian writer he saw no indication of divine blessing on the Roman Empire therein. Rather, he interprets this coincidence as proving the Satanic character of the empire, a Satanic imitation of the kingdom of Christ, a parody of the latter's unity and universal rule for all time.[5]

In the third century Western Christianity was interpreting the Roman Empire in the apocalyptic and anguished terms of an embittered minority. Time was running out before the coming of Antichrist and the end of the world. Similar views were to be found at the end of the century in Victorinus of Pettau,[6] and (if this is his correct date) stridently expressed by Commodian. Cyprian, too, saw the Empire in terms of corruption and the tiredness of old age.[7] The failure of the Great Persecution while bringing welcome physical relief to the Christians confronted them with a serious dilemma. Antichrist had certainly suffered a setback, but if the emperor was now a Christian what was to become of the old Jerusalem–Babylon tension; yet if it was to be retained how could the Church express its new relationship with the state? Lactantius, for all his praise of Constantine, could not recognize in Augustus his hero's

---

[1] Minucius Felix, *Octavius*, 25. 5.
[2] *Ibid*. 25. 5.
[3] *Comment. in Daniel* iv. 8. See R. A. Markus, 'The Roman Empire in early Christian Historiography', *Downside Review* (1963), pp. 340–53.
[4] *Comment. in Daniel* iv. 7. See also A. Santo Mazzarino, *The End of the Ancient World* (tr. G. Holmes, 1966), p. 40.
[5] *Comment. in Daniel* iv. 9; cf. *De Antichristo* 49.
[6] *In Apocalypsim* xi. 7 (Migne, *Patrologia latina* v, col. 335).
[7] Especially in *Ad Demetrianum*, written in 251.

predecessor and could never abandon his view that history lay in the hand of God and that it was God (not Constantine) who had triumphed over his enemies in the deaths of the persecuting emperors. His interpretation of history is dominated as much as Tertullian's by concepts of divine judgement and vengeance which render his account of events schematic and basically untrustworthy.[1] Diocletian and Galerius could do no right, Constantius and Constantine no wrong. His successors found it easier to write about the Empire in moments of persecution, such as occurred between 355 and 361 when Constantius attempted to impose semi-Arianism on the West, than in periods of co-operation. Behind this limitation lay the sense that Christianity was a religion of triumphant individual deliverance from the physical powers of evil that dominated the world represented by paganism and heresy. History was an account of their overthrow.

For the East, however, there was less difficulty. Though down to A.D. 150 there was still a strong apocalyptic current in Greek-speaking Christianity which was to assert itself in the Montanist movement in Asia Minor, the legacy of the more positive outlook of Hellenistic Jewish apologists towards the Roman Empire was ultimately to prevail. There is evidence for this outlook in Luke/Acts[2] and in Justin (c. 155) where one finds indications of the emergence of a political theory of a Christian empire and therefore of its positive evaluation in history. Justin even sees the Roman legions as the instruments of divine justice in Judaea, and he hints at a providential plan whereby Rome was beginning her rule of Judaea at the precise moment of the Incarnation.[3] Christians, he stresses, were loyal to the Empire and for good reason. Twenty years later, Melito, bishop of Sardes, stated in an apology to the emperor Marcus Aurelius written in a period of severe local persecution against the Christians, 'Our philosophy (i.e. Christianity) grew up among the barbarians, but its full flower came among your nation in the great reign of your ancestor Augustus, and became an omen of good to your empire, for from that time the power of the Romans became great and splendid'.[4] The contrast in the underlying historical and political assumptions between these sentiments and those of Tertullian and his contemporaries is striking. Melito like Justin sees Empire and Church as allies, and the proof of this lay in the coincidence of the reign of the Prince of Peace beginning in the period of earthly peace provided by Augustus.

One may follow this evaluation a step further in Origen's reply to the pagan Celsus written in c. 248. Origen was not concerned with the possible historical implications of the millennial celebrations in Rome of that year, but harks back to the significance of the reign of Augustus for Christians. In a well-known passage in which he comments on Jesus' command to the apostles to 'Go and teach all nations', he writes 'It is quite clear that Jesus was born in the reign of Augustus, the one who reduced to uniformity, so to speak, the many kingdoms of the earth so that he had a single

---

[1] The best description of Lactantius' philosophy of history is to be found in A. Moreau, *Lactance, De la Mort des Persécuteurs* (Sources chrétiens, 39), pp. 25 ff.

[2] Luke/Acts as an apology: see B. S. Easton, *Early Christianity* (London, 1955), pp. 41 ff.

[3] *I Apol.* 32. 3–4. See H. Chadwick, 'Justin Martyr's Defence of Christianity', *Bull. of the John Rylands Library*, XLVII (March 1965), 275–97 (at p. 286).

[4] Melito cited by Eusebius, *HE* IV. 26. 7.

empire'.[1] Jesus' teaching would have been hindered by the outbreak of local wars, he adds, and the end of internecine conflicts enabled the preaching of peace by the disciples to be effective. Origen indeed looked forward to a time when all would speak one language and Christianity would be the universal religion.[2] Polytheism and polyarchy were symbols of the continuance of the confusion of Babel, the work of the demons whom Christ had come into the world to conquer.

Origen indeed was a critic of certain aspects of Roman history and Roman rule. The attempts by some of the emperors supported by the Senate and Roman people to persecute the Church aroused his anger,[3] and he urged civil disobedience against laws which sought to prevent the Christians worshipping God.[4] But his fundamental appraisal of the Empire was positive. The rule of Augustus, by fusing and federating previously warring communities into one empire, had brought humanity a step nearer its ultimate destiny of regaining the likeness of God lost at the Fall. Origen's disciple Eusebius had therefore a long tradition to draw upon when in the first decades of the fourth century he wrote his classic statements on the harmony of Church and state in history.

Eusebius lived and wrote at one of the great watersheds of Christian history. He was an eyewitness of the last stages of the Great Persecution in the East, and an established writer when it ended with the defeat of Maximin at the hands of Licinius in the spring of 313. After Nicaea in 325 he seems to have supplanted Hosius of Cordoba as Constantine's religious adviser and must be considered with his namesake of Nicomedia as the architect of Constantine's religious policy in the final period of his reign. His *Life of Constantine* and *Theophania*, both written near the end of his life in 339, are important commentaries on the religious situation in the Empire in the last half of Constantine's reign. Eusebius himself must be one of the very few individuals who have seen the apparently complete vindication of a theory of history and have also been in a position to guide events.

Eusebius saw the Roman Empire as established by Augustus as the result of God's direct intervention in history. In words which strikingly recall Philo's assessment of Augustus' work, Eusebius points out how before his victory there had been multitudes of quarrelling nations, 'Egypt, for instance, was a kingdom apart under its own ruler, and so were the Arabs, the Idumaeans, the Phoenicians, the Syrians and other countries; and nation rose up against nation, and city against city, and thousands of towns were besieged and thousands of men made captive in every region and country'.[5] Then with the simultaneous appearance of Augustus and Christ the 'multitude of rulers for the most part disappeared and peace covered all the earth, according to the prophecy whereof we are speaking which says directly of Christ "Now shall he be great to the ends of the earth. And this...shall be our peace"'. These really were the days foretold by the psalmist when 'the righteous shall flourish and abundance of peace: he shall have dominion from sea to sea and from the river to the ends of the earth' (Ps. lxxii. 7–8)[6]—and Eusebius was witness to the fact.

---

[1] *Contra Celsum* II. 30.   [2] *Ibid.* VIII. 72.
[3] *Ibid.* II. 79.   [4] *Ibid.* I. I.
[5] Eusebius, *Demonstr. Evangelica* VII. 2.   [6] *Ibid.*

28

The conversion of Constantine was an immense liberating event, denoting the utter discomfiture of Satan who in the previous three centuries had done his utmost through stirring up persecutions and heresies to delay the triumph of the race of Christians. Constantine had been designated God's instrument to proclaim his law to the world and himself could be regarded as a reflection of the Divine Reason. As such he stood 'at the helm of all the affairs of this world'.[1]

It was an optimistic view of events, and it rested on an intricate cohesive pattern of prophecy, history and political facts. Eusebius' own theological position is relevant, for he and his fellow Origenist bishops regarded Christ in the Scriptural terms of 'Way', 'Shepherd' and 'image' of the Father through whom man gained his destined goal of communion with and restoration to the likeness of God. Constantine by 'forming the Roman Empire, as in the days of old, into a single united whole bringing under his (and his son's) peaceful rule all of it'[2] was to bring this nearer. The emperor's death, however, in 337 ended these high hopes. Constantius, his son and successor, was altogether a man of meaner clay, and Julian was an apostate. Meantime, the great outsider in the Eusebian scheme of things, Athanasius, triumphed; for nearly a century Eusebius had no successor as an historian.

Meantime the West, through its writers Optatus of Milevis, Hosius of Cordoba and Hilary of Poitiers, was gradually moving towards an alternative view of the Roman Empire. Church and Empire were seen as parallel powers, separate from each other, but supreme in their own spheres. The pragmatist Optatus willingly conceded superiority to the empire on whom the Church depended for protection,[3] but those Westerners who considered carefully the implications of the doctrine of the Fall could recognize that even if the Roman Empire might be regarded figuratively as the successor of the Israelite state, it also had come into being as the result of sin, and its rulers, like the Israelite kings before them, must be subject to the spiritual powers. 'God', one author, albeit a Donatist, pointed out, 'had given the trumpet to the prophet and not to the king.'[4] The historiography implicit in this theory of the relations between the Church and the Empire was systematized as the result of the fall of Rome to Alaric in 410. Pagans were not slow to point to a Christian responsibility for an event which appeared to contemporaries as a catastrophe. 'When we used to make sacrifices to our gods', they said, 'Rome was flourishing. Now when one sacrifices to your God everywhere, and our sacrifices are forbidden, see what is happening to Rome.'[5] There were plenty of martyrs' bones, others claimed, but they could not avert the capture of the City.[6] This was the challenge that evoked Augustine's *De Civitate Dei*. It was written over a period of thirteen years, 413–26, a period in

---

[1] *Tricennial Oration* 1. 6. See also H. Eger, 'Kaiser und Kirche in der Geschichtestheologie Eusebs von Cäsarea', *ZNTW*, xxxviii (1939), 97–115 (especially pp. 114–15).

[2] Eusebius, *HE* x. 9. 6.

[3] Optatus, *De Schismate Donatistarum* iii. 3.

[4] Gaudentius of Thamugadi cited by Augustine, *Contra Gaudentium* 1. 35. 45. See my article 'The Roman Empire in the Eyes of the Western Schismatics', *Miscellanea Historiae Ecclesiasticae* (Louvain, 1961), pp. 9–22.

[5] Augustine, *Sermo* 296. 7.

[6] *Ibid.* 296. 6. Also *Ep.* 137. 20 and *De Civitate Dei* 1. 1.

which he was occupied with the formulation of his doctrine of Grace, and his doctrine of the Trinity, both of which may be expected to have influenced his work.

Augustine was not a systematic historian, but for this reason what he says about the Roman Empire is interesting, for it indicates the persistence of a continuous tradition of historical thought as well as of doctrine in the West. Thus in the first three books Augustine follows Minucius Felix and Lactantius by citing evidence to show that pagan Rome owed nothing to its gods, nor even to the actions of its traditional heroes. History was a reflection of the action of Providence. 'Everything', says Augustine, 'must be referred to divine providence.'[1] Human beings and institutions merely illustrated the actions of God, and this applied to the Roman Empire. Its greatness like that of its predecessors was by God's decision.[2] Like all secular governments it would perish. Only the heavenly city would endure. Hard though Augustine tries to refute the charge of fatalism, it is difficult to see in these instances the difference between the working out of God's foreknowledge and fate.[3]

The Roman Empire, however, was not the centre of Augustine's stage. Like other westerners he regarded human society itself as the product of sin, and the working-out of its history not so much as the advance from a lower to a higher plane, but the story of two parallel conditions or 'cities', the *Civitas terrena* and the *Civitas Dei*. Here Augustine is also drawing on previous western thought—Tertullian would have used the term 'camps' for his division of humanity but the idea is the same—but he gives that tradition a new interpretation. A generation before, the Donatist exegete Tyconius had pointed to the eternal division of mankind into the City of God or the City of the Devil according to their wills. Augustine changes 'wills' to 'loves', meaning the underlying will that determines an individual's single acts, but otherwise keeps Tyconius' scheme.[4] Whether a society belonged to one or the other City depended on the 'loves' of its individual members.[5] Thus, pagan Rome by definition must be assumed to belong to the *civitas terrena* because its 'love' was not directed towards God, and its history was strewn with calamities brought upon it by God's judgement. True, there were noble Romans, like Regulus, but the object of the state that they served was bad, namely lust of domination and conquest. These men were only 'less wicked' than the rest, an example to Christians of the standards to which even pagans might attain.[6]

Augustine pauses at the accession of Augustus. 'From (Pompey) the chain of civil wars extended to the second Caesar, afterwards called Augustus, in whose reign Christ was born. For even Augustus himself waged many civil wars and in these wars many of the foremost men perished, among them that skilful manipulator of the Republic, Cicero.'[7] Augustus in fact earns no other comment than, though he was a

[1] *De Civitate Dei* v. 9. 10. See C. N. Cochrane, *Christianity and Classical Culture* (Oxford, 1944), p. 479.   [2] *Ep.* 137.   [3] *De Civitate Dei* v. 9–11.
[4] See A. Pincherle's art. 'Da Ticonio a Sant'Agostino', *Ricerche Religiose*, 1 (1925), 443–66.
[5] Augustine, *De Civitate Dei* XIV. 28. See N. H. Baynes, 'The Political Ideas of St Augustine's *De Civitate Dei*', *Historical Association Pamphlet* (1949).
[6] *De Civitate Dei* I. 24, and v. 12–13: 'They who restrain baser lusts not by the power of the Holy Spirit...but by love of human praise are not indeed yet holy, but only less base.' *De Civitate Dei* III. 30. 3.

man of genius, he allowed Cicero to be killed. The contrast between Augustine's treatment of his accession and that of Eusebius is significant. Eusebius had a theory of progress in which man's free-will plays a decisive part. Man has been made by God 'a little lower than the angels' (Ps. viii. 5) and history recorded his return to an understanding of his true nature that he had lost at the Fall. In this process Augustus and Constantine were key figures. For Augustine, however, the Fall predestined all but a few of mankind to Judgement and the prospect of everlasting torment. The historical process merely sifted those saved by Grace from the remainder. Neither Augustus nor Constantine therefore was important in his own right, for only God influenced events.

Christianity, however, did make some difference even to the destiny of the Roman Empire. Augustine was prepared to concede this. Emperors could repent, as Nebuchadnezzar had done,[1] and if they imitated the pious examples of Constantine and Theodosius, they also could assure themselves of true happiness. Augustine would have said they would cease to be part of the *civitas terrena*. Such happiness could only be found, however, in the service of the Church as the executor of its will.[2] If there were still to be two swords, the sharper always belonged to the Church.

Augustine had set out to refute the pagans. Though he was interested in the history of Rome, and Roman enough to be concerned with its future, his primary concern had been the working of God's providence for humanity. Just as his doctrine of Grace embraced the whole of humanity, so did his theory of history. It was left to his pupil, Paulus Orosius, to give a succinct account of world history from the point of view of western orthodoxy which was to be one of the textbooks of the European Middle Ages. He wrote his seven books of *History against the Pagans*, on Augustine's instruction, in 417 when he had returned to Hippo from a somewhat chequered anti-Pelagian mission to Palestine. He obviously enjoyed his task, and he worked rapidly, ransacking pagan authors for scandalous facts in Roman history. Disasters, earthquakes, hailstorms, plagues of flies were all grist to his mill, as also was a numerological symbolism based on far-fetched coincidence and too literal a belief in the importance of the number Seven in human affairs. His brief, as he describes it, was 'to set down from all sources, gleaned from histories and chronicles down to the present day, whatever disasters resulted from wars or catastrophes, from plague and famine, or horrible experiences from earthquakes or untoward occurrences from floods or fiery eruptions, and the dire effects of thunderbolts and hailstorms, or miseries engendered from parricides and crises in the past centuries'.[3] The object of this research was to show that the present ills were not as bad as those of the past, and hence pagan complaints against the Christians regarding the fall of Rome were without foundation.

The result was an *a priori* interpretation of events as basically determinist as any Marxist could hope for. It was rigidly schematic, the present age being divided into that of four great empires, of which the eastern (Babylonian) and western (Roman) were the greatest, but whose supremacy had been intercalated by two lesser

---

[1] In contrast to the Donatist contention that all kings were persecutors. Augustine, *Contra Litteras Petiliani* II. 210–11, written a decade before the *De Civitate*. See Baynes, art. cit. pp. 12–13.
[2] *De Civitate Dei* V. 24–6.   [3] Orosius, *Historia*, Prologue 10.

empires, that of the Carthaginians representing the south, and the Macedonians the north. This symmetrical arrangement was supported by an equally symmetrical chronology. The message which Orosius wished to preach was that all secular power was derived from sin and characterized by lust of conquest and the like. The disasters that characterized the pre-Christian age were just chastisements, and these chastisements had in fact grown proportionately milder as the world had become more Christian. The civil wars of the fourth century were not half so destructive as those in the Republican period, and the fall of Rome had been characterized by courtesies on the part of the conquerors unheard-of in the time of Brennus.[1] Orosius here and elsewhere indicates some sense of progress in history but this progress was never more than halting. Augustus' reign had indeed coincided with the Incarnation, and for just a few years the Roman world had enjoyed peace.[2] The respite over, it was back to calamity. Interestingly enough he is fairer in his estimate of Tiberius than the fourth-century pagan historian Eutropius.[3] But progress is very slow. The conversion of Constantine does not mark an epoch in world history. Constantine is given, so to speak, a good press, his execution of Crispus and Fausta is excused, but to Orosius his main importance is that he follows on another 'Christian' emperor, Philip (244–9).[4] One feels that he wishes to emphasize by his brevity and dry descriptive cataloguing of events that the Roman state and all its emperors and their deeds would pass away when God so declared.

In one important particular he looks beyond Augustine. The latter had hoped for the purging and reformation of Rome and the Romans; Orosius saw that the barbarians were now a political force in their own right.[5] In an interesting concluding chapter he looks forward to a sort of Romano-Gothic commonwealth obedient to the command of God and therefore prosperous. Athaulph, he relates, from being resolved to substitute Gothia for Romania changed his policy to one of restoring and increasing the Roman name through Gothic power, 'habereturque apud posteros Romanae restitutionis auctor, postquam esse non poterat immutator'.[6]

In his limited way Orosius had been an optimist. The last historian of the western world was not. Salvian, the presbyter of Marseille, wrote c. 440, and in the generation that separated him from Orosius the Romans had been beaten in Gaul and Spain, and Britain and most of Africa lost to them. Consequently, Salvian's view of God's judgement on the Roman Empire differed considerably from Orosius'. For him the situation was all black. This was not on account of anything in Rome's past; in fact he reserves a few words of praise for the heroes of the Roman Republic, the Cincinnati, Fabii and Fabricii, on the grounds that they were poor, hard-working men who directed all their efforts towards the common good.[7] Rather, the judgement of God

---

[1] *Ibid.* II. 19. 4.   [2] *Ibid.* VI. 20.
[3] *Ibid.* VII. 4. He attributes to Tiberius a plan rejected by the Senate of declaring Christ a god ('ut Christus deus haberetur'). Tertullian, *Apol.* V. 2 and XXI. 24 is probably his source for the story.   [4] *Historia* VII. 28.
[5] *Ibid.* VII. 43. See H. J. Diesner, 'Orosius und Augustinus', *Acta antiqua Academiae Scientiarum Hungaricae*, XI, 1 (1963), 89–102.   [6] *Ibid.* VII. 43. 6.
[7] *De Gubernatione Dei* (ed. and tr. E. M. Sanford), I. 2. He also praises 'even Greek philosophers' who went without luxuries and offered themselves to death for greed of glory rather than of wealth.

32

was directed to the extortion, corruption, luxury, and immorality of the Roman Christians of his age. The latter were entirely to blame for their own misfortunes, 'kindling the fire of celestial wrath and arousing the flames by which we are burned'.[1] The barbarians, free from these vices and only unwittingly heretics, were exempt from God's wrath and therefore had been uniformly successful. With Salvian one experiences the full force of the pessimism implied in the phrase 'the last century of the Western Empire'.[2]

A combination of personal experience and doctrinal tradition had brought about the western view of the Roman empire. It was to have an enormous effect on medieval thought. Without the De Civitate Dei and Orosius' seven books of History against the Pagans the outlook that led to the conflict between the Empire and the papacy would have been virtually impossible. It was an idea of history, however, that paid scant attention to facts. It remained schematic and impersonal. It dealt with universal and eternal contrasts between formalized types of peoples and institutions determined by a legalistic eschatology inherited from Rabbinic Judaism. Men and human progress, as such, hardly entered Augustinian calculations, for all tended towards a predetermined end directed through the inscrutable mind of God.

For the West then, Orosius and Salvian were symbols of their age. It is difficult to imagine the latter as a contemporary of Socrates and Sozomen, and his De Gubernatione Dei written perhaps in the same year as the Ecclesiastical Histories of these two lawyers of Constantinople. With their serenity, rigorous fairness towards their characters, sense of truth and accuracy, and healthy scepticism towards the pretensions of the ecclesiastics of their day, they demonstrate between them the enduring sense of security which was already characterizing the Eastern capital. Byzantium had a thousand years to run; the Roman West perished in 476. Socrates stops his history at A.D. 439 because he says things were going so well for the Church that there was nothing more to tell.[3] Like the doctrine of the Trinity he takes for granted the partnership of Empire and Church and the emperor's right to summon Church Councils.[4] He judges men and events on their merits. Julian and Valens get their deserts, but there is no universal condemnation of the past, and no sense of divine judgement and vengeance. Theirs is an historiography which is perhaps less a continuation of Eusebius than of Thucydides. In historiography as well as in matters of doctrine East and West had already gone their separate ways. Chalcedon, a dozen years later, merely confirmed the fact.

GONVILLE AND CAIUS COLLEGE

[1] De Gubernatione Dei, VIII. I.
[2] See S. Dill's view of Salvian in Roman Society in the Last Century of the Western Empire (London, 1919), pp. 319–22.
[3] Eccl. Hist. VIII. 48.   [4] Ibid. Prologue to Bk v.

X

The Roman Empire
in the Eyes of Western Schismatics
during the Fourth Century A. D.

« What has the Emperor to do with the Church ? » Donatus of Carthage's famous question to Paul and Macarius, the emissaries of the Emperor Constans in 347, was more than the outburst of a disappointed man. It was a theological and political challenge, posing in its sharpest form the problem of Church-State relations, which since the Council of Nicaea had been confronting Christians in the Roman Empire. Whereas in the East, Constantine's claim to the bishops at Nicaea to be « your fellow-servant and one of your number » [1]), had been received without apparent resentment, in the West, major re-appraisals of the hitherto prevalent Christian tradition were becoming necessary. There, the attitude towards the Roman Empire had been inspired largely by the Old Testament and late Jewish literature. It had emphasised the contrasts between the People of the True Israel and the World. It held no place for the ruler, absolute in religious as well as secular affairs, and under the pagan emperors the defiance of the Maccabees against the Seleucid kings served as a model for the Christian's relations to the Roman authorities [2]). Donatus' approach to theology was conservative, the

---

[1]) SOCRATES, *Eccl. Hist.*, I. 9. See S. L. GREENSLADE, *Church and State from Constantine to Theodosius*, London, 1954, p. 18.

[2]) Cf. for North Africa in the Great Persecution, Secundus of Tigisis' claims, cited in AUGUSTINE, *Breviculus Collationis cum Donatistis*, III, 13, 25, and the *Acta Saturnini* 16 (*P. L.*, VIII, 700B).

faithful upholder of the traditions of the bishop-martyr Cyprian, and this traditionalism must be taken into account in considering the violence of his attitude towards the Emperor Constans, even though the latter was an avowed supporter of Nicene orthodoxy. But, whether by the middle of the fourth century this anti-Imperial tradition was still representative of Christians in the West as a whole is another matter, which it is the object of this paper to discuss.

As is well known, by the time Donatus had been disappointed of receiving similar treatment to Athanasius, and recognised as sole bishop of Carthage, wholly different concepts of Church-State relationships were taking shape in the Latin and Greek-speaking parts of the Empire. The Eastern view was derived from the Origenist understanding of Logos theology. Optimistic in its premises, it interpreted human history as one of gradual ascent towards ideal harmony with God. All things were made by God. He ruled the Kosmos as well as Israel. The interests of both could be reconciled [3]). The birth of Christ in the reign of Augustus had seen the end of warring national states and the establishment of the *pax romana* [4]). The conversion of Constantine was nothing less than a realisation of the secular hope of men, the dream of perpetual and universal peace under the authority of the Emperor, who derived his own power from God. Constantine, to cite Eusebius of Caeserea's panegyric, « receives and bears the image of the Supreme Kingship, and so steers and directs in imitation of his Superior, the helm of all the affairs of this world » [5]), that is, religious as well as secular rule. Constantius II accepted this view of his position as Emperor without question.

The West had no Philo, no Origen, and no Eusebius of Caesarea. Far from having been foreseen as an intelligible step in the divine plan for human salvation, the notion of a Christian Caesar and Roman Empire had been looked upon as contradictions in terms. « The fact that Christ rejected an earthly kingdom », declared Tertullian, « should be enough to convince you that all secular powers

---

[3]) See E. PETERSON, *Der Monotheismus als politisches Problem*, Leipzig, 1935, p. 30 ff.

[4]) ORIGEN, *Contra Celsum*, II, 30; EUSEBIUS, *Demonstratio Evangelica*, III, 7, 30; E. PETERSON, *op. cit.*, p. 66. For a less flattering view of the same events, HIPPOLYTUS, *Comment. in Danielem*, IV, 9.

[5]) EUSEBIUS, *De laudibus Constantini*, I, 6 Cf. C. N. COCHRANE, *Christianity and Classical Culture*, Oxford, 1944, p. 185.

and dignities are not merely alien from, but hostile to, God » [6]).
« There can be no reconciliation between the camp of light and
the camp of darkness. No man can serve two masters, God and
Caesar » [7]). Hippolytus, more radical even than Tertullian, associated the rule of the Roman Empire with that of the Pauline « man
of sin ». Both would end together, he declared [8]). These are strong
words, and they were re-inforced by an almost complete cultural
barrier which encouraged the rejection of the Classical literary heritage by the convert to Christianity. The Western reaction to Constantine's conversion was therefore likely to be confused. Long-standing
ideas had to be modified. Nowhere was this more the case than in
North Africa.

Inevitably, the relationship between Church and State played a
considerable part in the long struggle between the Donatists and
their opponents. At the same time, the existence of a strongly-en-
trenched theoretical opposition to the authority of the Emperor
should warn the historian against attributing its continuance by the
Donatists to the circumstance that Constantine rejected their views.
It is difficult to see how the Emperor could, with the best will, have
harmonised his own concept of « the very office of a prince to cast
out error and... to cause men to agree together to follow true religion » [9]), with the eschatological views of the Church and its government which Donatus and his followers represented. The fact, however, that he did not do so, and supported the Caecilianist minority consistently, rendered the continuance of the third century attitude towards the State, among the Donatists inevitable. It also led
to the emergence of a loyalist and pro-Imperial sentiment among the
Caecilianists. Here, as in the doctrine of the Church, African Catholicism breaks with previous African tradition.

The new trend among the African Catholics is illustrated in the

---

[6]) TERTULLIAN, De Idololatria, 18 (C. S. E. L., XX, 53).

[7]) Ibid., 19. See, C. N. COCHRANE, op. cit., p. 213.

[8]) HIPPOLYTUS, Comment. in Danielem, IV, 7 (ed. BONWETSCH and ACHELIS).
See, S. MAZZARINO, La Democratizzazione della Cultura nel Basso Impero, in
XIe Congrès Internat. des Sciences historiques, Rapports, II, Antiquité, p. 37.

[9]) Letter to Domitius Celsus, A. D. 316 (ZIWSA, App. VII, p. 212): « Quid potius
agi a me pro instituto meo ipsiusque principis munere oporteat, quam ut discussis
erroribus omnibusque temeritatibus amputatis, veram religionem universos, con-
cordemque simplicitatem atque meritam omnipotenti Deo culturam praesentare per-
ficiam ? ».

striking passage of Optatus of Milevis, *circa* 365, replying to Donatus denial of the State's right of intervention in Church affairs. He asserted, « For the State (*respublica*) is not in the Church, but the Church is in the State, that is, the Roman Empire, which Christ in the Song of Songs calls Lebanon, where there is holy priesthood and chastity and virginity, which do not exist among the barbarian nations, or, if they do, are not safe » [10]). If St Paul urged Christians to pray for their pagan rulers, how much more was this service owed to Christian ones ? Optatus thus emphasized the decisive character of the change brought about by Constantine's conversion. He even appears to envisage the subordination of the Church to the State. In the Catholic Council of Carthage of 348, Constans was praised as being « the most religious emperor » and his emissaries were « servants of God » [11]). The African Catholics were, however, a privileged minority, dependent on Imperial favour for their existence [12]). Even moderate African opinion, represented by the Donatist exegete Tyconius, was ranged against them. Such views, he said represented members of an apostate church in the service of the Devil. These were clerics who « relying on royal favour had renounced Christ and confessed through their mouths and works, 'We have no king but Caesar' » [13]). Indeed, apart from the Roman Ambrosiaster near the end of the century, no Western theologian followed Optatus' lead in expressing so whole-heartedly the pro-Imperial point of view [14]).

Augustine himself is more cautious. « Christian times », he tells the Donatists, were different from pagan times. There could now be just persecutions directed by the authorities against those who disobeyed their righteous ordinances [15]). The Emperor was a brave sol-

---

[10]) OPTATUS OF MILEVIS, *De Schismate*, III, 3, p. 74.

[11]) *Concilium Carthaginense*, anno 348. Proem. *P. L.*, VIII, 774 D.

[12]) On the numerous African Catholic bishops thronging the Court of Constans at this time, Canon 8 of Council of Serdica (MANSI, *Concilia*, III, 67).

[13]) Tyconius, cited from BEATUS OF LIBANA, *In Apocalypsin Comment*. (ed. FLÓREZ), p. 409: « Non est... alius rex aut aliud regnum, cuius sint falsi fratres, quam mundi, et in Christum se dicunt credere et diabolo deserviunt, et regali amicitia freti ex se et ipsis confitentibus Christo recusato et veluti lege damnato ore confiteantur et operibus dicant: Nos non habemus regem nisi Caesarem » (See, T. HAHN, *Tyconius-Studien*, Leipzig, 1900, p. 72).

[14]) AMBROSIASTER, *Quaestiones* 35 and 91 (*C. S. E. L.*, L, p. 63 and 157), See S. L. GREENSLADE, *Church and State from Constantine to Theodosius*, p. 32.

[15]) AUGUSTINE, *Contra Cresconium*, II, 22, 27; *Contra Litteras Petiliani*, II, 92, 205, *Ep*. 105, 11, and 185, 5.

X

dier of Christ [16]), but at the same time he was a servant of the Church, only truly happy insofar as he served the Church's interest. Such a one was Theodosius I, who « did not cease to help the troubled Church against the impious by most just and merciful laws [17]). This being the case, Augustine was able to identify in general terms the cause of the Catholic Church with that of *Romanitas* in Africa. He insists on the virtue of the framework of Roman laws and institutions in which that Church was living. The towns and their magistrates are Roman towns and Roman magistrates [18]). He reproaches the Donatists for being supporters of the barbarian insurgents. Firmus and Gildo were denounced as « savage enemies of the Romans » [19]) ; and through the Circumcellions, the Donatists were also disruptors of the existing, divinely ordained, social order [20]).

The Donatists certainly had backed the losing side in both the great native rebellions of 372-75 and 397-98. But the evidence would lead us to think that their attitude towards their times was not entirely motivated by material and political considerations. Their appeals to Constantine in 313, and to Julian in 362 indicate that they were not uncompromisingly disloyal to the Roman Empire. One must look for other considerations which would account for their apparent inconsistencies. We would suggest, perhaps, that their attitude was the same conditional loyalty which we have already found among the African Christians of the previous century. Over the years, however, they had reduced this standpoint to a coherent and logical concept based on theological rather than political ideas.

Thus, the world-situation in which the Donatists found themselves corresponded to the *saeculum* of apocalyptic literature [21]). It was a finite world-age, dominated by the Devil and preceding his

---

[16]) AUGUSTINE, *Enarr. in Ps.*, 21, 4 (*P. L.*, XXXVI, 172): « Non est fortior miles (Christi) quam imperator ».

[17]) AUGUSTINE, *De Civitate Dei*, V, 24. See N. H. BAYNES, *The Political Aspects of St. Augustine's De Civitate Dei* (Historical Association Pamphlets, 104), 1949. p. 12.

[18]) *Contra Litteras Petiliani*, II, 19, 43; II, 83, 184 and *Epp.*, 34, 35. The Roman authorities are « Ordinatae potestates » and Hippo was a « Civitas Romana ».

[19]) *Contra Ep. Parmeniani*, I, 11, 17: « Hostem immanissimum Romanorum ».

[20]) *Ep.* 185, 4, 15; cf. H. J. DIESNER, *Studien zur Gesellschaftslehre und sozialen Haltung Augustins*, Halle, 1954, p. 67 ff.

[21]) Not an uncompromisingly dualist assumption, for the *saeculum* would have an end, and the Devil, or anti-Christ was subject to God.

final assault on the world. The Church dwelt in this world but was contrasted with it, and was surrounded by false brethren and hypocrites who sought to destroy it [22]. The earthly rulers were the *principes saeculi* or *reges saeculi*, and though it was not impossible for them to desert the *civitas diaboli* and accept the Christian way of life, the influences against them succeeding in doing so were strong [23]. Tyconius makes the point that the will alone decides a ruler's place either in the *civitas Dei* or *civitas diaboli*, and that earthly rulers might be found in both [24]. But generally, as in Hippolytus' time, Babylon, the world and the Roman Empire coincided as the *civitas diaboli*. In these circumstances the Donatists accepted the existing age as one of persecution [25]. Oppression of the Church was one of the signs of the approach of anti-Christ, and beyond that the triumph of the Righteous at the Divine Judgement. The personal conversion of Constantine did not alter the general situation, especially if the Emperor allied himself with the Caecilianists. Thus in *circa* 320, the Donatist writer of the *Passio Donati* claimed that the only difference between his own day and the preceding period was that the Devil, « finding that he could not conquer Christians in open persecution attempted to circumvent them by cunning frauds » [26]. The same obloquy was meted out to Constans and his court in 347 [27]. In the post- as well as the pre-Constantinian era, the Devil was the prime mover, the secular powers were his pawns. So too, a century later, the Donatist chroniclers who wrote successive editions of the *liber Genealogus* at Carthage between 409 and 463, associated indiscriminately the sufferings of the Donatists due to

---

[22]) Tyconius, *In Apocalypsin* (Beatus, p. 316): « Diximus quatuor angelos bipartitos esse, et invicem mixtos, id est ecclesiam et regna mundi : curabimus oportune commemorare mundi regna, vel maxime presens regnum, in medio esse ecclesiae, per orbem in falsos fratres ». See T. Hahn, *op. cit.*, p. 25.

[23]) Petilian of Constantine, cited by Augustine, *Contra Litteras Petiliani*, II, 92, 202. Also, *Gesta Collationis Carthaginensis*, III, 258 (P. L., XI, 1413 B).

[24]) Tyconius, *op. cit.*, Beatus, p. 506: « Ecce duas civitates, unam Dei, unam diaboli... et in utrasque reges terrae ministrant ».

[25]) Gaudentius of Thamugadi, cited by Augustine, *Contra Gaudentium*, I, 20, 22.

[26]) *Passio Donati* (P. L., VIII, 753) « [Diabolus] eos quos aperta persecutione superare non potuit, callida fraude circumvenire molitus est ».

[27]) *Passio Marculi*, persecution came from « de Constantis regis tyrannica domo et de palatii ejus arce », P. L., VIII, 761 A. The inspiration was the « Rabies antichristi ».

Honorius' rescripts of 405 and those of the Christians during the pagan era. The last compiler, writing long after the Vandal conquest, even discovered that the numbers of the Beast in *Rev.* 13 should be interpreted as an anagram for the name of Geneseric [28]). Both the Roman emperor and the Vandal king was a « rex saeculi ». Both could be regarded as hated precursors of anti-Christ.

The role of the secular ruler was a strictly limited one. It could be defined as the maintenance of freedom of religion and earthly peace, though the latter was portrayed as of only limited felicity [29]). The first requirement, that of freedom of religion, restricted political obedience, but once secured, the second duty assured the state of the passive support of the Donatist community. This accepted, the Donatist appeals to the Emperor, even Julian, to give them religious liberty become intelligible. Thus too, Gaudentius, bishop of Thamugadi (Timgad) when besieged by the Imperial tribune, Dulcitius, in his cathedral in 420, wished the emperor success in governing his dominions [30]), while pointing out that he had no right to coerce people in religious matters [31]). « God gave the trumpet of command to prophets and not to kings » [32]) he added. Petilian of Constantine too, could advise the emperor to use his soldiers against « Scythians and barbarians » and not Christians [33]). Even so, persecution unleashed by the State was not to be met by rebellion but by martyrdom. Penance and suffering were the hall-marks of Christian life, not recourse to arms [34]). In his extremity, Gaudentius could declare that « God never expected the aid of earthly military might » [35]) ; and that « Christ sent fishermen, not soldiers, to spread the faith ». He quoted the example of Razias in *II Macc.*, XIV, 42 to show that even suicide was justified, in order to avoid contamination with the ido-

---

[28]) *Liber Genealogus* (ed. MOMMSEN, *M. G. H., AA.,* IX), p. 195.

[29]) Gaudentius, cited by AUGUSTINE, in *Contra Gaudentium*, I, 24, 27. « Saeculi enim pax inter animos gentium dissidentes armis et belli exitu foederatur ».

[30]) AUGUSTINE, *Contra Gaudentium*, I, 8, 9.

[31]) *Ibid.*, I, 7, 8 and I, 33, 42.

[32]) AUGUSTINE, *Contra Gaudentium*, I, 34, 44.

[33]) *Contra Litteras Petiliani*, II, 85, 188.

[34]) Tyconius describes penance as « secret martyrdom », « Duo sunt genera martyrum, unum aperte per gladium, aliud in occulto per poenitentiam » (BEATUS, p. 287, HAHN, *op. cit.*, p. 47-48).

[35]) *Contra Gaudentium*, I, 35, 45; cf. I, 34, 44: « Salvator animarum Dominus Christus ad insinuandam fidem, piscatores non milites misit ».

latory of the existing age, even if this had been commanded by a ruler [36]).

It was therefore not the Roman Empire that the Donatists declared themselves against, but the age itself. « Odio saeculi gaudemus » [37]). They looked beyond this age towards the peace of Christ. This was not merely tactical, the mood of the moment, but the result of logically worked out belief. They regarded themselves as the heirs to the whole saga of persecution and righteous suffering which had typified the struggle between Christ and anti-Christ since the beginning of time. Like the writer of *IV Maccabees* (XVIII, 11 ff.), they interpreted their own roles in history as that of the heirs of Abel, of the prophets slain by unbelievers, down to the persecutions of their own day. This outlook was uniformly held among the Donatists, and is represented in extant sermons, tracts, and *acta martyrum* of the fourth century. The best example comes in an encyclical letter to his clergy by Petilian of Constantine. It forms part of a long, turgid, and confused requisitory against « the kings of this world, in whom Christianity has never found anything save envy towards her » [38]). In this, Petilian relates the persecution of the Maccabees by Antiochus, of John the Baptist's murder by Herod, and the trial and crucifixion of Jesus by the Jews and Pontius Pilate to the persecutions suffered by the Christians. He makes no break between those conducted by Nero, Trajan, Geta, Valerian and Diocletian and those by « Macarius and Ursacius » directed by Christian Emperors against the Donatists. All were acts against the saints to be avenged by God [39]). There was no place for « Christian times » in this philosophy.

In all these events, moreover, the secular rulers were abetted by apostates, whom Tyconius twenty years before had characterised as a « Church of Judas », and which also had existed from all time alongside the Church of Christ. This apostate body now instigated rulers « who might desire to be Christians », to persecute. « Nor indeed does the hand of the butcher glow, save at the instigation of your tongue », Petilian tells the Catholics [40]). In this majestic yet ter-

---

[36]) *Ibid.*, I, 28, 32.
[37]) *Ibid.*, I, 26, 29. Note too, the title of Vitellius Afer's defence of Donatism: « De eo quos odio sunt mundo, servi Dei », GENNADIUS, *De Scriptoribus Ecclesiasticis*, 4 (*P. L.*, LIX, 1059).
[38]) AUGUSTINE, *Contra Litteras Petiliani*, II, 92, 202 (*P. L.*, XLIII, 322).
[39]) *Ibid.*, col. 323.
[40]) AUGUSTINE, *Contra Litteras Petiliani*, II, 92, 202 (*P. L.*, XLIII, 324). See the

rible panorama of history, the outside world, whether represented by the Roman Empire or later, by the Vandal kingdom, was merely the expression of a hostile age destined, like the persecutors themselves, to perish utterly. If the Donatist was a rebel, he had no theoretical reason for taking up arms. He could remain passive, sure of ultimate vindication. His outlook towards the Roman Empire was theological, directed to the Last Days, forming an integral part of an exclusive doctrine of the Church and his hope of individual predestination to salvation.

One final point in this theology must be stressed. Towards the end of his tirade, Petilian links the concept of righteous suffering with that of poverty. « So too », he tells the Catholics, « you do not cease to murder us who are just and poor » [41]) and he goes on to warn Donatists who gave way to pressure, « out of love for their worldly goods » of the consequences of their act [42]). The equation is an interesting one, for among the Circumcellions the martyr's *agon* had become extended to the overthrow of anti-Christ represented by landowners as well as by idolatrous officials. Here, we find the Donatist outlook at one with that most enigmatic of Latin Christian writers, namely Commodian. To both, human fortunes would be reversed in apocalyptic fire [43]).

Were the Donatists isolated conservative fanatics whom the tide of events had left behind ? When one looks at the tracts written by Western leaders during the crisis years of 355-361 it is clear that this was not the case. The fact that Constantius' attempt to impose a non-Nicene formula on the Western Church in these years was short-lived, does not lessen the significance of the outburst of anti-Imperial feeling which this produced. In these years, there were repeated on a lesser scale the tensions among Western Christians which had characterised the period immediately after the Great Persecution and had resulted in the Donatist schism. The reply of Lucifer of Cagliari and Hilary of Poitiers to the defection of powerful bishops

interesting discussion of this passage in J. P. BRISSON, *Autonomisme et Christianisme dans l'Afrique romaine*, Paris, 1958, p. 376-377. Brisson compares Petilian's reservation that the Emperors might want to become Christian with Tertullian's protestations of loyalty towards the Roman Empire (*Apol.*, 32).

[41]) AUGUSTINE, *Contra Litteras Petiliani*, II, 92, 202 (*P. L.*, XLIII, 324).

[42]) *Ibid.*, II, 98, 225.

[43]) See J. P. BRISSON, *op. cit.*, p. 393 ff.

such as Saturninus of Arles and Epictetus of Centumcellae [44]), was similar in form and ferocity to the Donatist reaction to Caecilian and his supporters. These men were regarded as apostates. They were deserters to a religion which was not Christianity, but like the paganism of the persecutors fifty years before, was sponsored by the Emperor. Not only was the attack as unrelenting, but many of the ideas expressed by Constantius' opponents in the West were the same as those of the Donatists fifty years before. That the schism led by Lucifer of Cagliari, probably in opposition to Athanasius' policy of reconciling Old and New Nicenes after the Council of Alexandria in 362, did not become an Italian and Gallic Donatism, was due largely to the fact that the underlying Western doctrine of the Church and of Church-State relations in these provinces was still as exclusive and uncompromising as it had been in the previous century.

The Luciferians were Donatists in embryo. The same problems of the nature of the Church and its place in a hostile world which gripped Donatists and Catholics in Africa agitated them also. In the Luciferian and Orthodox spokesmen which Jerome wrote up in his *Dialogus Contra Luciferianos, circa* 378, much turns on the question of admission to the Church. Was Arian baptism valid ? The Luciferian begins, like his Donatist contemporary, with the assertion that « the entire universe belongs to the devil », and that, « the Church has become a brothel » [45]). Heretics were the equivalent of pagans, their meeting-place were « camps of the devil » [46]) and in consequence, their clergy could not be accepted without being reduced to penitent lay status and their laymen would be re-baptised [47]). These phrases and actions both remind one strongly of North Africa. So too does the exclusive view of the Church, in strict logic reduced to the real salt of the earth, namely Lucifer and his followers. The Catholics are blamed here also, for « opening the camp to the enemy » [48]).

---

[44]) LUCIFER, *De non conveniendo cum Haereticis* (*P. L.*, XIII, 777 C).

[45]) JEROME, *Dialogus contra Luciferianos* 1, *P. L.*, XXIII, col. 155: « Asserebat quippe universum mundi esse diaboli, et ut jam familiare est eis dicere, factum de Ecclesia lupanar ».

[46]) *Dialogus* 3 (*P. L.*, XXIII, 157 A).

[47]) *Ibid.* 4: « Recipimus laicos, quoniam nemo convertetur, si se scieret rebaptizandum » (col. 158 B).

[48]) *Ibid.* 10: « Vos hosti castra traditis », col, 165 D.

Lucifer's surviving writings, compiled before his breach with his colleagues, also show a remarkably similar theological approach to his environment to that which prevailed on the other side of the Mediterranean. Here, too, the Roman Empire is represented as part of the *saeculum*. Constantius himself is identified variously with the precursor of anti-Christ, an idolator and an apocalyptic beast [49]), just as his brother had been identified by the writer of the Donatist *Passio Marculi* some ten years before [50]). Thus, naturally, his intervention into ecclesiastical affairs must be resisted, and like the Donatists, Lucifer is never tired of citing as justification for his attitude the parallel of the Maccabaean rebellion against Antiochus [51]). The latter was regarded as a « persecutor nostrae religionis » [52]) and his times, like those of Constantius, were under the direct sway of antichrist [53]). Lucifer clearly considered the Christian Church of his day as the lineal descendant of the persecuted Jews in the Seleucid era [54]). Though he lacks the pungency of Donatus' attack, he leaves no doubt that he regarded the Church's duty of obedience to the laws of the Empire as limited, that Constantius was no « bishop of bishops » [55]), that on the analogy of the Old Testament prophets which, like the Donatists, he uses constantly, the bishops of the living God had the right and positive duty of command over the Roman Emperor [56]). If need be, they must defy him, together with the strength of the Roman Empire [57]). If they failed to get their way, then martyrdom was the only course. However, from the quotations from *I Maccabees* which Lucifer cites (especially *I Macc.*, II, 11, etc.) [58]) it is clear that he was prepared to go a good deal farther along the

---

[49]) LUCIFER, *De non conveniendo cum haereticis, Pro Sancto Athanasio* and *Moriendo esse pro Dei filio, P. L.*, XIII, 781, 783, 911, 1018.

[50]) *Passio Marculi (P. L.*, VIII, 761D).

[51]) E. g. in *De non Parcendo in Deum delinquentibus*, col. 964-967.

[52]) *De Non Parcendo*, 958 B.

[53]) For the survival of this view in the West until the end of the century, see Q. JULIUS HILARIANUS, *De Mundi Duratione Libellus*, XVII (*P. L.*, XIII, 1105 B).

[54]) *De non Parcendo in Deum delinquentibus*, col. 963 and 1006. Constantius hardly acted like Antiochus, contenting himself with surprised protests against Lucifer's insults, and pointing out that he had, after all, survived a goodly time !

[55]) *Moriendum esse pro Dei Filio*, col. 1032 C.

[56]) *De non Parcendo*, col. 957 B: « Quae hic tibi injuria fit a nobis ? quae ingeritur Imperatori Romano contumelia ab antistitibus Dei vivi ».

[57]) *Ibid.*, 963 B. Also, *Moriendum esse pro Dei filio*, 1037 A.

[58]) *De non Parcendo*, col. 960-961.

path of open rebellion than were the Donatist leaders. What would
have happened to Constantius if, he asks, he had fallen into the
hands of Mattathias or Phineas ? [59]). In any event, Constantius was
doomed as a blasphemer and apostate to divine vengeance.

At the same time, for all his abuse of the emperor, and the long
quotations justifying rebellion to his authority, Lucifer and his followers lacked the theological depth which their Donatist contemporaries possessed. In Lucifer, there is none of the considered relationship that we find among the Donatists between persecution and
the Christian's call to a life guided by the Holy Spirit, that was being
preached by Tyconius and even by Petilian. There is no theory of
martyrdom in Lucifer, only the lengthy assertion of its necessity in
face of an impious tyrant. Implicitly, he stands for the same principles as his Donatist contemporaries, but he prefers personal invec-
tive to theology. Only when his followers take the step of breaking
with the majority do we find the glimmerings of a system, and that
system follows the same lines as Donatus', namely opposition to
the contemporary world, and rejection of an « apostate Church »
which had sold the pass to the enemy.

The crisis, then, which followed the Councils of Arles and
Milan showed that the Donatist view of Church-State relations was
no mere aberration. It brought to the surface tendencies which
existed in Western theology as a whole, based on presuppositions
alien to both the Eastern and the African Catholic viewpoints. The
West had not reconciled itself to « Christian times », and did not
know how to do so. Confronted with the representation of Constantius as an idolatrous « apostate to Arianism », many Western bishops
reacted to Imperial policy in the same way as had Donatus to the
« idolatrous mission » of Paul and Macarius only ten years before.
The African Catholics with their loyalism and frequent attendance
at Court were out of line with this thought. The logical conclusion of
the Western theology of the Church at this stage was Donatism.

Though not all went so far as the Luciferians and broke communion with the majority, the attitude of many of the Western clergy towards the secular power was expressed by Hilary, when he wrote
his *Liber Contra Constantium Imperatorem* in 361. Here, there is not
only abuse of the emperor as « antichrist » (ch. 2) but more significantly, the view that his rule was a direct continuation of the age

[59]) *Ibid.*, col. 962.

of persecution. Constantius was the heir of Nero, Decius and Maximian. Only now, the Devil used guile and not force [60]). All this has
the ring of the Donatist martyrologists and of Petilian of Constantine
and his fellows. No wonder that in the early fifth century these found
justification for their doctrine of the Church in Hilary's writings [61]).

This brief analysis suggests that on both sides of the Mediterranean the adoption of Christianity as the religion of the Empire
produced a profound theological crisis. The Donatist majority among
African Christians were heirs to the doctrine of the Church held by
Tertullian and Cyprian and continued to express the resultant dualism
of relationships uncompromisingly. There might be co-belligerence
between individual rulers and the Church, but never an alliance.
Sooner or later the Devil would re-assert his sway. Constantius' religious policy in the West revealed that these same principles were
held by the majority of the Western Church leaders also and, indeed,
continued to be held by some until the end of the century [62]). No
one in the crisis of 355-361 expressed views concernig the Empire
similar to those of Optatus of Milevis. We may detect therefore, a
certain unity between fundamental attitudes of mind held by the
majority of Christians on both sides of the Mediterranean at this time.
Schism becomes a relative term, as the stress of crisis calls forth similar reactions to the secular power from men whose position with regard to Catholic orthodoxy differed as much as that of Donatus and
Hilary. It is thus not altogether surprising to find a non-African but
a Gaul or Spaniard, Parmenian succeeding Donatus as Archbishop
of Carthage in 355, and he rapidly became as convinced a Donatist
as his predecessor.

The dilemma of Western theologians was never wholly solved.
Its acuteness was, however, lessened by the end of the fourth century by the orthodoxy of Gratian and Theodosius, and by the assimilation of some measure of the Hellenistic view of the State through
Neo-Platonism. This was one of the great achievements of Ambrose and his pupil Augustine [63]). Only then, did the basically Jewish

---

[60]) HILARY, *Contra Constantium Imperatorem*, 5, 8 and 9 (*P. L.*, X, 585-586).
    [61]) AUGUSTINE, *Ep.*, 93, 6, 21 (referring to Vincentius of Cartenna, *C. S. E. L.*,
XXXIV-2, 467).
    [62]) For the survival of political millenarism as a living idea at the end of the
fourth century, see Quintus JULIUS HILARIANUS, *Libellus de Mundi Duratione*, 16 and
17 (*P. L.*, XIII, 1104-1105).
    [63]) For the relations between the two, and Augustine's debt to the thought of

and apocalyptic view of the State give way to the more philosophical concept presented by Augustine in the *De Civitate Dei*. To the Western schismatics, however, went the honour of representing what Brisson [64]) has so aptly described as « l'impatience populaire » of the Latin Christian congregations. And, this was not without its influence in the break up of the Roman Empire in the West.

Ambrose, P. COURCELLE, *Recherches sur les Confessions de Saint Augustin*, Paris, 1950, p. 106 ff.

[64]) J. P. BRISSON, *Autonomisme et Christianisme*, Ch. IV.

XI

RELIGION AND SOCIAL CHANGE IN THE LATE ROMAN EMPIRE

THE 'Dark Ages' have come into their own as a subject for research. Not only has the archaeologist enabled the historian to gain an insight into the unrecorded lives of the ordinary people of that period, but the barbaric itself exercises a baleful fascination over many minds of our own day. The Age of the Antonines is no longer golden. There are no modern Gibbons. The classics made their appeal to a dominant middle class, which was itself the product of a prosperous urban civilization. The life portrayed by the Latin and Greek authors was also the life of a citizen class, the rulers of the confederacy of city states which composed the Roman Empire in the Mediterranean basin during the first two centuries A.D. The one civilization is now showing signs of following the other along the road towards impotence and perhaps eventual oblivion. In the twilight of 'Western European culture', it is to be expected that the classics should lose some of their former predominance.

The student directs his inquiry into those forces which were largely responsible for the overthrow of the Romano-Hellenic world. He turns his attention to the rising village cultures of the Numidian High Plains and the Syrian hinterland, the revolutionary colonate of late Roman Spain and Gaul,[1] and to the Coptic peasants of the Nile valley. The fanatical, dissenting form of Christianity which many of these country folk professed, served much the same destructive purpose to the classical civilization as the Communist conception of life exercises on that of the modern middle classes.

Three great religious changes took place during late Roman and Early Byzantine times. First, in the latter half of the third century, the conversion of a substantial proportion of the inhabitants of the Mediterranean provinces of the Roman Empire to Christianity, secondly, in the fourth and fifth centuries, the progressive alienation of the masses from orthodoxy in favour of provincial schisms and heresies, and finally from the seventh to the tenth century, the gradual transfer of the allegiance of the majority of those same masses from Christianity to Islam. In each of these transfers of allegiance economic and social factors played a major role.

It is in Roman North Africa that recent archaeological research allows these processes to be most closely followed. The historian

[1] The Bagaudae. Peasantry driven to revolt by economic hardship. First mentioned in A.D. 285.

has always been well supplied from literary sources on the development of the Christian Church in that area. Tertullian, Cyprian and Augustine mark epochs in the Church's progress, and apart from their works, there are documents of first-rate historical importance which have survived. These include the complete account of the conference between the Donatists and Catholics which took place at Carthage in June 411 under the presidency of the Imperial Commissioner Marcellinus, and the documents which deal with the outbreak of the Donatist controversy in 312.

But the sources tell us mainly about the beliefs and evolution of a comparatively small Latin-speaking minority. Augustine's sermons for instance, were addressed to a literate audience who could appreciate quotations from the classics, wealthy people who could afford ivory beds, or evade ecclesiastical fasts by indulging themselves in fancy dishes. The Berber peasant spoke little if any Latin, slept on a mat as does his present-day descendant and ate a rough and scanty fare. Augustine's friends were members of the senatorial and land-owning class, his own ideal of life as expressed in the *Confessions* was an 'otium liberale' on some great landed estate, leisure for contemplation; his monasticism had little to do with evangelical poverty, but was rather a projection of this leisured ideal into the life of the African Catholic Church.

Yet Augustine had no contact with the mass of the people who adhered to his Donatist opponents, because he could not speak their language.[1] In addition, he made the mistake of believing that he was dealing with a purely intellectual movement which could be combated through debates, conferences and Imperial decrees, aided by a certain amount of pressure from the authorities. His acquaintance with Donatist beliefs, and even the works of Cyprian on which those beliefs were based, was the most elementary. In reality, he was faced with what we would call a 'communal' movement, burning with all the intensity of religious fanaticism combined with economic discontent. Finally, his efforts to restore Catholic unity in the African provinces failed. Even his own see of Hippo had ceased to exist within fifty years of his death. Whatever may have been his effect on Christian thought in Western Europe, his place in the history of North Africa is relatively small. He is a majestic, but in Africa an unremembered, leader of a movement whose decay and final dissolution he could not prevent.

The patient work of the French archaeologists has enabled various aspects of the other side of the story to be pieced together. From the mid-third century onwards the real wealth of the African provinces lay less in the settled corn-growing area peopled by Punic

---

[1] Proto-Berber was the language spoken by the peasants around Thagaste. The area is particularly prolific in Libyan and Latino-Libyan inscriptions.

and Latin-speaking town dwellers, than on the plains which form the interior of modern Tunisia and the Department of Constantine. This dry inhospitable country became in the late Roman period the main source for the supply of olive oil for Italy and Rome and probably for the whole of the western Mediterranean basin. The ruins of olive presses may be numbered in thousands, from the great factories on the plains of Tebessa to the single vat by a primitive hut belonging to some Romano-Berber peasant. The writer found eighty-five presses in a single village, and fifty per site is about the average. It was possibly little more than the truth when the Arab invaders of the seventh century claimed that they could ride across the plains from Tripoli to Tangier through a single vast forest of olive trees.

It was on account of their olive oil, coupled with Emperors' policy of granting a secure tenure in return for remaining on the land as a cultivator, that the African colonate increased and prospered.[1] The earliest inscriptions from the High Plains are dated to the mid-second century A.D., and the villages produce few if any datable objects before the third century. The writer found coins of Gallienus (253-268) on his lowest level in the Romano-Berber village of Kherbet Bahrarous near Batna in Algeria. But in the fourth and later centuries the situation must have been different. In the area of Constantine Department which lies between the main east-west railway linking Algiers and Tunis and the Aures mountains, more than 1500 Romano-Berber villages have now been located. Some of these are very large, extending over one hundred acres. The majority cover about twenty acres, but are very built over, like a modern Kabyle village. It was not for nothing that in 313 Constantine congratulated himself on the 'spontaneous surrender' of the 'most populous' African provinces; and the bulk of that population probably lived in Numidia.

In the early third century the inhabitants were scrupulous adherents of the cult of Saturn. As Toutain and Carcopino have long ago pointed out, this religion had nothing in common with that of the Italian deity Saturnus, but was a thinly disguised successor of the Berber Baal-Hammon. The god was not worshipped in temples like the gods of the classical pantheon, but in open sanctuaries and often on high places. He was a supreme deity who demanded complete subservience from his worshippers. It is interesting to note that most of the names used by the Numidians, even when the province was almost wholly Christian, such as Donatus, Rogatus, Fortunatus or

[1] Through the Lex Mancia. For the connection between the administration of this law in the second century A.D. in Africa and the increase in olive cultivation there, see J. CARCOPINO, 'L'Inscription d'Ain el Djemala', *Mélanges de l'École française à Rome*, Vol. XXVI, 1906, p. 366.

490

Concessus, are connected with the worship of Saturn and define man's relation towards the god as a slave. His wrath was signified to the unfortunate believer in dreams, and could only be appeased through blood of a lamb sacrificed as a substitute for ('pro vicario') the human victim.

In the mid-third century however the shrines of this formidable deity had become deserted. The last dated inscription in honour of Saturn is from a site near the French-Algerian township of Sillègue and was dedicated in A.D. 272. Most of the big sanctuaries such as those near Timgad, Theveste and N'gaous, were probably abandoned about this period or a little earlier. The last inscription in the grotto of Bacax near Thibilis is A.D. 283. It is interesting to record that the sites of these sanctuaries all became Donatist bishoprics in the fourth century.

The conversion of the vast majority of the Numidian villagers to Christianity must be placed in the second half of the third century. There is not only the negative evidence of the closing down of the pagan shrines, but evidences for organized Christianity in Numidia date only from A.D. 254.[1] Yet half a century later, the one area in the whole of the Western Empire in which there was a persecution under Diocletian on anything like the scale of what occurred in the East was Numidia, more accurately Numidia Militana, the district precisely covering the Algerian High Plains. Our evidence for this comes not only from literary sources which dilate on the crimes of the *praeses* Florus, but inscriptions show that in some villages 'the days of incense-burning' were remembered a century later by the inhabitants. Further, the names of those who were believed to have been executed during the Great Persecution can be numbered by scores on the inscriptions dug up in the village chapels.

No entirely satisfactory explanation can be found for the abandonment of the cult of Saturn by the African peasant. One is led, however, to suspect that the movement accompanied great social changes. In Africa, as elsewhere in the Roman Empire, the third century sees the decline of urban life and institutions, and the physical decay of the towns themselves. In the villages, the opposite occurs. In one area, on the plain of Medjana around Setif, inscriptions record a rising level of prosperity between A.D. 190 to 260 in the villages inhabited by Libyan tribesmen.[2] One even finds that in this period the legionary settlements, which were founded in central Numidia

---

[1] CYPRIAN, *Epistola* 59.3. (ed. Hartel).

[2] J. CARCOPINO, 'Les Castella de la Plaine de Setif', *Revue Africaine*, 1918, pp. 1-22. Another interesting fact is that the great majority of milestones found in Numidia date from the late third century, denoting probably increasing trade and also the increasing importance of the area from the tax-gatherer's point of view.

during the first and second centuries, completely lose their Roman character. Bou-Takrematem which I visited in 1939 and 1944 became an enormous village, fragments of temple and triumphal arches being used as building material for olive presses. It is in fact between A.D. 250 and 350 that Africa established herself as a great exporter of oil. Less famed for her wheat, she became in the words of a geographer, 'outstanding above nearly all other nations in the use of oil'. This change naturally benefited the villages which were the primary producers, rather than the towns.

It is possible that while many would simply have regarded Christianity as a superior form of magic (pagan magic symbols and formulae are not uncommon in African churches), there was an element of protest in the mind of the villager as he transferred his allegiance from Saturn to Christ. The bankruptcy of the cities caused increasingly heavy burdens to fall on the shoulders of the villager. An inscription from Ain Zoui, later a Donatist centre in southern Numidia, shows that the tax-collectors were not particular in their methods of enforcing payment. Lactantius records their brutalities in Africa on the eve of the Great Persecution. Resentment, too, may have been caused by the growing tendency to 'Romanize' the native worship which took place in the early third century. But these are matters for speculation. Certain it is, however, that the Great Persecution found the citizen class in Numidia apparently solid in support of the Imperial power and of paganism while the villagers took the brunt of the repression. The lifting of the ban on Christian practices in 305 revealed a clear cleavage in outlook between the inhabitants of town and countryside.

The attention of the student is directed to the fact that similar movements took place in other provinces at this time. In Egypt, Eusebius indicates that a state approaching civil war appears to have broken out during the Great Persecution, and we may not be far wrong in associating the devotion of many of the Egyptian peasants to the Christian faith with an aversion from Hellenism, and from the soldiers and tax-collectors who represented to him the culture of the Greek-speaking towns. Christianity and the rise of Coptic as a literature appear to have been parallel movements. But in the same epoch the Egyptian deities who had been worshipped for 3000 years lost their adherents in favour of Christianity. Similarly in the Tembris Valley area of Phrygia, those parts which in the second century A.D. seem to have been particularly under the spell of the national gods Men and Lairbenos become overwhelmingly Montanist or Novatianist in the third and later centuries. Phrygia also was one of the scenes of brutalities involving the inhabitants of the smaller towns and villages during the Great Persecution.

492

In North Africa one can follow the story in detail for another century. The Donatist controversy began with a disputed election to the see of Carthage in A.D. 312. In fact, within a few years Africa was divided religiously on exactly the same lines as during the Great Persecution. Donatus himself, the originator of the dispute, came from a settlement in the far south of Numidia where olive culture was already meeting the desert. His followers were the Numidian peasants and the Carthaginian lower classes. They and the Donatist clergy combined a veneration for the martyrs of the Great Persecution with disdain of classical learning and culture. Their opponents were to be found among the Romanized populations in the cities, who had either a pagan background or who had co-operated with the Roman authorities during the Persecution. The conversion of Constantine to Christianity and his immediate adoption of a standpoint hostile to Donatus divided the African Christians permanently into two warring camps.[1]

We are in fact able to set out an exact distribution map of the areas held by the Donatists and Catholics during the fourth and early fifth centuries. The main evidence is provided by a nominal roll of the six hundred or so bishops who took part on opposing sides at the conference held between the Donatists and Catholics at Carthage in 411. This evidence has been widely supplemented by that of inscriptions and other archaeological data. The Catholics are shown to have been in a majority in Proconsular Africa (modern Tunisia) and in the fertile river valleys of northern Numidia (the northern part of the Department of Constantine). They predominated in the Roman settlements of this area where Africa shared in the general Mediterranean civilization.[2] Cereals and vineyards were the major sources of income for these regions at that time as they are today.

The Donatist opposition was made up of men of a different stamp. Though the nominal leadership of the Church was at Carthage, and the Donatists maintained a bishop of Rome, their real centre of authority was in the olive-growing country in the Numidian High Plains. If their chiefs paid lip service to the principle of a universal Church, most of the more humble adherents considered that the glory of the Divine Kingdom was sufficiently represented by the vast Donatist cathedrals in the Numidian cities of Timgad and Bagai.

---

[1] The decisive moment was in April 313 when Constantine freed the African Catholic clergy from their financial obligations as members of local urban councils who were collectively responsible for the taxes. This put a financial premium on orthodoxy and automatically committed dissenters to opposition in some form or other to the Emperor.

[2] The Catholics predominated in exactly those areas which had an average yearly rainfall of more than twenty-four inches, and which could support an urban culture. The Donatists had the upper hand in the more arid country suitable for villages and olive and barley growing.

Was it not stated in the Song of Songs that the Lord rested 'in the south'?

Archaeological research leaves little doubt of the religion which was being practised in the densely populated Numidian villages. Between 1933 and 1939 fifty villages and seventy-two churches were investigated. Some villages contained not one, but half a dozen chapels, each built on the same plan, with earth walls whitewashed inside and out, and adorned with Scriptural texts and Donatist watchwords. Beneath the altar was always a tomb, that of a martyr, and close by, relics enclosed in a rough cooking pot and hermetically sealed with white plaster. One gained the impression of an intense and primitive religion having little in common with that adhered to in the Roman towns.

The Donatists combined an exclusive and biblical, one might use the same term as they did themselves, 'Evangelical', religion with a ferocious hatred for the prevailing social system. The real destroyers of the Roman world in North Africa were not the Vandals, but the revolutionary peasantry and the Donatist clergy who led them. Both Augustine and the other African Catholic writer, Optatus of Milevis, draw the same picture of the activities of the 'leaders of the saints'. 'No creditor could extort payment of a debt', masters were forced to change places with their slaves, the estates of unpopular land-owners were laid waste and their homes burnt to the ground. One Donatist bishop of Timgad, Optatus, earned an unenviable repute as a brigand, 'scorching', as Augustine says, 'all Africa with tongues of flame'. In complete control of southern Numidia for ten years between 388 and 398, he went on armed progresses, gave away lands, evicted unpopular proprietors, settled disputes and razed Catholic churches to the ground. He rather than Augustine typifies the last generation of Roman Africa. On the other hand, the laws of the Codex Theodosianus and the writings of non-Africans such as Zosi-mus show the African to have been subjected to every form of abuse and exaction by the Roman authorities. In the consequent native revolts of 372 and 398, the two Churches were ranged against each other. The Catholics backed the authorities, the Donatists the rebels.

Between Donatist and Catholic in North Africa there was a con-flict of civilizations expressed in terms of religious dogma. The language of the dissenters was Berber; they occupied precisely that area where Berber and not Arabic is spoken today. The magnificent stone carvings of the southern Numidian churches are derived from Libyan prehistoric motifs and survive today among the woodwork and pottery of the Kabyles. They were entirely non-classical in inspiration; whereas the mosaics in the Catholic churches on the coastal plains continued in the same tradition and designs of the Roman world.

494

Already in the fourth century one scents something of North African Mohammedanism. The Donatists regarded Donatus as a miracle-working prophet and a great reformer of the Church. His prayers were answered direct from heaven. He was in fact esteemed almost as Christ Himself. His followers were engaged in 'holy war' against the pagans and Catholics. The Donatist bishop was often the leader of armed forays and could well be compared with Moslem Mahdis. The chapels which dominated the villages resemble even down to details the Koubbas of a North African Moslem settlement. Brotherhoods of pilgrims grew up around the Christian martyr's tomb, as they do now around that of a Moslem marabout. Holy men, saints and pilgrims were characteristic of Christian Africa as they are of Moslem Africa. Donatist Christianity may perhaps be regarded as a transformed popular religion and to a certain extent the forerunner of Islam. In this it has its close parallels with Montanism and Novatianism in Asia Minor in the same period. The division of the Mediterranean between what is now the northern and Christian shores, and the southern and Islamic would appear to begin in the last half of the third century.

One has concentrated on North Africa, for much of the recent evidence bearing on the subject comes from there, and fresh discoveries continue to be made. But evidence for the rise of popular Christian movements which drew their support from the oppressed classes within the Roman Empire may also be derived from other provinces.[1] The history of the Coptic Church, for instance, is often the history of the religious dissent of the Coptic villages from the beliefs of the wealthier Greek-speaking classes. In the third century, when these latter remained pagan, the Copt became Christian. When the Alexandrine Greek became an Arian Christian, the Copts championed Athanasius, and as monks in the wilderness found refuge from their enemies the soldiers and tax-collectors. The Emperors declared the creed of Athanasius to be orthodox in 381; the Copt tended towards Monophysitism, until in 451 he finally broke with the rest of Christendom when only fourteen out of the hundred Egyptian bishops were prepared to sign the formula of Chalcedon. The language of the Coptic Church was Copt and not Greek, and the Saidish 'Life' of the great Egyptian leader of that time, Schnoudi, indicates that the antipathy of the peasant towards the Greek-speaking landowner and magistrate was one of the driving forces behind his rebellion against orthodox Christianity.

Indeed, orthodoxy in the later Roman Empire tended to mean

[1] In Britain, the decay of the Roman cities was accompanied by a renewal of interest in the old Celtic deities, indicated by the building of temples in abandoned Iron Age hill forts, such as at Lydney and Maiden Castle. This movement also coincided with a magnificent revival of Celtic art.

the dominant religion in the great maritime cities of the Mediterranean, and the beliefs of the official classes and Romanized landed aristocracy. Imperial support for these beliefs, combined with a relative ease of communications gave to the Catholics a decisive advantage over their 'backwoods' opponents. Augustine was never tired of informing his Donatist opponents that the Catholic Church was 'spread over all the world', while the heresies were confined to single provinces.

Yet, there are features in common which united the dissenting Churches throughout the Mediterranean world. The Holy Spirit played a predominant part in their theology. Martyrdom, which was regarded alike by African Donatist and Phrygian Montanist as the highest earthly reward and the supreme victory over evil, was the moment at which the believer could himself become filled with the Holy Spirit and partake in a fleeting vision of the future life. Stringent asceticism, complete renunciation of the culture of the world, the service of a priesthood sacramentally pure, 'without spot or wrinkle', and utter subservience to divine precept were all necessary conditions in the preparation for martyrdom. Donatists, Novatians and Syrian and Coptic Monophysites shared in these beliefs, and regarded the Church more as a brotherhood of militant believers than as an institution for salvation. It was, however, at no time possible for their beliefs to gain the title of 'orthodox', owing to the physical inability of the artisans and peasants who adhered to them to organize effectively. The next village or the banks of the river was too often the limit of their earthly horizon. On the other hand, in the fifth century, the great landowners in Italy, Spain and Gaul, such as Paulinus of Nola, and Sidonius readily became bishops, and with that development the pattern of Catholic feudalism which dominates the Middle Ages in Europe begins to emerge.

The conclusion that may perhaps be drawn is that at least at the period of the foundation of our present civilization, the development of religious belief cannot be separated from the development of general culture. Changes of religion accompany social changes, and must be set in the same framework as parallel literary and artistic movements. It seems to have been no more an accident that Donatism predominated precisely in the dry areas of North Africa where an urban civilization could not develop, than that Islam has in its turn supplanted Christendom in all the semi-desert country between the 37th and 10th parallel north. Religion regarded from this point of view ceases to be the revelation of absolute truth, and becomes relative to civilization as a whole. 'Heresy' and 'schism' become terms denoting social and political tension.

The acceptance of this relative view of religion might have a considerable influence on our attitude towards Christianity today.

496

We should have to ask ourselves, whether the commercialized superstitions which often pass for the Christian religion in many parts of Europe are worthy of defence. The fact is that the urban and mechanical civilization of Western Europe has created an environment which makes it difficult for us to grasp even the outlines of the Mediterranean desert religion preached by Christ. Yet progress towards formulating beliefs which will be understood by and inspire the people of our generation cannot be permanently successful so long as the conception of 'orthodoxy' remains. The relative failure of European Protestantism to become the predominant and living religion of the Western world may be partly due to its having substituted for the orthodoxy of Pope and Church an equally brittle and vulnerable orthodoxy of Council and Scriptural Word.

We need to realign our ideas to meet the impact of vast social, political and religious changes. It is doubtful whether for the Englishman the keys of salvation are to be found either in Rome or in Moscow. For him, the way lies in the rejection of all absolute conceptions of religion, and in a re-interpretation of that traditional middle road which brought him through the crises of the Reformation period, and may yet guide him through this present revolutionary era.

XII

The Gnostic-Manichaean Tradition in Roman North Africa

Throughout its history one may detect three principal tendencies at work in the African Church. First, and probably the strongest, was the traditional Cyprianic and Donatist view of Christianity. This was a Biblical religion, rejecting the culture and society of the surrounding pagan world and exalting the qualities of the prophet and the martyr. Its ideas can be traced in unbroken sequence through the Montanists of Tertullian's time and the confessor party during the primacy of Cyprian down to the Donatists themselves. This religion interpreted the ideas of the majority of the North Africans at least as late as the first decades of the fifth century, and in particular it appealed to the labouring population of Numidia for whom it provided means of voicing hostility to the Roman taxes and Roman institutions.[1]

Opposed to the Donatists were two other creeds. There were the Manichees, whom the Donatists regarded as heretical Christians and Mani himself as an impostor.[2] So far as one can tell, relations between them were those of mutual avoidance and abhorrence. Then there were the Catholics. The latter do not emerge as a predominant force until the great Persecution and fail to dominate the scene until after the Conference at Carthage in June 411. These divergent religious tendencies came into mortal conflict at the end of the fourth century, and, thanks mainly to St. Augustine, victory went to the Catholics, aided as they were by the imperial government. One has the impression, however, that Catholicism was never a popular movement in Africa and that the victory of Augustine and his friends over both Manichees and Donatists was a major factor in alienating the Berbers from the Church altogether.[3] In the long run, the natives found Islam a better vehicle for their traditional beliefs than the religion which the Roman and Byzantine administrations had tried to thrust upon them.

This article is mainly concerned with the heretical opposition to St. Augustine. The Saint reveals from his writings that he had far more

[1] The writer has worked out these views in detail in *The Donatist Church*, Oxford 1952 particularly in chapters v and xx.
[2] Augustine, *Contra Litteras Petiliani*, ii. 18. 40: P. L., xliii. 271.
[3] For the reaction against Catholicism on the arrival of the Vandals see Victor of Vita, *Historia Persecutionis Africanae Provinciae* (ed. Petschenig, C.S.E.L., vii), 1.1, and Possidius, *Vita Augustini*, xxviii: P. L., xxxii. 58.

interest in the problem of the Manichees than he had in that of the Donatists. If one turns to his *De Haeresibus* one finds three times as much
space devoted to a detailed description of Manichaeism, interspersed with
personal reminiscences, as to the uninspiring and purely factual account
given of Donatism.[1] The Donatists he never understood. He was inclined
to consider them as disciplinary offenders, heretics only through the offence
of 'inveterate schism'.[2] To some extent he was right. The questions that
divided them from the Catholics were those of discipline and politics, but
not of doctrine.[3] The person of Christ, the relationship between the Old and
New Testaments, the necessity for baptism, the sacrament of the Eucharist,
and belief in bodily resurrection were not in dispute. Even the liturgy of the
two Churches was probably the same. Donatist writers such as Donatus
himself, Macrobius of Rome, Vitellius Afer and Tyconius found their way
into orthodox galleries of 'Illustrious Men'.[4] Catholic writers from outside
Africa, such as Hilary of Poitiers, were included in Donatist libraries.[5]

When one turns to the African heretics, one is faced with an entirely
different set of relationships. From the time of Tertullian, probably as long
as Christianity lasted in North Africa, there was a minority drawn mainly
from the romanised town-dwellers who accepted none of the premises on
which the Catholics and the Donatists were agreed, and yet claimed to be
Christians. Their opponents they regarded as schismatics from pagan
idolatry.[6] They were unmoved by the controversies which to the outsider
seem to dominate the history of African Christianity in the third and
fourth centuries, such as the nature of the Church, the value of martyrdom
and the necessity for re-baptising converts. It is interesting that in Arnobius's works, written just before and during the Great Persecution, there
is not a hint of the problems which in a few years' time were going to cause
the Donatist controversy. In glaring contrast to the Donatist majority,
they regarded the 'right use' of the pagan classics and society rather than
their destruction as the duty of a Christian, while martyrdom was in itself
a useless act.[7] Instead, they found greater wisdom in the Gnostic Sibylline
oracles and in the cult of Hermes Trismegistos than in the Old Testament,
whose god they regarded either as a power of evil or as non-existent.[8] They
approached Christianity as the culminating point in a system of divine
revelation in which the Jesus of history represented most perfectly the
pattern of an immanent world-saviour.[9] He was the reflection of reality

---

[1] Augustine, *De Haeresibus ad Quodvultdeum*, xlvi and lxix: P. L., xlii. 34–38 and 43–44.
[2] Augustine, *Contra Cresconium*, ii. 7. 9: 'haeresis autem, schisma inveteratum'.
[3] The only doctrinal issue was the tendency remarked on by Augustine for the
Donatists to take the Arian view of the Trinity (Augustine, *Ep.* clxxxv.1), but the Catholics
had fallen into the same error at Sirmium and Ariminum.
[4] Jerome, *De Viris Illustribus*, xciii. Gennadius, *De Scriptoribus Ecclesiasticis*, iv, v and
xviii: P. L., lix. 1060 and 1071.
[5] Augustine, *Ep.* xciii. 31.   [6] Augustine, *Contra Faustum*, xx. 4: P. L., xlii. 370.
[7] Tertullian, *Scorpiace*, i. and x.
[8] Augustine, *Contra Faustum*, xiii. 1 and xv. 1, and *De Haeresibus*, xlvi. Cf. Lactantius,
Divinae Institutiones, vi. 25. 10 (ed. Brandt, C.S.E.L., xix. 579).
[9] See the important article by H. J. Polotsky on Manichaeism in Pauly-Wissowa, *Real-
enzyklopädie der klassischen Altertumswissenschaft*, Supplement vi, cols. 240–271 at col. 267.

and not reality itself, and knowledge of this reality through Him rather than the martyr's crown was the end of the Christian's life.

The subjects that interested these individuals were philosophical, such as the nature of evil, the relationship between the Saviour and the human soul, and the relative merit of Christianity as against Hermetism and Neo-Platonism as a means of personal salvation. Their hope was the achievement of a divine revelation, through which all the mysteries 'of the beginning, the middle and the end', and 'of the making of the world, the reason for the day and night and the course of the sun and moon',[1] as Felix the Manichee thought, would be made plain to the believer in a single momentary vision. In 391 Augustine wrote in his *Soliloquies*, 'he desired to know God and his own soul. Nothing else? Nothing whatever'.[2] It is this sentiment repeated in the *Confessions*, the desire for the overwhelming experience of divine knowledge, which links Augustine with the Gnostics of African Church history. It forms the common ground between him and Africans such as Arnobius and Lactantius, who may have come to Christianity by way of pagan gnosticism,[3] and not least with the Manichee, Faustus of Milevis.

Is it then possible to think in terms of a Gnostic-Manichee tradition in Africa, a tradition which appears, curiously, to have more links with the Catholic than with the Donatist Church? If that is the case, does it affect the generally held view of St. Augustine and his legacy to Western Christendom?

In the first place, there is the existence of historial continuity between the Gnostics and the Manichees in Africa. The Gnostics fade out at the time of the Great Persecution, and their place is immediately taken by the Manichees. Though Africa produced no Gnostic sects of its own, it prolonged the life and increased the vigour of a number of them. The great age of African Gnosticism is the period A.D. 190–220, a half century or so after the death of Marcion and Valentinus. There is no evidence to show when the doctrine of these two thinkers took root in Africa, but we do know that it was the steady propagation of their beliefs that roused Tertullian to write against them,[4] and then to spend the best part of twenty years of polemics in combatting their doctrines. The impression one gains is that in the early third century there were only two schools that mattered among the African Christians. These were the Montanists and the Gnostics. The future of the African Church lay between them. One was for or against the Old Testament and the Biblical approach to Christianity. The third party, which eventually emerged as the Catholics,

---

[1] Felix's statement during his debate with Augustine in 405. Augustine, *Acta cum Felice*, i. 9 (P. L., xlii. 525); cf. *Poimandres* i. 4 (ed. W. Scott, *Corpus Hermeticum*, Oxford 1924, i. 114).
[2] Augustine, *Soliloquies*, i. 7; cf. *Confessions*, i. 1.
[3] For this view, see J. Carcopino, *Aspects mystiques de la Rome païenne*, Paris, Artisan du livre 1942, 293; cf. Lactantius, *Div. Inst.*, ii. 15 and iv. 9 on Hermetism and Christianity.
[4] Tertullian, *De Praescriptione*, i.

consisted, so far as one may judge, of second-rate ecclesiastics such as the bishop of Uthina and the herd of semi-believers, the 'Psychics' of Tertullian's Montanist writings.[1] But Gnosticism did not stay the course. We know that the Marcionites and Hermogenists continued to exist[2] and that sects of every variety flourished in Carthage in the third century,[3] but in the period after Tertullian existing evidence suggests that a kindred form of Gnosticism, Hermetism, absorbed much of the native's revelationist aspirations.[4] By the time that Optatus of Milevis wrote his seven books against the Donatist bishop of Carthage, Parmenian, he could tell his opponent that the Gnostic heresies which he had denounced were 'dead and buried'. Not only their vices but their very names were forgotten.[5] He could hardly have said the same of the Manichees. His own town, Milevis, had produced one of the ablest members of the sect, the one-time friend of Augustine, Faustus.

Meantime, the Manichees had gained a footing in Africa at an exceptionally early date. Within twenty years of Mani's death, probably on 26 February 277,[6] his religion had established itself in Carthage and in other towns. Diocletian's rescript from Alexandria despatched to Julianus, proconsul of Africa, on 31 March 297, in which the burning of the 'Manichees and magicians' and their sacred books was ordered, was written in reply to official complaints from Africa the previous year.[7] Six years later, during the Great Persecution, when Mensurius of Carthage was able to satisfy the authorities by handing over the scriptures 'of the new heretics', we may assume reasonably that the works of the Manichees were meant.[8] Thus, the religion was established in Africa at the time of the earliest known Manichee missions to the Roman empire, those of Papus and Thomas in Upper Egypt,[9] and nearly twenty years earlier than the first reference to Manichaeism in Rome.[10] Moreover, despite every effort to discredit the sect, to destroy the philosophical foundations of its creed and to hunt down its adherents, Manichaeism persisted in North Africa until the last generation of Christianity there and probably beyond.

[1] Tertullian, *De Monogamia*, xii; *De Fuga*, ix and xiv.

[2] Even in Mauretania: Cyprian, *Ep.*, lxxiii. 4; Philastrius, *Panarion*, liv.

[3] See articles, 'Abrasax' and 'Adjuration' in Tome i. 1, and 'Jao' in Tome vii. 2, of the *Dictionnaire d'archéologie chrétienne et de liturgie*.

[4] J. Carcopino, loc. cit., 310. Hermetism was not regarded as in any way incompatible with Christian Gnosticism. Hermetic works were among those most in use by the Egyptian Gnostics of Nag Hammadi. See H. C. Puech, 'Les Ecrits Gnostiques Decouverts en Haute-Egypte', in *Coptic Studies in Honour of Walter Ewing Crum*, Byzantine Institute, Boston 1950, 91–154 at p. 143.

[5] Optatus, *De Schismate Donatistarum* (C.S.E.L., xxvi. p. 11), i. 9.

[6] Dating, H. C. Puech, *Le Manichéisme*, Publications du Musée Guimet, (Bibl. de Diffusion), lvi, Paris 1949, 53.

[7] Text of the rescript in Krüger-Mommsen, *Collectio libr. Juris antejustin.*, 1890, 187. Commentary P. Alfaric, *Les Ecritures Manichéens*, Paris, Nourry 1918, i.61 and Wm. Seston, *Mélanges H. Ernout*, Paris 1940, 345–54.

[8] Augustine, *Breviculus Collationis cum Donatistis*, iii. 13. 25; P. L., xliii. 638.

[9] Alexander of Lycopolis, *De Placitis Manichaeorum*, ii; P.L., xviii. 413. Dating, p. xv of Brinkmann's edition. Leipzig 1895.

[10] In the pontificate of Miltiades, 311–314. See L. Duchesne, *Liber Pontificalis*, i. 169, No. 3.

THE GNOSTIC-MANICHAEAN TRADITION

It was regarded as a danger to orthodox Christianity and to Islam alike as late as the first half of the eighth century.[1] Its persistence over this long period of four centuries suggests that it appealed to some traditional and widely felt need among the North Africans.

Apart from historical continuity, the Manichees of Augustine's time were concerned with precisely the same problems as the Gnostics of two hundred years previously, and they answered in precisely the same way. The famous description given by Tertullian of Gnostic speculation in *De Praescriptione* vii is closely paralleled by Augustine's account of Manichee arguments in *De Duabus Animis* viii. 10. The Gnostics ask, 'whence is evil, why is it permitted? What is the origin of man? And in what way does he come? Besides the question which Valentinus has lately proposed—whence comes God?' Augustine describes the Manichees as speculating, 'Whence are the sins themselves, and whence is evil in general? If from man, whence is man, and if from an angel, whence is the angel?' And, Augustine adds, by this question, they think themselves triumphant.[2] So, relates Tertullian, did the Gnostics. Both regarded the object of the individual's existence as the attainment of that divine knowledge which would answer these questions. Tertullian relates how the Gnostics of his day relied on the text 'Seek and ye shall find' (*De Praescriptione*, viii) to justify their speculations and their attacks on the Old Testament. During their debate on 24 August 392, the Manichee Fortunatus told Augustine, 'The reason must be sought how and wherefore souls have come into this world', and if evil was not a contrary substance, why need souls be liberated by Christ?[3] A statement attributed to Valentinus in the *Excerpta ex Theodoto* may sum up both the Gnostic and Manichee viewpoints. 'But it is not only baptism that frees (from the power of fate), but also knowledge; knowledge of what we were, why we have come into being, where we were and at what point we have been inserted into the scheme of things, whither we are hastening, from what we are redeemed, and what is being born and reborn.'[4] These ideas were completely alien to the mass of the African Christians to whom baptism was *the* essential sacrament and resurrection meant the bodily resurrection of each individual from his grave, whence any idea of individual rebirth on earth was excluded.[5] But they were faithfully echoed by the African Manichees contemporary with Augustine.[6]

[1] We know of the persecution of the Manichees in the Vandal period (Victor Vitensis, ii. 1), their survival under pope Gregory I (*Ep.* ii. 37) and their arrival in Italy under pope Gregory II (*Ep.* iv). In the mid-eighth century a Manichee 'Imam' arrived in Baghdad from Africa. See P. Alfaric, op. cit., 62.

[2] See also Augustine, *De Moribus Manichaeorum*, ii. 2.

[3] Augustine, *Contra Fortunatum*, i. 6; P.L., xlii. 115.

[4] *Excerpta ex Theodoto*, lxxviii; P.G., ix. 694–695.

[5] In the great Christian cemeteries, such as at Timgad, the body was placed at burial in liquid plaster so that its exact outline should be observed. For the literal belief in bodily resurrection see Tertullian, *Apologeticus*, xviii and xxiii.

[6] The Manichee view of baptism was stated by Augustine. 'Baptismum ... quod Manichaei dicunt in omne aetate superfluum': *Contra Duas Epistolas Pelagianorum*, iv. 4.5; P.L., xliv. 613, and cf. *De Haeresibus* xlvi; P.L., xlii. 38. For Manichaean denial of the resurrection of the body, Evodius, *De Fide*, xl; P.L., xlii. 1151.

What was the 'evil' the knowledge of which the African Gnostics and Manichees so diligently sought after? In the present writer's view, their pessimism had little to do with the current political situation, for the flourishing of Gnosticism in Africa coincides with the most prosperous era in the history of the province, and that prosperity was enjoyed throughout all classes, both in town and countryside.[1] Manichaeism too, was best represented among the wealthy and comparatively secure landowners and merchants in Africa.[2] Nor were the Greek philosophers as taught in the African schools the only influence that prepared the ground for the reception of Gnostic and Manichaean beliefs.[3] Neo-Platonists, such as Alexander of Lycopolis were careful to point out the distinction between the Manichaean conception of matter and that taught by Plato and Aristotle.[4] Augustine found in Neo-Platonism the antidote to the Manichaean assertion that evil was a substance.[5] The evils which the Gnostics and Manichees attempted to turn from themselves were considered to be demoniac forces, in whose existence the Berber has believed from remote prehistory down to the present day.

The evil of demons was personified in two ways. First, there was the almost universal belief in Africa that the life of a human being was minutely governed by the conjunction of planets and stars at birth. Death came when the demons who controlled the planets under which the individual was born, declared that it must.[6] There is quite a large number of funerary inscriptions of both the pagan and the Christian era in Africa which give the exact year, month, day and hour of the deceased's death. This is not pedantry on the part of the relatives, but, as Carcopino has pointed out, a means of showing that he or she had accomplished an allotted span on earth and no more. Religion aimed at providing the believer with a series of formulae to outwit the various demons he would meet on his journey through the planetary spheres on his way to Paradise. The formula prescribed in third century Hermetism was "Ev ter pius', that enjoined on the Christians of the same period was "Αγιος, "Αγιος, "Αγιος"[7]. The language of the heavenly powers was believed to be Greek. Failure to repeat the correct words would lead to the soul being for ever frustrated and dispersed through the endless labyrinth that extended between the circles of the skies. Astrology, therefore, was a necessary part of the Gnostic and Manichee religion, and as we learn from Tertullian, great was the attraction felt by African Christians for the astrological cults of the east.[8]

The second terror was even more dreaded. The evil eye and the evil mouth were believed to be the immediate cause of human suffering.

[1] See R. P. Festugière, *La Révelation d'Hermes Trismégiste*, Paris 1944, i, 'Le Déclin de Rationalisme.'

[2] See Possidius, *Vita Augustini*, 6. 15 and 16.

[3] Cf. Tertullian, *De Praescriptione*, vii.

[4] Alexander of Lycopolis, *De Placitis Manichaeorum*, ii.

[5] Augustine, *Confessions*, vii. 9, 13.

[6] J. Carcopino, op. cit., 214 and 224; and E. de Faye, *Gnostiques et Gnosticisme*, Paris 1925, 263-264.

[7] J. Carcopino, op. cit., 279-81.   [8] Tertullian, *De Idololatria*, ix.

THE GNOSTIC-MANICHAEAN TRADITION

Prophylaxy against them has exercised a profound effect on art in Africa from Roman times down to the present day.[1] A number of inscriptions found on mosaics from buildings, including churches, are directed against 'Invidus' or the evil eye, and some of the very finest decorative patterns, such as those in the House of the Birds at Dougga, or from the villa at el-Haouria, have the same object in view.[2] In the present century, sayings current among the Berbers include 'the evil eye owns two thirds of the graveyard'.[3] Even personal possessions are decorated with designs calculated to dispel its influence.

These are persistent and primitive beliefs, strong enough to form the background of religions fatalistically concerned with the problem of evil, and hopeless of bringing remedy in the present world. Moreover, there is one piece of direct evidence which would link the Gnostic trend in African religion with the traditional cults of Carthage. Over a generation ago, Bousset pointed out that Ialdabaoth of the Gnostic cults which has been interpreted as the god of the Old Testament or the Demiurge who created the world, was originally none other than Saturn.[4] He quoted the text of Origen, *Contra Celsum*, vi. 31 to show that the lion-headed god Ialdabaoth was to be associated with the planet Saturn. But the lion-headed deity is well-known in Africa as a representation of the supreme native god, Saturn Baal-Hammon. Clay statues dedicated to him and his female counterpart, Caelestis, have been found in this form on sites near Carthage.[5] The lion is represented among other attributes of the god on third-century inscriptions from the site of Novar . . . (Sillègue) in Mauretania Sitifensis,[6] while Arnobius refers to 'lion-headed Frugifer' (Saturn).[7] The usual Berber representation of Saturn as savage and morose, demanding appeasement by blood sacrifices and yet ruling all-powerful over creation, fits entirely Tertullian's description of Marcion's creator as known in Africa, 'judicem, ferum, belli potentem'.[8] His influence was never far from the surface. In the fifth century Augustine remarks that some Africans, particularly astrologers (*Mathematici*), regarded Saturn and the Christian God as one and the same being.[9] Perhaps the difference between regarding this Jealous God as God, or rejecting him as an evil Archon decided the

[1] E. Westermarck, *Ritual and Belief in Morocco*, London 1926, i. 417–478, at p. 475.
[2] See article 'Oeil' in *Dictionnaire d'archéologie chrétienne et de liturgie*, xii. 2, cols. 1936–43. Also, L. Poinssot, 'Les Mosaïques d'el Haouria' in the proceedings of *Premier Congrès de Soc. savantes de l'Afrique du Nord*, 1935, 183–206, and A. Merlin and L. Poinssot, 'Deux mosaïques de Tunisie', *Monuments Piot*, xxxiv, 1934, 129–176.
[3] E. Westermarck, op. cit., 414. For the 'eye' on Romano-Punic funerary urns see F. Missonier, 'Fouilles dans la Nécropole Punique de Gouraya', *Mélanges de l'école française de Rome*, l (1933) 104.
[4] W. Bousset, *Hauptprobleme der Gnosis*, Leipzig 1907, 351–355. See also Gilbert Murray, *Five Stages of Greek Religion*, London 1935, 147.
[5] E. F. Gautier, *Le Passé de l'Afrique du Nord*, Payot 1937, 147. The writer has seen these in the Bardo Museum.
[6] C.I.L., viii. 20437 and 20442. [7] Arnobius, *Adv. Gentes*, vi. 10.
[8] Tertullian, *Adv. Marcionem*, i. 6, and iii. 21.
[9] Augustine, *De Consensu Evangelistarum*, i. 21. 29–36; P. L., xxxiv. cols. 1055–1058; cf. Salvian, *De Gubernatione Dei*, viii. 2.

Africans' allegiance to Donatism or to the Gnostics and Manichees. For or against the Old Testament was also for or against Jehovah.

If the foregoing is correct, and the basic religious needs which many North Africans felt were freedom from the thraldom of a savage Creator-God and salvation from tangible powers of evil, then the attraction of Gnosticism becomes clearer. Both Gnosticism and Manichaeism promised the believer redemption from these powers and provided him with a logical explanation of events and physical phenomena based largely on astrology. That eventually the Gnostic Saviour was identified with Christ rather than Hermes Trismegistos may have been due to the natural yearning, so evident in the first book of Arnobius's *Adversus Gentes*, for a personal world saviour, even if impersonal and docetic in essence. It was Faustus of Milevis's 'Christ hanging from every tree', symbolising the suffering of the world, and of God himself.[1] In the second century as in the fourth, speculation regarding evil, coupled with distaste for the Old Testament, led straight to a heretical and dualistic form of Christianity.

There are, in fact, two tendencies one can trace right through the Gnostic and Manichee writings as they have survived in Africa. First, there is the hostility inspired by the Old Testament and Jehovah, and secondly, the reliance of the heretics on the words of St. Paul to support their teaching.

It is interesting that both the followers of Marcion in Africa and the Manichees raised precisely the same arguments against the Old Testament. So close are the parallels that it is possible to suggest that the Manichaean apostle to Africa, Adimantius[2] (possibly the Addas of *Acta Archelai*) lifted extracts *en bloc* from Marcion's *Antitheses* which were circulating in the country. Thus, the old dispensation ordained an 'eye for an eye': Christ commanded the believer to turn the other cheek. (Tertullian, *Adv. Marcionem*, ii. 18 and iv. 16; Augustine, *Contra Faustum*, xix. 3 and *Acta Archelai*, 44).[3] In the Old Testament divorce was permitted: in the New Testament it was not (*Adv. Marcionem*, iv. 34; *Contra Faustum*, xix. 3). Moses enforced the Jewish Sabbath and the Law: Christ freed believers from both (*Adv. Marcionem*, iv. 34; *Contra Faustum*, iv. 1). Moses cursed 'everyone that hangeth from a tree': Christ died on the Cross (*Adv. Marcionem*, iii. 18, and v. 3; *Contra Faustum*, xvi. 5 and *Acta Archelai*, 44). One finds, too, the same arguments used in *De Carne Christi*, vii and *Acta Archelai*, 55, against belief in Christ's physical birth, i.e. the revelation of His divine nature to St.

[1] Augustine, *Contra Faustum*, xx. 2; Evodius, *De Fide*, xxxiv, and see also W. Jonas, *Gnosis und spätantiker Geist*, Göttingen 1934, 303–312 (some Gnostic parallels).

[2] See F. Cumont, 'La Propagation du Manichéisme dans l'Empire Romain', in *Revue d'Hist. et de Littérature religieuses*, Nouv. serie, i. 1910, 31–43, and P. Monceaux, 'Le Manichéen Faustus de Milev. Restitution de ses Capitula' in *Mémoires de l'Institut National de France, Académie des Inscriptions et Belles-Lettres*, t. xliii, Part i, 1933, 20.

[3] The *Acta Archelai* (ed. Beeson, Leipzig 1906) are used here as corroborative evidence to *Contra Faustum* and *Contra Adimantium*. Hegemonius's Epilogue, with its dating of Mani as 'post dormitionem sancti martyris Cypriani, modicum ante Diocletianum', and his detailed reference to the Donatists in Rome (*Montenses*), suggests that he may have been himself an African, perhaps one of the African colony in Rome.

Peter as contrasted with the implied rejection of the Virgin related in Mt. xii. 47 and Luke viii. 20. The docetic character of Christ's birth was asserted both by the African Marcionites (*Adv. Marcionem*, iii. 8) and by the Manichaeans (*Contra Faustum*, xxvi. 1; *Acta Archelai*, 50) while both justified the fundamental dualism of their approach to Christianity by reference to the parable of the Two Trees (Mt. vii. 17).

It is very difficult to think that these similarities are accidental and do not spring from a common source, which would imply an element of direct continuity between the two heresies. There seems also to have existed a parallel but independent tradition in Africa of what might be called 'knockabout rationalism' at the expense of the Old Testament. In a curious pamphlet written by a 'disciple of Fabricius' which was circulating in Hippo, to which Augustine replied in 419, the Old Testament was attacked from another angle. The author considered ignorance rather than malice as the besetting characteristic of the Old Testament God. Why did he have to create a rainbow in order to remind himself of his covenant with Noah?[1] Was not the serpent in the garden of Eden a better judge of human character than he?[2] Why, if the world was made good was it allowed to deteriorate?[3] These are particular points which the Manichees were not making, and Augustine in his refutation explicitly acquits the author of Manichaeism.[4]

Rejection of the Old Testament led in Africa to an almost exaggerated respect for the Epistles of St. Paul, and also for the various Gnostic *Acta* of the Apostles. The latter, such as the *Acts of Paul and Thecla*, seem to have passed straight from the African heretics of the third century to the Manichees and their allies in the fourth and fifth.[5] To judge from the *Acts of the Scillitan Martyrs*, the Pauline Epistles were circulating separately from the Gospels even in the second century and were being studied by wide groups of the population.[6] The reliance of the Marcionites on St. Paul needs no further comment, but it is interesting to find that the African Manichees also used St. Paul extensively. To Felix he was the forerunner of Mani. African Manichaeism is almost a Paulinist heresy. One sees, for instance, that practically the whole of the debate between Augustine and his former friend, the Manichee Fortunatus, turns on the interpretation to be placed on Pauline texts. Support for docetic Christology, Fortunatus claims, is found in Phil. ii. 5–8;[7] for the necessity of prevenient grace for personal salvation in Eph. ii. 1–18[8] which he quotes

---

[1] Augustine, *Contra Adversarium Legis et Prophetarum*, i. 20. 43: P.L., xlii. 629.
[2] Ibid., i. 14. 18.   [3] Ibid., i. 21. 45.
[4] Ibid., i. 1. 1; cf. i. 3. 4. and ii. 12. 40: 'nam non eum puto esse Manichaeum.'
[5] Tertullian, *De Baptismo*, xvii, shows that Marcionites were quoting these *Acta* to justify women participating in the Church as ministers. Faustus (*Contra Faustum*, xxx. 4) quotes the same *Acta* in defence of the ideal of virginity. The Leucian *Acta* of Andrew, Peter and John, together with the *Acts of Thomas* and *Acts of Paul and Thecla* formed part of a pentateuch used in Africa by both the Manichees and their 'fellow-travellers', such as the disciple of Fabricius.
[6] *Acta Scillitanorum* (ed. Rendel Harris, *Cambridge Texts and Studies*, i. ii, 1891, 106).
[7] *Contra Fortunatum*, i. 7.   [8] Ibid., i. 16.

in full; of the impossibility of bodily resurrection, and hence of the Incarnation in I Cor. xv. 50;[1] of the antipathy between flesh and spirit in Gal. v. 17 and vi. 14.[2] Similar examples may be found in the works of Faustus of Milevis and in Augustine's debate with Felix the Manichee.

But the most interesting example of all is the use made of St. Paul by the writer of a fifth-century manuscript which was discovered in a cave over sixty miles south-west of Theveste (Tebessa). This manuscript is a treatise defining the respective rôles of the Manichee Elect and Hearers, the two grades (*gradus*) as they are called, in the Manichee hierarchy. It may be a local work and not merely a translation of one of Mani's epistles.[3] The manuscript is practically a list of Pauline quotations. The spiritual perfection of the life of the Elect is proved from Col. iii. 15–16; the necessary distinction between the rôles of spiritual and carnal men from II Thess. iii. 12–13; the Christian ideal of the wandering missionary (the Elect) from I Thess. v. 12, and Phil. ii. 16 and 25; the filling of the Elect with Grace from Phil. i. 15, and the rebuttal of the argument drawn from II Thess. 3. 10 that even the spiritual man must work, from Titus iii. 8. That the African Manichees regarded St. Paul as *the* Apostle, like their Marcionite predecessors seems perfectly clear. One wonders how far St. Augustine had studied the Pauline epistles during his ten years as a Manichee.

For, it is by no means evident that those opinions which would repel the African Donatists—not least because the Manichaean Kingdom of Darkness was placed in the 'south' which could be interpreted as their beloved Numidia—had the same effect on the Catholics. From statements made by Augustine we know that conversions to and from the heresy among the African Catholics were not uncommon, and evidence suggests that relations between the two communities were far closer than one would imagine. In 393, Canon 36 of the Council of Hippo was directed against the reading of non-canonical Scriptures in church, such as those used by the Manichees.[4] In 400, apart from Augustine himself, his friends such as the great landowner Romanianus, Alypius, bishop of Thagaste, Evodius, bishop of Vzalis, and the successive bishops of Constantine, the capital of Numidia, Profuturus and Fortunatus, were former Manichees.[5] From the Donatists we hear of the conversion of a Catholic *sanctimonialis* to Manichaeism.[6] A curious situation is revealed by Augustine in *Epistle* ccxxxvi. In this he describes how one of his sub-deacons had been a Manichee

---

[1] *Contra Fortunatum*, i. 19.   [2] Ibid., i. 21.

[3] P. Alfaric, 'Un Manuscript manichéen', *Rev. de l'Hist. et de Litt. rel.*, nouv. ser. vi. 1920), 62–98. Alfaric argues in favour of this remarkable manuscript being a translation of one of Mani's own works (p. 93). It seems, however, too full of Pauline quotations for this to be likely, and, moreover, the dropping of the senior Manichaean grades in favour of two categories only, Elect and Hearers, is an African expedient.

[4] *Breviarium Hipponense*, 36 (ed. Bruns, *Canones Conciliorum Apostolorum Selecti*, Berlin 1839, ii. 138). That this canon was intended to refer to apocryphal works used by the Manichees, see Augustine, *Ep.* lxiv. 3 (to Quintasius).

[5] Augustine, *Confessions*, vi. 7. 12; *De Unico Baptismo*, xvi. 29; *Contra Acad.* i. 1. 3.

[6] Augustine, *Contra Litteras Petiliani*, iii. 17. 20. The name too, Genethlius (i.e. skilled in casting horoscopes), of the Catholic bishop of Carthage (died 391) may be interesting in this connection.

Hearer for years, but none the less had continued to minister to his Catholic congregation without arousing the least suspicion.[1] The contemporary Donatist gibe that African Catholic congregations represented the 'multitude of waters' teeming with heretics of diverse sorts, and 'the vile dregs of Manichees' had a good deal of justification.[2] The story of Priscillian suggests that Africa was not the only province in the West where Manichaeism influenced Catholic clergy.

It is not possible at present to say why this should have been so. Something, however, may be learnt from Augustine's contact with Manichaeism, and from the imprint which the heresy left permanently on his mind. At an early period, he tells us, he became obsessed with the problem of evil, and in this mood he fell under the influence of the Manichees at Carthage.[3] He first sought an answer from the Old Testament, but this repelled him, and for a long time he was satisfied by the Manichee solution.[4] Here his experience seems to have been similar to that of Faustus of Milevis, who relates how diligently he had studied both Testaments before coming to the conclusion that the New Testament, purged of Jewish interpolations, alone sufficed for Christian belief.[5]

Then, Manichaeism was the religion of the inquiring mind, and of the ascetic, features which made it an attractive religion to Augustine and many of his middle-class contemporaries.[6] Professor Courcelle has shown by a comparison of Augustine's statements in the *Confessions* with those made in other works, notably the *De Beata Vita, Sermo* li and *De Utilitate Credendi,* that it was above all the desire for a faith explicable by reason that caused his conversion.[7] The Manichees, regarding the soul as consubstantial with the Father of Greatness,[8] naturally based their claims on an appeal to reason. When Augustine's Manichee friends pointed out that the Catholic Church taught the existence of an anthropomorphic god and argued the impossibility of reconciling the rules enjoined in the Old Testament with the religion of the New, the basis of Augustine's childhood faith was sapped. The idealism in him was awakened by the feeling of conversion and he returned to Thagaste a prosletysing member of the sect, ready, like Faustus or his Coptic Manichee contemporaries, to reject with contempt the religion of his parents.[9]

---

[1] *Ep.* ccxxxvi. 1–3: C.S.E.L., lvii. 524. Cf. Pope Leo I, *Sermo,* xlii. 5: P.L., liv. 279.
[2] *Contra Fulgentium,* xiii: P.L., xliii. 768. It is interesting that Tertullian aligns Gnostics and Catholics ('Psychics') as enemies of the church of the martyrs.
[3] Augustine, *De Libero Arbitrio,* i. 4: 'eam quaestionem quae me admodum adolescentem vehementer exercuit et fatigatum in haereticos impulit atque dejecit' (P.L., xxxii. 1311). Cf. K. Holl, 'Augustins innere Entwicklung', *Gesammelte Aufsätze,* iii. 54–116.
[4] *Conf.* v. 12–20.
[5] *Contra Faustum,* xxxiii. 1 and 2, and *De Moribus Ecclesiae Catholicae,* i. 2.
[6] See P. Alfaric's chapter on Augustine's Manichaeism in his *L'Evolution intellectuelle de St. Augustin,* Paris 1918, 65 f.
[7] P. Courcelle, *Recherches sur les Confessions de Saint Augustin,* Paris 1950, 60–67. See also *De Duabus Animis,* ix.
[8] Evodius, *De Fide,* xii; see also H. C. Puech, *Le Manichéisme,* 154n. 275.
[9] *Confessions,* iii. 11, 19. See also *Contra Faustum,* v. 1, and xiii. 1, and the Coptic Manichee Psalm, No. CCLXIX, lines 29–32 (ed. Allberry, Stuttgart 1938, 87.).

23

Two other factors may have played their part. First, Augustine as well as his friends like Alypius were fully convinced of the truth of astrological predictions.[1] Secondly, as a Numidian Catholic, a member of a ruling minority, there was less inherent compulsion, such as devotion to local martyrs or a treasured memory of persecution resisted, to hold Augustine to the Church once his intellectual assent had weakened. To many observers Numidian Catholicism in the 370s and 380s must have seemed a dying religion.[2] The Manichees, regarding previous experience as the tributaries to the true synthesis of religion,[3] were evidently more attractive to the young philosopher than were the Donatists. By becoming a Manichee Augustine had no thought of renouncing Christianity.

This attraction, though rigorously suppressed after his baptism, remained with Augustine throughout his life. As Holl has pointed out, Augustine spent ten of his most formative years as a Manichee. These years had not been wasted. He had pondered over the problem of evil and he had learnt of the essential order and harmony of the universe in which evil also had its place.[4] Mani had provided him with logical explanations for all phenomena, natural and supernatural, explanations neatly arranged in numerical sequences of fives and twelves. Augustine was not satisfied with the details of the scheme, which offended his scientific sense, but the concept he never forgot. Moreover, as a Manichee he had learnt to hate the flesh and to admire the Elects' ideal of chastity. He was disillusioned by their failure to live up to their rule, and not by the rule itself.[5] He had been content to remain an *Auditor* himself because he still desired worldly advancement.[6] The 'monastery' which he founded at Hippo on his return from Italy in 388 seems to have resembled the Manichee communities he had lived in or experienced in Rome.[7] Indeed, as in Egypt, the Manichees in the West may have had a considerable share in popularising the monastic ideal. Thus, with his knowledge and sympathy for his former creed, he was able to point out its weaknesses and actually convince its adherents of their errors by citing his own experience. That Manichaeism failed to survive in the West as an organised religion may be due largely to Augustine's writings and controversies in the years 387–399.

But, paradoxically, the most abiding legacy of Western Gnosticism

---

[1] *Confessions*, iv. 3, 4; *Contra Academicos*, i. 17.

[2] Optatus of Milevis, in his second edition of *De Schismate Donatistarum*, admits the weakness of Catholicism in Numidia. It existed 'licet in paucis', vii. 1 (Ziwsa, p. 159). Also, Possidius, *Vita Augustini*, vii.

[3] See *Kephalaion* 154 in the Coptic Manichee writings, described and published by K. Schmidt and H. J. Polotsky; 'Ein Mani-Fund in Aegypten', *Sitzungsberichte der Berliner Akademie der Wissenschaften*, 1933, Phil.-Hist. Kl. 4–89, at pp. 41–42.

[4] This is suggested among other things by the title of his work which he wrote while a Manichee, *De Apto et Pulchro*; cf. K. Holl, *Augustins innere Entwicklung*, 75.

[5] Augustine, *De Moribus Manichaeorum*, lxviii.

[6] *De Util. Cred.*, ii.

[7] The Manichaean monasteries in the West were a mixture of a seminary and a hostel in which the Elect might practise religion in preparation for their lives as missionaries. Augustine's aim at Hippo seems to have been similar; cf. *De Moribus Manichaeorum*, lxxiv and Possidius, *Vita* v.

THE GNOSTIC-MANICHAEAN TRADITION

and Manichaeism is probably to be found in the later theology of St. Augustine. For the sake of the original thinker it was unfortunate that after 400 he felt impelled to lay aside the doctrinal works on which he was engaged to seize the chance offered by Gildo's defeat to overthrow the Donatists.[1] For the next twelve years the politician dominated the theologian in him, and, when once more in 411 at the age of 57 he turned back to theological controversies, the ideas which came most readily to his mind seem to have been those of his youth, and not those of his maturity. He had become, moreover, in the strife with the Donatists, too ardent and too vindictive a debater to allow his Pelagian opponents to establish any claim whatever to the justice of their case.[2] This was fatal to a judicious assessment of the rôles of human free will and divine grace.

Augustine, it is true was at pains to point out the difference between the Catholic and Manichee viewpoints. Indeed, the fourth book of *Contra duas Epistolas Pelagianorum* and the first book against Julian of Eclanum are little more than a long and able defence against the charge of Manichaeism. Yet there was something in Julian's accusations, and it is curious to find in the mouth of this last great opponent of Augustine the very same charges that he himself was wont to make against the Manichees a generation before. How could Christian penitence be reconciled with predestination,[3] or traducianism with the non-substantiality of evil?[4] If marriage was essentially good, how could procreation be essentially wicked?[5] More and more one finds Augustine in difficulties, almost desperately attempting to establish a *via media* between Pelagianism and Manichaeism, but inescapably driven towards the conclusions of his youth by the logic of his anti-Pelagian argument.[6] Indeed, it seems hardly possible that one who had lived his early manhood as a member of a sect permeated by ideas of Grace and predestination, could have reacted differently when faced with the Pelagian challenge. So the argument that no meritorious action was possible without Grace led to the conclusion that the elect were small in numbers compared with the mass of the naturally damned. The Christian elect came to differ little from the Manichee *Electi*.[7] Like them, 'their

---

[1] The *De Genesi ad Litteram*, which was designed as a complete refutation of Manichaeism, and the *De Trinitate*. See G. Bardy, *Saint Augustin: l'Homme et l'Oeuvre*, Bruges 1948, 328.

[2] Augustine's view of the Pelagian case can be indicated by his question, 'Quid eis hoc prodest, per verum seducere ad falsum'? *Contra duas Epist. Pel.*, iv. 5. 9: P.L., xliv. 615.

[3] Julian, cited by Augustine in *Contra Julianum, opus Imperfectum*, iv. 126; cf. Augustine, *Contra Fortunatum*, i. 21.

[4] Julian in *Contra Julianum*, vi. 5. 11.

[5] Julian in *Contra Julianum*, vi. 2. 3.

[6] For instance, when he has to refute the Pelagian thesis, 'omne peccatum non de natura sed de voluntate descendere' (*Contra duas Epist. Pelagianorum* iv. 4. 5; P. L., xliv. 612). This had been the point he had tried to prove against the Manichees 30 years before in *De Duabus Animis*, xii. 16–18 and *De Moribus Manichaeorum* vii f.

[7] There is a contrast here between Augustine's immediate Post-Manichee ideas. In *De Ordine*, ii. 10. 29 he rebukes Alypius for not understanding how liberally God's grace was spread throughout all nations. Grace was not restricted to the few predestined ones, as in *Cont. Jul.*, vi. 24. 75 and v. 4. 14.

figure (εἰκών)' as the Coptic Manichee psalmist exclaimed, 'had been chosen out',[1] and sin involving loss of grace was next to impossible. To Augustine, the unredeemed *massa* were 'in the possession of the devil' and 'deserved to be burnt for eternity'. As Buonaiuti pointed out, this *massa* is none other than a literal translation of the Manichaean βῶλος to which the wicked adhered[2] and which would be consumed in the eternal fire. All who were born by natural process of birth were part of this *massa* and belonged to the 'jus diaboli'.[3] As in Manichaeism, concupiscence was the means by which this 'law' was perpetuated.[4] Finally, the 'two cities' into which mankind would become divided, were not merely 'Types' as described by Tyconius, but in Augustine's hands they become entities, peopled by good and evil elements, while the Kingdom of the Devil was portrayed as a place of smoky, noxious darkness, reminiscent of the Manichee's Hell.[5] There was much to be said for Julian's final gibe that no more than an Ethiopian could change his skin or a leopard change his spots could Augustine free himself from Manichaeism.[6] The Gnostic tendency which we have observed in African Church history in the third century was never quite extinguished.[7] If Augustine drove both Donatism and Manichaeism out of sight, he may to some extent have perpetuated the latter in his theology of Grace.

[1] Cited from Polotsky and Ibscher, *Manichäische Handschriften* (Stuttgart 1934), p. 3, l. 25.

[2] E. Buonaiuti, 'Manichaeism and Augustine', *Harvard Theol. Review*, xx. (1927) 117–127.

[3] Augustine, *De Nuptiis et Concupiscentia*, i. 21; also *Contra Julianum*, vi. 2. 3, and *Ep.*, clxxxvi.

[4] *De Gratia Christi et de Peccato originali*, ii. 33. 38; P.L., xliv. 404: cf. E. Buonaiuti, op. cit., 125n. 16.

[5] *De Civitate Dei*, xi. 33.

[6] *Contra Julianum, opus Imperf.* iv. 42; cf. G. de Plinval, *Pélage*, Fribourg 1945, 363.

[7] For the general continuity between the Gnostic and Marcionite communities in the West with Manichaeism, see Harnack's classic, *Marcion: das Evangelium vom fremden Gott*, Leipzig 1921, 193 f. and 272*.

XIII

Manichaeism in the Struggle between Saint Augustine and Petilian of Constantine

It is not easy to do justice to the opponents of St. Augustine. Faustus of Milevis, Petilian of Constantine, and Julian of Eclanum have all suffered through being the anvils on which the doctrinal truths associated with Augustinianism were hammered out. But Faustus and Petilian were Numidians like Augustine himself, and like him they represented religious ideas that had taken firm root in that province. In the end, both Donatism and Manichaeism were to last as long as Catholicism in North Africa, and towards the close of his life Augustine himself began to see that his great effort to establish Catholicism as the religion of his homeland had failed. Thus, the causes of the underlying weakness of Augustine's position in his own country are of real interest to the historian of the Church. In this paper we examine one possible line of inquiry which had special relevance to the resistance of Donatism to him, namely the suspicion that Catholicism in Numidia was not only a wilful and persecuting schism, but that it served as a cloak of respectability for the dreaded religion of the Manichees.

Though in 405 the Imperial Government meted out the same penalties to Donatists and Manichees[1], and Paulinus of Nola regarded them as the « twin horns of offence » in Africa[2], it would be difficult to find two more contrasting sets of belief.

The Donatists regarded themselves as the Catholic Church in Africa. They consciously took their stand on the practices accepted by the Church in the time of Cyprian and they denounced as heretical all doctrines condemned as unorthodox in the third and fourth centuries[3]. Hence, Marcionites, Cataphrygians, Novatianists, Patripassians, Valentinians, Arians and Manichaeans were all brushed aside, and the Donatist leaders rejoiced at the gradual disappearance of paganism throughout

---

1. *Codex Theodosianus* (ed. Mommsen and Meyer, Berlin, 1905) XVI, 5, 38. « Nemo Manichæum, nemo Donatistam, qui (ut comperimus) furere non desistunt in memoriam revocet ».
2. AUGUSTINE, *Ep.* 32, 2, CSEL, 34², 10, 8 : « ut cornua peccatorum, sicut per prophetam spondet, hoc est Donatistarum Manichæorumque, confringat.
3. E. g. Parmenian, in OPTATUS, *De Schismate Donatistarum*, I, 9, CSEL, 26, 10. Cresconius in AUGUSTINE, *Contra Cresconium*, II, 3, 4, CSEL, 52, 363 and IV, 61, 75, CSEL, 52, 574.

the world[1]. Their doctrinal and social outlook was not far different from that of Tertullian two centuries earlier. Their God was the Old Testament Jehovah, whose acceptable sacrifice was the blood sacrifice of martyrdom. Their Christology was subordinationist, probably due less to sympathy with Arius than to archaism[2]. They turned their backs on classical art and literature, accepting one book, the African Bible as containing all that was necessary to life here and hereafter. Beneath the surface of this mass movement smouldered the age-old cruelties and superstitions of Berber Numidia.

Just as Gnosticism and its allies within the Catholic Church had been anathema to Tertullian and to the African Montanists, so two centuries later, its successor, Manichaeism was abhorrent to the Donatists. The African Manichee rejected precisely those beliefs which the Donatist held most dear. Old Testament texts preaching defiance at persecution were to be found in plenty on the walls of Donatist chapels[3]. The Manichee, however, regarded the Old Testament as unnecessary for salvation, if not actually the work of the powers of darkness[4]. The Donatists buried their dead in great cemeteries, where care was taken to preserve the shape of the body in plaster for recognition at the last Day and offerings were made to the deceased[5]. The Manichee, in rejecting the humanity of Christ, rejected also the doctrine of the resurrection of the body. In daily life, far from requiring their converts to abandon previous pagan studies, they argued that such learning assisted the understanding of divine truth[6]. Not martyrdom, but a well-instructed mind, they argued, was the most acceptable sacrifice to God ; and Sibyl, Orpheus and Hermes Trismegistos rather than the Hebrew prophets were the forerunners of Christianity[7]. Faustus of Milevis scorned his Christian fellow-citizens, of whom the majority were Donatist, as mere schismatics from idolatry[8]. If Donatism drew its strength from the Numidian colonate who gloried in their faith and toiled for their living, the Manichees were mainly composed of urban and semi-clandestine groups, who saw physical labour as something to be rigorously avoided. Activity of any sort was a source of damage to the souls which inhabited things

1. Cresconius in AUGUSTINE, *Contra Cresconium*, IV, 61, 74, CSEL, 52, 573.

2. This might explain why they, like the African Catholics, accepted the Semi-Arian formulæ of Sardica and Sirmium but rejected Arianism.

3. Examples are quoted in Paul MONCEAUX, *Histoire littéraire de l'Afrique chrétienne*, IV, 455 f.

4. Faustus in AUGUSTINE, *Contra Faustum*, XV, 1, CSEL 25[1], 415.

5. See the writer's *The Donatist Church*, Oxford, 1952, 91, and A. BERTHIER, *L'Algérie et son passé*, Picard, 1951, 113.

6. Faustus in AUGUSTINE, *Contra Faustum*, XX, 3, CSEL 25[1], 537, 19. Cf. AUGUSTINE, *Confessions*, V, 6, 11, CSEL, 33, 97.

7. *Ibid.*, XIII, 1, CSEL, 25[1], 378, 28.

8. *Ibid.*, XX, 4, CSEL, 25[1], 538, 16.

associated with toil, such as beasts of burden or crops[1]. Not unnaturally, Manichaeism aroused horror among the Donatists, and not unnaturally too, a Manichaean background was not calculated to render the understanding of Donatism easy for the Catholic leaders. When in the summer of 392 the Donatists of Hippo approached Augustine to confound the Manichaean presbyter, Fortunatus, they showed clearly that they feared the Manichee more than they did the new Catholic presbyter[2].

Thus, to awake the suspicion in the minds of their followers that some of the Catholic clergy in Numidia had closer ties with the Manichees than they cared to admit, was an obvious line of propaganda for the Donatist leaders to adopt. In the twelve years of controversy between Augustine and Petilian of Constantine the charge of Manichaeism was persistently levelled at Augustine himself and his immediate friends, and it came to be taken up generally by the Donatists in controversy against the Catholics.

The duel between Augustine and Petilian begins about the end of A. D. 400[3]. Augustine had come into possession of the first part of a tract written by Petilian for his clergy, warning them against the activities of Fortunatus, the new Catholic bishop of Constantine. Both Fortunatus and his predecessor Profuturus were friends of Augustine, and like him had been Manichees before receiving Catholic Orders[4]. Fortunatus himself was a busy, proseletysing prelate, who kept Augustine fully informed of discreditable happenings in Petilian's diocese[5]. Petilian did not like him, and in one passage of his tract, he compares Fortunatus's claim to be a bishop with that of Manichaeus. Both represented the lineage of apostasy from Christ, which expressed itself by ensnaring souls and persecuting the true Church[6].

Augustine's reply to the first part of Petilian's letter which included the reference to Manichaeism, pointed out that the denunciation of the Manichees though welcome, was quite irrelevant[7]. The error of Donatus had no power to overthrow that of the Manichees. Petilian thought

1. *Acta Archelai* (ed. Beeson, Leipzig, 1906), 10. Cf. AUGUSTINE, *Confessions*, III, 10, 18, CSEL 33, 60, 3 and *Enarratio in Ps.* 140, 12, PL. 37, 1823.

2. POSSIDIUS, *Vita Sancti Augustini*, 6, PL. 32, 38.

3. I am accepting P. MONCEAUX's dating, *Histoire littéraire*, VI, 16, leaving slightly wider margin between the time Augustine received PETILIAN's *Ad Presbvteros. Epistola* and his reply.

4. AUGUSTINE, *De unico Baptismo contra Petilianum*, XVI, 29, CSEL 53, 31. Profuturus was a pupil of Augustine, *Ep.* 32, 1 and 38, CSEL 34², 8, 21 and *ibid.* 14, 15.

5. For instance, the case of Splendonius, AUGUSTINE, *Contra Litteras Petiliani*, III, 38, 44, CSEL 52, 198, 10.

6. Petilian in AUGUSTINE, *Contra Litteras Petiliani*, II, 18, 40, CSEL 52, 42. This is an obscure passage whose interpretation is made difficult by the allusion to the sixty disciples who left our Lord (cf. John. VI⁶⁶), in connection with Mani. Possibly, apocryphal works were circulating whose authorship was attributed to members of the sixty and were being used by Manichæans.

7. AUGUSTINE, *Contra Littercs Petiliani*, I, 26, 28, CSEL 52, 21-22.

otherwise, for the first and only extant book[1] against Augustine's reply contains the assertion that Augustine himself was a secret Manichee[2], and he linked this personal attack to his main theme, that the sacraments dispensed by Catholic ministers did not have their origin in Christ and were not, therefore, instruments of salvation.

The main accusations in Petilian's *Ad Augustinum* have already been discussed by Professor Courcelle in his brilliant study of the *Confessions* of St. Augustine[3]. Much of the material which Petilian used was taken from books III and IV of the *Confessions*, and was embroidered upon so as to leave the impression that Augustine's conversion had been insincere, and that the only baptism he had ever received had been a Manichaean rite in Africa. Since in the Donatist view « it was the conscience of the giver (of baptism) giving in holiness that cleansed the conscience of the recipient », Augustine who « had knowingly received faith from the faithless, had received not faith but guilt[4] ». It seems, however, that for some time past, perhaps even before the *Confessions* had been written, the weak points in Augustine's career had been receiving attention among the Donatists. In any event, a substantial dossier drawn from various sources stood ready to Petilian's hand when he entered the lists against him, probably in the latter part of 401.

It is clear, for instance, that in the 380 S. Augustine had been well enough known as a Manichee in Carthage for his name to have been cited by the defence in the *cause célèbre* against the Manichees tried by the proconsul Messianus in 386[5]. The incident was remembered. It was easy to assert fifteen years later that Augustine's journey to Italy had been an opportune withdrawal to avoid difficulties with the authorities. More compromising to a Numidian audience was the letter which the Catholic primate of Numidia, Megalius, bishop of Calama, had written to Valerius of Hippo in 395 or 396 when the latter proposed to make Augustine his co-adjutor[6]. If Megalius had suspected Augustine's conversion, why should not Petilian ? This letter was one of the most prized pieces of evidence in Donatist possession. Many copies apparently existed[7]. It was used by Cresconius in his reply to Augustine's

---

1. That he intended to write a second book is shown in *Contra Litteras Petiliani*, III, 36, 42, CSEL 52, 196, 9. « Licet hoc secundo libro demonstrem... »
2. AUGUSTINE, *Contra Litteras Petiliani*, III, 16, 19, CSEL 52, 177, 4, « Manichæorum immunditias libentissime exaggeret, easque in me latrando detorquere conetur. »
3. P. COURCELLE, *Recherches sur les Confessions de Saint Augustin*, Paris, 1950, pp. 238-245. I owe a great debt to this work both in regard to my book on the Donatist Church and in the present paper.
4. Petilian in AUGUSTINE, *Contra Litteras Petiliani*, II, 3, 6, CSEL 52, 25 ; 4, 8, *ibid.*, 25 and III, 20, 23, *ibid.*, 179, 24.
5. AUGUSTINE, *Contra Litteras Petiliani*, III, 16, 19 and 25, 30, CSEL 52, 177, 6 and *ibid.*, 185, 15. P. COURCELLE, *op. cit.*, 240.
6. AUGUSTINE, *Contra Litteras Petiliani*, III, 16, 19, CSEL 52, 177, 15.
7. AUGUSTINE, *Contra Cresconium*, III, 80, 92, CSEL 52, 495, 8.

first book *Contra Litteras Petiliani*[1], and also by Petilian at the conference of Carthage in 411[2] in order to challenge the validity of Augustine's ordination. The rest of the evidence which Petilian put forward was calculated to complete the desired impression of St. Augustine — that of the Manichee presbyter and rhetorician turned Catholic bishop. The confession of a Catholic *sanctimonialis* in his diocese to Manichaeism evidently gave him some valuable, if inaccurate, information about local Manichaean baptismal practices[3]. Most damaging of all, however, may have been the extract of a letter written by Augustine possibly to Paulinus of Nola in 396. This Petilian interpreted to mean, that he had sent bread polluted in Manichaean eucharistic rites to his correspondents, at a time when he was ostensibly a candidate for episcopacy in the Catholic Church. Such « sacraments » would certainly be regarded as « venenosa turpitudo ac furor » by any Christian, and could hardly have commended the claims of the Catholics to administer a true sacrament[4]. As Augustine himself pointed out in another connection, among the practices of the Manichaean Elect was the liberation of the soul in bread and its despatch heavenwards[5]. They pitied the bread rather than the hungry beggar who implored it.

Augustine had a sound answer to all Petilian's charges. He had openly and sincerely repented his Manichaeism, he had written many anti-Manichaean works, he had left Africa three years before the trial before Messianus had taken place, Megalius had withdrawn his strictures against him and apologised to a Council. On the other hand, as is clear from his writings, he remembered for more about Manichaean literature and ideas than would be expected in an African Catholic bishop[6]. His past laid him open to unscrupulous attacks. As he was forced to admit, Petilian was supreme in the capital of Numidia, and his word carried weight in Hippo[7]. Whoever had handed over to him Megalius letter to Valerius, or had had long enough access to Augustine's correspondence to copy letters which might be compromising, had rendered signal service to Donatism.

---

1. *Ibid.*, and IV, 64, 79, CSEL 52, 577.

2. *Gesta Collationis Carthaginensis*, III, 234-247, PL. II, 1405.

3. AUGUSTINE, *Contra Litteras Petiliani*, III, 17, 20, CSEL 52, 177, 25. Inaccurate, because Augustine himself states, « Baptismum... quod Manichæi dicunt in omni ætate superfluum » in *Contra duas Epistolas Pelagianorum*, IV, 4, 5, PL. 44, 613.

4. AUGUSTINE, *Ep.* 31, 9, CSEL 34[2], 8, 10 and *Contra Litteras Petiliani*, III, 16, 19, CSEL 52, 177, 11. I have followed COURCELLE, *op. cit.*, p. 239, n. 2, though this solution suggests an astonishing degree of ability or luck on the part of the Donatist agent, who managed to secur copies of these particular letters ans convey them to Petilian without apparently being detected. The attack clearly took Augustine off his guard.

5. AUGUSTINE, *Enarratio in Ps.* 140, 12, PL. 37, 1823.

6. B. ALTANER, *Augustinus und die N.T. Apokryphen*, dans *Analecta Bollandiana*, 67, 1949, pp. 236-248.

7. AUGUSTINE, *Contra Litteras Petiliani*, III, 11, 12 and 59, 72, CSEL 52, 173, 19 and 227, 7. Also, *Epistula ad Catholicos*, I, *ibid.*, 231, 15.

In Carthage also, a formidable reception awaited Augustine when he went there in the summer of 403 to attend a Council and preach against Donatism. Primian made substantially the same accusation as Petilian, though emphasizing most his disorderly past in Carthage itself and the suspicion that he had not been baptised into the Catholic Church in Italy[1]. Augustine replied that even if all the rumours about him were true, that would only make him straw rather than wheat in the Church ; but he was grievously shaken by Primian's onslaught and it was seven years before he preached against Donatism in Carthage again.

The debate showed no signs of flagging in the following years. The influence of the accusation of Manichaeism is perceptible in Augustine's reply to Cresconius about the year 406. Apart from the allusions to Megalius' letter, one finds Augustine having to defend his own record when commenting on Petitlian's original reference to Manichaeism in his *Ad Presbyteros Epistola*[2]. It will be remembered that in his reply to Petilian (*Contra Litteras Petiliani*, I, 28) in 401, he had dismissed this reference as quite irrelevant. Now, he could not afford to take this line, even though the statement had not been aimed at him. In Constantine itself, Petilian resumed his attack on Fortunatus. The *De Unico Baptismo* (*Circa* A. D. 409) pointed to the fact that both he and his predecessor had been Manichees[3]. How could a Church which had *traditores* for its founders and secret Manichees among its priests claim to be Catholic ? By now the argument had become general, and in the anonymous pamphlet entitled *Contra Fulgentium*, the Donatist representative denounced the Church, of his Catholic opponent as « teeming heretics of all sorts, and the vile dregs of the Manichees[4] ».

Are we justified in dismissing these charges as purely polemical calumny, or were there factors in the religious situation in Numidia which made them appear credible ? Two points stand out. First, there is consistent evidence for the attraction which Manichaeism exercised on individual Catholics, and vice versa, for which there is no parallel in the history of Donatism[5]. Among the spurs which drove Augustine to write his anti-Manichaean works of the period 387-399 was the reconversion of Catholics who had gone over to Manichaeism, and in many

1. AUGUSTINE, *Sermo* 3 in *Ps.* 36, 19, PL. 36, 393-394. P. COURCELLE, *op. cit.*, p. 244.
2. AUGUSTINE, *Contra Cresconium*, IV, 64, 79, CSEL 52, 577, 23. « Tibi certe ipse non succenseo, quod mihi ex obliquo Manichæos objicendos putaveris, propter adolescentiæ meæ. » The reference had not been aimed at Augustine in the first place, but at Fortunatus, but Augustine had become sensitive to any mention of Manichæism by his opponents. Cf. *ibid.*, III, 78, 90, CSEL 52, 493.
3. AUGUSTINE, *De Unico Baptismo*, XVI, 29, CSEL 53, 31.
4. PSEUDO-AUGUSTINUS, *Adversus Fulgentium Donatistam*, 13, CSEL 53, 299. Written *circa* 412.
5. For further details I would refer the reader to my article on « The Gnostic-Manichæan Tradition in Roman North Africa », *Journal of Ecclesiastical History*, IV, 1, 1953, 13-26.

cases he was successful[1]. In the climax of the struggle with Donatism the chief Catholic leaders in Numidia, Augustine, Alypius and Fortunatus had all been Manichees. Unlike conversion from Donatism, a Manichaean background does not seem to have constituted an effective barrier to promotion in the Catholic Church, even to important bishoprics such as Constantine. Catholicism in Numidia would have been in a poor way without its Manichaean converts.

Secondly, despite the efforts of St. Augustine and his friends to expose the Manichees, there is evidence to suggest that a certain amount of secret Manichaeism persisted within the Catholic Church. The case of the Catholic *sanctimonialis* in the diocese of Constantine has been mentioned. Augustine himself relates an extraordinary affair which seems to have taken place some time after 411[2]. One of his sub-deacons, the incumbent in the village of Mallia, confessed to having been a Manichaean Hearer for years, and to have taught Manichaean doctrine throughout his career in the Church without apparently awakening the least suspicion. The sort of thing which was going on is indicated from a letter written by Augustine to his colleague Quintasius some years before. Quintasius had been allowing non-canonical scriptures, including those read by the Manichees to be used in his diocese, where Manichaeism was rife[3]. In 393 the Council of Hippo had forbidden the use of all but canonical Scriptures in churches, with the aim of preventing just such abuses[4]. The suspicion against the Afri;an Catholic clergy never quite died out. Both Pope Gregory I[5] and Gregory II[6] issued warnings against accepting African priests entering Italy without investigation, as they might turn out to be Manichees.

The reason for this association lies outside the scope of this paper[7]. But the fact that such suspicions were widespread in Africa at the height of the Donatist controversy has prompted us to look closely at Petilian's arguments. They throw some light on what Augustine and his friends represented in the eyes of those whom they were trying to convince, and that they ultimately had to rely on force in order to prevail is not surprising. As we know from the sermons and letters of Pope Leo, Rome itself contained numerous Manichees who behaved outwardly as Catholic

---

1. Particularly noticeable in the *De Utilitate Credendi* addressed to his friend Honoratus, and the *De Moribus Manichæorum*.

2. AUGUSTINE, *Ep.* 236, CSEL 57, 523, addressed to Deuterius of Cæsarea with whom Augustine first enters into contact after the conference of Carthage.

3. AUGUSTINE, *Ep.* 64, 3, CSEL 34², 231.

4. *Breviarium Hipponense*, 36 (ed. Bruns, *Canones Conc. Apost. selecti*, Berlin, 1839, II, 138).

5. GREGORY, *Ep.* II, 37 (ed. Ewald and Hartmann, Berlin, 1891, vol. I, 133).

6. GREGORY II, *Ep.* 4, PL. 79, col. 502.

7. I have suggested some of the reasons in my paper in the *Journal of Ecclesiastical History*, 1953, *art. cit.* p. 24-26.

Christians[1]. This was the case in Africa also. It should be taken into account as one of the underlying factors in Augustine's controversy with Petilian, and to have contributed to the bitterness and tenacity of the Donatist resistance to him.

Cambridge.

1. Pope Leo, *Sermo,* 16, 4, PL. 54, 178 and *Ep.* 7, *Ad Episcopos per Italiam, ibid.,* 620.

XIV

A NOTE ON THE BERBER BACKGROUND IN THE LIFE OF AUGUSTINE

In North Africa during the Roman occupation, as in our own day, there were three distinct languages spoken. Latin had been brought in by the conquerors from the northern shores of the Mediterranean as the official language, and it was probably spoken with the same fluency and enthusiasm by the native town-dwellers as is French by their Arab successors. But among themselves, whether in town or country, the normal speech of the natives seems to have been either a Semitic language, Punic, or the African language, Libyan, which is the direct ancestor of the modern Berber.

It has generally been assumed that Punic must have succeeded in ousting Libyan as the spoken language even in fairly remote areas of Roman North Africa. Recent discoveries of Libyan and Latino-Libyan inscriptions suggest, however, that the distribution of African native languages in the Roman Empire was not so very different from the modern distribution of Arab-speaking and Berber-speaking districts, though Arabic is now spoken over a rather wider area than Punic ever was. It seems that the Semitic language was favoured then, as at present, in the coastal areas from Homs (Leptis Magna) to Oran, and in the earlier colonized districts of the Algerian and Tunisian river valleys. Outside these areas the language and culture of the people remained Libyan. Some discoveries of Libyan inscriptions made in the years preceding the war are of particular interest as shedding light on the social background of the Africans in northern Numidia among whom St. Augustine spent his life.

Between 1932 and 1937, M. Paul Rodary, administrateur in the Commune Mixte of Souk-Ahras (Department of Constantine), the ancient Thagaste, carried through a series of searches for Libyan inscriptions within the bounds of his administration.[1] As a result of his investigations, 213 new Libyan inscriptions were found in cemeteries in the country lying north of Souk-Ahras. These make a substantial addition to the large collection of Libyan texts already known from sites near that town.[2] Souk-Ahras itself has produced six.[3] Many of these stones were doubtless pre-Roman, but M. Rodary found a number of bilingual, Latino-Libyan, inscriptions from the cemeteries of Djentoura, Chabet el Mkous, Dar Tebala, Kef beni Fredj, and Sidi Abdallah.[4] All these places are in the hills north and west of Souk-Ahras. These latest discoveries help to dispel the confusion caused by Augustine's statements concerning the speech of the peasantry in this part of North Africa in his day.

Augustine describes the native farmers who lived in the hill forts ('castella') such as Fussala,[5] or in villages on the great estates such as Sinitum and Figuli,[6] as speaking 'Punic which is African',[7] and in view of M. Rodary's researches there seems every reason for identifying 'Punic' with the Libyan or proto-Berber of the inscriptions.[8] Punic or neo-Punic inscriptions are almost wholly confined to the Algerian towns or, if they are found in the country-side, as in the case of the Bordj Hellal inscription, are the work of citizens.[9] At present the number of Punic or neo-Punic inscriptions discovered

[1] P. Rodary, 'Recherche des Inscriptions libyques dans la Région de Souk-Ahras', *Premier Congrès de la Fédération des Sociétés savantes de l'Afrique du Nord*, Alger, 1935, pp. 173–81, and pp. 415–23 in the transactions of the Third Congress held at Constantine, 1937, published at Algiers, 1938.

[2] See S. Gsell, *Atlas archéologique de l'Algérie*, Alger, 1911, feuille 18 (Souk-Ahras), nos. 185, 200, 218, 235, 236, 249, 267, &c.

[3] Dr. L. Reboud, *Recueil de Constantine*, xvii, 1875, p. 21 ; S. Gsell, *Atlas archéologique*, feuille 18, no. 340.

[4] P. Rodary, op. cit. [5] *Ep.* 209, 2–5; *C.S.E.L.* lvii, pp. 348–50.

[6] *Ep.* 108, 5, 14; *C.S.E.L.* xxxiv, part 2, p. 628; also *Ep.* 105, 2, 3–4; *C.S.E.L.* xxxiv, part 2, pp. 597–8.

[7] 'Latinam et Punicam, id est Afram', *In Epistolam Ioannis ad Parthos, Tractatus*, ii. 3 ; *P.L.* xxxiv–xxxv, col. 1991.

[8] Ernest Mercier, *Recueil de Constantine*, xxx, 1895, p. 146, makes this point. There are in addition practically no Punic loan-words in the Berber language, such as might have been expected if Punic had ever superseded Berber as the speech of the country-side. There are on the other hand a few Latin loan-words in modern Berber. On this subject see H. Basset, 'Les Influences puniques chez les Berbères', *Revue Africaine*, lxii, 1921, pp. 340–75.

[9] Père J. Chabot, note in *Recueil de Constantine*, lxiii, 1935–6, p. 197.

outside ancient cities of Algeria and Tunisia is very small, while on the other hand Libyan inscriptions are numerous. Indeed, no area in the whole of North Africa is so rich in these inscriptions as that within a twenty-mile radius of Souk-Ahras. One rather suspects that Augustine regarded all native speech as 'Punic', just as the majority of Frenchmen in Algeria do not distinguish between Arabic and Berber. To them, both are 'Arabic'.

The vitality of Berber culture during the late Roman or post-Roman periods in the area in which Augustine was brought up, is further suggested by the finding of the characteristic Libyan dolmen constructed from the stone of ruined Roman buildings, as at Guelaat bou Atfane and Sigus, two sites lying south and south-east of Souk-Ahras.[1]

One may regard Thagaste in the time of St. Augustine as typical of the decaying Roman towns of fourth-century North Africa. A few large town houses would be inhabited by Latin-speaking citizens. These were the landowners, such as Romanianus, or Alypius' family, who owned great estates outside the city, with whom Augustine, though himself the son of poorer parents, was closely associated.[2] Beyond the town walls the peasant lived a not very different life from that of his descendant to-day; he was a Berber, almost wholly uninfluenced by Roman civilization and often hostile to its representatives.

One would welcome some attempt to assess Augustine's importance as an African in the history of North Africa, and to consider his thought in the light of his Berber background. How far do Augustine's ideas show traces of the Berber surroundings in which he grew up? Underlying the Latin rhetoric of his sermons, is there any trend which links his thought with that of later North African thinkers such

---

[1] S. Gsell, *Monuments antiques de l'Algérie*, vol. 1, Paris, 1901, pp. 33–4. An interesting Romano-Berber cemetery was excavated just outside Hippo. The finds revealed an extreme poverty and barbarity on the part of those who were buried there. See M. Belorgey, 'Découverte des Caveaux funéraires dans le Terrain de la Société des Lièges et Produits Nord-Africains', *Actes du troisième Congrès de la Fédération des Sociétés savantes de l'Afrique du Nord*, 1937.

[2] *Confessions*, vi. 14, and vi. 7, 11. Augustine himself was the son of a curial, but apparently both he and Alypius were able to avoid taking their place in the Curia of Thagaste. Augustine's friends, as revealed in his letters, all appear to have been members of the Latin-speaking upper classes, with the exception of Bishop Samsucius (*Ep.* 34, 6). Compare Augustine's description of the status of his next door neighbour, the Senator Julianus, 'de domo clarissimi et egregii iuvenis Iuliani quae nostris adhaeret parietibus', *Ep.* 99; *C.S.E.L.* xxxiv. 2, p. 533.

At Cuicul (Djemila) the mansions of the aristocracy and the church are the only surviving trace of the fourth- to fifth-century dwellings in the town.

as Roudh el Q'rtas and Ibn Khaldoun, or connects it with what some scholars regard as the *Africitas* of Tertullian and Apuleius? Or, must one accept the position that the Roman civilization which Augustine represented was extraneous to the main stream of North African history, and that it is only through the Donatism of the Libyan peasantry, and of the African intellectuals who hated the Roman Empire, that the continuity of North African thought is to be traced?

We must remember that the Church which Augustine so vigorously defended was already doomed to disappearance in North Africa when he died. Fifty years later Hippo had probably ceased to be a bishopric.[1] The Catholic Church in Africa could not survive the Roman cities and the Roman villa-owning aristocracy. The strength of Christianity among the African peasants lay in the Donatist Church. Here they could at one and the same time vent their antipathy to their Latin-speaking masters, and express beliefs which had inspired their fore-fathers, beliefs which indeed form the basis of North African religion to-day.[2]

The opposition to Donatism which Augustine led was not sufficient to destroy the movement, but it prevented it from becoming the Church of all North Africa. The conversion of North Africa to Islam may perhaps have been aided by the fact that while Catholicism died out, Donatism was too much weakened by continual harrying to take its place.

M. Rodary's discoveries give an insight into the more neglected native aspect of Roman North Africa, into an African culture which, surrounding the Latin cities, finally strangled their influence and against which even Augustine struggled in vain.

[1] Hippo is not included among the Numidian bishoprics listed by Victor Vitensis in 484, *C.S.E.L.* vii, pp. 119–23. See also Père J. Mesnage, *Le Christianisme en Afrique, Déclin et Extinction*, Alger, 1915, p. 14. Augustine's memory seems to have inspired no Catholic resistance to Huneric's persecutions, nor any revival in the Byzantine period, in contrast to the part played by the memory of Marculus and Parmenian in the times of Donatist persecution.

[2] An example of the continuity of beliefs among the North Africans throughout the pagan, Christian, and Mohammedan periods can be found in the cult of holy men and martyrs and the practices related thereto. Herodotus, iv. 172 (ed. Gsell, Alger, 1915, pp. 183–4) mentions the practice among certain tribes of sleeping round and taking oaths at the tombs of holy men, just as the Donatists did at the tombs of their martyrs. See Optatus, ii. 21; *C.S.E.L.* xxvi. p. 59; *C.I.L.* viii. 27333 (Dougga). The same rites are common in North Africa to-day in connexion with the Moslem cult of saints (marabouts).

XV

*The Two Worlds of Paulinus of Nola**

The last century of the Roman empire in the west has exercised
a fascination on generations of historians since Gibbon. Why
did the Roman provincial system that had brought vast areas,
such as the Prefecture of the Gauls, under a single administration
that held sway from Hadrian's Wall to the mountains of the Rif,
give way to the divisive régimes of the Germanic kingdoms?
From the effects of military defeat and economic and social
ills, the search for factors that led to the western empire's collapse
has returned to the psychological and personal, the failure of
will among the potential governing class in the west to fulfil
its traditional role in the empire's service. Gibbon's charge
against 'Christianity and barbarism' as the villains of the piece
has been heard again.[1]

The career and literary work of Paulinus of Nola might be
put forward to justify this accusation.[2] Paulinus as much as any
of his contemporaries may be said to reflect the change of mood
which seems to have overtaken members of the western aristocracy in the last two decades of the fourth century, and his
writings provide many clues why he opted out of Gallo-Roman
society and a tradition of service to the Roman empire. His
renunciation of a career as an imperial governor and his position
as a wealthy, aristocratic and supremely talented literary figure, for
the comparative seclusion of the shrine of St Felix near Nola
caused a sensation and also some bitter recrimination. Ambrose,
Bishop of Milan, wrote in 395, 'I have ascertained from reliable
sources that Paulinus, whose rank in Aquitaine is second to none
has sold both his properties and those of his wife . . . and has
bidden farewell to home, country and kindred to serve God
more zealously. And he is stated to have chosen a retreat in the

city of Nola where he may pass his life in seclusion from the tumult of the world.'³ But Ambrose also believed that there would be plenty of leading men who when they heard, would denounce Paulinus' act as a shameful deed. Both the action and the reaction were signs of the times.

Meropius Pontius Paulinus was born about A.D. 355 into a wealthy land-owning family in Aquitaine. Their estates also included land at Fundi in Campania near Nola, at Ebromagus between Toulouse and Narbonne, as well as near Bordeaux. These holdings were vast in extent and could be described as 'kingdoms' (*regna*) by his friend and fellow-aristocrat Ausonius.⁴ Paulinus' father was a senator and he was trained as a lawyer so as to be able to take his place in the senior administration of the empire. It may be assumed that he studied rhetoric at the university of Bordeaux. There, owing to his father's influence, he met the poet Ausonius, who became his mentor. Having practised law for a short time, in 378 he was appointed *consul suffectus* the year before Ausonius himself attained the Consulate. Paulinus later attributed his success to Ausonius.⁵ In 381 he moved from Rome to Campania where he had been appointed *consularis* (governor). In this relatively prosperous and peaceful province he had his foot firmly on the first rungs of the administrative ladder.

Paulinus, however, was a Christian, and so was Ausonius, though Ausonius had been born *circa* 310 before Constantine's victory at the Milvian Bridge. This raises some questions about the christianisation of western Gaul, for the life Paulinus was to reject was not paganism, but the same type of conventional and non-assertive Christianity that had driven Jerome from his native town of Stridon *circa* 373 to semi-solitude and asceticism on an island in the Adriatic.⁶ Paulinus' education had been as rooted in the Scriptures as in the classics. One finds perhaps a trace of early influences in his prayer to 'the almighty creator of all things' for 'a contented mind not given over to base gain' to personal purity and rejection of 'lewd jokes'⁷ and hope for a beloved wife and children and the tranquillity of the countryside.⁸ To be moderate in food and dress and dear to friends and in good health filled his horizon. His object was a quiet life, but there was no hint of rejection of his obligations. Indeed his prayer was for the '*patrias virtutes*' of his station in life.⁹ Ausonius too was a

Christian, punctilious in his observance of Easter celebrations at Bordeaux, if little else.[10]

How and when had formal observance of Christianity replaced formal observance of the cult of the Roman and Gaulish gods? The picture is not clear. Ausonius has left some celebrated character-sketches of his colleagues among the professors at Bordeaux.[11] There was Minervius the *rhetor* who came from Rome and Constantinople to teach at Bordeaux, a 'second Quintilian' Ausonius calls him, two thousand of whose pupils entered the senate.[12] Two others rose to provincial governorships like Ausonius himself. A wide variety of religious opinions were represented. Association with the Druids and the Romano-Gallic gods was regarded as a mark of distinction, and Ausonius' friends wrote verses in honour of Jupiter and the pantheon.[13]

Christianity, however, including the extreme asceticism of the Priscillianists from Spain, was gaining ground in the 370s. We hear of Euchrotia, the wife of a celebrated pagan lawyer, Delphidius, and her daughter who became Priscillianists and were executed under Magnus Maximus (383–388).[14] From the middle of the fourth century there had also been a noticeable movement towards Christianity among the people of south-western Gaul. Thus Hilary of Poitiers testifies (*c.* 356), 'Every day the believing people grow in numbers and multiply the profession of their faith. One abandons pagan superstitions and the vanity of idols. Everyone moves along the road to salvation.'[15] Allowing for exaggeration, it looks as though the 350s saw the trickle of converts grow into a stream. The usurper Magnentius would hardly have chosen the Christogram as the device for his coinage in his final fling of defiance to Constantius in Gaul in 352–353, had Christianity not had a large and influential following in the Gallic provinces.

At first Gallic Christianity was not an intolerant creed. Ausonius' appointment by Valentinian I as tutor to his son Gratian *circa* 365 reflects perhaps the open policy of that emperor, pro-Christian but not aggressively so. His officials in Britain even lent their aid in building the great temple to Nodens near Lydney in 364–67.[16] While he ruled (he died in 375) Christianity in the west tended towards the same slow absorption of pagan culture that characterised its progress in the east. Only the North African Donatists still maintained the traditional western rejection of any alliance between Church and empire. For the rest, Christianity in western Europe seemed destined to continue and build upon the religious and philosophical traditions of the past. Martin of Tours in his cell was far away from the mind of the writer of the *Moselle*.

During the next generation the picture changed dramatically. Ausonius' influence waned while that of Martin of Tours increased beyond belief. Indeed, in his old age Ausonius was to sense that his grandson Paulinus of Pella would be following the example of Martin. The goal of the ambitious young provincial was tending to become less a position in the public service than a bishopric or the monastic cell. Religious orthodoxy supplemented aristocratic connections as the road to a high career in the imperial service. Relics of saints would be regarded as equally effective defences against the barbarian invaders as military skill. Augustine of Hippo was one of the very few North Africans to make good at the imperial court. [17] Despite his provincial origins, and we may assume his provincial accent, in 384 he had become at the age of thirty the official spokesman at the court of Valentinian II and Justina at Milan. On his mother's arrival in Milan the choice before him had defined itself clearly as one between a great administrative career backed by an Italian wife and estates in north Italy, combined with a non-asssertive commitment to Christianity, or dedication to lifelong service of the Catholic Church in ascetic retreat in his native North Africa. Such were the real issues behind the famous conversion scene in the Milanese garden in August 386, and victory went to the call of religion. The empire was robbed of its most promising younger representatives, and for Augustine's circle of friends, the judge Alypius, the *agens in rebus* Evodius and the remainder, the same choice was made. In the reign of Theodosius 379–95, the claims of Church and State were beginning to look like two competing and contrasting alternatives.

In many respects Paulinus' course was to resemble that of his friend, Augustine, and like Augustine he was to persuade others to follow his example. There was Aper, also a lawyer and former provincial governor, Sanctus, Amandus and Desiderius among his correspondents. Others such as Victricius, Bishop of Rouen, and Sulpicius Severus, Martin of Tours' biographer, had already come to the same conclusion. [18] The Aquitanian clergy with whom

Paulinus corresponded were pietists like Bishop Delphinus and the presbyter Amandus, men to whom events in the outside world meant little. Even as the barbarians were sweeping across Gaul, Paulinus' correspondents were writing about the erection of new churches and monasteries and their aspirations towards the monastic life. Their escape from the realities of the world was complete. The change of outlook which was affecting the higher reaches of provincial society in the 380s was to spread even to the old Roman aristocrats in the next two decades. The will to resist the barbarians had been eroded years before Radagaisus and Alaric invaded Italy.[19]

The steps by which Paulinus abandoned his career as provincial governor and devoted himself to a dedicated religious life under the protection of St Felix of Nola may be followed closely. His was not the single crisis of Augustine's conversion. There seem to have been a series of small but cumulatively significant incidents that persuaded him ultimately to make a complete change in his life. Felix's shrine appears to have been located on or near part of Paulinus' family estates. He had visited it as a boy and been awestruck by the services in the saint's honour.[20] Felix himself was reputed to have been the son of a Syrian immigrant and to have been martyred probably during the Decian persecution of 250–1. The shrine had been set up by the Christians of Nola in remorse for the mistreatment the saint had suffered at the hands of their fellow-citizens during the persecution. When he was governor of Campania Paulinus had had the road from Nola to the shrine repaired and a new hospice built for pilgrims.[21] Perhaps at this period or on his return home he may have visited Ambrose at Milan and imbibed some of the enthusiasm the bishop felt for the ascetic way of life.[22] Only ten years before, Ambrose also had been a provincial governor.

Paulinus' return to Gaul may however have been connected less with religious convictions than with violent political changes. which occurred in the summer of 383. At that time Magnus Maximus, the commander of the troops on Hadrian's Wall, made a successful bid for power. The Emperor Gratian was captured and murdered at Lyon on 25 August. The whole of the Prefecture of the Gauls fell to the usurper. In Italy the vacuum was filled by the arrival in Milan of Valentinian II and his mother Justina. Able diplomacy by Bishop Ambrose stayed Magnus

Maximus on the western approaches of Italy. It may be assumed that Paulinus' return to Gaul in 384 was connected with the political changes there as well as family affairs.[23] Ausonius as Gratian's tutor and ex-consul was suspect to Magnus Maximus and Paulinus was a close friend of Ausonius. On his return, he retired to his estates, and soon after married the Spanish heiress Therasia. The match extended his already wide holdings beyond the Pyrenees, and more important even, it brought him a relationship with the wealthy and pious Melania the Elder and through her to the doyen of Roman Christian families, the Anicii.[24]

Therasia too, was a resolute woman and a convinced Christian who from now on was to be the predominant influence in his life. For a year or two, however, Paulinus was content to manage his estates and maintain friendly contact with fellow-landowners. His earliest verses follow in the footsteps of Ausonius. He writes to his friend Gestidius partly in prose and partly in elegant verse thanking him for his gift of fish and oysters. In return, he sends him wildfowl and looks forward to their meeting.[25] There was nothing ascetic in the presents or exchange of good wishes. Nor, in the fragment of composition which Paulinus sent to Ausonius, can one detect anything more than half-hearted condemnation of Egyptian mysteries, 'wizards of vain mysteries', which Ausonius might have made himself – 'quique magos docuit mysteria vana Nechepsos et qui regnavit sine nomine moxque Sesostris' (*Carmen* III = Ausonius *Ep.* 23). He was developing into a narrative poet with a sense of the epic. His interest lay in Rome's remote past, and the pride he felt in her history was reflected in the long poem on the kings of Rome which he sent to Ausonius. The latter was enthusiastic. Paulinus had compressed three books of Suetonius into a single 'longe iucundissima poema', he wrote. In the fluency of his style and the natural cadences he produced in his lines Paulinus excelled all youthful Roman rivals. Paulinus too, was seized with a sense of the grandeur of the Latin language.[26] In a passage, preserved by Ausonius, where he dwells on Sallust's inclusion of Libya as an apanage of Europe, he had written that fame had blotted from her page the uncouth names of the Libyan kings which could not be perpetuated in Roman speech.[27] His master had every reason to be proud of his pupil.

Meantime, however, events were gradually drawing Paulinus

towards a more intense commitment to Christianity. First, he came into contact with Martin of Tours, then at the height of his fame. Shortly before, Martin had destroyed paganism in northern Gaul in a swift succession of missions and then in 384 had defied Magnus Maximus in an effort to save Priscillian from execution. Paulinus, afflicted by a disease of the eyes, met the great man at Vienne and was cured;[28] and there he also met Victricius, future Bishop of Rouen, who like Martin himself had renounced his military career for service in the Church.[29] His example was not lost on Paulinus. Soon after, perhaps in 388, occurred the first of two family tragedies that left an indelible mark on his memory. His brother was murdered. Years later, Paulinus still felt the weight of accusation on his conscience.[30] In all probability he was innocent, for he received the condolences of Delphinus, Bishop of Bordeaux, and his presbyter Amandus. Both remained his firm friends. Momentarily he was in serious danger. In his poured-out confidences to Felix he recalls how his lands and his life were threatened. The public assessor had already come to view his possessions prior to putting them up to auction.[31] The incident, together with the executions on the grounds of Priscillianism that struck the intellectuals in Bordeaux, highlights the insecurity that prevailed in Aquitania in the last years of Magnus Maximus' reign.

The effect of these tribulations was to deepen Paulinus' religion. The two earliest of his surviving letters, Letters 35 and 36, are addressed to Delphinus and Amandus at Bordeaux.[32] To Delphinus he writes briefly thanking him for his affection shown towards him after his brother's death and hoping his prayers would be answered. His real grief was not so much that his brother had died but at his spiritual indifference. He was 'more anxious about the anxieties he had to abandon here than of the cures he could look forward to in heaven'. Clearly Paulinus had already marked out his own future career as that of one dedicated to the Christian religion, and in his slightly longer and more intimate letter to Amandus he leaves no doubt of this. Paulinus asks the presbyter to 'be his brother in the Lord', i.e. prepare him for baptism, and in a letter containing no less than thirty-one Scriptural quotations hopes that he himself will not die untimely so that he must face the awful 'Lord our Judge' while still a Christian only in name. In this frame of mind he took the decisive step of baptism at the hands of Delphinus at Bordeaux in 389, and the same year left with his wife for Spain. Despite Magnus Maximus' overthrow he had no wish to resume his official career, and he bade farewell to Aquitaine where such deep tragedy had befallen him.

The group of six poems (*Carmina* IV–IX) which may reasonably be attributed to the next few years show Paulinus profoundly Christian in his outlook but still enamoured of the joys of country life and his home in the new setting of his wife's estates.[33] 'Adsit laeta domus epulisque adludat inemptis', he writes (*Carmen* IV, line 15). He came to enjoy and admire Spain with its combination of wild country, rich agriculture and fine cities,[34] valuable evidence for the continued prosperity of parts of the province on the eve of the barbarian invasions. His mind, however, was turned towards God. God was still addressed in somewhat Vergilian terms in *Carmen* IV as 'omnipotens genitor rerum, cui summa potestas' (compare *Aeneid* X, line 100, 'pater omnipotens rerum cui summa potestas'), and in the neutral Constantinian invocation, 'summus pater' (*Carmen* VI), but familiar classical lines were being imperceptibly transformed to carry new Christian meanings. Thus in *Carmen* VII Paulinus uses the theme of Horace's second epode, that rural life is to be preferred to soldiering, trade or a public career, to express his own distaste for public life. The iambics,

> Beatus ille qui procul vitam suam
> ab inpiorum segregarit coetibus
> et in via peccantium non manserit
> nec in cathedra pestilenti sederit
> sed corde toto fixus in legem dei
> praecepta vitae nocte volvit et die
> mentemque castis institutis excolit
>
> (*Carmina* VII, 1–6)

(Happy is he who has separated his life far from the crowds of the ungodly and has remained not in the way of the sinners nor has sat in the seat of pestilence, but having fixed his whole mind on the law of God and desiring (to keep) His commands each night and day of his life, ennobles his mind with chaste injunctions.')

may be paralleled by Horace's second epode but the message is now that of Psalm 1.1.

Beatus ille qui procul negotiis,
ut prisca gens mortalium
paterna rura bobus exercet suis
solutus omni faenore

(Happy is he who, far from business cares, like the ancient
race of mortals, works his ancestral acres with his steers,
from all money-lending free.)

Already, however, Paulinus was contrasting the lot of any of
those who relied on worldly success with those who fixed their
hopes on God alone. The impious would not rise to glory. They
would be judged and consumed in the flames. The poem ends
significantly, with another reminiscence of Psalm 1,

Vias bonorum laetus agnoscit deus
at inpiorum pronum iter delebitur.

(A joyful God acknowledges the ways of the just but the
downward path of the impious will be destroyed.)

Therasia did not have to drag her husband from pagan altars,
but Ausonius may have been right in suspecting that 'Tanaquil'
as he calls her had influenced her husband's withdrawal from his
old love of the classics and from Ausonius himself. Between
390 and 394 contact between the old tutor and pupil slackened
and then lapsed. Maybe part of the fault was simply communications, for though Ausonius wrote four letters at least to Paulinus
in these years, Paulinus points out that four summers had passed
since he heard from him, when at last three letters arrived at the
same time.[35] Ausonius had written movingly, seeking to persuade
Paulinus to return to Bordeaux. 'What more shall I not righteously
call down on thee, O land of Spain! May Carthaginians ravage
thee . . . Here dost thou, Paulinus, establish thy robe consular
and Roman chair and wilt thou bury thy native honours?'[36]
Gradually, however, the truth was dawning on the old man.
'We are shaking off a yoke, Paulinus, which its tried equableness
once made easy . . . which mild Concord used to guide with even
reins.'[37] It was Therasia who was responsible for this change.
'Let thy Tanaquil know nought of this',[38] he urges, 'Let Paulinus
baffle his inquisitor, and let him abandon his solitude and the

gloomy delusions of a Bellerophon, and return to the "men of Roman name"[39] and the world of Latin literature that he had left behind at Bordeaux.'

It was the summer of 394 before Paulinus replied in two letters. By this time he had had his fill of the classics and the death of his infant son had thrown him into despair. In 393 he had reopened correspondence with Delphinus and Amandus after four years,[40] telling them of his desire to devote himself to Christ. 'I am planted in Christ and am Christ's dark toil', he tells Amandus.[41] Thus he was in no mood to heed Ausonius. In the first letter, he defends himself against the reproach that he had shaken off the yoke that had bound him to Ausonius in the common pursuit of letters.[42] That was never the case. He could not match Ausonius' graceful verses. He was unworthy of his master's praise. 'If thou dost match calves with bulls or horses with wild asses . . .' he writes. He would always be yoked in love to his old friend, but it would be a love between souls, 'linked together in worship of Christ'. In the emphatically Christian view of friendship Paulinus was reflecting the difference between his generation and that of Ausonius. The second letter finds Paulinus in a more sombre mood. Ausonius' three letters contained 'things sweet though somewhat soured by manifold complaints', and these hurt him. None the less he would write first in light iambics to repay his master his debt of words, but the more serious reproaches made against Therasia and himself must be answered in the 'sterner metre of hexameters', the 'avenging heroic metre'.

> Ista suo regerenda loco tamen et graviore
> vindicis heroi sunt agitanda sono.

Then to quote:

Why dost thou bid the deposed Muses return to my affection, father? Hearts consecrated to Christ give refusal to the Camenae, are closed to Apollo. Once there was accord betwixt me and thee, equals in zeal but not in power – to call forth deaf Apollo from his Delphic cave, to invoke the Muses as divine, to seek from groves or hills the gift of utterance by the god's gift bestowed. Now 'tis another force that rules my heart, a greater God that demands

another mode of life, claiming for himself from man the
gift he gave, that we may live for the Father of life.
(*Carmen* X = Ausonius *Ep.* 31, lines 20–32,
tr. H. G. Evelyn White)

The new life demanded renunciation of empty business and
pleasure, and idle tales of literature

> vacare vanis otio aut negotio
> et fabulosis litteris . . .
> (lines 33–4)

The alliteration and play on words conceals Paulinus' resolve.
It was God's will that he abandon the tradition in which he had
grown up. In terms which he was to use more than once in his
letters from Nola, he stressed the utter incompatibility of ordinary
service to the world and obedience to the commands of Christ.

> . . . de vanis liberat curis
> otia amant strepitumque fori rerumque tumultus
> cunctaque divi inimica negotia donis
> et Christi imperiis et amore salutis abhorrent . . .
> (lines 165–8)

(They love repose void of empty cares and shun the din of
public life, the bustle of affairs, and all concerns hostile to
the gifts of Heaven, both by Christ's command and in the
desire for salvation.)

(tr. H. G. Evelyn White).

Let Ausonius blame the Creator if he did not like these commands.
Paulinus repudiated the charge that he wished to live as a solitary
in desert places. His was not the disturbed mind of a Bellerophon.[43] Therasia was no Tanaquil, but a chaste Lucretia,[44]
and there was more to Spain than craggy heights and ruined
cities. It had its Saragossa, its pleasant Barcelona and Tarragona
looking down from majestic heights to the sea.[45] To live for
Christ was not perversion but delight, and indeed the only way
to avoid the certainty of 'the severe wrath of the heavenly
Judge'.[46] 'If thou dost approve', he ends, 'rejoice in thy friend's
rich hope; if otherwise, leave me to be approved by Christ.'[47]
Together, the two letters bade a solemn farewell to his old

tutor and to the outlook that he represented. It was to be many generations before the Classical world and Christianity would come to terms again in the west.

Rejection apart, we may perceive two main aspects of Paulinus' intellectual evolution which affected his religion. First, the nostalgia for a primitive rural golden age, derived originally from Vergil's *Georgics* and Horace is heightened and provided with a Biblical background by reference to the first chapters of Genesis and the life of John the Baptist. Second, Paulinus was becoming ever more influenced by the sense of approaching Judgment. In *Carmen* VI written as a Panegyric of John the Baptist one finds both elements and also examples of how Paulinus was converting Biblical texts into Latin hexameters. Thus, 'Behold I shall send my messenger before thy face' (Isaiah 40: 3–4) becomes

> Mittam, ait, ante tuos oculos, o nate, ministrum
>
> (line 309)

Primitive nature corresponded to God's handiwork and was good. The superstructure added by man was the cause of evil. The values of the pagan world were thus turned upside down. [48] John, Paulinus urged, had forsaken the wretched crowds of milling individuals for the wilderness. His garments of camel hair protested against the luxury of the world. His innocence cried out at the intrigues of the secular age. And, perhaps in a flash of anguished memory of his sufferings in Aquitaine, Paulinus expatiated on human violence and strife that merited God's eternal condemnation.

> Hinc odia, hinc lites, hinc fraus, hinc livor et irae,
> Caedes, arma, cruor, conflictus proelia mortes
> Hinc offensa dei quam tartara saeva piabunt
>
> (lines 244–6)

(Hence hatreds, hence lawsuits, hence fraud, hence envy and hatred, murder, arms, blood, strife, battle and death. Hence the offence against God which they will expiate in savage hell.)

Judgment, indeed, was vividly impressed on his mind. He feared that his soul would be 'shackled with paltry cares for the body', he told Ausonius, 'and weighted with a load of business, if perchance the awful trump should peal from the opened heaven, it should fail to raise itself' to meet the Lord.[49] This was another feature which divided Paulinus and his age from that of Ausonius. Judgment was beginning to play the same overwhelming part in western European religious thought that it had always played hitherto in North African Christianity. The onset of the barbarians seemed to believers such as Paulinus more of an irrevocable sign of the approaching end than a military challenge to be overcome. The fall of empires was in the nature of Providence, but to save one's soul was the duty of every individual.

At some stage Paulinus had made contact with Jerome far away in Palestine. In 393/4 he had received from him the latter's works *Against Jovinian* with their exuberant defence of asceticism as the sole means of approach to God.[50] Now he determined to sell his estates and those of Therasia. This must have become public knowledge in Barcelona. The estates of a newly ordained presbyter were supposed to pass to the church in which he was ordained. At Christmas 394 Paulinus found himself forcibly ordained 'through the sudden compulsion of the crowd'.[51] As at Thagaste in 411, when Pinianus, reputedly the richest man in the west, took up residence and Alypius schemed for his ordination, Barcelona believed itself on the brink of a massive windfall.[52]

Paulinus, however, was not to linger in Spain. For some months he hesitated. On the one hand, early in 395 he wrote the first of a series of thirteen *natalicia* or commemorative poems for the anniversary of Felix' martyrdom reputedly on 14 January (*Carmen* XII). At the same time he allowed himself a final, perhaps self-revealing panegyric[53] devoted to the Emperor Theodosius following his victory over the alliance of aristocratic Roman paganism and barbarian Arianism on the river Frigidus on 6 September 394. The work is lost. It praised, however, Theodosius' (orthodox?) legislation as a model for future ages. Jerome to whom he sent a copy was enthusiastic in his praise; the work reflected Ciceronian diction and often that master's sentiments, but he also told Paulinus he was 'only a beginner' in Christ's service.[54] If he continued, however, he foretold that he would outshine every hitherto Latin Christian writer, pungently criticising each from Tertullian to Hilary.[55] He urged him to progress in his reading of the Scriptures and turn his genius exclusively towards their understanding. 'I will not be satisfied with any mediocrity in you. I shall look for complete perfection'[56] – a life, that was, devoted to asceticism and scriptural study. Writing was to be in the medium of God's word, not Cicero's.

This may have given Paulinus the final impulse he needed. Previously, he had written to his friend Sulpicius Severus, himself an Aquitanian landowner who had fallen under the spell of Martin of Tours and become his biographer. Paulinus had sent, replete with Scriptural quotations, a long and fulsome letter (*Ep*. I). He praised him for abandoning secular affairs, and justified his own decision to do likewise, but finally invited him to spend Easter with him. It was after all only eight days' journey from his estates at Eauze (Elusione) near Narbonne to Paulinus' home. The Pyrenees were less formidable than their name.

Severus did not come. Not long after, Paulinus and Therasia sailed for Italy, making for Nola by slow stages. The trend of Paulinus' thought may be revealed from a later letter to Sulpicius (*Ep*. 5.4). Physical frailty had taken the edge off enjoyment of pleasures: secular life was full of troubles and trials. These taught him 'to hate what perturbed me and increased my practice of religion through my need for hope and fear of doubt. Finally, when I seemed to obtain rest from lying scandal and from wanderings, unbusied by public affairs and far from the din of the forum I enjoyed the leisure of country life and my religious duties.' These had made it possible for him to advance still further towards obedience to Christ's command. He had opted out. Augustine might have written the same from Cassiciacum. Arrived at Milan the couple were welcomed by Ambrose and Paulinus was invited to accept enrolment among Ambrose's clergy. He declined reluctantly. At Rome, however, his welcome from Pope Siricius was icy. The Pope and his clergy refused to see him. No satisfactory reason has been found to account for this. It has been suggested that Siricius feared that Paulinus might be a Priscillianist or that he just disliked aristocrats turned ascetics, or that Paulinus' association with Jerome prejudiced him. Perhaps a simpler explanation is that Paulinus had been a provincial governor and had been ordained presbyter. In the tradition-inspired minds of Siricius and even the more worldly-wise Innocent I (401–417) tenure of such an office could debar the holder from the priesthood, because it would normally involve him in bloodshed through his responsibility for ordering the punishment of criminals.[57] Paulinus makes the point of stating that during his office he shed no blood.[58] He found the rebuff he suffered at Rome mortifying. In the autumn of 395, the party at last reached Nola and there Paulinus was to spend the remaining thirty-six years of his life. Part of his remaining patrimony he devoted to building a magnificent new basilica in honour of Felix, which was dedicated in 403. Five years later Therasia died, and in 409 following the death of the Bishop of Nola, Paulinus was consecrated in his stead. The calm of his existence was ruffled briefly by the appearance of numbers of refugees from Rome fleeing from Alaric's forces as they pressed southwards after capturing Rome. He died in 431 without ever returning to Gaul, and he was buried in the church of Felix on which he had lavished so much of his energy and wealth.

For more than a quarter of a century, however, Paulinus maintained a thriving correspondence with like-minded Christians throughout the western world. He had friends and correspondents from the Channel coast of Gaul to Jerome's cell in Palestine. They included such opposites as Jerome and Rufinus, Augustine and Pelagius, Alypius and Julian of Eclanum. There were writers such as Sulpicius Severus, practical missionary bishops such as Victricius of Rouen and Nicetas of Remesiana in Illyricum, devout clergy such as Delphinus and Amandus of Bordeaux, pious laymen such as Aper and Amanda, Sanctus and Eucher and his relative Jovius, a man of letters and probably a pagan, the only link with his life at Bordeaux.[59] Between 395 and 415 Paulinus had placed himself in a unique position to influence Latin Christianity and Christian literature at a crucial period. It is unfortunate, perhaps, that he had so few ambitions in that direction. He was neither a speculative thinker nor a controversialist. He accepted orthodoxy as he had learnt it and criticised known heretics like Apollinaris with more vigour than understanding.[60] He failed, however, to think through his own position and draw conclusions from his religious experience. In the crisis of the Pelagian controversy in 416–18 he allowed his deference to Augustine to get the better of his judgment. The power of grace he acknowledged fully, but it had been 'assisting Grace'[61] (*adjutorio divinae gratiae*) and his life had been directed by the same search for perfection through personal endeavour that inspired Pelagius and his friends.[62] His also was the cult of the serious, and his aim, like that of Pelagius, was to avoid the penalties of Judgment due to failure to use his free-will aright. Though he accepted the fact of Original Sin he shared the Pelagian ideal of personal approach to God through imitation of Christ as revealed in Scripture, and he took a positive view of the virtues of the pagan ancestors of his friends. 'We see the seeds of light sparkling out of the darkness of unpious minds,'[63] he writes of the forebears of Melania the Elder. He alone had the prestige to uphold the position of his south Italian colleagues when confronted with the full force of Augustinianism in 416. Had he risen to the occasion, western Christendom might have been spared the final fateful injection of theological rigorism from North Africa.

Paulinus' genius, however, lay in personal relations. He was a superb liaison-officer, able to act as a clearing house for the exchange of opinions and books, and contact between personalities. He had a gift for friendship and an ability to enter into a sympathetic bond with like-minded people whom he had never seen.[64] Even Augustine admired his friendship with Pelagius.[65] Paulinus believed that personal relationships were predestined and in many respects Alypius and Augustine whom he never met became as much his friends as Severus and Delphinus whom he had known in Gaul.

Forty-five of Paulinus' letters survive from the period of his stay in Nola, all except one fall within the span 395–413 – the last letter in the series, No. 51 to Eucher, the future bishop of Lyon and Galla, may be as late as 421–3.[66] Little significance, however, may be attached to this apparent gap, as a great deal of Paulinus' correspondence has not survived. Most of the letters are written to his old friends in Gaul, no less than thirteen to Sulpicius Severus, to Delphinus five, Amandus six, Sanctus two, Jovius one, and Victricius of Rouen two. Significantly perhaps, those to Severus are the only group which are not signed jointly by Paulinus and Therasia. Was there perhaps some deep jealousy that prevented Therasia even associating herself with any reminder of Paulinus' earlier years in Aquitaine?

Severus held a special place in Paulinus' affections. Like him he had been a lawyer, and from the leisured existence on his estates with his aristocratic wife had turned towards a religious life.[67] The correspondence extends over ten years (395-404) and some of Paulinus' letters are lengthy documents, a type of composition that one finds in other western Christian authors of the day such as Augustine and Jerome. As we have seen, before he left Barcelona, Paulinus had invited Severus to stay with him and compared his conversion to the ascetic practice of Christianity with the similar experience of his friend. By the summer of 396 Paulinus wrote again, another long and intimate letter (*Ep.* 5). This time he invited him to visit Nola. There is much mutual congratulation that each had found a similar service to Christ. Paulinus wondered indeed if the coincidence of recent illness does not prove the completeness of their mutual harmony. Finally, there is an interesting and revealing account of Paulinus' reception at Rome the previous year (*Ep.* 5.14), and the writer does not hesitate to call the Roman clergy envious and hate-inspired. Fortunately, their influence did not extend to the clergy in Campania nor to Africa whose bishops had sent two couriers to him since his arrival at Nola.

This letter is typical of much that Paulinus wrote to his more intimate friends. It is wordy, introspective and moralising, but also sincere and in its way moving. Paulinus does not hide his feelings. It contains also considerable information about the life and thought of western Christian intellectuals at the time. Incidentally, these letters to Gaul reveal something of the silent religious revolution which was taking place there and of which Paulinus himself was a prime example. The Christianisation of the rural areas was evidently proceeding apace. In another letter to Severus written *circa* 402 (*Ep.* 32) he congratulates his friend on building two basilicas and a baptistery in the village of Primulaicum (Premillac in Perigord) where he owned an estate. He elaborated on the symbolism of the twin-roofed basilicas representing the Church with its two Testaments[68] and enquired after the relics of the saints and the fragment of the Cross brought back by Melania from Jerusalem, and which he had sent.[69] In a spirit of competitive holiness Paulinus went on to describe the basilica he was building in honour of Felix at Nola, a vast building which he described to the last detail of the choice of inscriptions to be painted on the walls for purposes of meditation, an unconscious but priceless aid towards understanding the features of early fifth-century Christian architecture.[70] Elsewhere one may detect the quickening interest in the monastic vocation among the one-time leaders of Gallic society. Aper and Amanda his wife followed Paulinus' example, shrugged off the cares of high office and accepted the ideal of religious poverty.[71] For Paulinus the 'bustle of the churches' was almost as worldly as the crowds in the forum.[72] Devotion to religion implied also a solitary's existence. In the final letter in the collection, to Eucher and Galla, he praised his correspondents' decision to betake themselves to a monastic settlement on the islands of Lerins off Marseille which was being organised by the presbyter Honoratus. He goes on to name three other young men who intend to follow suit. This was the means of perfection and of avoiding the penalties reserved at Judgment for the unrighteous.

Paulinus also shows considerable interest in missions to the heathen. His letter to Victricius of Rouen (*Ep.* 18) demonstrates, however, more than simple enthusiasm for their conversion. He associated Christianisation with pacification. In this he found himself at one with Ambrose of Milan for Ambrose had written to Queen Fritigil of the Alemanni asking her to use the influence of her Christianity to persuade her husband to live in peace with the Romans.[73] Paulinus praised Victricius for having rendered the Channel coast safe by spreading Christianity among the still unconverted Nervii,[74] and similarly the Morini, more picturesquely than accurately described as dwelling 'at the edge of the world battered by a deafening ocean', had also abandoned their barbarous ways. Again, in a poem addressed to Nicetas of Remesiana he praised the latter for having preached successfully to the barbarous Bessi who dwelt round Nish. Now these men 'harsher than their winter snow were led as sheep into the hall of peace'.[75] Barbarism and aggression against the Roman empire were to be cured by acceptance of the Christian faith, a missionary strategy that came too late.

Paulinus' letters to his Gallic friends throw light on his ultimate thoughts and attitudes. The more public aspect of his life at Nola is illustrated by the correspondence he maintained with members of the Roman nobility, such as the senator Pammachius and the African episcopate, and notably Augustine. Thanks very largely to the researches of P. R. L. Brown it is becoming evident that Paulinus' relationship (through marriage ?) with Melania influenced his friendships and activities.[76] It drew him away, for instance, from the powerful patronage of Jerome and though, so far as we may judge, Paulinus took no part in the Origenist rumpus, it placed him alongside Rufinus and the most powerful of the senatorial Christian families, the Anicii.[77] This in turn drew Pelagius into his circle. Pelagius, Brown believes, may have come to know the contents of Augustine's *Confessions* from Paulinus,[78] and Paulinus' library may have been where Julian of Eclanum studied Augustine's anti-Manichaean works in preparation for launching the great controversy that occupied the last fifteen years of Augustine's life.[79] Certainly Pelagius and Paulinus were on good terms and corresponded about the year 404, and his friendship with Julian of Eclanum and his family is well-known. Paulinus, however, revered Augustine. His were 'verba caelestia'.[80] If Alypius was 'his brother,' Augustine was 'his master'.[81] Pierre Courcelle has been able to trace an exchange of 36 letters between Paulinus and Augustine spread over the years 395–421[82] and of these Paulinus' surviving contribution consists of 4, 6, 45 and 50 from his collection of letters and 24, 25, 30, 94 and 121 from Augustine's correspondence. He had first heard of Augustine from Alypius, who, impetuous as usual, had sought contact with Paulinus very soon after his arrival at Nola.[83] He had written asking him to borrow for him a copy of Eusebius of Caesarea's *Chronicle* translated by Jerome which he knew to be in the possession of Paulinus' relative Domnio in Rome, and eventually sent him the corpus of Augustine's anti-Manichaean works in exchange.[84] Paulinus was greatly impressed and opened a correspondence with Augustine which lasted for more than a quarter of a century. A friendship was established which was proof against differences of opinion and interest, and even the dire suspicion about 400 that Augustine might after all be a secret Manichee.[85]

This was an example of instant and lasting understanding; not surprisingly the question has been asked how far Paulinus influenced Augustine to write the *Confessions* and dictated, as it were, the form these took. The *Confessions* are unique in Latin literature. Augustine in 396–97, imagining himself on the verge of old age although he was only 42–3, wrote a stylised autobiography divided into periods representing the six ages of man,[86] in each of which he believed he saw God's guiding hand moving him towards the ultimate haven of rest in Him. It was a long prayer poured out by one who believed himself saved only by the overwhelming power of God's grace. Previous Christian autobiographies there had been: Perpetua's self-revealing account of her thoughts in prison awaiting martyrdom at Carthage in 203, Cyprian writing to his friend Donatus, *circa* 245, about his conversion, Gregory of Nazianze communing with himself in his *Poemata de Seipiso*, but none of these combines the prayer and sense of divine Grace that permeates the *Confessions*.[87] In Paulinus' early writings, however, one may detect the germ of a similar approach. Augustine retained Paulinus' letters and in the heat of the Pelagian controversy quotes an interesting passage back at him in order to show that he too had been conscious of the depth of his sin. Erubesco pingere quod sum: non audeo pingere quod non sum; odi quod sum sed non sum quod amo (I blush to depict what I am. I do not dare depict what I am not. I hate what I am but I am not what I love). The passage is almost Augustinian both in introspection and in its style.[88]

Paulinus' early poems also take the form of prayers addressed to God. He did not shun self-criticism. The long reply to Ausonius and the earlier letters to Sulpicius Severus already discussed are deeply self-revelatory, and he was interested, as he indicated to Alypius, in hearing of the spiritual experiences of the others.[89] In Alypius, too, he found someone who was ready to oblige but then despite Paulinus' pressure drew back.[90] Augustine's *De Utilitate Credendi* written *circa* 390 already contained autobiographical aspects, written to justify his one-time adherence to and his rejection of Manichaeism. Now, in 396 as his old friends left the monastic surroundings of Thagaste to take up duties as Catholic bishops in Numidia, Augustine felt the solitude. Paulinus' suggestion to Alypius caught his own mood.[91] Augustine told Paulinus he would set down how he too 'had been made separate' by God.[92]

Paulinus may be included therefore among the major influences that had led Augustine to write the *Confessions*. His remaining correspondence with his contemporaries is less significant. Prolix and rhetorical, replete with good spiritual advice, it is often more interesting for what it omits than what it says. References to the growing political and military crises that threatened Italy from Alaric and Radagaisus, and of the battles that were being fought in north and central Italy are absent. The religious vocation, prayer and the attitudes necessary for the soul's salvation, avoidance of sin, advice regarding temperance and humility, and above all attention to the text and interpretation of Scripture filled his pages. As Walsh points out, even when writing to political figures like Pammachius and the elder Melania's son, the senator Publicola, his words were directed to their souls and not to their activities in Rome.[93] Even so, the style is in the ornate late-classical tradition, and though no longer admitted, it continues to be modelled on the authors of the past. Paulinus revels in his account of Victricius' renunciation of his military career in favour of that of dedication to Christ, writing more like a hagiographer of the previous century as he described Victricius' defiance first of his commanding officer and then of the general himself.[94] Now, to transform Rouen 'into the appearance of Jerusalem' and convert it into a place of crowded churches (*Letter* 18.5) was comparably greater service than defence of the frontier in the Roman army.

On the other hand, Paulinus tells his readers a good deal about his life at Nola. It has been pointed out that this was austere rather than ascetic.[95] His library was well stocked. There were lively exchanges of books with Jerome and with his friends in Gaul. There were no exaggerated privations. Paulinus and his family fasted until 3 p.m., and then had a simple meal with wheaten bread, vegetables, wine served in vessels of pottery and boxwood, but the wine was a vintage product from his remaining estates near Narbonne.[96] He had brought servants with him. Some of these, such as Julianus who acted as his emissary to Alypius and the North African clergy (*Letter* 3), were quite important people capable of negotiating on behalf of their master. Another courier was the presbyter Vigilantius, who was entrusted with a message to Jerome at Bethlehem. He became disenchanted with asceticism and had sufficient independence of mind to accuse Jerome of Origenism and write a criticism of a whole range of what he considered useless and superstitious practices. He has been preserved for posterity in Jerome's vitriolic *Contra Vigilantium*, written *c.* 403.[97] Other servants named in the correspondence as couriers to and from Nola were humbler but equally colourful individuals. There was the monk, Victor, originally a disciple of Martin of Tours, who carried letters annually between Paulinus and Severus. He tried to put Paulinus on a more rigorous diet than wheaten bread and Paulinus describes the horrible concoctions he prepared and still more horrible smells that emanated from his kitchen.[98] Victor and Bishop Delphinus' servant Cardamas provide an element of comic relief in Paulinus' correspondence. Cardamas,[99] an actor turned exorcist who drank heavily and purported to terrify demons, foreshadows similar characters in mediaeval monastic life.

Solitude also was a relative term only. Nola was the centre of conferences and discussions. Paulinus craved company. He was anxious for his friends to visit him. On several occasions he pressed Severus to do so and similarly Nicetas of Remesiana twice stayed at Nola, in 398 and 402. In 404 occurred a notable family gathering of Melania the Elder and her relations under Paulinus' roof. Locally Paulinus was on excellent terms with the bishops of Campania including of course Memor and his son Julian of Eclanum. Every year too, the family journeyed to Rome partly on pilgrimage to the shrines of Peter and Paul but also on semi-diplomatic business involving visits to Christian senators and to the successive Popes, Anastasius I and Innocent I. Altogether his life at Nola bore little comparison with those of adherents to a monastic rule.

The heart, however, of Paulinus' existence was Felix's shrine. For nearly a decade (395–403) he devoted all his zeal and energy to constructing the great complex of buildings that replaced the original shrine.[100] Nothing, not even respect for poor people's property, was allowed to stand in the way. The saint's aid, usually invoked to counteract natural calamities, was called upon to bring down fire to consume a peasant's hut that stood in the way. The owner had declared himself readier to die than give in! The occupant of another was so harried that he destroyed his dwelling in disgust and moved away.[101] Felix was not an unmitigated blessing to the community. When it was complete, however, the memorial to the saint must have been an imposing sight. The new church had been built to join the east end of the original basilica erected over the tomb of Felix so that there was, as Paulinus pointed out, a view from one church into the other, in order that worshippers could also look upon the saint's tomb. There was a baptistery adjoining and in front extended a court in which fountains played, and a hospice for pilgrims and guests.[102] Not surprisingly the upkeep, especially the water supply, was more than the town of Nola was willing to undertake. Paulinus, however,

was proud of his handiwork and in 402 before it was completed
he was describing to Nicetas in a style reminiscent of Statius'
description of villas in the first century A.D. a walk through the
porticos to the church, mentioning on the way the useless vege-
table patch the fine building had replaced.[103] At heart, Paulinus had
little feeling for the hard grind of peasant life. Everything he did
had the stamp of the aristocrat born to have his way.

Poetry was always Paulinus' true medium of self-expression.[104]
Some of his letters, like those of Ausonius, break into verse, and as
we have seen, it was through alteration of metre that he expressed to
his master his change of mood and meaning. Elegiacs denoted
a lighter vein, hexameters were reserved for a more serious
message. There is far more classical allusion and far more imitation of the Classics in the poems than in the letters. After his
conversion he might assert that the Muses were closed to him
but he made ample use of the arts he had learnt from them. He
felt no impropriety about continuing to write poetry or of deriving pleasure from this, but the aim was now to fix the reader's
mind on Christ or on his saving mercy through his servant Felix.

Of thirty-three surviving poems, thirteen written between 395
and 407 commemorated the *natalicia* of Felix, and a few fragments
of others on the same theme have survived and are collected in
Carmen XXIX. In general these are long and rather tedious works
designed by Paulinus to be orated to the great concourse drawn
from all classes including numerous peasants who came to the
shrine each year on the occasion of the *natalicia*. There were good
classical precedents for this type of poem. Vergil put into Aeneas'
mouth the wish to observe the anniversary of his father's death
(*Aen.* V.49ff), and significantly Paulinus imitated this passage
(*Carmen* XXVII, lines 148–50). Ausonius also had written one
such commemorative poem. Paulinus, however, transformed completely this literary tradition to serve his purpose of honouring
Felix and of reaching the widest possible audience in language
most calculated to impress it. In North Africa, Augustine had
exploited the popular type of alphabetical poem to win maximum
propaganda effect at the outset of his campaign against the Donatists in 393.[105] Paulinus without a controversial motive wished to
leave his hearers no doubt as to the sanctity and power of Felix
and his own debt to him. Felix's miraculous career was described
in detail, how during the Decian persecution he found safety in a

ruin concealed behind a spider's web and then in a cistern between two houses where he was fed by an old woman for six
months.[106] In another poem, the theme was Felix's funeral, his
assumption into heaven and the building of his tomb. Declama-
tory addresses are frequent. In the two poems devoted mainly to
Felix's career, speeches are given to the ailing bishop of Nola,
Maximus,[107] and a rapid-fire question and answer between pur-
suers of Felix[108] and his well-wishers. The power of the saint is
brought home to the rustic audience by descriptions of his
recent miracles. A thief who tried to steal a cross is paralysed, lost
cattle are returned to a farmer and a pig makes its way to the shrine
after having been left behind by the herdsman because it was too
fat.[109] Paulinus tells even of a cow that had fled the sacrificial
altar returning of its own accord.[110] Behind the miracle stories
lies the fact of the conversion of the Campanian countryside by
the influence of the saint's shrine. Henceforth there would be
the intimate relationship between the rural population and the
cult of the saint. Old forms were not abandoned. Now, however,
the saint was on the side of the rural community. The 'public
enemy' could be depicted in vivid terms as the local big-wigs
at Nola who refused to sanction water-supply for the baptismal
cella. In the course of a few years, paganism had been conquered
for good. Felix was installed as patron saint and protector of
the whole area, sovereign alike against the power of the invading
Goths and the ordinary hazards of farming life.

At heart Paulinus would have liked to apply to himself the
advice he gave to his kinsman Jovius. 'Be a Peripatetic for God and
a Pythagorean as regards the world. Preach the true wisdom that
lies in Christ, and be silent finally towards what is vain.'[111] This
may be shown from poems which seem to follow the classical
traditon most faithfully. At a date between 401 and 404 Paulinus
blessed the marriage of the young Julian, son of Bishop Memor,
to Titia, daughter of Bishop Aemilius of Beneventum (*Carmen
XXV*). The occasion could have come straight out of *Barchester
Towers*. The first decade of the fifth century saw the emergence
of at least one clerical dynasty in south Italy allied to an aristocratic Christian household in Rome with Nola as the focus of
their religious life. Paulinus' *Epithalamium* written for the happy
events adopts the form but reverses the message of its classical
model. While his contemporary Claudian, in 398 writing the

Epithalamium of the most Christian emperor Honorius to Maria, could still depict the bride as 'not ceasing under her mother's guidance to unroll the writers of Rome and Greece',[112] and enjoin her to listen to the marital advice of Venus, Paulinus banished Venus, Cupid and Juno from the feast. They were replaced by *pax*, *pudor* and *pietas*.[113] There was no place for Claudian's 'rude crowd of Nereids' thronging around Venus, however tastefully described.[114] The true examples of marriage were Eve, Sarah, Rebecca and above all, the Virgin Mary; and while Claudian ends with the hope 'of a little Honorius born in the purple, to rest on his grandsire's [Stilicho's] lap',[115] Paulinus urges sexual abstinence on Julian and Titia, or if children did come then they should be dedicated to an ascetic life. The keynote was contained in the opening lines – 'Concordes animae casto sociantur amore Virgo puer Christi, Virgo puella dei'. Solemnity replaced joy, emotional intensity gave way to ascetic caution and the decorations and dancing in the city's streets gave way to celebrations more in keeping with a Christian occasion. Paulinus was following the teaching of Ambrose rather than Jerome. Marriage was not denigrated, but its object was the production only of Christians dedicated to God.

Paulinus' *Consolatio* (*Carmen* XXXI), written for Pneumatius and Fidelis who had lost their son, conformed to the same pattern. Paulinus cannot help reminding himself of his own loss years before, but the parents of the dead child are bidden to put away grief and to mourn instead the sin of man. The deceased is indeed praised, and the untimeliness of his death due to Invidia has a distinct pagan flavour, but Christian spirituality prevails. Paulinus depicts the resurrection in terms of Ezekiel's vision of the restoration of the dry bones (Ezekiel 37)[116] and of Christ's promises. At the Coming of Christ the parents would see their son again. While both poems show Paulinus drawing on Classical authors to add style and embellishment, his aim was to adapt their words exclusively to Christian ideas while rendering these acceptable to his educated readers.

The language of his other poems, such as the exhortations (*Protreptici*) addressed to Jovius (*Carmen* XXII) or the young Licentius, or the *Propemptikon* written on Nicetas of Remesiana's departure for Dacia in 400, contains the same mixture of Classical and Christian elements. In particular, Paulinus' poem to Jovius

has the swing of one of Horace's letters and as one would expect
in this context, the text is full of Classical allusions. All the same,
Jovius is told to put away childish things. 'Non modo iudicium
Paridis nec bella gigantum falsa canis. Fuerit puerili ludus.'[117]
He should be writing of Creation not with the dreams of Epicurus
as his source but of Moses and St John. In the *Propemptikon* also
there are reminiscences of Horace, Propertius, Ovid, Tibullus and
Statius which educated readers would recognise, but there is also
the missionary motive of Nicetas' journey in Christ's service – to
bring 'the faith that gleams before Christ to the remainder of
humanity buried in error'.[118] Altogether, though in style, vocabulary and metre Paulinus imitates the classics, he was also bor-
rowing from the new generation of Christian poets, such as
Juvencus and Prudentius. Up to this moment, North Africa as
in so many other aspects of western Christian civilisation had
been the seed-bed of Christian poetry, and familiarity with its
use had extended far down Christian society there. Tombs and
churches were dedicated in verse by individual Christians and
moral exhortations preserved for posterity in mosaics in verse.
In making verse his normal vehicle of expression, even to the
inscriptions on the walls of the basilica in honour of Felix,
Paulinus pioneered the emergence of a Latin-Christian poetry
outside Africa in what was to be the last creative age in the
Western Empire.

In particular he influenced the development of a specifically
Christian terminology through which the Scriptures could be
naturalised into the former classical educational and literary traditions. In this he widened the foundations already laid down by
the North African Christians.[119] He differentiated clearly between
the use of words in a pagan and Christian context. The Christians
were *fideles*. They worshipped in a *basilica*, *cella* or *aedes*. *Templum*
is confined to a pagan temple. Curiously, *domus* for *domus Dei*
common in North Africa in the sense of 'church' or 'chapel' does
not appear to have been used. *Altaria* and *mensa* (the latter in
common use in North Africa) are the terms for 'altar': the more
traditional *ara* is neglected except for a Jewish altar. *Propheta*
tends to displace *vates* in Paulinus' later works for 'prophet' and
the Old Testament prophet's message is a *praedicatio*. The term
sacramentum, beloved by Tertullian to describe the Christian's
commitment to the exclusive service of Christ, was used by

Paulinus in the mediaeval sense for the sacraments of the Church, such as baptism and marriage or for the great occasions in the Church's year, such as Easter and Trinity. Pagans were still 'the nations' (*gentes*). *Paganus* used in North Africa for 'those outside the *militia Christi*' was not yet given its later popular meaning of 'pagan'.[120]

Paulinus' literary legacy may be traced through the North African poets of the Vandal period, Luxorius and Dracontius. North Africa, however, was destined to pass out of Latin Mediterranean civilisation, and it was to be many centuries before western European Christendom sought once more to harmonise Christianity with its classical heritage. Not until the last quarter of the eleventh century would something like a school of poets emerge who consciously drew their inspiration from the former greatness of Rome.[121] Paulinus gives no hint that he was aware that catastrophe overhung the western world in which he had grown up. South Italy is depicted in the same terms of peaceful prosperity as Gaul and Spain.[122] His conclusion that service to the Roman empire was incompatible with service to Christ had been influenced by a sense of futility resulting from his abundance of material wealth and power. His complaint was against the luxury and useless bustle of contemporary society. He was not in despair at its decline and fall. 'Let them enjoy their pleasures', he wrote to Severus while he was still at Barcelona in 395, 'their high offices and wealth, if indeed these are theirs. For they prefer to have those on earth where our life ends than in heaven where it abides.'[123] He shows that the contemporaries that he influenced such as Aper thought likewise.[124] His approach to life was purely individual. Like Augustine, his concern was with his inner self and how to save it from 'what is called the second death, nothing other than a life of punishment'.[125] He conceived this as requiring a complete abandonment of secular duties, and so far as possible the heritage of pagan Roman civilisation. There was no spark of the provincial patriotism that lights through the pages of Paulus Orosius. Like some antiquarian romantic, in his mind's eye he saw himself welcoming death at the hands, not of the barbarians but of persecuting authorities of a long past era.[126] In one letter to Severus he dwells on the wickedness of the Emperor Hadrian, believing that in building a temple of Jupiter over the spot where Helena found the True Cross he aimed at destroying the Christian faith. [127] Radagaisus and Alaric do not figure in his correspondence, though *Carmen* XXI written in 400 rejoices in the defeat of the Goths thanks to the saints and martyrs. When one compares his letters and poems with the writings of Prudentius one appreciates the gulf that was opening between the Christian in the west who believed that Rome purged of aristocratic paganism might still be mistress of the world, and those like Paulinus and Augustine who denied any such possibility.

For the historian who believes that human history is in part directed by the wills of individual men and women, the collapse of the Roman empire in the west resulted not only from military disaster and economic and social tensions, but from the alienation from public duty of a considerable number of the traditional governing class. Alienation was due largely to theological attitudes, a fatal attempt to maintain the otherness of Christianity in the changed situation following the Constantinian revolution. What had once been a specifically North African interpretation of Christianity, emphasising with fatalistic insistence the universal penalty of Judgment except for those saved by Grace as the prime result of the Fall, became the accepted doctrine of western Christians, including the Roman aristocracy. It shared with more material causes the undermining of the will to resist the Germanic invaders in the west that resulted in the fall of the Roman empire. Paulinus of Nola, Romano-Gallic aristocrat, Christian man of letters, and seeker after perfection, fully represented the spirit of his times.

Notes

* In this paper I have drawn on my article, 'Paulinus of Nola and the last century of the Western empire', *JRS* 60 (1969), pp. 1–11. I have also been encouraged by my colleague, Professor P. G. Walsh, and Dr R. P. H. Green of St Andrews University to whose contributions on Paulinus I am greatly indebted. I have used P. G. Walsh's translations of Paulinus' *Letters*, published in *Ancient Christian Writers*, vols 35 and 36 (Westminster, Maryland, 1967). See Note p. 133.

1 E.g. by A. Momigliano in his essay in *Paganism and Christianity in the Fourth Century* (Oxford, 1963), pp. 1–16.

2 The standard works on Paulinus remain Pierre Fabre's *Saint Paulin de Nole et l'amitié chrétienne* (Bibliothèque des écoles françaises d'Athènes et de Rome, fasc. 167, 1949) and *Essai sur la chronologie de l'œuvre de saint*

Paulin de Nole (Publication de la Faculté des Lettres de l'Université de Strasbourg, fasc. 109, Paris, 1948). See also Walsh, *op. cit.*; C. H. Coster, 'Paulinus of Nola', *Late Roman Studies* (Harvard, 1968), pp. 183–204, and R. P. H. Green's monograph, *The Poetry of Paulinus of Nola, a study of his Latinity* (Collection Latomus, vol. 120, Brussels, 1971). The text of Paulinus' *Epistulae* and *Carmina* are published by G. von Hartel in *CSEL* XXIX and XXX.

3 Ambrose, *Ep.* 58 ad Sabinum. For a full collection of *elogia* of Paulinus' decision to withdraw from the world, see Migne *PL,* LXI, col. 125ff.

4 Thus, Ausonius' description, *Ep.* 27, line 116 (ed. and Eng. tr. by H. G. Evelyn White). For Paulinus' estates and secular career, see A. H. M. Jones, J. R. Martindale and J. Morris, *PLRE* (Cambridge, 1971), pp. 681–2. That in addition, Paulinus had an estate near Narbonne, see Paulinus, *Ep.* 5.21.

5 Paulinus acknowledges his debt in *Carmen* X (ed. W. Hartel, *CSEL* XXX, Vienna, 1894), lines 93–6.

6 Jerome's view of a conformist provincial Christian society in north-east Italy is bitingly expressed in his *Ep.* 7.5. 'In mea patria rusticitatis vernacula deus venter est et de die vivitur. Sanctior est ille qui ditior est.'

7 Thus, *Carmen* IV, lines 8–12:
  Mens contenta suo nec turpi dedita lucro
  Vincat corporeas casto bene conscia lecto
  Inlecebras, turpesque iocos obscenaque dicta
  Oderit illa nocens et multum grata malignis
  Auribus effuso semper rea lingua veneno.

8 *Ibid.*, lines 15ff. Compare also *Carmen* XXIII.

9 *Carmen* V, lines 26–30.

10 Ausonius, *Ep.* 4, lines 9–10.

11 Ausonius, *Commemoratio Professorum Burdigalensium* (ed. H. G. Evelyn White). For Aquitaine in this period, see C. Jullian, *Histoire de la Gaule,* vol. VIII, pp. 130ff.

12 Ausonius, *Professores*, II, lines 9–12.

13 *Ibid.*, IV.

14 Sulpicius Severus, *Chronicon* II.48.3, For Ausonius' description of Delphidius and his family, *Professores* VI, 37–8.

15 Hilary, *Tractatus in Ps. 67.20* (*PL* IX col. 457).

16 For Lydney, see R. E. M. and M. V. Wheeler, *Lydney Park* (Reports of the Research Committee of the Society of Antiquaries of London, vol. 9, 1932), pp. 103–4.

17 For Augustine at Milan, see P. Courcelle. *Recherches sur les confessions de S. Augustin* (Paris, 1950), pp. 78–95 and *Les Confessions de S. Augustin dans la tradition littéraire* (Paris, 1963), ch. I, and P. R. L. Brown, *Augustine of Hippo* (London, 1967), pp. 79ff.

18 Paulinus, *Ep.* 38, 39 and 44 (to Aper), 40 (to Sanctus and Amandus), and 43 (to Desiderius). For Sulpicius Severus, see *Ep.* I and Victricius, *Ep.* 18. See P. G. Walsh's 'Paulinus of Nola and the conflict of ideologies in the fourth century', *Kyriakon (Festschrift Johannes Quasten)* P. Granfield and J. A. Jungmann (Münster, 1970), pp. 565–71.

19 An example of the fatalistic attitude of Christian bishops to these events is provided by Maximus of Turin when he told the wretched city councillors of Turin trying to prepare the defences of their city against Radagaisus in 402 that they would be better employed preparing their souls in readiness for the approaching Last Day (*Sermo*, 85.2, ed. A. Mutzenbacher, p. 348).

20 *Carmen* XXI, lines 367ff.

21 *Ibid.*, lines 381ff.

22 Ambrose's description of Paulinus' 'conversion' (*Ep.* 58) suggests an acquaintanceship but not a close one. To suggest a meeting during Paulinus' stay in Italy seems reasonable. There is no evidence for a later visit to Milan, about 387 (see N. K. Chadwick, *Poetry and Letters in Early Christian Gaul* (London, 1955), p. 70).

23 He emphasises the latter in *Carmen* XXI, lines 397-8: 'te [Felix] revocante soli quondam genitalis ad oram sollicitae matri sum redditus'.

24 Melania was a Spaniard, like Therasia, and the connection with Paulinus would seem more probably to come through her. Paulinus (*Ep.* 29.5) is vague enough in claiming kinship: 'cuius (Melaniae) fides illi magis quam noster sanguis propinquat'. Another clue is perhaps given in *Carmen* XXI, lines 281ff, where Paulinus appears to associate the noble family of Albina which was connected by marriage with Melania, and Therasia. 'Prima chori Albina est cum pare Therasia; iungitur hoc germana iugo,' Therasia it would seem had the closer connections with the Christian Roman aristocracy than Paulinus.

25 Paulinus, *Carmen* I.

26 Ausonius, *Ep.* 23.

27 *Ibid.*

28 Paulinus, *Ep.* 18 to Victricius.

29 *Ibid.*, 18.7.

30 *Carmen* XXI, lines 416ff. Compare also, *Ep.* 5.4, with its reference to the 'lying scandals' from which Paulinus was now finding rest.

31 *Carmen* XXI, lines 419-20.

32 For the early dating of these letters, see Fabre, *Essai sur la chronologie*, pp. 66ff.

33 These poems contain no reference to Felix or to Paulinus' various concerns when he was living at Nola. Paulinus was, however, adapting the classical metre to the requirements of a devout Christianity. See Fabre, *St Paulin de Nole*, p. 27, placing *Carmen* IV in the period 384-9.

34 As demonstrated in his defence of his life in Spain when he wrote his reply to Ausonius, *Carmen* X, lines 199ff.

35 Paulinus, *Carmen* X, lines 1-5, = Ausonius, *Ep.* 31. Another factor that undoubtedly affected Paulinus at this time was the death in infancy of his son (*Carmen* XXXI, line 603: 'exoptata diu soboles').

36 Ausonius, *Ep.* 29, lines 54-61.

37 *Ep.* 27.

38 *Ep.* 28, line 31: 'Tanaquil tua nesciat istud'.

39 *Ep.* 27, line 60: 'Romana procul tibi nomina sunto'.

40 Paulinus, *Ep.* 9 and 10. Dating, see Fabre, *Essai sur la chronologie*, pp. 62ff.

41 *Ep.* 9.5.

42 *Carmen* XI = Ausonius, *Ep.* 30.

43 *Carmen* X, line 191.

44 *Ibid.*, line 192.

45 *Ibid.*, lines 202ff.

46 *Ibid.*, lines 330-1.

47 *Ibid.*, lines 285-6.

48 Thus Varro, *De re rustica* III.1.4, 'divina natura dedit agros, ars humana aedificavit urbes', and man had improved on the original divine handiwork.

49 Paulinus, *Carmen* X, lines 305ff.

50 Jerome to Paulinus, *Ep.* 58.6 (ed. I. Hilberg, *CSEL* liv, p. 535).

51 Paulinus, *Ep.* 1.17, and compare *Ep.* 2.2.

52 For the scenes at Thagaste, see Augustine *Ep.* 126 and 127.

53 This is suggested by Jerome's opinion (*Ep.* 58.8) of the work that 'cumque in primis partibus vincas alios, in paenultimis te ipsum superas'. There was clearly some evidence of inward strife whether Paulinus was willing to continue in the public service of even the most Christian emperor.

54 Jerome, *Ep.* 58.8: '[tu] qui talia habes rudimenta, qualis exercitatus miles eris'.

55 *Ibid.*, 58.10.

56 *Ibid.*, 58.11: 'Nihil in te mediocre contentus sum: totum summum, perfectum desidero', a very shrewd thrust touching Paulinus' vanity as a writer.

57 For the continued association in the minds of western Christians of public office with 'the world of the devil' and consequently debarring the holders from the priesthood, see Pope Innocent I, *Ep.* 2.2, to Victricius of Rouen and also *Ep.* 6.11 (*PL* XX, col. 500). Pope Siricius gave his view in *Ep.* 5.2: 'Item si quis post remissionem peccatorum cingulum militiae saecularis habuerit ad clerum admitti non decet'. Paulinus could, of course, claim that his period of office took place before his baptism. Compare, too, Lactantius, *Div. Inst.* VI.20.16.

58 Paulinus, *Carmen* XXI, lines 395-6:
Ergo ubi bis terno dicionis fasce levatus
Deposui nulla maculatam caede securim.

59 *Ep.* 17. Paulinus, however, seems to have known precisely what was happening in ecclesiastical Gaul, who was a newly appointed bishop and what were his views. See *Ep.* 48 (fragment).

60 *Ep.* 37.6.

61 Cited by Augustine in his long letter to Paulinus, *Ep.* 186.34.

62 For the essential spirit of Pelagianism in south Italy see Brown *op. cit.*, pp. 381ff.

63 Paulinus, *Carmen* XXI, lines 234-5.

64 Shown for instance by Paulinus in his letter to Alypius, *Ep.* 3. See Fabre, *St. Paulin de Nola*, pp. 138ff.

65 Augustine, *Ep.* 186.1 and 4.

66 His Letters 1, 9, 10, 35 and 36 were written before his departure to Spain, while Letter 34 is a sermon.

67 Severus had abandoned his career as a lawyer 'with a sudden urge to break the deadly bonds of flesh and blood' (Paulinus *Ep.* 5.5). The correspondence ends in 404 perhaps because of the growing insecurity of the countryside immediately preceding the great Germanic invasions of 405–6.

68 *Ep.* 32.5.

69 *Ibid.*, 32.8.

70 *Ibid.*, 32.10–23. On the basilicas see H. Belting, *Die Basilica der SS. Martiri im Cimitile* (Wiesbaden, 1961).

71 *Ep.* 39.

72 *Ep.* 38.10.

73 Paulinus the Deacon, *Vita Sancti Ambrosii* 36 (PL XIV, col. 42): 'In qua epistola [Ambrose] etiam admovuit ut suaderet viro Romanis pacem servare'.

74 Paulinus, *Ep.* 18.4.

75 *Ibid.*

76 *Carmen* XVII, lines 206–8, and compare lines 225–6:
Mos ubi quondam fuerat ferarum
Nunc ibi ritus viget angelorum.

77 P. R. L. Brown, 'The patrons of Pelagius', *JTS*, n.s. 21.1 (1970), pp. 56–72.

78 *Ibid.*, pp. 57–9.

79 *Ibid.*, p. 60.

80 Paulinus and Therasia to Romanianus, published among Augustine's correspondence as *Ep.* 32, at para. 2, 'verba caelestia Augustini'.

81 Paulinus, *Ep.* 8 to Alypius, line 83 (Hartel, p. 51).

82 Courcelle, *Les Confessions*, pp. 559–607.

83 Paulinus, *Ep.* 3.

84 *Ep.* 3.2, and compare Paulinus' letter to Alypius (=*Ep.* 24 in Augustine's correspondence). Alypius like nearly all westerners did not know Eusebius' work at first hand but attributed it to his namesake Eusebius 'of Constantinople' (i.e. of Nicomedia), as did Paulinus.

85 The incident which took place *circa* 399–400 is discussed by Courcelle, *Les Confessions*, p. 567.

86 On this important aspect of the *Confessions*, see L. F. Pizzolato, *Le Confessioni di sant' Agostino: da biografia a 'confessio'* (Milan, 1968).

87 See Brown, *op. cit.*, p. 159. These works would, however, seem to contribute only indirectly to the literary genre of the *Confessions*. The latter would appear to be the culmination of Augustine's ten-year crusade against the errors of Manichaeans and should perhaps be read in conjunction with *De Genesi contra Manichaeos*, both of which embody his own reprobation of his nine years with the sect.

88 Augustine, *Ep.* 186.40.

89 Paulinus, *Ep.* 3.4 to Alypius: 'Send me the whole account of your holy person.' Compare also the passage in another letter to Alypius, preserved in Augustine's correspondence as *Ep.* 24.4 (Goldbacher, p. 76).

90 Augustine to Paulinus, *Ep.* 27.5.
91 See Brown, *op. cit.*, p. 161–2.
92 Augustine, *Ep.* 27.5.
93 See Walsh, *Letters*, introduction, pp. 10ff.
94 Paulinus, *Ep.* 18.7.
95 Chadwick, *op. cit.*, p. 72.
96 *Ep.* 5.21. On the daily meal attended by Paulinus' household at Nola see *Ep.* 15.4 and 23.8, and the vegetarian diet observed, *Ep.* 19.4 and 23.5.
97 For Vigilantius see G. Bardy's article in *Dictionnaire de Théologie Catholique* XV, 2992, and Chadwick, *op. cit.* It may be reasonably assumed that the presbyter Vigilantius and Jerome's later opponent are the same person.
98 Paulinus, *Ep.* 23.7 and 9.
99 For Cardamas and his eccentricities, *Ep.* 14, 15 and 19.
100 The literary evidence is analysed by R. C. Goldschmidt, *Paulinus' churches at Nola* (Amsterdam, 1940), and the results of the excavations at Cimitile are analysed by H. Belting, *op. cit.*
101 *Carmen* XXVIII, lines 61ff. That peasants possessed no clear-cut property rights in Campania at this period is an interesting sidelight on prevailing social conditions in what has been generally thought to have been an impoverished province.
102 As described in *Ep.* 32.13ff.
103 *Carmen* XXVII, though no direct quotations from Statius are recognisable. Vergil *Aen.* V seems to be the most frequent source of Paulinus' inspiration here. See, however, Helm's article in Paulinus in Pauly-Wissowa *RE* 18.4, col. 2340, suggesting a reminiscence of Statius, *Silv.* I.3 and II.2.
104 For much of the information in this section I am indebted to R. P. H. Greene's book, especially ch. II. See also Helm, *op. cit.*, cols. 2336–44.
105 Augustine, *Psalmus contra partem Donati*, PL XLIII, cols 23–32.
106 Paulinus, *Carmen* XVI, lines 100 and 155–92.
107 *Carmen* XV, lines 309ff and 351ff.
108 *Carmen* XVI, lines 66ff, and compare lines 105ff for the exasperated ruminations of the pursuit party.
109 *Carmen* XIX, lines 378ff., and *Carmen* XX, lines 301ff.
110 *Carmen* XX, lines 388f.
111 *Ep.* 16.7.
112 Claudian, *Epithalamium*, lines 231–3.
113 Paulinus, *Carmen* XXV, lines 9–14. See also Helm, *op. cit.*, col. 2339, for Ovidian influence on this composition.
114 Claudian, *Epithalamium*, line 171.
115 *Ibid.*, lines 340–1.
116 Paulinus, *Carmen* XXXI, line 313.
117 *Carmen* XXII, lines 13–14.
118 *Carmen* XVII, lines 51–2.
119 For these, see A. A. T. Ehrhardt, 'Quaker-Latein', in *Existenz und Ordnung* (*Festschrift Erich Wolf*) (Frankfurt, 1962), pp. 167–71, and for

the Latin used in Christian communities as a jargon, see C. Mohrmann, *Augustinus Magister* (Paris, 1954), vol. I, pp. 111–16.

120 See, for these and other examples, Green, *op. cit.*, ch. IV.

121 See Colin Morris, *The Discovery of the Individual* (Church History Outlines 5, SPCK, 1972), pp. 51ff.

122 As showing Paulinus' description of the early spring breaking in on the countryside around Nola.

> Hinc vernat hiems, hinc undique nobis
> Spirat odoratos vegetabilis aura vapores;
> Hoc de corde venit benedicti spiritus agri
> (*Carmen* XXVII, lines 164–6).

123 *Ep.* 1.7.

124 *Ep.* 38.

125 *Ep.* 40.11.

126 *Ep.* 1.8. 'I pray, brother, that we may be found worthy to be executed in the name of Christ.'

127 *Ep.* 31.3.

NOTE: Professor Walsh's edition of the Poems of Paulinus of Nola, publ. 1975 (Ancient Christian Writers, 40) was not available for use in this article.

XVI

ATHANASIUS AS AN EGYPTIAN CHRISTIAN LEADER IN THE FOURTH CENTURY[1]

The century and a quarter that separated the Council of Nicaea in 325 from that of Chalcedon in 451 saw changes in the direction of western civilisation that have lasted until our own day. In this period, the Christian Church that previously had suffered intermittent persecution became the predominant factor in the lives of the rulers and peoples of the Roman empire. The age-old patronage of the 'immortal gods of Rome' was replaced by that of God and Christ, to be acknowledged and worshipped as the councils of the Church prescribed. Between them, the emperor Constantine and his friend and counsellor, the historian Eusebius of Caesarea (circa 269-339) reflected a coherent view of a world governed by the providence of God through His chosen representative, the Emperor.[2] The application of this view to all aspects of the empire's authority after the Council of Nicaea in 325 marked the beginning of a new era. During the years that followed, the inhabitants of the eastern provinces in particular, found an inner solidarity as members of a 'race of Christians' that was proof against otherwise divisive forces of regional rivalry and social antagonism.

The Christian leaders were drawn from sundry backgrounds that emphasised the complete and universal character of the Church's triumph. There were high imperial officials such as Ambrose of Milan, ex-soldiers like Victricius of Rouen, former Jewish farmers such as Epiphanius of Salamis, but by far the greatest proportion came from the provincial middle class, the *curiales*, men who by tradition were important in their own cities and were educated in either Greek or Latin. These men, like Augustine, Jerome and the Cappadocian Fathers formed an essential bridge between the pagan and Christian civilisations before the onset of the barbarian invasions, and they provided social mobility in an era of increasing ossification of class and caste.[3] In culture if not in status (for this is not accurately known) and among the greatest of this generation of

---

[1] The annotated text of a lecture given at an evening conference organised by the University of Edinburgh Department of Extra-Mural Studies in association with the Faculty of Divinity on 5 November 1973.

[2] For the relationship of the emperor to God in Eusebius' mind, see *Oration on the Tricennalia of Constantine* (ed. I. A. Heikel) 2. 1-5.

[3] See A. H. M. Jones, *The Later Roman Empire*, Oxford, 1964, p. 920-29.

Christian leaders, was Athanasius, whose 1,600th anniversary we recall this evening.[1]

Athanasius died on 4 May 373 after having been Archbishop of Alexandria for just under forty-five years. He had been born in circa 295 when the Greco-Roman world was still pagan and placed by the emperors Diocletian and Maximian under the patronage of Jupiter and Hercules. He lived through the Great Persecution (303-312) and the valour of the Egyptian confessors made a deep and lasting impression upon him. In the *De Incarnatione* he recalls in words similar to Eusebius (with whom he had little else in common!) how men 'weak by nature leaped forward to death', not fearing torture and how their wives and children did the same demonstrating the power of Christ's religion.[2] He saw the end of the old religion, the desertion of its temples and the irrevocable growth of popular enthusiasm in Egypt for the most exacting form of Christianity, monasticism. His shrewd comment on the pagan reaction under the emperor Julian (361-363) that it was like a cloud that would soon pass, has found its place in popular history.[3] For him Christianity was liberation from the thraldom of a world hitherto dominated by idolatry and magic.[4]

Victory, however, did not bring peace to the Church. Athanasius' episcopate was singularly stormy. He spent seventeen years in exile from his native Alexandria. His writing betrays the bitterness of the controversies in which he was engaged. He did not shrink from the use of violence against opponents. Only in the final decade of his life does the mellowness of statemanship show through the embattled personality, and he becomes something of the Grand Old Man of orthodoxy. Until that time, *Athanasius contra mundum* is no inept description of his career.

Yet the blame for strife does not lie at his door alone. He had a passion for the truth of the creed of Nicaea and a determination that this should be vindicated. And nowhere did he succeed more thoroughly than in Egypt. More than half a century after his death, at the beginning of the Nestorian controversy in 429, Cyril of Alexandria wrote to the Egyptian monks. They were suspicious of the term *Theotokos* (God-bearing) as applied to the Virgin Mary. Was it

---

[1] Athanasius is described by Sozomen, *Hist Eccl* ii. 17.10 (ed. J. Bidez and G. C. Hansen, Berlin, 1960) as being 'well educated in grammar and rhetoric', and fitted in every way to succeed Alexander as archbishop through his 'learning and wisdom'. An Alexandrian middle-class background can therefore be assumed.

[2] *De Incarnatione* 29.4; compare Eusebius, *HE* viii.9.4 (referring to the martyrs of the Thebaid).

[3] Theodoret, *Hist Eccl* iii.9.

[4] *De Incarnatione* 31.2.

22

scriptural or not? Cyril's case was weak. In the course of this long letter he could cite hardly a single text to support his view, but he assured his readers that Athanasius would have agreed,[1] and that was enough to win them over.

How did Athanasius achieve this reputation in Egypt? At first sight it is not easy to see. The problems raised by the Council of Nicaea were hardly intelligible to those who lacked an education through Greek philosophy and in many cases spoke no Greek at all. Moreover, Alexandria was not Egypt. As a city, the representative of the former Macedonian ascendancy, it was bitterly resented. There exists indeed, a third-century version of a traditional Egyptian oracle known as the Oracle of the Potter, that castigates the 'city by the sea', rejoices in its humiliations and prophesies its ruin.[2] Athanasius was an Alexandrian brought up in the Christianised philosophic tradition of Origen and his successors. It is no little part of his claim to genius that by his death he had transformed the none too popular hegemony of the Church of Alexandria over the rest of Egypt into an unbreakable alliance between the Coptic and Alexandrian Christians. In this, somehow or other, the Biblicism of the Copt and the philosophic theology of Alexandria were welded into harmony and the foundations were laid on which Cyril established the power of the Alexandrian Church during the fifth century.

This aspect of Athanasius' work concerns us this evening. One instance first, to show how far the internal and external issues confronting Athanasius were interlocked during the first years of his rule. In 334 he had been bishop for six years. Storms had gathered thick around him. He had aroused the intense distrust of the majority of the eastern bishops, the foremost representatives of Constantine's Christian revolution, and the anger of a large section of the Christians in Egypt. Unity, however, was the key to Constantine's policy towards the Church. In 334 he was preparing to celebrate thirty years of reign as Augustus—that span once prophesied for him by a Gallic oracle of Apollo.[3] It had been, however, the God of the Christians that had given him his great victories over his rivals Maxentius and Licinius, necessary for its fulfilment, and Constantine intended to celebrate his thirty-year rule with due acknowledgement of divine favour. A magnificent church had been built on the

[1] Cyril, *Ep* 1, *P.G.* 77, col 13C.

[2] *Pap. Oxy.*, 2332, and see the discussion by E. Lobel and C. H. Roberts in *Oxyrhynchus Papyri* xxii, published by the Egypt Exploration Society, London, 1954. For another indication of antipathies between rich and poor in Egypt during the third century, see *Pap Oxy* 2554, an astrological text with its references to 'tumult and war' and 'things going badly for the rich'.

[3] Anon., *Panegyrici Latini* (ed. Baehrens) 6 (7) 21.3-6.

site of the Holy Sepulchre at Jerusalem, and the emperor planned to be baptised like Christ himself, in the waters of the Jordan.[1] As a prologue he instructed his friend, Eusebius of Caesarea, to hold a council of bishops including bishops and presbyters from Egypt 'at which complaints against Athanasius could be heard' in his episcopal city of Caesarea.[2]

By now Constantine regarded Athanasius as the chief obstacle to his grand design of Christian unity. Athanasius' refusal to receive Arius back into communion and restore him to his former position as presbyter was the main grievance, for it involved the emperor personally as well as the considered judgment of the great majority of the eastern bishops. Combined with this, however, were the grievances of Athanasius' domestic opponents, the Meletians, who illogically had made common cause with Arius' supporters. Athanasius, however, had stood his ground, refusing to attend the Council of Caesarea. It was packed by his enemies, he claimed.[3] The emperor was patient. Another council was summoned to meet at Tyre in July 335 on the very eve of the Tricennalia celebrations. Constantine appealed for peace and unity. He upbraided those who, inflamed by a spirit of contention, endeavoured to throw everything into confusion. More to the point, he sent a senior official, the Count (*Comes*) and former consul, Dionysius, to supervise proceedings and maintain order. After a long hesitation Athanasius yielded and decided to attend. A papyrus, a chance find, a letter written by a Meletian presbyter to a Meletian monastic leader, describes vividly the state of his mind.[4] 'Athanasius', a correspondent wrote, 'is very despondent . . . They have often come to fetch him and so far he has not started. He put his luggage aboard as if he was starting, and again he took the luggage off the ship a second time'. Like Cyril before the Council of Ephesus in 431, Athanasius feared for his position once he left Alexandria. He took the precaution of having forty-eight Egyptian bishops accompany him; but his enemies were even better prepared.

The Council of Tyre was a model of many similar meetings that took place in this and in the next century. In essence it was a court. The president was a layman and he was supported by lay assessors. At the Council of Chalcedon in 451 the contending bishops addressed

---

[1] Eusebius, *Vita Constantini* (ed. Heikel) iv.62, and *Pap Lond* 1913.

[2] Sozomen, *Hist Eccl* ii.25.1, Theodoret, *Hist Eccl* i.28. 2-4.

[3] Theodoret, *Hist Eccl* i.28. See also K. Holl, 'Die Bedeutung der neuveröffentlichten melitianischen Urkunden für die Kirchengeschichte', *Gesammelte Aufsätze* ii. (Tübingen, 1928) p. 284.

[4] H. I. Bell, *Jews and Christians in Egypt*, Oxford, 1924, p. 38 ff, and Holl, *op cit.* p. 286.

24

the emperor or his representatives who were senior secular officials and they took the decisions though with the agreement of the bishops present.[1] Already, however, under Constantine, Church and State were being integrated as a single body, and Athanasius himself never questioned the lay authority in the council. The charges, too, concerned ostensibly his conduct in Egypt and not his orthodoxy. A man who claimed to be a presbyter of a church in Mareotis (a status Athanasius denied him) named Ischyras complained that a chalice used for the Eucharist had been broken wantonly by one of Athanasius' priests and that Athanasius had imprisoned him and charged him falsely before the prefect of Egypt. Callinicus, a Meletian bishop who had been reconciled to Athanasius' predecessor, Alexander, complained that Athanasius had deposed him because he refused to communicate with him until he had cleared himself of the charge relating to the chalice. Five other Meletian bishops stated that they had been beaten by Athanasius' agents, and Bishop Arsenius whom Athanasius had been accused eighteen months previously of murdering was now said to have been kidnapped and beaten.Finally, Athanasius' election as archbishop seven years before was challenged. His consecration had been carried through secretly against the will of the majority of Egyptian bishops.[2]

Violence and uncanonical consecration were sufficiently grave charges to secure the deposition of a bishop, and Athanasius' enemies among the Syrian and other eastern bishops were clever enough to embroil their quarry in misdemeanours allegedly committed in Egypt rather than attempt to convict him of unorthodoxy. The creed of Nicaea might be circumvented but not attacked openly. They succeeded. A partisan and vigorously led commission was sent to Mareotis to investigate the chalice affair, and it reported in Ischyras' favour, though it transpired that Ischyras himself was ill in bed when the incident was supposed to have happened. Witnesses agreed, however, that Athanasius' presbyter, Macarius, had overturned the holy table in the church.[3]

Meantime, Athanasius and his bishops withdrew from the Council in protest and repaired to Constantinople. Not surprisingly he was condemned to deprivation in his absence. The Meletian bishops and clergy were received into the communion of the Council. The emperor was informed of its decision. Athanasius was removed from

[1] See for instance, R. V. Sellers' description of the sessions of the Council of Chalcedon, *The Council of Chalcedon*, London, 1961, p. 103 ff.

[2] Socrates, *Hist Eccl* i.28-30, Sozomen, *Hist Eccl* ii. 25, Philostorgius, *Hist Eccl* ii.11 (Athanasius' consecration).

[3] Socrates, *Hist Eccl* i.31, though Socrates claims their evidence was 'deficient of proofs'.

office and forbidden by the Council to return to Alexandria.[1] The way was clear for Arius' return eased by the latter's allegedly orthodox confession before the emperor himself. The arch-heretic was received once more into orthodox communion and Constantine went on to fete the peace and brotherly unity of the Church at a massive celebration in Jerusalem.[2] Early in November 335, his dramatic personal appeal to the emperor rejected,[3] Athanasius was on his way to the first of his five exiles in the western city of Trier.

What had happened? How was it that the theological opponents of Athanasius had been able apparently to destroy him through convicting him of an obscure misdemeanour committed in an out-of-the-way village in the Nile delta? Who were the Meletians? How did they come to play so fateful a part in the first decade of Athanasius' episcopate, and survive to harass him until he passed from the scene?

To answer these questions we must go back to the generation before the outbreak of the Great Persecution in 303. Just as Alexandria and the remainder of Egypt represented different, indeed contrasting cultures, so the Christianity that developed in these two areas was also radically different. Of the Alexandrian contribution to Christian thought and teaching represented by Clement, Origen, Dionysius and their successors sufficient has been said,[4] and it is enough to remind that it represented a Christian Platonism, Greek in language and expression, that looked back ultimately to the work of Philo and the school of Alexandrian Hellenistic Judaism. Christianity in the Nile valley also seems to have looked back to Judaism, but of a different type. The monastic ideal of the *Therapeutae* described by Eusebius (*Hist Eccl* ii.17) was so akin to the monasticism with which he was acquainted in Egypt that he believed it to be actually Christian. He was not, however, far off the mark. Fragments of more than one copy of the *Gospel of Thomas* were found at Oxyrhynchus, in Athanasius' time an important Christian centre, long before the complete gospel was recovered among the books

---

[1] Sozomen, *Hist Eccl* ii.25.19, Socrates, *Hist Eccl* i.32. See K. Holl, *art cit*, and L. W. Barnard, 'Athanasius and the Meletian Schism in Egypt', *Journal of Egyptian Archaeology*, 59, 1973, p. 183-89.

[2] *Ibid* ii.26, Socrates, *Hist Eccl* i.33.

[3] Athanasius was accused by his enemies at this point of withholding part of the corn supply from Alexandria to Constantinople. The accusation was also made by the Meletian monk Callistus (*Pap Lond* 1914) and there may be some truth in it.

[4] See for instance H. Chadwick's chapters on Clement and Origen in *Cambridge History of Greek and Early Mediaeval Philosophy*, (ed. A. H. Armstrong), 1967, p. 168-195. Later.

preserved by the Sethite sect in their library at Nag Hammadi.[1] The *Gospel of Thomas* was a collection of Logia attributed to Jesus that emphasised how the ascetic virtues practised as a solitary were the key to knowledge of the Kingdom of Heaven. This Jewish-Christian work was circulating already in parts of the Nile Valley by the mid-second century A.D. The Jewish-Christian influence was to be important. Coptic Christianity was to owe more to it than to any resurgence of national Egyptian sentiment. By the end of the century Clement of Alexandria (circa 190 A.D.) preserves traces of other Jewish-Christian writings such as the *Gospel according to the Egyptians* and the *Gospel according to the Hebrews*, that were circulating at his time. Their legacy was also a lasting one.

During the third century one can trace the continued existence of this non-Hellenistic and non-Platonic element in Egyptian Christianity and the mutual suspicion between the Bishop of Alexandria and his suffragans. There was the incident in about A.D. 260 when Dionyius of Alexandria rebuked Bishop Nepos of Arsinoe for preaching millenarist doctrines on the grounds that these were unsound, resting on a false literalist understanding of scripture and were Jewish inspired (Eusebius, *Hist Eccl* vii.24). Biblical literalism was, however, precisely the understanding of the Bible espoused by the monastic movement whose foremost representative decided on his vocation a decade later. Antony, despite his name (probably Aurelius Antonius), was a Copt, the son of wealthy farming parents (300 arourae was a considerable holding for the time).[2] When he established himself as an ascetic and a solitary on the edge of his village in 270, he not only opened a new chapter in the history of Egypt but ensured that this chapter would be linked to the already existing prophetic and Biblical strain in Christianity that prevailed outwith Alexandria.

He had 'sold all' in order to fight demons, perhaps identified in his mind with the gods of ancient Egypt as well as Greco-Roman importations. His method was ascetic conflict inspired wholly by the Bible whose pages were enough for all instruction, he claimed.[3] The

---

[1] For the original Oxyrhynchus papyri, see B. P. Grenfell and A. S. Hunt, *Oxyrhynchus Papyri* iv, p. 10-22. An excellent study of Thomas *logia* has been made by H. W. Montefiore, 'A comparison of the Parables of the Gospel according to Thomas and of the Synoptic Gospels', *New Testament Studies*, 7, 1961, p. 220-48; see also my article, 'The Gospel of Thomas: Is Rehabilitation possible?' *Journal of Theological Studies*, NS xviiii, 1967, p. 13-26.

[2] Thus, for comparison, at Theadelphia, a village of the city of Arsinoe, 270 arourae was divided between twenty-five owners and lesser office-holders at Hermopolis were assessed for taxation at about 60 arourae apiece, see A. H. M. Jones, *op cit*, p. 454 and 596.

[3] Athanasius, *Life of Antony* 16.

followers he gathered round him in the twenty years before the Great Persecution (we are told by Athanasius after his death in 356) sang psalms, loved reading, fasted, prayed, rejoiced in the hope of things to come and laboured in alms giving . . . There was neither the evil-doer, nor the injured, nor the reproaches of the tax-gatherer; but a multitude of ascetics and the one purpose of them all was to aim at virtue.[1] One can see here in the pursuit of perfection through the ascetic life, combined with a withdrawal from the normal obligations to society, the makings of a profound revolution in Coptic Egypt.

In 270 when Antony started upon his work, Christianity was still a minority religion. In the ensuing decade, this too was to change. The exact reason for the massive turning away from the deities that had watched over the destinies of countless generations of Egyptians is unknown. All one can say is that during the third century the traditional rites connected with the cults seem to have become perfunctory while if we may believe the writer of the *Life of Pachomius* these rites had begun to evoke positive aversion among some.[2] Most of the disillusioned and discontented flowed towards Christianity, and in particular, towards monasticism. Eusebius describes how from being a land full of the most opprobrious idols Egypt was turning visibly towards the true faith,[3] and Antony's self-denying creed based on a literal reading of the command, 'Go, sell all that thou hast . . .',[4] found many imitators.

There was, however, another channel attracting the idealism of the time. In the 280s, the first Manichaean missionaries are said to have reached Egypt.[5] Within a few years they had established communities in the Nile valley. The soulful, haunting hymns these have left behind combined with a radical dualistic theology which placed the body and all its works on the side of evil found a responsive echo among the Copts. Marriage was abominated.[6] and poverty

---

[1] *Life of Antony* 44.

[2] *Vita Pachomii* 4 (ed. Th. Lefort, *Corpus Script. Christ. Orientalium, Script. Coptici*, iii.7, Paris, 1924, Louvain 1936).

[3] Eusebius, *Demonstratio Evangelica* vi.20.9 and ix.2.4.

[4] Athanasius, *Life of Antony* 2. Contrast the sentiments expressed by Clement towards the use of wealth in *Quis dives salvetur?*

[5] Alexander of Lycopolis, *De Placitis Manichaeorum* 2 (P. G. 18, col 413). See *A Manichaean Psalmbook* (ed. A. J. Allberry), Stuttgart, 1938; like Christianity the Manichaeans encouraged feelings of conversion among their adherents and rejection of the evil ways of their parents; cf Psalm 269, lines 29-32 (Allberry, p. 87).

[6] *Pap Rylands* 469 = *Texte zum Manichaismus* (ed. A. Adam), Berlin, 1954, No 35, p. 52. The Manichaeans were not the only Coptic ascetic sect that opposed marriage. Compare, for instance, the followers of Hierakas of Leontopolis. See Epiphanius, *Panarion* (ed. K. Holl) 67; Hierakas' teaching was said to resemble that of both the Gnostic Valentinus and Mani. Also, Ps. 277, lines 30-34.

enjoined. Before 300, Theonas, archbishop of Alexandria, denounced them and in particular, their condemnation of marriage in an encyclical. Their attraction, however, like that of Gnosticism which they superseded, was evident. Their hymns and psalms passed straight into Coptic, and they presented Athanasius with the challenge of winning Egyptian asceticism for orthodoxy.

The Great Persecution of 303 broke upon Egypt in the midst of ferment of religious and cultural change. Already Christianity had become a vehicle for Coptic self-expression with the Bible translated into Sahidic. There is an interesting example also of a late third-century school exercise book which contains exercises in grammar and literature in Greek, but a fragment of Psalm 46 (v 3-10) in the Akhmin dialect of Coptic.[1] Coptic even at this time was becoming the 'Christian language'—another reason perhaps for believing that Athanasius was conversant in it. At first, however, the persecution was relatively mild. Churches were seized and scriptures burnt, but as a papyrus from Oxyrhynchus shows, civil disabilities to which Christians were subjected, such as prevention from pleading in court were often evaded.[2] In 304, however, the authorities became stricter. More clergy and monks were sought out and imprisoned. Among those who found themselves in gaol were Peter, Archbishop of Alexandria since circa 300, and Meletius, Bishop of Lycopolis (Assiut) in Upper Egypt, the one representing Alexandrian orthodoxy, the other, the emergent Coptic Christianity. They did not get on. Seventy years later, Epiphanius of Salamis records an incident during that time. The confessors had no doubt that they would survive the persecution. They were concerned, however, about the treatment that the lapsed would receive when it ended. Meletius stood for a rigorous policy. Perhaps he had seen clerical lapse and hypocrisy at Lycopolis. Peter stood for a milder one. The dispute became bitter as each attracted supporters from among the other prisoners. At last Peter had had enough. He hung his pallium across the cell and ordered all those who refused to accept his rulings to leave his half of the prison. The majority of both clergy and monks did so. The two parties ceased to be on speaking terms.[3]

Shortly after, Diocletian abdicated (1 May 305); the prisoners were released, and for about eleven months there was an uneasy truce. Just before Easter 306, Peter published his regulations for re-admitting the lapsed to communion. As anticipated they were mild. Those who had given way under torture could return after a forty

[1] P. J. Parsons, 'A School book from the Sayce Collection', *Zeitschrift für Papyrologie und Epigraphie*, 6, 1970, p. 133-69.
[2] *Pap Oxy* 2601 (= *Oxyrhynchus Papyri*, vol xxxi, p. 167).
[3] Epiphanius, *Panarion*, 68.2-3.

days' fast, those who yielded on imprisonment had to undergo what was in effect a three-year catechumenate. Those who got their slaves to sacrifice for them were to be subjected to three years' penance. This was much too tolerant for Meletius. He went into formal schism. He began to ordain presbyters in dioceses other than his own. He intended clearly to render the see of Alexandria and its incumbent of no effect.[1] One of those Christians who supported him was an earnest cleric named Arius.

In the next few years Meletius' cause prospered. The second half of the persecution between 306-312 was terrible in the extreme and in particular for the Copts in Upper Egypt. Eusebius of Caesarea has left an eyewitness account of ten, twenty, or even one hundred being executed in a single day, with the executioners growing utterly weary and their axes becoming blunt from over-usage.[2] This was when the Coptic Church was born and the era of Diocletian became the Era of the Martyrs. Those who escaped execution were often sent to work in the mines in Palestine and Cilicia. There they formed the spearhead of resistance among the Christians. But under stress it was to the Old Testament that they turned, proclaiming as their personal names, not those of ancient Egypt but of the Hebrew prophets—Jeremiah, Elijah, Daniel and Isaiah.[3] Copts though they were, these new Christians were as disdainful of their Egyptian past as they were of the idolatry of the imperial authorities. Coptic self-identity was not associated with any surge of Egyptian national feeling.

Meletius himself was re-arrested and sent to the copper mines of Phaeno in southern Palestine,[4] and there he ordained more clergy and consecrated a bishop. The schism in the Egyptian Church was now complete. But one event more than any other checked Meletius' progress. On 25 November 311, Bishop Peter was executed. The Church of Alexandria had its bishop-martyr, and Peter's martyrdom seemed to set the seal of divine approval on his policies. Those who had deserted him began to return to serve his successor, among them the presbyter Arius. The Meletians did not forget.[5]

As important as Peter's martyrdom in frustrating Meletians, was the fact that in Egypt there was no tradition of conflict over the nature of the Church as there was in the Latin Church in North

---

[1] For a summary of this period. see A. H. M. Jones, *Constantine and the Conversion of Europe*, London, 1948, p. 147-8.

[2] Eusebius, *HE* viii.9.4.

[3] Eusebius, *Martyrs of Palestine* (ed. H. J. Lawlor and J. E. L. Oulton), 11.8.

[4] Epiphanius, *loc cit*, 68.3.

[5] For Meletius' denunciation of Arius to Archbishop Alexander, see Epiphanius, *loc cit*, 68.4.

Africa. If there was jealousy of Alexandria and incomprehension of the theology of its bishops, there was no history of schism in the Egyptian Church and none of the actual rejection of the leadership of Alexandria. Meletius represented tendencies and aspirations among the Copts which none the less remained largely inarticulate. His followers were not destined to play the part of the African Donatists. Even so in the 320s, Meletius' movement posed a threat to the hegemony of the archbishop of Alexandria. A list of his supporters made out in 327 shows that he could claim one bishop in every six episcopal towns in the Delta but one in every second or third city in the more purely Coptic-speaking province of the Thebaid.[1] His mission extended as far down the Nile as Coptos (Q'ft).[2]

By Nicaea, however, Meletius was prepared to come to terms with Alexander of Alexandria. The Council was very fair. Meletius was allowed to retain his title of bishop but not to carry out episcopal functions. His bishops, however, subject always to Alexander's confirmation might retain both, and where two rival bishops existed, the Meletian should rank as the junior but with power to replace his opposite number should the latter predecease him.[3]

The Meletian Church was thus kept in being, but the arrangements required a bishop of Alexandria with monumental tact and patience to absorb these former rebels into a united Church. Athanasius lacked these essential qualities. He was elected as Alexander's successor (perhaps against a Meletian candidate in the person of John Arcaph) as a 'good man and a pious and one of the ascetics'.[4] This was true enough but he was also vigorous to the point of brutality. Of the three problems besetting the Church in Egypt—Arius' supporters, the Manichees, and the Meletians—he came to the conclusion that the Meletians were the most pressing and he turned the full force of his authority and personality against them. He had the wit to recognise that the key to success both against them and against the Manichees was the support of the monks. The Arian menace was confined to a large extent to the Greek-speaking towns. So in the first year of his episcopate he went straight to the Thebaid, the centre of the Meletians. There he concentrated on winning the support of the monks. This proved to be decisive for his future success. As archbishop of Alexandria he had immediate advantages

---

[1] Athanasius, *Apol. contra Arianos* 71, and see E. R. Hardy, *Christian Egypt, Church and People*, New York, 1952, p. 53.

[2] L. W. Barnard, *art cit*, p. 185.

[3] See Hardy, *op cit*, p. 54.

[4] Athanasius, *Apol. contra Arianos* 6.

over any Egyptian opposition. Alexandria had long been recognised as the focus of Christianity for the whole of Egyptian Christianity, and this position had just been formalised at the Council of Nicaea.[1] No one could claim otherwise without being reckoned a schismatic and even a heretic. Moreover, in the previous sixty years, since the time of Bishop Dionysius (247-264), the custom had grown up for the archbishop of Alexandria to announce the date of Easter and its attendant fast in a letter addressed to all Christian communities, and this letter could be used to inform them also of the bishop's views on other matters. Athanasius used this facility to the full. His earliest letters of 329 and 330 exhort his readers to virtue with a moral earnestness, expressed in vigorous Biblical terms. Interestingly the Jews were the main objects of his criticism, with their 'fables' and literalism; the Christian sanctified his soul with nourishing virtues. He uses his free-will to achieve the virtues of generosity, temperance and justice. Above all he remembers the poor and the strangers.[2] Athanasius set before his hearers precisely the virtues that the emperor Julian was to credit the Christians with, and already one sees the combination of Platonist theology with social idealism with which he was to unite the Alexandrian with the Coptic sections of the Egyptian church. But with this idealism went a streak of anger and intolerance. The letters were vehicles of propaganda. Already in 330 Athanasius was criticising 'the dissemblers', those in sheep's clothing, the whited sepulchres, the followers of unlawful heresies.[3] He came to enjoy associating all his enemies in a single concatenation of wickedness. Thus even as an elder statesman he wrote in 365 (*Letter* 41) of 'the Arians and their successors, the Meletians are also their rivals in misdeeds because they have acquired the arrogance of the Jews'. In one sentence he pinpointed three of his principal enemies and held them up to popular execration.

Athanasius was a superb populariser and propagandist. He gives the impression of a vast detailed knowledge of his enemies' deeds and motives. He writes as though his supporters knew all about them before he started to expound and they need only to be reminded of the salient facts. Thus of the events in 327-328 he was to write: 'Five months, however, had not passed when the blessed Alexander died and the Meletians who ought to have kept quiet and to have been grateful for what they had received on any terms began, like dogs unable to forget their vomit, to trouble the Churches again' (*Apol. against the Arians* 59.71). The truth was not so simple, but the

---

[1] Canon 6.
[2] *Letter* (ed. Lefort) 1.11.
[3] *Letter* 2.6.

version stood. Or again, in 358, dealing with events far away from Egypt, he affects to assume that his monkish readers were fully in the picture, 'And I suppose no one is ignorant of the case of Paul, Bishop of Constantinople, for the more illustrious any city is, so much the more what takes place in it cannot be concealed'.[1] It sounds fine and it must have meant something even to the Coptic peasant to whom the nearest town would be as distant as Constantinople. And propaganda could be, and was, supplemented by strong-arm methods, such as those employed against Meletian bishops visiting the military camp outside Alexandria when they were attacked, beaten and imprisoned by a band of Athanasian supporters.[2] The kidnapping of Arsenius was in the same vein.[3]

Such was the popular leader who went boldly into the centre of his opponents' power in 329 and 330. There in the Thebaid he met the Bishop of Tentyra who asked him to ordain a young man whose ideas of monasticism differed from those of Antony. On this occasion Pachomius absented himself and escaped[4] but a few years later he gave in. As presbyter he was soon among Athanasius' loyal supporters and on his death in 345, his successor Theodore followed his example. For his part, Antony is said to have sought out Athanasius immediately after his consecration, and 'evinced unlimited friendship for him'.[5] The immediate effect of Athanasius' successful wooing of Pachomius and Antony was that the Meletians were outbid for monastic support. When Meletius' successor as their leader, John Arcaph, failed to win Constantine's favour and was banished in 336 despite the emperor's exile of Athanasius, their cause became destined to steady decline. The eclipse of this largely Coptic opposition to the Alexandrian archbishop may be explained partly in terms of Athanasius' personality. Whatever his inclination for strong-arm methods, he was also a many sided individual who possessed a unique insight into the ecclesiastical problems of the fourth century in their widest perspective. It is not easy to credit the same hand with writing the high speculative theological discourses against the Arians and the *Life of Antony*. In the latter one is transported to a monkish fairyland, peopled by demons who took the forms of a dragon, a black boy, a wild beast or tempting woman, who cajole, tease and threaten the monks. Antony's theology too

[1] *Historia Arianorum* 7, P.G. 25, col 701A.
[2] *Pap Lond* 1913-4, H. I. Bell, *Jews and Christians*, p. 45 ff.
[3] See Sozomen, *HE* ii.25.
[4] *Vita Pachomii* 28. His eventual ordination, see B. J. Kidd, *History of the Church to 461*, ii, 105
[5] Sozomen, *HE* ii.31.

and his non-episcopal view of Church order stand in sharp contrast to Athanasius. Their unity, however, was based on mutual personal regard, combined with the acceptance of martyrdom and its substitute, the ascetic in permanent combat against the forces of evil,[1] as the true ideal of a Christian life. One thing is certain, however, namely that Athanasius was the true archbishop for the great majority of the monks. Countless stories arose to demonstrate his ready wit and wisdom. 'How is the Son equal to the Father?', one monk is supposed to have asked him. 'Like the sight of two eyes', flashed back Athanasius.[2] Greek theologian though he was, Athanasius was able also to preach on occasions in Coptic which no doubt enhanced his reputation with the monks[1]. They became the eyes and ears of the archbishopric.[3] He kept in constant correspondence with their leaders and appointed his leading bishops, such as Serapion of Thmuis, from their ranks. His successors wisely followed his example. And behind sheer personality was a theology that corresponded to the needs of the monks. Their fight against demons demanded a Christ who was God without reservations. Just as they rallied eventually to Cyril's Christology, so the Homoousios (of the same substance) of the Creed of Nicaea was essential to them. Had Athanasius not stood firm, then they might have looked elsewhere, and if not to the Meletians once more, then to the Manichees whose psalms full of references to Jesus and the Virgin and stringent asceticism were as much a temptation to the monks' orthodoxy as the demons themselves.

Fortunately for Athanasius his officially-backed supplanters in the years 339-345 and 356-361 were hardly calculated to seize popular loyalty from him. Gregory (d. 345) and George (murdered 361) were outsiders, Cappadocians, who neither knew nor cared for the Egyptian scene. They counted for little outwith Alexandria. Thus, the field was left to Athanasius, and his return by slow stages through Syria and Palestine from his second exile in October 346 provoked one of the most astounding demonstrations of popular support that ever fell to the lot of anyone in the ancient world. The magistrates of Alexandria led out a great concourse of Christians from all over Egypt more than a day's journey from the city to greet the hero. A lesser distance, ten miles, sufficed usually, even for an

[1] *Apophthegmata Patrum*, reproduced by F. Nau, 'Histoire des solitaires egyptiens', *Revue de l'Orient Chrétien* 12, 1907, p. 48, n 1.

[2] See T. Lefort, *Le Muséon* 42, 1929, p. 197-224, 46, 1933, p. 1-33, and 48, 1935, p. 55-73.

[3] Thus his question to Theodore, Pachomius' successor, 'Quid agit ecclesia?' during a visitation aimed at assessing the Arian menace (*Vita Pachomii* 96).

emperor.[1] The scenes on his return were indeed compared to honours paid to the emperor, Constantius.

The next decade, the 'ten glorious years' of Athanasius' rule, enabled him to discomfit the local Arians and rally the Egyptian episcopate and people to his rule. How great was the enthusiasm he says, in which the multitudes vowed themselves to asceticism and the people abounded in practical works of Christian charity.[2] There was 'wonderful, profound peace' in the churches.[3] In Alexandria itself churches no longer sufficed for the congregations. In 355 Athanasius had to use the unfinished and undedicated basilica based on the Caesareum for his Easter services.[4] Beyond Egypt, in this period he consecrated Frumentius as bishop of Axum in Ethiopia, thus opening the way to missions beyond the southern frontier of the empire and down the Red Sea, and these Christianised lands would look to Alexandria for leadership. On his deathbed in 356 Antony bequeathed his sheepskin mantle to Athanasius, a symbol of the alliance between Alexandria and Christian Egypt. It stood Athanasius in good stead, for in February 356 Constantius had moved against him once more and ordered the Prefect of Egypt to arrest him.

The course of the quarrel with Constantius which led up to this event lies outside the scope of this lecture, but a word may be said about the relationship between church and empire as Athanasius wanted his hearers to conceive it. There was nothing particularist, let alone Egyptian nationalist about it. Athanasius, as we have noted, occasionally preached in Coptic, but incompatibility between this and a Greek-thinking theologian never seems to have crossed his mind. He accepted the loyalist tradition of the eastern episcopate as a whole, and only because the facts as he saw them left him with no other conclusion did he at last turn on Constantius to denounce him as Antichrist. Thus in his *Defence against the Arians*, written circa 351, he is glad to include every document that testified to imperial words and actions in his favour. His immediate reaction to his life of exile in 356 was to blame the general Syrianus rather than the emperor. Indeed nothing could be more deferential than his Defence before Constantius (*Apol. ad Constantium*).[5] The emperor he recognised as a 'long standing Christian': he addressed himself humbly to his piety. He had never

[1] Gregory Nazianzene, *Oratio* xxi, 27-29 (P.G. 35, cols 1113-1116).

[2] Athanasius, *Historia Arianorum* 25 and 27; Hardy, *op cit*, p. 61.

[3] *Ibid* 25 = P.G. 25, col 724A.

[4] Athanasius, *Apol. ad Constantium* 13-18.

[5] See the excellent summary in S. L. Greenslade, *Church and State from Constantine to Theodosius*, London, 1954, p. 47.

calumniated Constantius to his brother (ch-2-3). He regarded the usurper Magnentius (350-353) as a devil and a murderer (ch 6-10). Truth indeed, was the defence of kings (ch 12) but there is no suggestion that Constantius did not possess it. Indeed, he was a lover of it. Athanasius would have appealed like Paul had done to Caesar if he had been confronted with an accusation (ch 12). Disobedience was far from his mind. 'I did not resist the commands of your Piety', he went on, 'God forbid, for I am not a man to resist even the Quaestor of the city, much less so great a prince' (ch 19).

A year later in 358, however, the tone has changed, and significantly Athanasius tells the monkish recipients of the *Historia Arianorum* (ch 3) not to copy the document but to return it to him. Constantius was denounced in those Old Testament terms beloved of western polemists as worse than Saul, worse than Ahab, the forerunner of Antichrist. In the *De Synodis* of 360 when Athanasius discusses the synods of Ariminum and Seleucia, Constantius is named as the patron of heresy, 'most irreligious emperor'. It is in the *Historia* that the documents are preserved recounting Pope Liberius' speech to Constantius and Hosius of Cordoba's equally famous letter, 'Write no letters, send no counts . . . Remember that you are a mortal man . . . God has put into your hands the kingdom. To us he has entrusted the affairs of His Church, and as he who would steal the empire from you would resist the ordinance of God, so likewise fear on your part lest by taking on yourself the good of the Church you become guilty of a great offence. It is written "Render unto Caesar the things that are Caesar's and unto God the things that are God's" (ch 44).[1] Athanasius had moved far.

It would be going against the weight of evidence to suggest that for the last three years of Constantius' reign Athanasius did not espouse the dualistic theory of Church and State. But it was a temporary mood only, occasioned by anger and frustration with the emperor and the apparent successful emergence of the Arian cause under his patronage. His was a duel with Constantius himself and he used such weapons as came to hand. So far as one can see, there was no deeper correlation in his mind between the creed of Nicaea itself and the rejection of the theory of divinely appointed imperial autocracy. If he upbraids Constantius he does not disparage the imperial office. Given an emperor favourable to Nicaea, such as the short-lived Jovian, he was once more the loyal subject. In the east the import of the writings of the period 358-360 was quietly forgotten. The challenge to the emperor's power to arbitrate in the affairs of the Church was not repeated. At Chalcedon not even

[1] See Greenslade, *op cit*, p. 45.

Dioscorus cited Athanasius' *Historia Arianorum* to justify opposition to the emperor Marcian. Only in the sixth century was Athanasius' concept of the Church as a divine and autonomous society independent of the state revived by another Alexandrian, the Monophysite philospher, John Philoponus, and then again only as a *tour de force* and a literary exercise.

It was in this period of exile that the Egyptian legend concerning Athanasius took shape. Hidden by the monks, and secure from discovery by the emperor's agents he poured out a series of treatises designed to rally popular opinion to his cause. *The Life of Antony*, *The History of the Arians to the Monks*, his encyclical *To the Bishops of Egypt and Libya* against the Arians, the *Defence of his Flight*, his denunciation of the Synods of Ariminum and Seleucia, date to this time. No section of the Christian population were left in doubt as to his views.

Shortly after the death of Constantius in November 361, he was once more recalled to Alexandria, this time by the pagan emperor Julian. He used the few months before he was sent into exile again, to win at last the moderate Origenist bishops of Asia Minor and Syria (supporters of the Homoiousios) to an acceptance of the creed of Nicaea. In this he displayed the arts of diplomatist and conciliator lacking in his earlier days.

With the death of Julian in June 363 Athanasius' troubles were nearly over. He was recalled from exile by Jovian (363-364) and despite a further brief period of exile under Valens in 365-366, his final years were undisturbed. He rebukes his colleague Serapion of Thmuis for failing to give due place in the Trinity to the Holy Spirit but this gave rise to no serious controversy in Egypt. However, on the horizon was appearing the new Christological issue arising from the ideas of Athanasius' friend Apollinarius, which was to convulse the east half a century later. As yet that had no effect on his complete control of Egypt. This he retained until his death on 4 May 373.

When he became archbishop in 328, the Church in Egypt might have fragmented and foundered. The two great movements within Christianity of the previous half century, the conversion of the countryside and the growing controversies as to what constituted orthodoxy, were combining to cause unprecedented tension within the Church. The Great Persecution brought all the latent differences to the surface. In North Africa permanent schism between Donatists and Catholics had resulted. A more pliant man than Athanasius would probably have come to an agreement with the eastern bishops, but thereby have forfeited the confidence of the Coptic monks for whom no Arian type of Trinitarian doctrine could guarantee the individual against the powers of evil. Athanasius' *Life of Antony* shows how strongly he could identify himself with the ideals of the Coptic monks. The strife with demons, the arguments with the philosophers, the rejection of traditional Egyptian rites, and the struggle for social justice were his ideals as well as Antony's. But he also describes Antony's friendly relations with the emperors Constantine and Constantius, which he regards as the natural state of affairs. Athanasius was not Donatus of Carthage nor were the monks Circumcellions. His quarrel with Constantine did not lead to separatist revolt. He shows, indeed, what could be accomplished within the framework of the Constantinian settlement, as interpreted in the east. Of the two worlds of Athanasius, Greek and Egyptian, the Egyptian may have lain nearer to his heart and he saw beyond Egypt the vision of Christianity far beyond the frontiers of the empire inspired and guided by Alexandria. His defence of Nicaea was conducted against a background of pressures within the Church in Egypt. Though his character was hard and methods often deplorable, he brought a unity to the Nile Valley based on common Christianity at a crucial moment of its people's history. At a distance of 1,600 years one cannot withhold admiration for the genius of this leader of true heroic status of Egyptian Christianity.

XVII

POPULAR RELIGION AND CHRISTO-
LOGICAL CONTROVERSY IN THE FIFTH
CENTURY

HOW far does the great religious controversy of the fifth century centred on the mystery of the Incarnation reflect popular religious ideas of the east Roman world? It is well known that factors that had little to do with theological speculation, such as the rivalry for prestige and leadership between Constantinople and Alexandria, played a large part in bringing the controversy between rival concepts of christology to their climax in the twenty years that separate the councils of Ephesus and Chalcedon.[1] More discussion, perhaps, is needed concerning the contribution of articulate public opinion to the course of events, and in particular, to the persistence of the opposition to the Chalcedonian definition after 451.

In the fifth century there was no longer the same gap between the outlook of the theologians and that of more ordinary Christians, as there had been in the time of Origen. The great Alexandrian theologian had been conscious of his isolation, and had ruminated on the vast mass of the faithful who knew nothing but Jesus Christ and him crucified, who were separated from those who partook of the divine Logos as He was in the beginning with God.[2] To Athanasius belongs the credit of making the theology of Alexandria also the religion of the Coptic-speaking monk. His deep religious sensitivity had enabled him to demonstrate the *Homoousios* in a way that satisfied the needs of Trinitarian definition and those of the simple Christian, who wanted assurance that Him whom he worshipped needed no redemption Himself, and was indeed God. In the last part of the fourth century both halves of the Roman Empire witnessed religious debate developing as one of the predominant aspects of society, and in addition, the political and social problems

---

[1] See N. H. Baynes, 'Alexandria and Constantinople: a study in Ecclesiastical Diplomacy', *Byzantine Studies and other Essays* (London 1955) pp 97–116.

[2] See H. J. Carpenter's article, 'Popular Christianity and the Theologians in the Early Centuries', *JTS*, new series XIV (1963) pp 294–310, especially p 309.

of the Roman Empire were often interpreted in religious terms. Even Arianism, whose arid progress through the reign of Constantius II seemed to be more the concern of the emperor and his bishops than their congregations, roused fervent discussion among the populace in the capital[1] as well as deep interest among the ever-increasing numbers of educated and highly placed laity.[2] In Africa the Circumcellions of Optatus of Milevis's and Augustine's day provided visible proof that the popular quest for the millennium and the rule of the saints and martyrs of the church, could also involve overturning existing social structures on earth.[3]

The christological controversy could be expected to arouse deeper concern among ordinary Christians, since questions of personal salvation were even more directly involved than in Arianism. How was the saving work of Christ to be understood in terms of His own being? As in the arian controversy Alexandria spoke for the majority. Athanasius's ability to interpret subtle theological concepts successfully to people of an entirely different religious and cultural outlook from himself was perfected by Cyril. The essence of the Alexandrian appeal to popular opinion was put by the latter in the spring of 429 in a superb lawyer's brief addressed to the Egyptian monks. Cyril aimed at convincing them that even though the term *Theotokos* (bearer of God) was nowhere to be found in Scripture it was nonetheless an essential element of belief from the point of view of salvation. If, he said, Christ was not by nature God, but equal to us and nothing more than an instrument of God, how could he overthrow death, and how could we be exhorted to worship a mere man? Nicaea had implied that what was born of the Virgin was 'of the same substance as God', and hence the title *Theotokos* was justified. Moreover, the great Athanasius had used the term. Could he err?[4] The medicine worked. The doubts of the monks were stilled, and at Ephesus I and II they were prepared to dare all to destroy 'the divider of Christ', Nestorius.

Even so, Cyril's argument ran into serious difficulties outside Egypt which his Antiochene opponents were quick to point out. In the con-

---

[1] For Gregory of Nyssa's well-known description of his experiences with Arian-minded tradesmen in Constantinople, see *De Filii Deitate*, PG, XLVI (1863) col 557.

[2] Such as Count Terentius, to whom Basil wrote one of his most interesting letters on the Trinity, Ep 214, ed R. J. de Ferrari (London, Loeb ed, 1930).

[3] For instance, see Optatus of Milevis, *De Schismate Donatistarum*, ed C. Ziwsa, CSEL, XXVI (1893) III, 4, p 81.

[4] Cyril, *Ep I AdMonachos*, PG, LXXVII (1864) cols 3–40, and *ACO* (1914–40) I, l, i, p 5; dated by L. S. Lenain de Tillemont, *Mémoires pour servir à l'histoire ecclésiastique des six Premiers Siècles*, XIV (Paris 1690–1712) p 330 to 'a little after Easter 429'.

Popular religion and christological controversy

troversy that spanned nearly a quarter of a century between 428 and 451, the opposition had found a champion in the historian and philosopher Theodoret, bishop of Cyrrhus in northern Syria. At the time of Ephesus Theodoret had already characterised Cyril's views as a compound of arian and apollinarian heresy.[1] Sixteen years later, in the course of a Dialogue (*The Eranistes* or *Beggarman*) ostensibly between a representative of Cyril's theology and an Antiochene, he demonstrated in popular form that Cyril's assertion of the essential (hypostatic) union of Godhead and manhood in one incarnate nature of Christ led to the complete separation of Christ from humanity and thus an inability to save.[2] How could, he asked with others, He save what He did not assume? Christ saved by His assumption of entire humanity and destroyed sin and death through the complete harmony of His will with that of God. Where to Cyril Christ was the Word made flesh of John 1:14 manifesting the fullness of God to a worshipping humanity, to the Antiochenes He was the great high priest and pioneer of the Letter to Hebrews, who pointed the way to salvation by his own example and obedience to God.

Antioch and Alexandria represented two different ideas of salvation. They continued to do so despite verbal concessions on each side which found their expression in the Formula of Reunion in 433 that restored communion between them after the council of Ephesus. The Alexandrine looked forward to the ultimate divinisation of humanity and its reabsorption into God as the ultimate source of its being. Antioch, on the other hand, was concerned to preserve the reality of man, each individual moving by the right exercise of his will towards communion with God, and receiving the merited rewards and punishments on the way.

There is, however, no doubt that in the Roman east in the fifth and sixth centuries Cyril's conception of salvation corresponded more to popular religion than the Antiochene, despite the skill and dedication of Theodoret. One hint of this may be gathered from the manner in which writings either by Apollinarius himself or by his disciples were fathered on figures as orthodox and respected as popes Felix and Julius, and Athanasius himself, and were accepted as genuine by both the mass of the people and by theologians. Cyril's Twelve Anathemas, for instance, would hardly have been conceived without the authority of the

---

[1] Theodoret, Ep 153, *PG*, LXXXIII (1864) col 1444D.

[2] For an account of the debate see A. Grillmeier, *Christ in Christian Tradition*, Eng tr . S. Bowden (London 1961) pp 419ff.

apollinarian forgeries to support them![1] The part which these played in shaping the christology of Cyril and his adherents needs no emphasis. The ground had been well prepared for Cyril's triumph at Ephesus. At the council itself both Theodoret and Cyril have left graphic descriptions of the dramatic events of 22–7 June 431 when Nestorius was condemned by Cyril's council as 'the new Judas' and deposed on 22 June, while four days later John of Antioch declared Cyril and his ally Memnon of Ephesus deposed as heretics and disturbers of ecclesiastical order. The populace of Ephesus and to a lesser extent of Constantinople had a major say in the eventual decision favouring Cyril. The latter was very conscious of the need of carrying popular opinion with him and immediately wrote an account of the events to the clergy and people of Alexandria.[2] In this letter he describes how the populace of Ephesus demonstrated night and day in favour of his vindication of Mary as *Theotokos* (God-bearing). He was preceded, he said, from the church dedicated to the *Theotokos* where the council had met, by a torchlight procession, men and women rejoicing at Nestorius's downfall. The picture was not exaggerated. Theodoret's accounts written to the emperor and the court of Constantinople tells the same story from the opposite point of view.[3] The bishops of the oriental diocese (i.e. the patriarchate of Antioch) had arrived in Ephesus to find the city in turmoil. Cyril and Memnon had 'banded together and mustered a great mob of rustics' who had closed the churches of the city against them and prevented the celebration of Pentecost. In Constantinople also there were rejoicings at Nestorius's deposition. Whatever part was played by ecclesiastical rivalries and the ability of Cyril to bribe his way to success, popular devotion to Mary as *Theotokos* and the equally deeply held belief reflected in Cyril's teaching that the Word of God truly suffered in the flesh to redeem mankind, carried the day. Theodoret's charge that Cyril's ideas were simply a development of Apollinarianism fell on deaf ears.

When the crisis was renewed in 447 Alexandria continued to hold the trump cards, and had Cyril's successor Dioscorus been an abler diplomat and less vindictive a character, Alexandrian theology might well have become the standard of christian orthodoxy. That popular

---

[1] Grillmeier suggests the period 429/30 (i.e. during the interchanges with Nestorius) as that in which the apollinarian formulas find their way into Cyril's theological language: *Christ in Christian Tradition*, p 400.

[2] Ep 24, PG, LXXVII (1864) col 137 (*ACO*, I, l, i, pp 117–18).

[3] Ep 152, PG, LXXXIII (1864) col 1441, compare Epp 153, 154 and in 157 where Theodoret protests to Theodosius II that the Antiochene bishops were becoming 'a prey to tyranny'.

Popular religion and christological controversy

opinion continued to favour Alexandria, this time supported by the emperor himself, is evident from the events surrounding the summoning of the notorious second council of Ephesus in August 449. In the spring of that year a striking demonstration in favour of the one-nature christology took place at Edessa, the capital of the province and former client-kingdom of Osrohene.[1] Cyril's adherent Rabbula who had been metropolitan had died in 435, and his successor, Ibas, was an equally convinced Antiochene. For thirteen years, however, he presided over the see uneventfully, though there was an undercurrent of discontent, and certain unwise statements he had made were eagerly remembered by his enemies. In 448 the storm broke over him. Dioscorus was determined to root out all traces of Antiochene teaching and assert the primacy of Alexandria over Antioch and Constantinople. He had the full support of Theodosius II; and Ibas, the metropolitan of the see celebrated in history and legend as the 'city of the believing people of Mesopotamia',[2] was among his prime targets. Ibas was accused by Dioscorus's agents, the local monks and by some of his presbyters of blasphemy, nepotism and embezzlement of church property. He had been heard to say in the presence of presbyters, 'I do not envy Christ that he became God, for I have become that, as he is of my own nature.' He did not believe in hell, it was said, regarding it only as a threat, and had asserted that the Jews had only crucified a man. He had also sold church plate for his own benefit. Ibas was acquitted, however, by two ecclesiastical tribunals, the last of which was composed of bishops in no way favourable to his views. When he returned to his see in March 449 there were vast demonstrations against him. So hostile was the crowd that he had to withdraw, and on 12 April the provincial governor of Osrohene entered the city accompanied by his staff to conduct an inquiry; the verbatim report shows what transpired. Amid loyal shouts of 'Long live the Roman Empire', 'Many years to Theodosius', there were others more menacing: 'To the gallows with the Iscariot', 'Ibas has corrupted the true doctrine of Cyril', 'Long live arch-bishop Dioscorus', 'The Christ-hater to the arena', 'Down with the Judophile', 'The works of Nestorius were found with Ibas', 'Where has the church property gone?'.[3]

The cries show a strongly pro-imperial and anti-nestorian tendency,

---

[1] Recorded in detail in the *Acta* of the second council of Ephesus, ed [J.] Flemming, *Akten [der Ephesinischen synode vom Jahre 449]*, in *Abhandlungen der Königlichen Gesellschaft der Wissenschaften zu Göttingen*, neue Folge xv (Göttingen 1914–17) Phil. Hist. Klasse, pp 15–55. [2] See Rufinus, *Historia Ecclesiastica*, PL, xxi (1849) ii, 15, col 513.
[3] Flemming, *Akten*, p. 19.

and were supported by an abundance of sworn testimony by city magistrates, clergy, monks and artisans. Edessa had at one time been pro-Parthian in sentiment, yet there was now no doubt as to the loyalty of its people to the empire. This loyalty was associated in their minds with adherence to the christology of Cyril.

These instances of public feeling help one to understand the attitude of the 135 bishops who assembled at Ephesus in August 449 where, amidst lurid and violent scenes, they reinstated the Constantinopolitan archimandrite Eutyches, who held extreme Cyrilline views, deposed his judge, the patriarch of Constantinople and those who had been his accusers, and acclaimed Dioscorus the true champion of orthodoxy. 'Let him who preaches Two Natures himself be cut in two', so the assembly cried out.[1]

Despite the violence of their proceedings, Dioscorus and his collea-gues spoke for the east, a fact which Theodosius II recognised when he told his distracted relatives at the western court at Ravenna that at Ephesus 'in full respect for the truth various disturbers of the peace had been removed from the office of the priesthood', and that 'nothing contrary to the rule of faith or of justice had been done there'.[2] The council had in fact been a large-scale disciplinary body whose membership had been restricted to ten bishops from each metro-politan area. Though the faith of Cyril had been vindicated, and in particular, his Twelve Anathemas declared canonical, it had not been intended as a general council such as was its successor at Chalcedon held by Theodosius's successor Marcian in October and November 451.

Here too, despite the combined influence of emperor, pope and episcopate, the popular verdict against the *Tome* of Leo and the defini-tion of Christ as subsisting in two inseparable and unconfused natures was overwhelming. The bishops had not spoken for the people and the subsequent bitterness ending in the monophysite schism during the sixth century was a reflection of this fact. Half a century after the council the Monophysite, John Rufus, bishop of Maiuma near Gaza, collected and wrote down a part of the mass of floating tradition surrounding the reception of the definition in the various eastern provinces.[3] Strongly

[1] See L. Duchesne's summary in *The Early History of the Church*, III (Eng tr L. Jenkins, London 1924) pp 288–91.

[2] Theodosius II, Letter included in Pope Leo's correspondence, Ep 62 'Nihil igitur ab his (episcopis) contrarium regulae fidei aut justitiae factum esse cognovimus', *PL*, LIV (1846) cols 875–7. Compare Epp 63 and 64.

[3] Edited by F. Nau, in *PO*, VIII, (1912) pp 1–161.

Popular religion and christological controversy

prejudiced against Chalcedon though he was, these *Plerophoria* (*Revelations*) as they were called ranging from province to province are impressive in their unanimity. It was not only in Egypt, and in Palestine where the monks had a special grievance against the turncoat bishop Juvenal, that feeling was strong. In Isauria for instance, the monks found it impossible to understand how their bishops drawn from their own ranks could have restored Ibas and Theodoret to their sees after condemning them to deposition now and hell hereafter only two years before.[1] In Pamphylia, where there was to be a long history of anti-chalcedonian feeling, a layman openly rebuked the metropolitan for preaching heresy.[2]

Monks in the same province saw visions of Christ cursing Chalcedon as Chalcedon had denied him, or of Satan asking them why they did not follow the example of their bishops and worship him.[3] All over the east families were divided, no greetings exchanged in the streets between adherents and opponents of Chalcedon, and in particular the latter refused to receive communion at the hands of bishops who had signed the definition.[4] Only the Jews were reported to be pleased with the decision. They were said to have written to Marcian in the following terms:

To the merciful emperor Marcian: the people of the Hebrews: – For a long time we have been regarded as though our fathers had crucified a God and not a man. Since the synod of Chalcedon has assembled and demonstrated that he who was crucified was a man and not a God we request that we should be pardoned this fault and that our synagogues should be returned to us.[5]

All this was in addition to the riots and popular execration that greeted the return of Juvenal, bishop of Jerusalem,[6] who had betrayed both Dioscorus and his own strongly expressed convictions in order to safeguard the patriarchal status of his see, and the even worse disorders that greeted the promulgation of the definition by the new patriarch of Alexandria Proterius. The latter was popularly regarded as a 'wolf', and an 'anti-Christ'.[7]

Why was this the case? Why was any christology that deviated from Cyril's rejected by the populace? The clues are to be found in the utterances of contemporaries. Antipathy to anything that smacked of

---

[1] *Plerophoria*, xxiii, PO, VIII (1912) pp 54–7. Compare *ibid*, xxi, p 44 and lix, p 115.
[2] *Ibid*, lxiv, p 120. [3] *Ibid*, ix, p 22.
[4] *Ibid*, lxx and lxxii, lxxv, lxxvi, lxxviii, lxxiii, etc.
[5] Michael the Syrian, *Chronicle*, ed J. B. Chabot (Paris 1901) VIII, 12, p 91.
[6] *Plerophoria*, xvi–xx. [7] *Ibid*, lxvi and lxix.

Judaism was one reason, and Chalcedon was regarded by its opponents as acceptable to Judaism,[1] but behind this was a deeper theological ground. The one-nature christology implied confession in unequivocal terms that 'Christ is God', and associated the suffering and redemption of mankind with divine suffering and glorification, whereas 'two natures inseparably united' either seemed nonsense or implied the existence of 'two Christs' (pre- and post-Incarnation) one of which could not be God. At Chalcedon the distraught cries of the Egyptian bishops against the proposed two-nature christology make this clear. 'As he was begotten, so he suffered. Let no one divide the king of glory. Let no one divide the indivisible. Let no one call the one Lord two. Thus Nestorius believed.'[2] Nearly a century later, in 541, Silko king of the Nobatae explained why he accepted the monophysite christology preached by missionaries sent by the empress Theodora in preference to those from Justinian representing Chalcedon. The latter did not preach monotheism, he explained. If God was one, and Christ saved as God, then he must also be God.[3] There could not be two natures, one divine and one not. Similarly, twenty years before in 523, the monophysite christian confessors at Najran in Yemen explained why they preferred martyrdom to embracing Judaism (or Nestorianism). 'You must know', said the Christian Habsa, 'that not only will I not say that Christ was a man, but I worship and praise him because of all the benefits He has shown me. And I believe that He is God, maker of all creatures, and that I take refuge in His Cross.'[4] Cyrilline theology as interpreted by the opponents of Chalcedon touched the sources of popular Christianity in the east. Once again, the behaviour of the Egyptian bishops at Chalcedon itself is revealing. Pressed to sign the definition of faith that Christ subsisted 'in two natures' without separation that had been accepted by the remainder of the bishops they gave way to despair. 'We shall all be killed if we subscribe to Leo's epistle', 'Every district in Egypt will rise against us.'[5] The fate of the ambitious but luckless presbyter Proterius who accepted consecration in Dioscorus's stead, torn to pieces by the Alexandrian mob on Maundy Thursday 457, showed that they were speaking the truth.

If one probes deeper and asks why popular religion in the east in the

[1] Ibid, xiv.
[2] Schwartz, ACO, II, l, i, paras 171–5 = Mansi, VI, col 636.
[3] John of Ephesus, Historia Ecclesiastica, ed E. W. Brooks, CSCO, 3 series III (Paris 1935) IV, 7.
[4] See The Book of the Himyarites, ed A. Moberg (Lund 1924), Introduction p cxxiv.
[5] Schwartz, ACO, II, l, ii, pp 110–13 = Mansi, VII, cols 58–60.

Popular religion and christological controversy

fifth century preferred Cyril's ideas to those of Nestorius and Flavian of Constantinople, the answer is complex. Monasticism certainly accounts for much, and one can indicate a tendency for the mysticism of the monks to lead towards the glorification of Christ and the *Theotokos*. This is particularly the case in Palestine, where, in the sixth century, despite the loyalty of the great majority of monks to Chalcedon, owing perhaps to the fact that Jerusalem's standing as a patriarchate like that of Constantinople depended on a decision of that council, a very large proportion of churches built at that time are dedicated to the *Theotokos*,[1] and Cyril's theology was regarded as canon. It is not quite adequate as a complete explanation. A considerable minority of monks in Syria and in the capital sympathised with the two-nature christology, and monks in Syria are recorded as having used their influence on popular religious belief to prevent the spread of the extreme one-nature christology taught by Apollinarius.[2] Moreover, the dogmatic writings of the leaders of Egyptian monasticism, particularly Shenoudi of the White Monastery, show all the literalist milleniarism of a biblical fundamentalist with no concern at all for the Mary of the one-nature christology. Yet Shenoudi could imagine himself striking down Nestorius at Ephesus.

Perhaps at the back of these monks' minds and the popular religion which they expressed was the fear of the old gods dispossessed of their power by Christ, but ever-menacing in the form of demons. Only Christ as God and wholly God could avail against them. The demons, whether dwelling on the edge of the Egyptian desert or in the upper atmosphere, were a constant threat in the minds of all classes. They were responsible for all irrational aspects of life from the onset of plague or earthquake to the outbreak of civil disturbance. Both at Antioch in 387[3] and Edessa in 449[4] the presence of demons – at Edessa 'Nestorian' demons – proved a welcome alibi for the ill behaviour of the citizens. In the plague at Antioch early in the sixth century, one arch-demon was identified. It was Phoebus Apollo now associated with destruction of life and not with healing.[5] After death, as Severus

---

1 See G. M. Armstrong, 'Fifth and Sixth Century Buildings in the Holy Land,' in *The Greek Orthodox Theological Review*, XIV (Brookline 1969) pp 17–30.

2 Sozomen, [*Historia Ecclesiastica*] ed J. Bidez and G. C. L. Hansen, *GCS*, I (1960), VI, 27, 10, p 276.

3 *Ibid*, VII, 23, 4, p 337.

4 Flemming, *Akten*, p 33.

5 John of Beith-Aphthonia, *Life of Severus*, ed/trans M. A. Kugener, *PO*, II, 3 (1904) p 246. For the old gods as 'demons' who had been dispossessed of their temples and

the monophysite patriarch of Antioch pointed out, failure to receive the sacrament at the hands of a truly orthodox priest would entail the soul being captured by demons and frustrated in its efforts to move towards God.[1]

Such ideas lay at the back of popular religion in the fifth and sixth centuries in the east. The emphatic christology expressed in the formula 'out of two natures, One' guaranteed the believer against the victory of the irrational powers of chaos and evil in the universe which surrounded him. In the minds of many too, the unity and continuity of the imperial monarchy was also associated with a one-nature christology. As James of Sarug, the monophysite bishop of the east Syrian see of Batnan pointed out to the emperor Justin, the symbol of the cross which he wore on his diadem had no meaning unless Christ was one and was God.[2] The emperor Marcian was abused by the Monophysites precisely because he broke the unity of the empire and Christendom through the decisions of Chalcedon.[3] There was a clear tendency in the fifth and sixth centuries for the people to associate themselves with the imperial monarchy through their concept of Christ, for just as Christ was One, so the emperor His vice-regent was also one.

The emperors themselves were not blind to such ideas. Theodosius II shifted his support from Nestorius to Cyril in 431 once he saw that opinion favoured the latter, and from that time on his aid to the adherents of the one-nature christology was unstinted. In touch with public opinion throughout the eastern provinces through the monks who acted as standing channels of complaints from the provincials, the eastern emperors were far better able than their western counterparts to inform themselves of situations and remedy wrongs. In 387 Antioch survived the wrath of Theodosius I thanks to the intervention of Macedonius the Barley-Eater. Thessalonica in 390 had no monastic intercessor and suffered massacre. The existence of these relationships between emperor and provincials, together with acceptance of common religious ideas,

---

rendered powerless by the word of Christ, see the sixth-century inscription from Ezraa near Bostra in the province of Arabia, published by C. Mondésart, *Syria*, xxxvii (Paris 1956) pp 125–8. In the capital, Atlas, believed to be responsible for earthquakes, came readily to the lips of the people in moments of crisis. At the time of the Nika riot the spokesman of the Green fraction claimed he actually ordered baptism in the name of the 'One God'. See Theophanes *Chronicle, Sub anno mundi* 6024, ed J. Classen (Bonn 1839) p 280.

[1] *Select Letters*, ed E. W. Brooks (London 1902–4) III, 4, pp 246–7.
[2] Cited from A. Vasiliev, *Justin the First* (Dumbarton Oaks 1950) p 234.
[3] Michael the Syrian, *Chronicle*, VIII, 14, ed/trans J. B. Chabot, 4 vols (Paris 1899–1924) II, p 122. Compare pp 88–9.

Popular religion and christological controversy

contributed much to the maintenance of popular loyalty to the empire. The demonstrations at Edessa in 449 in favour of Cyril's doctrines were significant in this regard, and we are fortunate in having a full contemporary account of what took place. A study of popular religious sentiment in the fifth-century east Roman Empire may throw a good deal of light on why Byzantium survived while Rome fell.

XVIII

THE MONKS AND THE SURVIVAL OF THE EAST ROMAN EMPIRE IN THE FIFTH CENTURY *

FOR THE ECCLESIASTICAL HISTORIAN THE CONTRASTING DESTINIES OF the eastern and western provinces of the Roman empire during the fifth century are of absorbing interest. In the east all roads lead to Chalcedon where in October and November 451, "five hundred and twenty or more"[1] bishops drawn from the whole area from Mesopotamia to the Balkans met in turbulent but constructive sessions to discuss the fundamentals of Christian doctrine and discipline under the presidency of the Emperor Marcian or his officials. The only westerners were the three papal legates, whose defective knowledge of Greek, however, prevented them from exercising effectively the honorary precedence over the debates that was theirs. Their colleagues in the west were concerned meantime with events of a different order. Only four months previously, on 20 June 451, Attila and his Huns had been checked in a titanic struggle with the Roman and Gothic forces under Aetius on the Catallaunian plains near Troyes.[2] Attila's army, however, was still in being, and next year Pope Leo was himself to take part in the embassy that persuaded him to spare Rome from siege and probable sack. In the east, the Huns had done their worst in the previous decade, but one way or another the boundaries of the empire had been restored and were not to be threatened seriously again for another century. In the west, the Visigoth and Vandal settlements in Gaul and Africa respectively had taken root. Within a quarter of a century there were to be no more western provinces for an emperor at Ravenna to govern.

In these great events, the attitude of the provincials towards the Roman empire was almost as important as the skill of the military commanders. From a military point of view the east was not much

---

* A revised version of a paper read at a Conference organized in the University of Birmingham on the theme of "Asceticism in the Early Byzantine World", 19-20 March 1971.

[1] This figure is given by the bishops themselves in a letter to Pope Leo informing him of the Council's decisions. Among Leo's correspondence, *Ep.* 98.1 (second version), Migne, *Patrologia Latina* (hereinafter cited as *P.L.*), liv, col. 959c.

[2] Dating and description, see E. A. Thompson, *Attila and the Huns* (Oxford, 1948), p. 141.

4

better placed than the west to withstand a sustained onslaught. Despite the defensive strength of Constantinople the eastern provinces were vulnerable from two directions. From the south-east the Persian monarchs never gave up entirely their dream of re-establishing the empire of Darius and Xerxes and extending their rule to the Bosphorus which they were so nearly to achieve in the reign of Heraclius. Across the Danube were the barbarians, the Goths, and the still more formidable Huns. For both of these the Balkan provinces presented a tempting prey comparatively near at hand, and not at the end of long and wearisome marches as Gaul and Italy lay. At Adrianople in 378 the Roman forces had been defeated utterly and the Emperor Valens had been killed. In 399-400 there had been a further threat in the heart of the empire itself through the revolt of the Gothic leaders Gainas and Tribigild. A generation later, successive imperial armies had been overthrown and the emperor's authority mocked at openly by Attila's Huns. Through the last twenty years of Theodosius II's reign, the east Roman provinces lay under the constant double threat from Attila on the Danube and Gaiseric's control of the seaways across the Mediterranean from Africa.[3]

Yet the empire had survived, and amidst all these disasters few if anyone in Constantinople believed that it would fall. John Chrysostom writing his *Homily on Isaiah* around A.D. 400 expressed his own hopes for its continuing prosperity, "Now those vast spaces the sun shines upon, from the Tigris to the Isles of Britain, the whole of Africa, Egypt and Palestine, and whatever is subject to the Roman Empire lives in peace. You know the whole world is untroubled, and of wars we hear only rumours".[4] Had he been in Italy or Britain, or indeed almost anywhere else in the west, he would have experienced more than rumours. But his attitude is typical of the times. Bishops like Synesius of Cyrene and the historians Sozomen and Socrates and even the pagan Zosimus, had confidence in the future and they wrote with a sense of detachment and ease unmatched by their western contemporaries. Socrates indeed ends his *Ecclesiastical History* with the comment that so far as the Church was concerned, the situation was so good that there was nothing more to write about, and this, he indicates, applied to cities and nations governed by

[3] See E. A. Thompson, "The Foreign Policies of Theodosius II and Marcian", *Hermathena*, lxxvi (1950), pp. 56-75.

[4] John Chrysostom, *Homil. in Isaiah*, 2, *Patrologia Graeca* (hereinafter cited as *P.G.*), lvi, col. 33. Compare Zosimus, *Historia Nova* (ed. L. Mendelssohn), ii. 36, 1-2 writing *circa* 460 and congratulating himself on living in Constantinople, in a city that was prospering as none other.

Theodosius II also.[5] It was the year 439, the year of the fall of Carthage and the definitive success of the Vandal venture in Africa.

This confidence and resolve were reflected in many aspects of east Roman provincial society.[6] In particular, contemporary authorities often suggest the existence of an active and articulate public opinion that atoned for the military incompetence of the generals. Acts of treachery indeed, there were, especially among the population of the Danube provinces even in favour of the Huns,[7] but these were counterbalanced by the loyalty and vigour of others. The inhabitants of Constantinople had clamoured for arms to defend the city against the advancing Goths just before the Adrianople disaster in 378,[8] and had turned on the supporters of Gainas in the city a quarter of a century later.[9] In the crisis of the Hunnish inroads in 447-448 the Thracian provincials harassed Attila's war-bands.[10] In the frontier province of Osrhoene, the Bishop of Edessa described as "confessor and monk" pointed out with pride to his visitor Etheria, *circa* 390, where fountains had appeared miraculously in the city when "the Persian enemy" had cut the water-supplies during a siege.[11]

One cause of this astonishing resilience may be found in the close interconnection of state and religion that prevailed in the east, which counteracted forces of separatism and revolt arising from social and regional discontents which contributed to the downfall of the western empire. Since the middle of the fourth century Christianity had been the predominant religion. The well-directed and not unintelligent effort by the Emperor Julian to restore paganism had proved a fiasco. Julian himself paints a vivid and depressing picture of the collapse of paganism in town and countryside alike, deserted temples, a decaying and indifferent priesthood, a goose instead of a hetacomb to be offered at the shrine of Daphne at Antioch.[12] In this great religious revolution the eastern monks had played a vital part. They were the people whom

---

[5] Socrates, *Hist. Eccles.*, vii.48.

[6] For an interesting general discussion of the differing attitudes of the eastern and western provincials towards the Germanic barbarian invaders, see F. Millar, "Dexippus", *Jl. Rom. Stud.*, lix (1969), pp. 12 ff.

[7] Sozomen (ed. Bidez/Hansen), *Hist. Eccl.*, ix. 5. 2. The treachery of the Bishop of Margus in 442 threatened the entire Danubian defence system. Compare also Priscus, frag. 1 (Bonn edn., p. 140).

[8] Socrates, *Hist. Eccl.*, iv. 38.

[9] Zosimus, *Hist. Nova*, v. 19.3.

[10] Priscus, frag. 2, pp. 143-4. For the defeat of the Byzantine generals by the Huns, see Theophanes, *Chron.* A.M. 5942 (Bonn edn., pp. 158-9).

[11] Peregrinatio Silvae, 19.10 (*Corp. Script. Eccl. Latin.*, xxxix, pp. 62-3).

[12] For instance in *Letters* (ed. Bidez), 22 and 89, and *Misopogon* (ed. W. C. Wright), 362c.

6

Libanius describes as clothed in black and with the appetites of elephants who destroyed the shrines of rural paganism.[13] They came down in Alexandria in their crowds to witness the destruction of the Serapeum by the Patriarch Theophilus in 391. "Their doctrines", we are told by Sozomen, "were invariably received and followed by the people on account of the virtue they exhibited in their actions".[14] They represented popular Christianity and indeed, popular opinion in the east.

The interpretation of Christianity, however, that triumphed there favoured the consolidation of Church and State round the person of the emperor. If Eusebius of Caesarea himself had no direct heir, his ideas of the Christian monarchy and the place of the emperor in the divine order of things won almost complete acceptance. The fifth century east Roman emperor like Constantine was "friend of God", and elected "by divine providence".[15] His monarchy had its due place of authority in the divine order together with that of the Church and its clergy. His duties involved the "common oversight" of his subjects, and the duty of leading them spiritually as well as materially towards salvation both on earth and in the Beyond. The "stability of the state depends upon the religion by which we honour God".[16] In writing thus to the First Council of Ephesus in 431 Theodosius II merely echoed the ideas of Constantine a century before, and represented fully those of educated provincials in the east. In contrast to the situation in the west there was no divergence of outlook between emperor and Church, and for the bishops who accepted the current Platonic and Stoic philosophic values as an essential background to their Christian belief, the idea of a universal Church ruled by the emperor was natural. The Christian society on earth was a reflection of the polity of heaven.[17] There were no "Two Swords" theories in Byzantine statecraft, no tradition of the jealous separation of powers between the secular and ecclesiastical, no belief that the state as the product of Original Sin was intrinsically inferior to the Church. The examples of Pope Liberius

[13] Libanius, *Pro Templis* (ed. R. van Loy, *Byzantion*, viii, 1933, pp. 7-39), ch. 8.
[14] Sozomen, *Hist. Eccl.* (ed. Bidez/Hansen), vi. 27. 10.
[15] Eusebius, *Hist. Eccl.*, x. 9. 2; compare Sozomen, *Hist. Eccl.*, Prologue, 9, Theodosius II as "imitator of the Heavenly Emperor". For Marcian elected "by divine providence" see Marcian to Pope Leo, Leo, *Ep.* 73.
[16] Mansi, *Conciliorum Collectio* (Paris/Leipzig edn., 1902), iv. 1112. For Socrates's view that Theodosius II's goodness merited his military successes, see *Hist. Eccl.*, vii. 18.
[17] On this theme, see N. H. Baynes, "Eusebius and the Christian empire", *Byzantine Studies and Other Essays* (London, 1955), pp. 168-72.

and Ambrose of Milan defying the Emperors Constantius II and Theodosius I were admired by historians as heroic deeds,[18] but were not preached as examples to be followed. Belief in a divinely appointed society dominated by emperor and Church had slowly percolated to all levels of the population in the east. Here too, Eusebius had spoken for his age. Confronted by the pagan and barbarian Persians and Huns the east Roman provincial regarded himself as belonging to "the race of Christians", whether he was an Armenian, Syrian, Egyptian or Illyrian. The aim of all human society was to become "Christian and holy", an image of heaven.[19] The barbarians, like the "envious demons", might cause damage and destruction but the Christian *oecumené* was inviolable. This sense of a common Christianity proved a powerful factor in consolidating morale in the face of external threats and nerving the ordinary citizens to self-defence; and it also enabled the individual emperors to be judged by qualities other than those of a successful general. Arcadius even was remembered as a "good emperor" who founded monasteries and orphanages,[20] and Theodosius II as a humane and just ruler, qualities that assured him the loyalty of his subjects whatever the adversity.[21] In the sixth century John Malalas, himself a man of the people, spoke of Theodosius II as one who was "held in high respect being loved by all the people and the senate".[22] This was true. For three days 12-14 April 449, Edessa, once a pro-Parthian centre, provided an astonishing manifestation of enthusiasm for Roman authority when in April 449 a commission headed by the governor of Osrhoene, *Comes* Thomas Chareas, visited the town to investigate complaints of a part of the citizens, clergy and monks regarding the orthodoxy and conduct of their bishop, Ibas.[23] The commission was met with shouts of "One God, victory to the Romans". "Multiply the victories of Theodosius". "Long live the Roman Empire". "Long live the Patrician Anatolius.

[18] For instance, by Theodoret, *Hist. Eccl.*, ii. 15-16 and v. 18.
[19] Eusebius, *Hist. Eccl.*, I.4, 4 ff., and x. 9, 8-9.
[20] Socrates, *Hist. Eccl.*, vi. 23; compare Michael the Syrian, *Chron.* (ed. J. B. Chabot, Paris, 1899-1911), viii. 1. Arcadius practising justice and "loving the monastic life".
[21] Note Sozomen's stress on Theodosius II's *philanthropia* (love for mankind) and "greatness of soul", that ensured that his reign was "less tainted with blood or murder than all the reigns of your predecessors": *Hist. Eccl.*, Prologue 21. Similarly, John of Antioch, frag. 193 (ed. Müller). See W. E. Kaegi, *Byzantium and the Decline of Rome* (Princeton, 1968), pp. 202-4, and C. D. Gordon, *The Age of Attila* (Ann Arbor, 1966), pp. 26-8.
[22] John Malalas, *Chron.* (Bonn edn.), xiv. 58, p. 358.
[23] The text of Chareas's reports, see J. Flemming, "Akten der ephesinischen Synode von 449", in *Abh. der Gesellschaft der Wissenschaften zu Göttingen*, new ser., xv (1917), pp. 15-55.

8

May he be preserved to Romania".[24] Edessa was to be strongly
Monophysite a few years later, but the monks and clergy who
demonstrated so volubly and shouted "One God" as a Monophysitiz-
ing slogan, also had in mind one Roman empire whose "God-loving"
sovereign commanded the complete obedience of his subjects.
For a century before, however, the monks in the east had been in
the forefront of the defence of the empire against Persia. Thus the
successive defences of the frontier fortress of Nisibis between 349 and
360 were inspired largely by the monastic bishop Jacobus and the
civilian population who urged on the Roman troops. Jacobus's
prayers resulted in the Persian army being stung by swarms of gnats
and forced to retreat in disorder.[25] When, after the Emperor
Julian's fiasco in 363, the city was handed over to the Persians, the
population begged to be allowed to carry on the struggle themselves.[26]
Nisibis was not the only instance of active defence. Monks manned
the defences of Amida in Anastasius's war against Persia in 502 —
though not successfully, as the Persians caught a section drunk at
their posts and were able to storm the town.[27]

The significance of the loyal demonstrations in favour of the eastern
emperors can best be realized when compared with the spirit of the
population in the west. Not many provincials shared the "groans of
the Britons" at the departure of the Roman legions. Indeed, authors
as different as the Gallic senator Rutilius Namatianus, the Constantinopolitan civil servant Zosimus and the South Gallic presbyter
Salvian, leave the impression that the provincials by the early years
of the fifth century in large parts of Gaul, Spain and Britain were in
a state of exasperation and revolt even before the serious onset of the
barbarians.[28] In Gaul in particular once the barbarians had
established themselves many of the provincials were only too glad to
join them.[29]

[24] Ibid., pp. 25 ff.   [25] Theodoret, Hist. Eccl., ii. 30.

[26] See R. Turcan, "L'Abandon de Nisibe et l'Opinion publique", Mélanges
André Piganiol (Paris, 1966), pp. 875-90.

[27] Chron. Edessenum (ed. Guidi), ch. lxxx; compare Michael the Syrian,
Chron., ix. 7 (ed. Chabot, p. 156).

[28] Aim of Gallic Bagaudae as one of "a Romana societate discessit", i.e. "to
secede from the Roman community": see Chron. Gallica, ad ann. 435, Chron.
Min., I. 660. Separatism in Armorica, see Rutilius Namatianus, De Reditu suo,
i, pp. 213-16, Zosimus, vi. 5, and in Britain, Zosimus, Hist. nova, vi. 5. 3. See
J. N. L. Myres, "Pelagius and the end of Roman Britain", Jl. Rom. Stud., 1
(1960), pp. 21-36 (especially pp. 32-6).

[29] Salvian, De Gubernatione Dei, v. 5. 22 (Monumenta Germaniae Historica, i,
p. 59): "So you find men moving over everywhere, now to the Goths, now to the
Bacaudae, or whatever other barbarians have established themselves anywhere,
and they do not repent their move". Salvian has said, ibid. 5. 21, "They [the
provincials] seek among the barbarians the Roman mercy, since they cannot
endure the barbarous mercilessness they find among the Romans" (trans.
Sanford, p. 141).

The reasons for the spirit of defection and separatism were largely economic. While the material remains of farms and villages in the western provinces of this period suggest a fair measure of prosperity in many parts, livelihoods were seldom secure. Few farmers were sure of making enough to pay their taxes and guard against the hazards of storm, drought or barbarian inroad. They were often at the mercy of the bailiffs of absentee landowners whose vast holdings extended over provinces rather than individual city territories. The picture Salvian paints for Gaul, of crushing taxation and extortionate collectors, could be applied elsewhere.[30] So, too, could the dilemma confronting the city councils whose members were responsible for a fixed quota of revenue from their estates on pain of making good the deficit themselves.[31] They must either squeeze the cultivators or go to the wall themselves. Intrinsically the eastern provinces were little better off. Urban patrons in Syria seem to have been no more kindly disposed to the villages dependent on them than were their Gallic counterparts. From the pagan side Libanius[32] and from the Christian John Chrysostom[33] and Theodoret of Cyrrhus[34] speak of the plight of the rural population of Syria and the tyranny of chronic debt and excessive rates of interest, of peasants being treated no better than beasts of burden, of oppression by officials, especially in respect of matters that affected their ordinary daily lives such as billeting and requisitions. The picture is very similar to that which can be gleaned about Numidia during the mid-fourth century.[35] The reaction, however, of the populations in the two halves of the empire differed considerably. The west produced the protest movements of the Circumcellions and Bagaudae, both of which aimed at the destruction of the existing social order, and there were movements in Armorica and perhaps Britain for separation from the Empire. All these inevitably weakened the ability and resolve of the western populations to resist the barbarians.

[30] Salvian, *ibid.* iv. 6. 30 and v. 7. 28: "The enemy is more merciful to these than are the tax-collectors" (*Leniores his hostes quam exactores sunt*). For a similar situation in the Danube frontier provinces, see Priscus, frag. 3 (Bonn edn. pp. 190-5). The merchant of Viminacium who had deserted to the Huns complained how in the Roman Empire "more painful conditions existed in peacetime than the evils of war, namely the most burdensome exaction of taxes and the insults of worthless individuals".

[31] Salvian, *De Gubernatione Dei*, v. 7. 28.

[32] Libanius, *Or.* 50. 36 (ed. Forster, iii, p. 487).

[33] John Chrysostom, *Homil. in Matth.*, 61. 3, *P.G.*, lviii, col. 591: Landowners "were more cruel than the barbarians because they imposed intolerable and unending taxes and *corvées* on the working population on their lands".

[34] Theodoret, *Epp.* 42 and 43.

[35] From Optatus of Milevis, *De Schismate Donatistarum* (ed. C. Ziwsa, *Corp. Script. Eccl. Latin*, xxvi), iii, 4.

In the east, however, the monks, drawn largely from non-Greek speaking rural populations, identified themselves with the religious and economic needs of the people. They were the "men of God", enjoying the privilege of divine revelation and even converse with the prophets and the Lord himself, whose powers enabled disease of body and soul to be cured, even death itself to be overcome, natural disasters mitigated and the victims to be housed and helped.[36] They protected the people against the worst abuses by officials and patrons and, claiming like the western bishops the right of free speech to every grade of authority, they acted as channels of communication by which grievances could reach even the emperor himself; coming from this source, the latter paid heed. They also provided a safety valve for urban turbulence and enabled otherwise revolutionary disturbances to be attributed safely to the agency of demons whose evil the monk could exorcize.[37] They formed thus an essential buffer between the state and the vast majority of its subjects, and so long as they continued to do so, the eastern provincials had neither the incentive nor the desire to desert to Persian or Hun.

At first sight it is not easy to see how the monks came to play this important rôle in the crisis of the empire during the fifth century. The ideals that fired Antony and his companions were solely those of the New Testament. "If thou wilt be perfect, go sell all that thou hast and give to the poor and thou shalt have treasure in heaven" (Mathew xix.21), or the injunction found in the *Gospel of Thomas* which circulated both in Syria and in the Nile valley, "Blessed are the solitary and the elect" (*Logion* 4).[38] Antony (251-356) began as a solitary on the edge of his village in 270, aiming at achieving a spiritual life through contemplation and progress towards victory over the demons. The vast popularity of the movement he initiated was partly the outcome, however, of current economic conditions. From the middle of the third century onwards the situation had been worsening in the Nile valley. Examples are numerous and well-known.[39] Questions addressed to an oracle at Oxyrhynchus included such pleas as, "Shall I be sold up?" "Am I to become a beggar?" "Am I to become a member of a municipal council?" "Shall I take

[36] See H. Lietzmann, *Geschichte der alten Kirche*, iv (Berlin, 1944), ch. vi, as the best account of these aspects of monasticism, and for a letter from a certain Ammonius asking for a cure for sickness from ascetics, see H. I. Bell, *Egypt from Alexander the Great to the Arab Conquest* (Oxford, 1948), p. 110.
[37] As at Antioch in 387, see Sozomen, *Hist. Eccl.*, vii. 23. 4.
[38] See my "The Gospel of Thomas. Is Rehabilitation possible?", *Jl. Theol. Stud.*, new ser., xviii (1967), pp. 25-6.
[39] See M. Rostovtzeff, *Social and Economic History of the Roman Empire*, 2nd edn., revised by P. M. Fraser (Oxford, 1963), pp. 479-86.

flight?"[40]   Land was in a poor state, and in abandoning his family's
300 *arourae* when he chose the solitary life Antony was more likely
to have been abandoning burdens rather than wealth. It is
interesting that his biographer, Athanasius, notes one of the benefits
of his settlements was that the grumbles of the tax-collector were not
heard there.[41]   This was even more to the point in the vast agricultural
settlements that Pachomius (*c.* 290-346) had called into existence.
These were self-supporting social and economic units where every
type of trade and work was organized among the monks.[42]   The
inmates now performed in security exactly the same tasks as they
had previously as villagers at the mercy of tax-collectors and soldiers.
Whatever their relations with officials or the bishops might be, the
monks were accepted by society from the emperor downwards as
essential for the well-being of the whole community. In return, so
long as Christianity prevailed they accepted that society while
attempting to end its abuses.

Despite their ideas of poverty, self-abnegation and disregard for
the needs of the moment, feats of asceticism and self-inflicted hardship
were only one aspect of the monks' struggle against the demons.
Antony himself had accepted the need of manual work through his
understanding of 2 Thess. iii.10 ("if any will not work, let him not
eat"). He was never idle, Sozomen claims, and defence of the
oppressed and representation of their cases to the authorities were
among his main activities.[43]   In all this, his example was universally
followed by his disciples, not least by Shenute and the monks of the
White Monastery. Elsewhere it was the same story. "All my life
I have spent in sowing, reaping and making baskets", said the monk
Serenus.[44]   The Syrian, Eusebius, when asked why he worked so
hard and lived so wretchedly, replied with the text "Love thy
neighbour as thyself", and went on to explain how the heavy iron
collar he always wore was to keep his eyes on the ground to remind
him of the virtue of manual toil.[45]   In both Egypt and Syria the

---

[40] *Pap. Oxyrhynchus,* 1477.
[41] *Vita Antonii,* 44, *P.G.,* xxvi, col. 908.
[42] *Vita Pachomii,* 7; compare 25 (mat weaving), Palladius, *Hist. Lausiaca,*
32, 12 (trades carried out in the monasteries and surplus sold for charity).
[43] Sozomen, *Hist. Eccl.,* I. 13.
[44] *Apophthegmata Patrum* (*P.G.,* lxv, col. 417). Another monk visiting
Apa Silvanus on Mount Sinai, claimed that Mary was better than Martha
and was told he could go without his lunch on the grounds that he did not need
any (*ibid.,* col. 409). For monks working in the harvest, see Rufinus, *Historia
Monachorum,* 18, and for Syrian monks working for their living and looking
after the sick, see John Chrysostom, *Homil. in Matth.,* lxiii. 4, *P.G.,* lviii, col.
672.
[45] Theodoret, *Hist. Religiosa,* iv, = *P.G.,* lxxxii, cols. 1341-5.

12

combination of the rôles of Old Testament prophet and "truly philosophic life" aspired to by the monk produced an active concern for the current needs of the population to an extent neither appreciated nor practised in the west at this period. In addition to Scripture, the works of Clement of Alexandria and Origen were to be found among the Egyptian monk's library, both emphasizing that knowledge of God and true piety were the result of human activity as well as the renunciation of all those things that fed the passions.[46]

Besa's *Life of Shenute* and Shenute's sermons (*circa* 430-450) give instances of the monks using these supernatural powers with which they were credited to improve the lot of the rural population. The picture is often that of a fervently Christian Egyptian population suffering various forms of extortion and oppression from a still pagan aristocracy of Greek-speaking landowners.[47] A prophetic word from Shenute and vineyards belonging to the latter whence high rents were being extorted, would sink below the waters of the Nile.[48] The monasteries too, served as refuges for the surrounding population in the event of Blemmyes and Beduin raids. Where the "Greek generals" as Shenute calls them, had failed to defeat the enemy, the monasteries were there to run a food and hospital service for some twenty thousand refugees.[49] The tendency of *Life* and sermons alike is to portray Shenute as a great prophetic figure and the leader of his people critical of the secular authorities but loyal to his patriarch who in his turn was loyal to the Byzantine monarch.

For Syria the similar activities of the more anarchic and individualistic monks are recounted by Theodoret in his *Historia Religiosa*, written *circa* 435. Much of what he says relates to northern Syria within reach of his diocese of Cyrrhus, north of Antioch. He shows how there also monks were accepted as leaders of the communities in which they settled down and acted as benefactors in a great variety of ways. Thus, the monk Abraames settled in a pagan village called Libanus somewhere near Emesa.[50] Hiding his identity, he managed to establish himself as a seller of walnuts. Then one day

[46] Palladius, *Hist. Lausiaca*, ch. 60. Also, *ibid.*, 11 and 47, and Cassian, *Collationes*, x. 2-3.

[47] For the relations between the two communites, see J. Leipoldt, *Schenute von Atripe, Texte und Untersuchungen*, xxv (Leipzig, 1904), p. 26.

[48] Besa, *Life of Shenute*, ch. 85 (ed. H. Wiesman, Louvain, 1951).

[49] Shenute, *Sermo* (ed. H. Wiesman, *Corp. Script. Christ. Orient.*, Scriptores Coptici, ii. 4, Paris, 1931), 21 and 22, pp. 37-41.

[50] Theodoret, *Historia Religiosa*, xvii (*P.G.*, lxxxii, cols. 1420-1). For the social importance of the Syrian monk, see A. Vööbus, "A History of Asceticism in the Syrian Orient", *Corp. Script. Christ. Orient.*, Subsidia 17 (Louvain, 1960), pp. 161 ff. and 317 ff.

the tax-collectors moved in. The villagers were in a weak position. It is specifically stated that "they had no lord", and owned their lands, often an advantage, but in this case a powerful urban *patronus* was essential. Defaulters found themselves being beaten and manacled. Abraames went to Emesa and raised a loan of 100 solidi which cleared the arrears. The village was converted, he himself was elected priest and a church was built. Abraames went on to settle disputes, not least concerning the distribution of water-supplies, a key fact in village life, and reconciling the parties in law-suits, and was eventually visited by Theodosius II in person.[51] He had had good luck and good connections, but his career illustrates how a monk could become the accepted leader of a community and use his authority to act as a channel of information and complaint to the emperor himself. He was not exceptional. Another Syrian monk, Maisumas, by means of a miracle, was able to prevent the carriage of an exploiting landlord leaving a village from which he had been extracting rents. Maisumas always kept near him a jar of grain and a jar of oil full for the use of the needy, and he also had wider horizons, prophesying correctly the defeat of a Persian invasion.[52] Another, Palladius, was successful in a piece of detective work, unveiling the murderer of a wealthy merchant who had visited a village whose livelihood depended largely on the prosperity of a periodic fair.[53] The prince of ascetics of this period, Simon Stylites, is recorded as acting as advocate and arbitrator, as well as exercising an enormous influence on otherwise predatory Arab tribes.[54] Again, from the eminence of his fifty-foot pillar, the saint maintained a lively contact with officials, forwarding petitions to them, acting as a court of appeal in cases over disputed weights and measures and unjust judicial decisions, and above all, he had direct access to the emperor. Theodosius II was persuaded by Simon to countermand the instructions of the *Praefectus praetorio per Orientem* that synagogues taken over by the Christians in Antioch should be restored to the Jews.[55]

While the bishops, fearing for their own authority, attempted to curb the secular activities of the monks,[56] east Roman society

---

[51] Theodoret, *ibid.*, col. 1424.
[52] *Ibid.*, xiv, cols. 1412-13.
[53] *Historia Religiosa*, vii, col. 1365. Also, Peter Brown, *The World of Late Antiquity* (London, 1971), ch. viii.
[54] *Historia Religiosa*, xxvi, col. 1476.
[55] Evagrius, *Hist. Eccl.*, I. 13.
[56] For instance, Canon 4 of the Council of Chalcedon and Canon 15 of the Canons of Rabbula which forbade monks to hear lawsuits. (See A. Vööbus, *op. cit.*, pp. 375-6.)

recognized them for the men of power that they were, the inter-
mediaries between the Christian people including the emperor and
his officials and the unseen world. They acquired foreknowledge of
future events and their opinions and decisions reflected the justice
of heaven. No wonder villagers would try to kidnap a monk so as to
have his authority on their doorstep.[57] Moreover, they were unique
to the east. In an interesting statement, Sozomen points out that
while in the west there were many good philosophers (that is
ascetically minded Christians), there was an absence of monks in the
European provinces of the empire.[58] To a great extent he was right.
Outside incipient Celtic monasticism and the settlements at Lerins
and elsewhere in southern Gaul, monasticism in the west was in
an early stage of development. It was still the personal choice of
a few rather than a mass movement. The monastic life, too, had a
sense of alienation and positive renunciation of estates, position and
responsibilities towards others foreign to the outlook of the east.
Paulinus of Nola's aim to renounce "the business of the forum" and
to "break the chain of whatever retained him in the present age",
was inspired more by the negative consideration of avoiding
Judgement to come rather than the positive aspiration of raising one's
soul towards contemplation of and absorption into the divine.[59] He
had no word of encouragement for those Christians still working
strenuously to shore up the tottering frame of the western empire.
The only counterpart to popular monasticism in the west was the
"soldier of Christ", or "athletes", the African Circumcellion, whose
rough-cast habit and life of pilgrimage from martyr's shrine to
martyr's shrine attracted the comparison.[60] His hopes, however, for
an apocalyptic reversal of fortunes between rich and poor found little
echo in the east. The Syrian monks whose activities included, like
those of the Circumcellions, freeing slaves and destroying debtors'
bonds,[61] would hardly have accepted armed attack on the villas of the

[57] Theodoret, *Historia Religiosa*, xix (Salmanes), cols. 1428-9.
[58] Sozomen, *Hist. Eccl.*, iii. 14. 38.
[59] For instance, Paulinus, *Carmen* x, lines 166-8 and his fear of Judgement,
ibid., lines 316 ff. See my "Paulinus of Nola and the last century of the
Roman Empire in the West", *Jl. Rom. Stud.*, lix (1969), pp. 1-11.
[60] Circumcellion as a "Miles Christi", see P. Monceaux, *Rev. de Philologie*,
xxxiii (1909), pp. 116 and 132. As "athlete" (*agonisticus*) see Optatus, *De
Schismate Donatistarum* (ed. C. Ziwsa, Vienna, *Corp. Script. Eccl. Latin.*, xxvi),
iii. 4. As pseudo-monk, Augustine, *De Opere Monachorum*, ii. 28. 36 (*P.L.*,
xl, col. 575), and my note, "Circumcellions and Monks", *Jl. Theol. Stud.*,
new ser., xx. (1969), pp. 542-9.
[61] Cited from A. Vööbus, *op. cit.*, p. 376. For the Circumcellions, Optatus,
op. cit., iii. 4.

rich or tempting martyrdom at the hands of a magistrate as a necessary corollary of their activities.

The emperors as men of their time shared to the full their subjects' awe of the monks. Almost from the moment he arrived in the east, Constantine had grasped the importance of the monastic movement as a force for the consolidation of the Christian monarchy. At Nicaea he received ostentatiously the Egyptian confessor Paphnutius. The latter had been condemned to the mines by Maximin and had lost his right eye and the use of his left leg, but he had survived, become an ascetic and had acquired a vast reputation for effecting miraculous cures and expelling demons.[62] Constantine's action symbolized his complete rejection of the ideology of the past and emphasized the future alliance of throne and monk representing official and popular religion respectively which was to continue as long as the Byzantine empire lasted. In the same period one can detect the first indications of the power that was to be placed in the hands of the monastic leaders when Sozomen records that Constantine sought the friendship of Antony, exchanged letters with him and urged him to put forward any request he might desire.[63] Rufinus adds the detail that the emperor wrote to Antony "as to one of the prophets"[64], asking his prayers for himself and his family. Another monk, Eutychius, who had established himself in Bithynia, went to Constantinople. There he visited Constantine with whom he had also exchanged letters and successfully pleaded for the pardon of a prisoner accused of plotting against the emperor.[65] The monk was on the way towards becoming the emperor's conscience.

The fourth-century emperors continued to keep in close contact with the monks. Valens was an exception, but his death at the hands of the Goths, duly foretold by the Egyptian monk, Isaac, was remembered.[66] The story is well known how, in the reign of Theodosius I, the monk Macedonius the Barley-eater, a rustic ascetic who spoke only Syriac and was popularly known as Gubba, saved the city of Antioch from dire punishment in 387 after the affair of the Statues. Where the eloquence of John Chrysostom could only secure for the inhabitants a respite and a hope of the emperor's mercy, and Bishop Flavian pleaded for their lives to the imperial commissioners with scant hope of success, the monk spoke out in their defence without the slightest hesitation. Theodosius himself

[62] Socrates, *Hist. Eccl.*, I. 11, and Rufinus, *Hist. Eccl.*, I.4.
[63] Sozomen, *Hist. Eccl.*, I. 13.
[64] *Hist. Eccl.*, I.8.
[65] Sozomen, *Hist. Eccl.*, I. 14.
[66] Sozomen, *Hist. Eccl.*, vi. 40.

was reminded curtly that he was mortal like everyone else, that the statues had been replaced and restored but that human beings could not be, and that he had no cause to be angry.[67]   The city of Antioch was spared.   The monk had shown his worth as a tribune of the people.   The importance of this initiative as a means of bringing the grievances and fears of the people direct to the emperor can best be judged when contrasted with the fate of the citizens of Thessalonica four years later.   There were no monks to beg for their lives.   Seven thousand inhabitants were massacred, and Ambrose's sole resort was to excommunicate the emperor for a deed he could not prevent.

In the fifth century monks played a decisive rôle in the Christological and ecclesiastical controversies in the east, and an important one in the day to day decision-making at the imperial court.   Both Theodosius II and Leo I took them into their confidence, and received good advice and loyalty in return.   Theodosius II's claim to a measure of statesmanship is that, like Constantine, he recognized the power of the monks to influence public opinion.   In 434 his letters to the Syrians, Simon Stylites, James and Barodotus contributed far more than threats of exile to get the Formula of Reunion accepted by all parties in the Nestorian controversy and a schism between Alexandria and Antioch averted.[68]   In 449 his invitation to James and Barsaumas to be present at the Second Council of Ephesus was a popular move and Theodosius II was never forgotten by the Monophysites: he remained their hero.[69] Leo I, though more Chalcedonian-inclined, followed his example and asked the advice of Simon Stylites and James before deciding to send Timothy the Cat into exile in 460.[70]   In all this the emperor kept his finger on the pulse of public opinion through the monks.   When one considers in addition his sympathies for the non-aristocratic classes in his empire, craftsmen, merchants and manufacturers,[71] it is not

[67] Theodoret, *Hist. Eccl.*, v. 20, and *Hist. Religiosa*, xiii, col. 1404; compare Sozomen, *Hist. Eccl.*, vii. 23 (Flavian's embassy) and see R. Browning, "The Riot of A.D. 387 in Antioch", *Jl. Rom. Stud.*, xlii (1952), pp. 13-21, for the causes of the riot, particularly the tension between rich and poor in the city and the heavy burden of taxation at this time.
[68] Texts in Mansi, *Conc. Collectio*, v. 929 ff.
[69] Thus, Michael the Syrian, *Chron.* (ed. J. B. Chabot, Paris, 1899-1911), viii. 8, p. 35, and in 583 the "Green" faction in the capital prevailed upon the emperor Maurice to name his son "Theodosius", rather than "Justinian". See P. Maas, *Byzantinische Zeitschrift*, xxi (1912), p. 29, n. 1.
[70] Evagrius, *Hist. Eccl.*, ii. 9.
[71] See E. A. Thompson's analysis of the evidence provided by Priscus, John Malalas and Lydus for Theodosius II's social policy, *Attila*, pp. 190-7.

altogether surprising that Theodosius II survived for a reign of forty-two years and handed over his realm intact to his successor.

Meantime in the capital the growth of monastic houses was providing the monks with even more direct means of access to the emperor. The household officers, the eunuchs of the court, who wielded immediate influence with the emperor were often of a monkish disposition. A near contemporary describes them as "living in the palace as though a monastery", and they were open to monastic pressures from without. Thus Dalmatius and Eutyches were decisive influences in turning Theodosius II against Nestorius in the months of crisis that followed Ephesus I in 431. A decade later Eutyches emerged as the *eminence grise* in the court of Constantinople. His godson was the Grand-Chamberlain Chrysaphius, in whose hands both the foreign policy of the empire, especially regarding the Huns, and its religious policy lay. This formidable partnership gradually wore down the opposition. The Augusta Pulcheria narrowly escaped being ordained deaconess and her rival, the Empress Eudocia, was worked upon, to quote the medieval historian Nicephorus Kallistos, "with a persistence of drops of water that wear away a stone".[72] Cyrus, the Pretorian prefect whose buildings and fortifications made him famous, was forced to convert to Christianity, resign his offices, and become Bishop of Cotiaeum in Phrygia.[73] Eutyches's policy was to make the religion of Cyril of Alexandria uncompromisingly stated in the Twelve Anathemas the religion of the empire regardless of the damage inflicted on the patriarchate of Constantinople, and the impossibility of securing western assent. In this he had Chrysaphius's support.[74] That the pair were foiled only by Theodosius II's sudden death (July 450) is a witness to the strength of the position which monkish influence had now attained at the imperial court.

Eutyches might be compared with some evil genius of latter-day Byzantine or Russian Tsarist history. From now on, the imperial court was seldom to be without its monastic politicians. Daniel the Stylite, Severus before he became Patriarch of Antioch, the Syrian stylite, Zooras, and Theodora's son Athanasius, play similar rôles during the next hundred years. Together they illustrate the closeness of the connections between religious and political action

---

[72] Nicephorus Kallistos, *Hist. Eccl.*, xiv. 47 (*P.G.*, cxlvi, col. 1424).
[73] See, *Life of Daniel the Stylite* (ed. and Eng. trans., E. Dawes and N. H. Baynes, Oxford, 1948), ch. 31.
[74] For this period see, P. Goubert, "Le Rôle de Ste. Pulchérie et de l'eunuque Chrysaphios", in (ed.) A. Grillmeier/H. Bacht, *Das Konzil von Chalkedon* (Würzburg, 1953), vol. i, pp. 303 ff.

in the east at this period.   Daniel illustrates also how eminence as a
monk could open the way to a Syriac-speaking villager to the exercise
of enormous political power in the capital.   Daniel ultimately became
the arbiter between rival emperors.   He was born in the territory of
Samosata *circa* 409.   At an early age he was offered by his parents to
the local monastery to be trained in the religious life.   He became
a disciple of Simon Stylites.   After twenty-five years in a Syrian
monastery he was persuaded to go up to Constantinople "as to a
second Jerusalem", with its martyrs, shrines and "great houses of
prayer"[75] — that is, the capital was regarded as a great centre of
religious life and orthodoxy as well as the residence of the emperor.
On arrival his Syriac speech at first made him suspect of heresy
(Nestorianism?)[76] and only after nine years in what had been a pagan
temple did his reputation as an expeller of demons enable him to amass
sufficient reputation so that he could mount a column and establish
himself as a true ascetic (*circa* 455).   From that moment he
prospered.   Courtiers who benefited from his miraculous healing
powers brought him to the notice of the Emperor Leo, and when his
prayers were believed to have secured a son for the Empress Verina
his position with Leo was unrivalled.[77]   He was, we are told by his
biographer, instrumental in settling a dispute between Leo and the
client ruler of Lazica when the latter visited Constantinople in 466.[78]
By this time important decisions were being remitted to him for his
advice.   The most important was in 468 when, in the grim aftermath
of the failure of Leo's expedition against Gaiseric, Daniel was asked
his opinion whether or not Gaiseric would now attack Alexandria.
Daniel told him that he would not — and he was right.   In the following year he showed his political finesse by supporting the Zeno faction
at Leo's court against that of the ruling Germanic clan of the Alan,
Aspar, and his son Ardaburius.[79]   In view of Zeno's character his
zeal on his behalf appears remarkable, but the Gothic Alan clique
could be suspected of Arianism and this was anathema to Daniel.
In view of this, it is not perhaps suprising that he warned Zeno about
plots against him when the latter became emperor in 474 and used his
influence decisively on his behalf in the crisis of his reign in the next
year.
   The episode reveals the tangled web of political, religious and even
military cross-currents which characterize the history of the east

[75] *Life of Daniel the Stylite*, ch. 10.
[76] *Ibid.*, ch. 17.
[77] *Ibid.*, ch. 38.
[78] *Ibid.*, ch. 51.
[79] *Ibid.*, chaps. 56, 55, 65-8.

Roman provinces in the fifth century. Since the Council of Chalcedon the object of the Alexandrians had been to get the emperor to renounce the Two-Nature Christological Definition and the *Tome* of Pope Leo. They had found that though the Emperor Leo was rather more sympathetic to their cause than Marcian had been, its acceptance was impossible without at the same time depriving the see of Constantinople of its title deeds to precedence next to Rome accorded to it in the 28th Canon. No emperor could do this, and Zeno, despite his leanings towards Cyril's theology, was not to be an exception. A palace revolution put a nominee of the senate and kinsman of the Dowager Empress Verina on the throne in January 475, and Zeno had to flee for his life. His rival, Basiliscus, then proceeded to do exactly what the Alexandrians wanted. Timothy the Cat was recalled from exile, and given a triumphant entry into Constantinople. The usurper's Encyclical promulgated in April 475 condemned the *Tome* of Leo and Chalcedon and pronounced the One-Nature Christology of Cyril's Anathemas as the orthodoxy of the empire. It was silent about the rights of the see of Constantinople.[80] While the Patriarch Acacius protested, Daniel acted decisively. A Syrian like Simon Stylites, his leanings were towards the Two-Nature Christology of Antioch and Chalcedon was for him the touchstone of orthodoxy. He told Basiliscus's envoy who visited him that his master "had adopted Jewish ideas" and was unworthy of his blessing.[81] Public opinion in the capital began to turn against Basiliscus. The cry went up, "The holy man for the Church. Let the new Daniel save Susanna in her peril. Another Elijah shall put Jezebel and Ahab to shame".[82] Then on the petition of Acacius, Daniel came down from his column. Crowds turned out to see him. He preached against the "new enemies of Moses" (that is, the Egyptians). He compared the existing situation with that of the persecuted under Diocletian.[83] One of the emperor's Gothic guardsmen who mockingly called on the "new Consul" was struck dead.[84] This was power in action. Timothy left the capital for Alexandria. Basiliscus capitulated. The Anti-Encyclical annulling the Encyclical was despatched. In a few months Zeno was back and Basiliscus on his way to prison and death.

The career of Daniel demonstrates the extraordinary power which

---

[80] For the events, see Zacharias, *Chron.*, v. 1-5 (ed. Brooks, Paris/Louvain, 1919-24, pp. 145-52).
[81] Daniel Stylites, *Life*, ch. 71.
[82] *Ibid.*, ch. 71.
[83] *Ibid.*, ch. 73.
[84] *Ibid.*, ch. 75.

20

had fallen into the hands of the monastic leaders. Even so formidable a patriarch as Acacius might not have succeeded without his help. Certainly the Anti-Encyclical embodying Basiliscus's abject surrender would never have been sent. In the next reign, that of Anastasius, we find Severus, though a scholar with a legal training but of no higher status than a monk, coming to Constantinople on the urgent business of his monastery, and within a short time dominating completely the religious policy of the emperor. The Patriarch Macedonius, popular though he was and fifteen years in office, found himself deposed and exiled in 511. The Monophysite addition to the *Gloria* ("Holy God, Holy and almighty, holy and immortal, *who was crucified for us,* have mercy upon us") was intoned in the churches of Constantinople and Severus himself became Patriarch of Antioch (November 512).[85] With Justinian and Theodora monkish politics return to something approaching the level of activity of the reign of Theodosius II.

For an emperor to whom "the interests of the Church were no less valuable than life itself", the monks were trusted advisers.[86] In the early part of Justinian's reign St. Sabas led an important delegation of Palestinian monks to the capital to counterbalance the increasing influence of their Monophysite rivals. It was one of the latter, however, who for a few years between 533 and 536 attained a situation of almost unrivalled eminence at the emperor's court. Like Daniel the Stylite, Zooras was a Syrian peasant and a pillar-saint, but between the period of Zeno to that of Justinian, the province of Syria I had become almost entirely Monophysite in loyalty, and Zooras was if nothing else a fanatical opponent of the "Synod" (of Chalcedon). The policy, however, of Justinian and his uncle Justin had been based on the restoration of communion between Constantinople and Rome, which involved the maintenance of the canonical status of Chalcedon. Justinian's wife Theodora, for her part, was a woman of the people and shared the basic Monophysitism of the populace. The Monophysites could always count on her as an ally, and it was her favour that Zooras enjoyed while in the capital. His *Life* as recounted by John of Ephesus a generation later, is doubtless full of exaggerations and embroideries but it leaves no doubt as to the influence which the monks could exert on the Byzantine government. Justin had harassed the Monophysites and made life thoroughly uncomfortable for their monks and clergy, especially in Syria. Zooras had no hesitation in taking up their cause personally with the emperor. He

---

[85] For the Patriarch Macedonius's fall, see Evagrius, *Hist. Eccl.*, iii. 32 and 44.
[86] Justinian, Novel 7.

descended from his column. "I will not rest", said he, "until I go up to him who holds royal authority and testify to him before the Lord Jesus Christ concerning the persecution of the whole Church and concerning the distresses and mockery of the saints in every place".[87] To the capital he went. Again, no protocol stood in the way of his direct access to Justinian. He preached against Chalcedon, defied the emperor's anger and struck him down with a painful sickness.[88] Like his predecessor Daniel, he became rapidly a power in the land. John of Ephesus points out that "as in his own country" he was "protector of the poor", and this guaranteed his influence among the populace.[89] He became Theodora's confessor and confidante. We are told "that many of the great affairs were resolved by him before the king and all the senators, while every day he was engaged in the same contest on behalf of the faith".[90] The height of his influence came when Anthimus became Patriarch in 535 and turned towards Monophysitism. The political reunion, however, of Africa and Italy with the eastern provinces of the empire made the formal acceptance of the Monophysite position by the Court impossible. Zooras's successes were ended by the arrival in the capital of Pope Agapetus (March 536) described by John of Ephesus as "a worse heretic than Paul of Samosata".[91] Eventually, he was exiled from Constantinople and had to accept asylum from the Empress Theodora.

With Zooras, as with Daniel, political influence primarily rested on an enormous reputation for sanctity, "the hidden power of grace",[92] achieved through ascetic practices. The monks were in communion with the unseen world which gave them the power to "bind and loose" even the emperor himself. They had the free speech (*parrhesia*) reserved to the bishop in the west before the emperor. There was also the monks' social concern, the championing of the peasants and poor of the cities from whose ranks they were often drawn, and their ability in some degree to make known the hardships of the people to their rulers. For Justinian the sanctity and inner power of a monk like Zooras outweighed his dislike of those who rejected Chalcedon. Later in his reign he accepted the monk John of Amida as a missionary and titular bishop of Ephesus despite his anti-Chalcedonian views.

[87] John of Ephesus, *Lives of the Eastern Saints*, ii (*Patrologia Orientalis*, vol. xvii), p. 21.
[88] *Ibid.*, p. 24.
[89] *Ibid.*, p. 26.
[90] *Ibid.*, p. 26.
[91] *Ibid.*, pp. 26-7.
[92] *Ibid.*, p. 23.

It is not perhaps too much therefore to point to the monks as among the forces that enabled the eastern empire to survive the crises that overwhelmed the west in the fifth century. If one asks why no similar movement developed in the west, the answer lies as we have seen in the different character of popular religious movements there. Behind these popular attitudes lay differences of ultimate belief that had divided Latin and Greek Christianity from the early third century onwards. Whereas in the east Christianity and the concept of the powers and duties of the emperor coincided, the west had never accepted Constantine's conversion with much conviction. If one excepts on the one hand, the loyalist utterances of Prudentius,[93] almost as fervent as those of his eastern counterparts, and the outright comparison by the Donatists of any secular ruler whether Roman or Vandal with Anti-Christ, one is left with a broad conspectus of western Christian opinion which regarded the Roman empire as of temporary value only, and was prepared to regard its demise more or less with indifference. Though for some periods of history the interests of the *Civitas Terrena* and the *Civitas Dei* might run parallel, there was no inevitability about this, and if Rome fell and the imperial armies were defeated it was a matter for Providence.[94] The prosperity of Christianity did not depend on the survival of the empire. Even its Christianization, though in fulfilment of prophecy, was of little moment in the history of human salvation. The Christian's duty was to renounce the world and fix his gaze on the coming Judgement which no one could evade, and from which there was no appeal.

These attitudes, while they existed in the east, could be softened by the use of allegorical interpretations of Scripture and by the equally profound belief that man's true destiny lay in the restoration in him of the likeness of God lost at the Fall. The emperor was neither repentant Nebuchadnezzar as Augustine would have him,[95] nor representative of Anti-Christ, but the reflection of the Divine Word. Whatever his personal defects, loyalty to him was as loyalty to God.

[93] Prudentius was attempting to appropriate for triumphant Christianity the patriotic rôle which traditional paganism had hitherto played in moulding the attitude of the senatorial aristocracy. See R. Klein, *Symmachus* (Darmstadt, 1971), pp. 140-60.
[94] For recent discussion of these attitudes and Augustine's rejection of Eusebius's Rome-theology, see R. A. Markus, *Saeculum* (Cambridge, 1970), pp. 45 ff.
[95] Augustine, *Contra Litteras Petiliani*, ii.92.204-5. Compare N. H. Baynes, *The Political Ideas of St. Augustine's De Civitate Dei* (London, Historical Association, 1949), pp. 12-13.

The different attitudes and rôles of the monks in the eastern and western provinces of the empire in the fifth and sixth centuries contribute much to their respective histories. In the west monasticism was avowedly escape. Neither Paulinus nor Melania could rid themselves of their worldly responsibilities fast enough. Where the Church exerted political influence it was through ecclesiastical statesmen such as Ambrose or Pope Leo. In the east on the other hand, monastic power was popular power, exercised in a state where the solidarity of the Christian people against Jews and barbarians was demonstrated by unswerving loyalty towards "the God-loving emperor", however deficient in those qualities he might be. Renunciation of the world entailed taking up the challenge presented by the demons and an active life in the service of causes where demons threatened. These could be the defeat of heresy or the defeat of barbarians or the defeat of various forms of oppression. In this age where the necessities of accuracy in religious belief were all-important for worldly success and an emperor would vie with the citizens of one of his provincial cities for the possession of a monk's body,[96] it was no more incongruous for a monk to be at the emperor's side at his court, than it was for a eunuch such as Narses to lead his armies, or for a rival to the throne or a fallen minister to find himself in a bishopric. One of Justinian's odder appointments towards the end of his life was that of Photion, described as a "monk of high rank" to deal with Samaritan rebels in 564, and he did his work well.[97] The monks thus provided a much needed flexibility in an otherwise increasingly hierarchical and hieratic society. Through them the Syrians and Copts, the submerged races in the Byzantine east, were enabled to exert an appreciable influence on religious and secular politics. This was the case, moreover, almost regardless of whether the monk accepted the emperor's *credo* or not. Their loyalty was thereby secured until the inability of the emperor and the authorities to renounce the hated *Tome* of Leo and the Council of Chalcedon rendered acceptance of second-class citizenship under the Moslems preferable to continued harassment by the Byzantines.

In the fifth century, however, such possibilities were not even on the horizon. The monks, whether Chalcedonian or Monophysite, were indispensable. Technically they were neither courtiers nor priests, but in the event they were more powerful than either.[98] In Eutyches,

---

[96] Evagrius, *Hist. Eccl.*, 1. 13, concerning the efforts of the Emperor Leo I to secure the body of Simon Stylites.
[97] John of Nikiou, *Chron.* (ed. R. H. Charles), 95. 17.
[98] See Brown, *The World of Late Antiquity*, p. 102.

24

Simon and Daniel the Stylite, and Zooras and his companions, the east Roman provinces produced popular leaders who, in a curious way, were exactly adapted to their times. By perceiving how the ultimate strength of their Christian peoples, their religious identity, their secular aspirations and will to survive, were reflected in the monks, the eastern emperors of the fifth century proved more statesmanlike than they are sometimes thought to have been. They confronted the challenges that defeated their western colleagues, overcame them and survived.

University of Glasgow

XIX

SEVERUS OF ANTIOCH AND THE ORIGINS OF THE MONOPHYSITE HIERARCHY

In a learned contribution to Alois Grillmeier's and Heinrich Bacht's classic work on the Council of Chalcedon,[1] Professor Albert van Roey traced the origins of the establishment of a separate Monophysite Church during the sixth century.[2] Though conceding that James Bar'adai " took the decisive step " towards creating a Monophysite hierarchy by his consecration of the monks Eugenius and Conon as metropolitans of Tarsus and Seleucia respectively,[3] he considered that much more was due to the work of John of Tella a generation before in the 530s, whose mass ordinations of clergy provided the Monophysites with a permanent ecclesiastical organisation independent of the Chalcedonians. In this period, however, Severus of Antioch though in exile in Alexandria was still at the forefront of the Monophysite cause. The object of this contribution is to examine more closely the part which he and his colleagues in Alexandria played in this momentous development and the context in which their actions took place.

The Council of Chalcedon in 451 had seen the emergence of a Monophysite movement but not of a separate Monophysite Church. The acceptance by the Council that the *Tome* of Pope Leo was orthodox and that Jesus Christ was to be acknowledged " in two natures inseparably united " had caused great satisfaction in the west but profound divisions among the churches in the east. There the great majority of bishops and their congregations accepted the Christology of Cyril of Alexandria (d. 444) as the touchstone of orthodoxy. Cyril had spent a lifetime in demonstrating that in the Incarnate Logos which was Jesus Christ there was only one nature (*physis*) and one individuality (*hypostasis*), namely

---

[1] A. Grillmeier and H. Bacht, *Das Konzil von Chalkedon*, Geschichte und Gegenwart, Würzburg, 1953, three volumes.

[2] A. van Roey, " Les debuts de l'Eglise jacobite " = *Das Konzil von Chalkedon*, Vol. ii, pp. 339-360.

[3] *Ibid.*, p. 357.

that of the Logos itself. He had triumphed over Nestorius at the Council of Ephesus I in 431, and his successor Dioscorus had brought about the downfall of the Patriarch Flavian of Constantinople at Ephesus II in 449 precisely because it had been possible to persuade the bishops in both assemblies that " Two nature " Christology implied the existence of " Two Christs." The division of Logos from manhood in two distinct natures in Christ necessitated the worship of a being other than God, and could imply the inefficacy of the sacraments. The Definition of Chalcedon seemed either to consecrate the doctrine of Nestorius or to be nonsensical. Nonetheless, because the emperor Marcian had approved it, the majority of the episcopate was prepared to acquiesce in the formula at least as a guard against the contrasting heresies of Nestorius and Eutyches.

Their views, however, were not accepted by a large proportion of their people. News of the Council's decisions were received with an outburst of popular wrath rare in the history of the Roman and Byzantine worlds. The indignation extended far beyond Egypt where the deposition of the Patriarch Dioscorus at Chalcedon had fanned the flames of discontent. In Palestine, Juvenal, the ambitious patriarch of the newly created patriarchate of Jerusalem, was believed to have betrayed Dioscorus and had to flee for his life. For two years the monk, Theodosius, established himself as patriarch in his place. A remarkable collection of " Witnesses " (*Plerophoria*) to events of the time assembled by John Rufus, Bishop of Maiuma near Gaza *circa* 512, show that the trouble also spread to Asia Minor and that in the provinces of Isauria and Pamphylia Christians had been aghast at what appeared to have been a corrupt volt-face on the part of their bishops and a betrayal of Cyril.[4] Indeed, wherever monasticism was powerful in the east discontent with Chalcedon was strong. Cyril's affirmation " One is the nature of the Incarnate Logos " became the rallying cry of the opposition.

Despite the depth of popular anger, however, there was no permanent schism. The monk, Theodosius' attempt to establish an anti-Chalcedonian episcopate in Palestine was short-lived. For sixty years after Chalcedon, except in Egypt no rival hierarchy emerged to challenge the Chalcedonian bishops approved by the emperor. Whatever their relations with the successors of Pope Leo at Rome, the four eastern patriarchates strove to remain in

---

[4] Published by F. Nau in *Patrologia Orientalis* viii, p. 11-161. See in particular, *Plerophoriae*, 16-20 (regarding Juvenal) and 21-24 (Isauria).

communion with each other. Even the Egyptians through Timothy the Cat (d. 477) and Peter Mongus (d. 489), aimed only at the restoration of the status quo in the last years of Theodosius II at the height of Dioscorus' power, by winning the emperor to Monophysitism and obtaining from him the denunciation of Leo's *Tome* and the Council of Chalcedon. There was no thought of setting up a separate Egyptian Church. During the usurpation of Basiliscus 475-476 they very nearly succeeded.[5] They were baulked, however, constantly by the fact that the title deeds to the claims of the see of Constantinople to supremacy over the other eastern sees and also Jerusalem's status as a patriarchate rested on the decisions of Chalcedon. The Council could not be denounced therefore without endangering the position of the see of the capital, and no emperor could afford to do this. Within this crucial limitation, however, the successors of Marcian were prepared to go a very long way towards meeting the Egyptian standpoint, supported as it was by a huge weight of popular opinion in the provinces.

The *Henotikon* of Zeno, the letter despatched by the emperor Zeno to the bishops, monks and laity of Egypt and Cyrenaica in July 482, marked the climax of these efforts. This, while not denouncing Chalcedon explicitly, declared the One Nature teaching of Cyril's *Twelve Anathemas* orthodox, affirmed that Jesus Christ was " one and not two," and anathematised " every person who has thought or thinks anything else either now or at any time either in Chalcedon or in any other synod whatsoever." [6] Not surprisingly the Papacy which had regarded the slightest deviation from Chalcedon as heretical, denounced the *Henotikon*, and two years later in 484 formally withdrew communion from the eastern sees. The Acacian Schism was to last for the next thirty-five years until a western-minded emperor sat on the throne of Constantinople.

The studied ambiguities of the *Henotikon* enabled communion to be restored between Constantinople and Alexandria and hence the religious unity of the east. However bitter pro- and anti-

---

[5] See Zacharias Rhetor, *Hist. Eccl.* (ed. and tr. E. W. Brooks, *Corpus Scriptorum orientalium christianorum*, 88 (= *CSCO*) Script. Syri. iii.5, Louvain, 1924 Bk. V. I do not regard him and his namesake Zacharias Scholasticus, Severus of Antioch's friend and biographer, as the same person.

[6] Evagrius, *Hist. Eccl.* iii.14. For the complete text see E. Schwartz, " Codex Vaticanus gr. 1431 " in *Abh. Bayer. Akad. der Wissenschaften*, Phil. Hist. Kl. 32, 6, München 1927, p. 52-4. Eng. tr. and notes in P. R. Coleman-Norton, *Roman State and Christian Church* iii, p. 924-33.

Chalcedonian factions in the cities, any ideas of establishing " altar against altar " in the western style or separation from the rest of the empire would have been completely repudiated. The emperor was vice-regent of God and the boundaries of his realm coincided with the *orbis christianus*. The Monophysites were to become separatists despite themselves, and characteristically they were to blame the emperor Marcian both for dividing Christ and dividing his empire.[7]   Similarly, it is not true to describe them at this stage as representing the outlook of the non-Hellenic populations of the empire, still less revolutionary ideals.[8]   Neither Cyril nor his successors in the Alexandrian patriarchate during the fifth century were Copts, though all were able to claim the loyalty of the majority of the Coptic monks.   Indeed, when one looks closely at the composition of pro- and anti-Chalcedonian even in Egypt one is struck by the manner in which both parties crossed barriers of race and class.   The people of Alexandria (the " demos ") was on the anti-Chalcedonian side.[9]   The Chalcedonians, however, included a proportion of Pachomian monks, Copts like the rest of the Egyptian monks, but retaining vivid memories of Dioscorus' misdeeds in the years 444-49,[10] and the official classes and "nobles" who formed the backbone of Alexandrian Chalcedonianism [11] were by no means all foreigners.   Nor were the Chalcedonian minorities in the provincial towns of Egypt such as Peter the Iberian encountered at Oxyrhynchus.[12]   The division during the fifth century ran through families and friends rather than along hard and fast community boundaries.

---

[7] Michael the Syrian, *Chronicle* (ed. J. B. Chabot, Paris, 1901) viii.14 (p. 122). " The unity of the empire was broken by Marcian, at the same time as he divided the faith."

[8] For this view, see E. L. Woodward, *Christianity and Nationalism in the Later Roman Empire*, London, 1916, p. 41-66, and also A. Vasiliev, *History of the Byzantine Empire*, Madison, 1958, p. 105-06.   I find no evidence to support the claim, however, that " the Egyptian Church abolished the use of Greek in its services and introduced the native Egyptian (Coptic) language," after Chalcedon.   Nor that " the Egyptian and Syrian populations were gradually becoming convinced of the desirability of seceding from the Byzantine empire."   This does not seem to have been the case even in the years immediately before the Arab invasions.

[9] Zacharias Rhetor, *Hist. Eccl.* iv.1 (Brooks, p. 118).

[10] See the letter of the presbyter Athanasius addressed to the Council of Chalcedon and read at the third session.   Mansi, *Conciliorum Collectio* (Florence, 1759) vi, col. 1021 and following.

[11] See Zacharias Rhetor *Hist. Eccl.*, iv. 3. (Brooks, p. 120).

[12] Zacharias Scholasticus, *Life of Peter of Iberia*, ed. Raabe, Leipzig, 1895, p. 68.

The equilibrium established in the east by the *Henotikon* was an unstable one, and during the last decade of the reign of Anastasius (491-518) it came increasingly under strain. The individual most responsible for its breakdown through the re-emergence of fundamental religious differences throughout the east was the brilliant intellectual, originally from a noble and episcopal house in Pisidia, named Severus.

Severus' early career gave little hint of the role he was to play in eastern Christianity.[13] The family tradition had been pro-Cyril ; his grandfather as Bishop of Sozopolis had been among Cyril's supporters at Ephesus I in 431, but Severus was destined for the law. He studied at Alexandria and Berytus, and though later rumours of his paganism were not true, his adherence to Christianity was little more than nominal. It is not known even whether he was in communion with Peter Mongus at Alexandria ; Egyptian monasticism seems to have made little or no impression on him. He left Alexandria *circa* 485 firmly attached to his legal studies and, as he told his biographer after a year at Berytus, he wanted to be a lawyer even if this involved delaying baptism.[14] His change of heart was due apparently to meeting the aged and venerable Peter of Iberia, Bishop of Maiuma, who visited Berytus shortly before his death in 489. Severus was gained by the arguments and example of an aristocrat like himself, accepted the ascetic life, and moved steadily in the direction of Monophysitism. Years later when he was in exile in Alexandria, Severus recalled how he came to reject "the Chalcedonian impiety" and draw near to (Monophysite) orthodoxy thanks to Peter. "This communion I so hold, I so draw near in it with the highest assurance and a fixed mind, when our holy father Peter of Iberia was offering and was performing the rational sacrifice." [15]

In 508 circumstances connected with the decline of Monophysitism in Palestine in face of the vigorous propaganda inspired by St. Sabas,[16] which threatened the existence of his own monastery near Maiuma, sent him to Constantinople. There, simple monk though he was, he soon became the leading religious influ-

---

[13] For this period see Zacharias Scholasticus, "Vie de Sevère" (ed. H. A. Kugener, *P. O.* ii, p. 7-115) and W. Bauer, in *Aufsätze und kleine Schriften* (ed. G. Strecker, Tübingen, 1967) p. 210-228.

[14] Zacharias Scholasticus, op. cit., p. 51.

[15] Severus, *The sixth book of Select Letters* (ed. E. W. Brooks, London, 1902-04) v. ii, p. 328.

[16] On this important phase in the history of Monophysitism see D. V. Chitty, *The Desert a City*, Blackwell's, Oxford, 1966, Ch. vi.

ence in the capital, with the ear of the emperor Anastasius. Severus was by now an uncompromising Cyrillian. " Firm assurance and fixed mind " meant for him the rejection of both the *Tome* of Leo and the Chalcedonian Definition however they might be presented. Gradually the aged emperor was persuaded to accept the formula that Christ existed " out of two natures, one " instead of " in two natures inseparably united." In 510[17] he permitted the recitation of the Monophysite addition to the doxology in the Eucharist " who was crucified for us," [18] he had banished the Henoticist patriarch of Constantinople, Macedonius, at Severus' behest on the charge of " falsifying Scripture " on 7 August 511, and finally the equally staunch Flavian Patriarch of Antioch in the autumn of 512.[19] On 6 November 512 Severus himself was consecrated Patriarch of Antioch.

If he had left the capital seething with religious dissensions, his six years as Patriarch were to ensure that this great area, extending from the Taurus mountains to the Egyptian border, was also to be riven permanently into pro- and anti-Chalcedonian factions. There can be little doubt that the populace of Antioch itself was already prepared for the establishment of a hierarchy unequivocally devoted to Monophysitism. Severus' other biographer, John, Superior (*Hegemon*) of the monastery of Beit-Apthonia describes how Severus entered Antioch amid scenes of unparalleled enthusiasm. " Anathematise the Council of Chalcedon. Anathematise the Council that has turned the world upside down. Anathematise the apostate Council. Cursed be the Tome of Leo. Deliver the city from heresy. We want to participate in the holy mysteries. We want to baptise our children." [20] The sting was in the tail. Once ordinary Christians became convinced that the sacraments administered by a priest who accepted the Council of Chalcedon could be invalid, it was only a short step to the formation of a permanent anti-Chalcedonian hierarchy on a territorial basis. So long, however, as the *Henotikon* remained in force, religious differences might continue to be blurred by interpreting

---

[17] See Ch. Moeller, " Le Type de l'empereur Anastase I," *Studia Patristica* 3, = Texte und Untersuchungen Vol. 78, Berlin, 1959, p. 240-7.

[18] Evagrius, *Hist. Eccl.* iii.44 and Theodore Lector, Extract 3 (ed. Kugener *P. O.* ii. p. 362). Compare, G. Bardy, " La politique religieuse d'Anastase," in ed. A. Fliche and V. Martin, *Histoire de l'Eglise*, Paris, 1948 Vol. iv, p. 311-12.

[19] Liberatus, *Breviarium*, xix (*Patrologia Latina* 67).

[20] John of Beit-Aphthonia, *Life of Severus*, (ed. H. A. Kugener, *P. O·* ii, p. 207-64), p. 241.

liberally its comprehensive formulations. No bishop of this period, not even Severus himself rejected the *Henotikon* outright. Severus merely interpreted it as " cancelling Chalcedon." A further point relating eastern and western beliefs also worked against the development of schism. Unlike the situation in the west where the Eucharist had tended to become a social act involving the whole Christian community at regular times, in the east, participation in the elements remained highly personal, perhaps to be accepted as seldom as once a year.[21] The blessed elements could therefore in case of need be carried to the faithful from a central source or left in a safe place ; many of Severus' letters written while in exile deal with the problem of conveying the Eucharist to the faithful through the agency of loyal priests and monks. In addition, the eschatology of the eastern Fathers was optimistic and forward looking. It involved only the soul's frustration if it accepted sacraments at the hands of an unorthodox cleric and not its destruction and everlasting damnation in hellfire.[22] The emotional aspect of religious division was less drastic and a general schism could be postponed.

Severus, however, was not a man for peace and reconciliation. For him " accuracy " of belief, meaning the rejection of Chalcedon, was everything. Early in his rule he ordered that " every bishop should remove from the sacred tablets (i. e. from recitation during the celebration of the Eucharist) the names of those who signed the impious deeds of Chalcedon." [23] This forced large numbers of clerics who would gladly have let sleeping dogs lie to choose sides. Though Severus was prepared to argue with those who he believed had honest scruples, his repeated insistence on theological " accuracy " combined with a tremendous drive and energy ensured that he made enemies as well as friends. Arguments that Chalcedon was not all bad and that it had at least disciplinary uses were brushed aside with merciless logic.[24] He even had scruples whether to visit a dying colleague whose strict orthodoxy he suspected.[25]

---

[21] Indicated by John Rufus, *Plerophoriae* 38 (the lawyer Anianus of Alexandria received an annual present of Eucharistic elements from Peter of Iberia). Also ibid. 78 and John Moschos, *Pratum Spirituale* Ch. 79. = *P. G.* 87, iii, col. 2936.

[22] Thus, Severus to Caesaria (niece of the emperor Anastasius) *Select Letters* iii.4 (p. 246-7). Constrast the fate awaiting those who accepted sacraments at the hands of *traditores* in Africa after the Great Persecution, *Acta Saturnini* 16 (= *Pat. Lat.* viii, col. 700).

[23] *Select Letters* i, 19, p. 68.

[24] For example, see Severus' account of his discussion with John of Claudiopolis in Isauria, *Select Letters* i.1, p. 4-5.

[25] *Select Letters* 1.11, p. 47-51.

In all this he was abetted by the Metropolitan of the frontier province of Euphratesia, an east Syrian named Xenaias (Hellenised into Philoxenus) Bishop of Hierapolis (Maboug) from 485-519, a fanatic who had made life intolerable for Severus' predecessor Flavian II and finally had engineered his dismissal. Philoxenus, however, drew support from the masses of monks who thronged the frontier area between the Roman and Persian empires. His ability to express Monophysitism in the Syriac idiom, which Severus could not, together with his Biblicism and puritanical morality ensured that Monophysitism would be the dominant creed among the Syriac-speaking Christians in the vital areas of Rome's frontier with Persia.[26]

Throughout the six years of Severus' rule one can detect a steady deepening of existing religious divisions throughout his diocese. Severus' vast correspondence and sermons demonstrate clearly that in some areas he was far more popular than in others. West of Antioch, for instance, at Q'ennaserim (Chalcis) he received a tremendous ovation from " the God-loving people " there when he came to preach in 514.[27] This was to be an area of great importance in the development of Monophysitism, dominated by no less than sixty monasteries within a radius of twenty five miles. These monks were to form the backbone of Syrian Monophysitism then as later in the century. The same was true of Euphratesia, heavily populated with monks, six of whose bishops were present with Philoxenus at Severus' consecration as Patriarch.[28] In Asia Minor, Pamphylia also was his, and the Metropolitan communicated with the Alexandrian Patriarch,[29] Dioscorus II, when the latter was on his way to the capital in 516. Isauria, however, though favourable, was rather less reliable ; some of its clergy gave Severus a disproportionate amount of trouble with their disciplinary failures and doctrinal doubts.[30] The real opposition to Severus came however from Cilicia, the homeland of the Antiochene theological tradition at the time of the Nestorian controversy, and the province of Syria Secunda dominated by Greek and often still strongly pagan cities. At Tarsus, Severus found Nestorius not only was

---

[26] For Philoxenus' life see A. de Halleux' monograph *Philoxène de Mabbog, sa vie, ses écrits, sa théologie*, Louvain, 1963, and for his activities during Severus' period as Patriarch, see A. van Roey, op. cit., p. 345-6.

[27] Sermon LVI (ed. R. Duval, *P. O.* iv, p. 78-82).

[28] See the list drawn up by M. A. Kugener, " Notices relatives à Sévère," in *P. O.* ii, p. 316-25.

[29] Severus, *Select Letters*, iv. 3, p. 259.

[30] For instance, *Select Letters*, 1.19.

included on the diptychs but commemorated among the martyrs.[31] In Syria Secunda his ideas were openly rejected, and near the end of 517 the bishops and monks of the province wrote to Pope Hormisdas (514-423) pledging their support to "the holy synod of Chalcedon," and the *Tome* of "our blessed father Leo," and requesting the Pope to anathematise not only the traditional heretics, but the former patriarch of Constantinople, Acacius, and all who had remained in communion with him.[32] As the sequel showed, this was welcome advice indeed.

It is doubtful whether outright schism between pro-and anti-Chalcedonian areas could have been avoided even if Anastasius had been succeeded by a likeminded emperor. In fact, the elderly soldier Justin who found himself chosen on 9 July 518 was a Latin-speaking westerner, more interested in restoring ecclesiastical relations with Rome than working out religious formulae designed to satisfy Severus. The religious revolution that took place in the first three years of his reign accelerated the establishment of a rival Monophysite hierarchy. The *Henotikon* was abrogated and the Acacian Schism formally ended. Old and New Rome were henceforth to be united in one faith. From the list of 55 expelled bishops in Severus' patriarchate, one may see the extent to which religious division there had been tending to take on territorial complexion. In Euphratesia on the Persian frontier six out of eight known incumbents, including Philoxenus, were exiled, in Cicilia Secunda (immediately north of Antioch) the same proportion, in Mesopotamia three out of four, Osrhoene all six, Isauria, nine out of eleven, Syria Prima (including the city of Antioch) four out of seven, Phoenicia Libanese (inland Phoenicia) all six. In contrast only one bishop from Syria Secunda was exiled, and none from Cilicia Prima, Arabia and Maritime Phoenicia.[33] One can detect from this how division was forming along provincial and cultural lines, the mainly Greek-speaking provinces remaining true to Chalcedon, while the mainly Syriac areas were opting for Monophysitism.

---

[31] *Ibid.*, 1.24, p. 84.

[32] The text of the letter is included in the *Collectio Avellana* (ed. A. Guenther, Vienna, 1895-98), No. 139. Pope Hormisdas' answer written in Feb. 518 is preserved, ibid. No. 140.

[33] For the list of bishops who were exiled at this time see *Chron. ad ann.* 846 pertinens, ed. E. W. Brooks and J. B. Chabot, *CSCO*, Script. Syr. iii.4, Paris 1903, p. 171-3, and E. Honigmann's tabulation and commentary in " Evêques et Evêchés monophysites d'Asie antérieure au VIe siècle," *CSCO*, Subridia 2, Louvain, 1951, p. 87.

This development was assisted by far reaching changes that had been taking place in the role of the Syrian monasteries. In its origins Syrian monasticism had been individualist, not to say anarchic. Individuals representing every sort of extravagance would set up as monks, and some would become renowned as saints throughout the Byzantine world. This tendency was now altering as in time the more viable of the foundations became permanent, and themselves became considerable landowners. Tchalenko's fundamental studies of the monasteries in northern Syria [34] has shown that by the beginning of the sixth century the Syrian monasteries, like their Egyptian counterparts, had become large economic and social units dominating the life of the villages in their immediate vicinity. Around Chalcis where Jerome had found nothing but quarrelsome hermits circa 375 were now buildings almost palatial in character. The old largely pagan landowning class chastised so richly by Theodoret [35] in the mid fifth century had been displaced by monastic holdings. These great monasteries in northern Syria were outward-looking, open institutions, hospitals and orphanages as well as refuges for contemplatives and ascetics.[36] The monks were also immersed in doctrinal discussions and furiously partisan in favour of Severus. Their overriding influence on the outlook of the people reinforced other factors making for territorial divisions between Monophysite and Chalcedonian in the patriarchate of Antioch.

Severus had not waited to be arrested on Justin's order but had left Antioch secretly for Egypt. He arrived in Alexandria on 29 September 518 to find the city and country united in opposition to Justin's religious policy " the Egyptians stripping themselves for action," [37] as he describes them. He was joined by seven other bishops and was to stay until his death in February 538, except for a visit to Constantinople lasting from the winter 534-35 to the autumn of 536. His first objective as patriarch in exile was to continue to administer his diocese from Alexandria through clerics who remained loyal to him. A stream of instructions, often involving minutiae of administration flowed from his headquarters in the city, a permanent Monophysite council that he and other exiles established to deal with disciplinary problems.

---

[34] G. Tchalenko, *Villages antiques de la Syrie du Nord*, Paris-Beyrouth 1953, Vol. i, pp. 145-182.

[35] Theodoret (ed. Y. Azéma, Sources Chrétiennes) *Ep.* 42.

[36] Jerome, *Epp.* 16 and 17.

[37] *Select Letters*, v. II, p. 328.

" As to the sub-deacon under a decree of separation from the miserable and wicked Cyriac, if he repent of the sins he has committed, the merciful sentence of God will absolve him through your holiness," he tells Bishop Sergius of Cyrrhus, whose city however had demonstrated in favour of Chalcedon on hearing the news of Justin's accession.   Cyriac was to be healed with a mixture of severity and a mild drug of penitence.[38] In this same letter we find perhaps the earliest indication that Severus was thinking in terms of establishing a rival hierarchy to combat the Chalcedonians in Syria.   He emphasised to Sergius that archimandrites in the monasteries must take seriously their responsibilities for appointment to the diaconate and presbyterate.   In yet another letter of this period, he lays down that clergy who " were of heretical (Chalcedonian) ordination " were not to be re-ordained, but allowed to retain their orders after due penance.[39] This was another point that differentiated religious conflict in the east from its counterparts in the west.   Rejection of the validity of Catholic orders and sacraments as being those of apostates was one of the factors that rendered the Donatist movement immediate and lasting after the Great Persecution.   In the east there was far more scope for the maintenance of personal ties between religious opponents.   Moreover, Severus himself was strongly opposed to anything that looked like ecclesiastical disorder.   The Christians of Emesa, one of the few places in Syria Secunda where he had any support, were warned against the arrival of wandering bishops without properly authorised credentials.[40] Severus regarded himself not as the leader of a sect or party, but as duly accredited Patriarch of Antioch.

The change of attitude which led to his acceptance of the creation of a permanent anti-Chalcedonian hierarchy in Syria and parts of Asia Minor was due to circumstances rather than design. The persecution continued spasmodically through the whole of Justin's reign.[41] After the expulsion of the Monophysite bishops in 518-519 it was the turn of the monks.   From 521 onwards thousands were expelled from their monasteries and turned out into the desert.   In self-defence Severus' supporters had to organise themselves for survival.   The monks set up what the Syrian

---

[38] *Ibid.*, v. 15, p. 351.
[39] *Ibid.*, v. II, p. 326.
[40] *Select Letters* ii.3, p. 208.
[41] See A. Vasiliev, *Justin the First*, Dumbarton Oaks, 1950, pp. 221 ff., for the main phases of Justin's policy towards the Monophysites.

continuator of Zacharias Rhetor calls, " quasi politeia sacerdotum insignium et fidelium," [42] that is organised communities that rejected the Chalcedonian communion and functioned under their own clergy, and for whom a continuity of ministry would be required. We find an important grouping of future Monophysite leaders in the hills around Mardin, a monastic centre near the Persian frontier.[43] With these Severus maintained close contact.[44] The survival of this group which included several bishops and other leaders was to be vital for the establishment of a Monophysite hierarchy on a permanent footing.

Justin died in August 527 and was succeeded by his nephew Justinian. The latter, though personally drawn towards Monophysite Christology saw the interests of the empire in terms of religious and political unity between the two Romes (i. e. Rome and New Rome or Constantinople). This involved an unshakeable loyalty to Chalcedon modified, however, by every concession man could devise to appease the Monophysites. Severus, however, came increasingly to suspect that the emperor was not be trusted and that no fundamental shift of policy would take place while he reigned.[45]

The crisis came in 529/530. To quote John of Ephesus' *Life* of John of Tella written with a hindsight of a generation later ;

> " At the end of ten years of persecution (i. e. 529/530), the faithful who remained in diverse places began to be concerned about ordinations and consulted the faithful bishops : but these latter feared to bring down on themselves even fiercer flames of persecution, and they refused to make ordinations openly, although they had made some in secret. Then complaints from the faithful persecuted arose from all sides against the blessed bishops because of the great deficiency of clerics ; and they wrote and besought the bishops to make ordinations for the faithful, for the matter was urgent." [46]

Severus had never made secret of his view that " true ordination " [47] was not a matter of see but of belief. The ending of

---

[42] Zacharias Rhetor, *Hist. Eccl.*, viii.5, Brooks, p. 56.
[43] Listed by A. van Roey, *op. cit.*, p. 350, n. 39.
[44] *Select Letters* v. 14, p. 345-6.
[45] John of Ephesus, reporting Severus' indecision whether to go to Constantinople or not in 535 and his statement " Do not be deceived. In the lifetime of these emperors no peace will be found." *P. O.* 18, p. 687.
[46] John of Ephesus, *Lives of Eastern Saints*, = *P. O.* 18, p. 516-17.
[47] *Ep.* 57 (Brooks, *P. O.* xii, p. 338).

the *Henotikon* period had confronted him with the consequences of this stand. Even before John of Tella's challenge he had attempted to palliate the lack of clergy. Probably still during Justin's reign he had written to Julian, presbyter and archimandrite of the famous monastery of Mar Bassus, advising him to take steps to maintain a cadre of clergy during the persecution. " Know therefore in times of persecution," Severus wrote, " anyonesoever of the God-loving bishops who is of the same communion with us may properly supply the need of any among the orthodox that is in need." [48]   Meanwhile, he had written to instruct two of his supporters, still active in the diocese, Marion of Sura and Sergius of Cyrrhus, to co-operate in ordaining clergy at Mar Bassus.[49]   Thus the principle of an independent hierarchy had already been conceded by the time John of Tella had taken up the issue with the leaders in Alexandria.

The results of the decision of Severus' council were sensational. To quote John of Ephesus again, hundreds of people came to him " like a flooded river that has burst its banks." [50]   " Every day fifty, a hundred and sometimes as many as two or three hundred men, came to him for ordination." Supporters in areas where John was intending to come were secretly warned of his arrival and asked to bring to him suitable candidates in their neighbourhoods. All those produced were examined in reading the Scriptures and reciting the psalms and obliged before acceptance to show some evidence of literacy. Candidates, we are told, came from as far afield as Armenia, Phoenicia, Cappadocia and Arzanene on the Persian frontier.[51]   Even if the number of ordinations, 170,000, is greatly exaggerated, the foundations of a Severan Church extending throughout the whole of the Roman east had been laid. John of Tella himself claimed to have admitted no less than 840 members of his monastery to the diaconate in a single year (530 ?).[52]

The years 530-531 mark the turning-point in the fortunes of the Monophysite movement. It seems that John of Tella's success had some influence in persuading Justinian to suspend the persecution.[53]   It was the period of unsuccessful war with Persia.

---

[48] Severus, *Select Letters*, i.59 (p. 178-9).
[49] *Ibid.*, v. 15, especially p. 357.
[50] *Lives of Eastern Saints*, p. 518.
[51] *Ibid.*, p. 522.
[52] *Ibid.*, p. 521.
[53] Elias, *Life of John of Tella*, (Ed. E. W. Brooks, *CSCO*, iii,25, Paris 1907), p. 39.

He could not risk an alienated and well organised population in the vital frontier areas. Next year the Monophysite leaders were summoned to a conference in the capital. They went as an organised group conscious of their strength and also their loyalty to the emperor. At court they had the support of Theodora. There was no submission to Chalcedon. From now onwards there was always to be a Monophysite hierarchy. After the failure, first of this conference and then in 535-36 with the deposition of Anthimus, Severus' friend and pro-Monophysite Patriarch of the capital, Severus decided on the final step. John of Tella was permitted to consecrate not only priests and deacons, but bishops, including a bishop for the Monophysites in Persia. By this act he showed that unlike the Chalcedonians the bounds of the Monophysite communion would not be confined to those areas under imperial control or influence. The doctrines of Cyril should be the doctrines of the whole Christian world. Whether Rome, Persia, (or the Arabs) ruled over men's bodies, orthodox doctrine must be sustained. John indeed was apprehended and died a martyr's death in Antioch in 537, but there was to be no looking back. The consecration of James Bar'adai in 541 and the despatch of the presbyter Longinus to the Nubians two years later were part of the same Severan legacy.

For historians of the western tradition the early history of the Monophysites presents great difficulties. Used to discussing situations in which there appear to be immediate connections between religious and political and social discontent resulting in schism, it is natural to seek for similar causes lying behind Monophysitism. This would seem to be justified also when by the end of the sixth century Monophysitism had become to all intents and purposes the national religion of Armenia, of much of Syria with the Arab tribes, of Egypt, Nubia and Ethiopia, just as Donatism occupied a similar situation in North Africa before the advent of Augustine. Appearances, however, only deceive. Chalcedon brought about a schism of minds and hearts but not of organisations. No " altar was set up against altar " [54] as happened in Carthage on the morrow of Caecilian's election as bishop in 312. It took eighty years for the Monophysites to reach a similar situation. To-day the ecumenical movement and the efforts of individuals such as Professor Georges Florovsky to whom this piece is dedicated, can only succeed as

---

[54] The phrase is from Optatus of Milevis, *De Schismate Donatistarum* (ed. C. Ziwsa, Vienna, 1894) 1. 19, " altare contra altare erectum est."

a result of painstaking attention to the origins of divisions in the Church as well as to the existing religious situation.   History can be a hard taskmaster.   In the study of the great religious traditions within Christianity there are few easy answers.

The University of Glasgow

XX

Old and New Rome in the Age of Justinian

For those who believe that 'a week is a long time in politics', Byzantine history is a wearisome business. For generations the same problems of theology and ecclesiastical precedence are argued between Rome and Constantinople without any apparent progress being made, while for centuries after the event Coptic and Syrian historians were treating the Council of Chalcedon with as much abuse as though it had only met the previous day. From the West, in his requisitory against Michael Cerularius, Cardinal Humbert did not fail to point out that six hundred years before, the see of Constantinople had abused its powers by consecrating Maximus as patriarch of Antioch without notifying the see of Rome.[1] No wonder Gibbon was exasperated with Byzantium, for such concern for the rights and wrongs of the remote past tended to ossify thought and action. Whether one turns to the art of war, to political thought or historical writing the evidence for the backward-looking tendency in Byzantium is clear. It must be accepted as one of the factors that led to the extinction of its empire and itself.

We begin near the origins of the great crisis in European history symbolised by the formal breach between Rome and Constantinople in 1054. The reign of Justinian (shared at first with his uncle, Justin, 519–27) 527–65 marks the climax of the first period of Byzantine history. Justinian and Theodora peer down the ages from the mosaic walls of San Vitale challenging romantic and historian alike, for their reign and their era had the attributes of greatness in struggle, endeavour and ultimate failure. In purely material terms the achievement of the emperor in the first ten years of his reign as sole ruler 527–37 was impressive. In a series of sweeping military successes, Africa, Sicily, Dalmatia and southern Italy, including Rome had been reconquered and reality given once more to the idea of the 'Roman world'. Old Rome and New Rome were united politically and ecclesiastically. The road taken by his predecessors Zeno and Anastasius in accepting the Acacian schism had been demonstrated to be false. Moreover, these reconquests had not been the results of mere greed for power. Given the western orientation of Justin and Justinian, it is difficult to see how the latter could have reacted differently to the situation presented by the progressive collapse, first of the Vandal kingdom in Africa and then of Ostrogothic power in Italy and the Balkans. Moreover, this was combined with powerful Catholic appeals, especially in Africa, for intervention, and it was the western Catholic 'lobby' in Constantinople that according to both Zacharias Rhetor and Procopius was mainly responsible for Justinian's decision to send Belisarius's expedition to Africa in 533.[2] Its amazing success, like other similar military situations, then developed a momentum of its own. Twenty years later Procopius could point out how pre-occupations in the West had denuded the Danube frontier for the benefit of the Huns and Slavs, but this was hindsight which few shared at the time. Most of Justinian's subjects probably shared the pride which John Lydus and Cosmas Indicopleustes voiced in the imperial restoration.[3]

The restoration of the Roman world, based on the Catholic religion as defined in the first four general councils and interpreted by the emperor himself as intermediary between God and the human race, is the keynote of the reign.[4] It is no accident that the first years should see at one and the same time a ruthless drive against pagan-ism and heresy of all sorts, and the accomplishment of a revision and codification of the law. There was to be one Church and one standard of Christian law for humanity. In fourteen months during 529–31 Tribonian revised the *Codex Theodosianus* and the subse-quent legislature extending over a century to produce the *Codex Justinianus*, as a single code of law for the whole empire, and by 534 had established in the *Digest* and *Institutes* a complete revision of the *ius antiquum*. As a visible climax of the endeavour of his age the vast, new and imposing church of Sancta Sophia rose slowly but steadily from its foundations, between 532 and 537. It won Pro-copius' praise as providing 'so brilliant a vision, that one might say that instead of being lit by the sun's rays, it enclosed the source of light within itself', and that 'when one entered it to pray, one looked upon it as a work of the wisdom of God rather than the handiwork of men'.[5] The example was taken up all over the By-zantine world. 'Église paléo-chrétienne' means more often than not a church with mosaics built in the first decade of Justinian's reign. Symbolic, too, of the direction of Justinian's thought, the dedications were more often to the *Theotokos* than to Christ Himself.[6]

In the spring of 532 Justinian had summoned six of the Mono-physite leaders to Constantinople to discuss their differences with an equal number of champions of Chalcedonian orthodoxy, in the hope that reconciliation could be achieved on the basis of an ac-knowledgement of the Council of Chalcedon of 451. The discus-sions, according to Zacharias Rhetor, lasted for rather over a year, but the results were inconclusive.[7] The Chalcedonians were able to point to inconsistencies in their opponents' case relating to the origins of the dissension. They were, however, unable to rebut the counter-claim that the doctrinal definition of the Council of Chalcedon represented a novelty, in the sense that it added to the Creed of Nicaea which all in the East agreed was the sole criterion of orthodoxy. Even the emperor's personal pleas had not prevented a breakdown. Justinian had been unable to unite his eastern dominions in a single faith before he turned his energies towards the reconquest of the former western provinces.

The Monophysites by now held the key to any restoration of religious, and ultimately political, unity between the east and west Roman worlds. The issues that divided them and the orthodox were already a century old and they concerned fundamentals of doctrine and ecclesiastical life. The Council of Chalcedon in 451 had resulted in major realignments. It had defined the Person of Christ as 'made known to us in two natures' inseparably united, rejecting by implication the view that Christ incarnate was formed 'out of two natures' one. In doing so, the bishops had indicated that they preferred a definition associated with Pope Leo, and set down by him in a letter (known as the *Tome* of Leo) to the erstwhile patriarch of Constantinople, Flavian, to that upheld by Cyril of Alexandria and his successor, Dioscorus.[8] There was, however, an element of ambiguity. The bishops at Chalcedon, apart from the papal legates, were all easterners. They had been willing to accept a definition which in fact meant little to them in order to rid themselves of the tyranny of Dioscorus, but they had no intention of abandoning the theology of Cyril. The *Tome* of Leo had been accepted even with enthusiasm because it could be argued that 'it agreed with Cyril'. Faced with the alternatives 'Leo or Dioscorus' by lay commissioners who presided over the council, the bishops had opted for Leo, but it was always Cyril's doctrine that was regarded as the yardstick against which all else had to be measured. Yet only by tearing fragments of certain of Cyril's letters from their context could his doctrine be made to accord even verbally with that of Leo. This had no doubt been realised, for many bishops at the council explicitly refused to accept the doctrinal definition as a Symbol of Faith, to be placed on the same level of importance as the Creeds of Nicaea and Constantinople and the decisions of the first Council of Ephesus in 431.[9] It was a statement of lesser value, something to be employed in baptismal interrogations and as a shield against the twin heresies of Eutyches and Nestorius. For the West and Pope Leo, however, the Definition represented a binding document beyond all discussion and negotiation,[10] and here East and West were to part company.

The dangers implicit in this divergence of interpretation became clear immediately, for Leo treated all those who had reservations over the Definition as heretics. At this time the 'hesitants' or *Dia-koinomenoi*, as they came to be called, comprised a large proportion of the bishops throughout the Byzantine world as well as the majority of the ordinary provincials, represented by the monks, who were later to form the backbone of the Monophysite movement. In addition to the doctrinal issue, Chalcedon had focussed attention on the ecclesiastical standing of the capital, Constantinople, or as it was more usually known, 'New Rome', and this also was to be a lasting bone of contention.

At the end of the council, partly to protect the capital from aggression on the part of Alexandria but equally as a general tidying up of existing practice, it was agreed that New Rome should enjoy ecclesiastical privileges next in rank to Old Rome. In the view both of the bishops and the lay commissioners, Rome was one, and it was unthinkable that New Rome should not enjoy the same dignities and honours as her venerable sister on the Tiber. Moreover, the canon said no more than what the Fathers had agreed at the Council of Constantinople, and its decision corresponded to reality. For the previous half-century Constantinople had been the court of appeal to which aggrieved clerics from all over the east had brought their cases, while the patriarch had similarly been represented at important hearings, such as that of Ibas, metropolitan of Edessa, tried at Berytus in 448 for heresy and peculation in the eastern provinces. Old Rome, however, could still assert the primacy congruent with its status as elder partner. This decision, known as the 28th canon, while acceptable to the eastern bishops aroused the strongest opposition in Rome, on the grounds that Constantinople had no canonical standing.[11] It was not an apostolic see and at the time of Nicaea when the precedence of the major bishoprics had been laid down, it was only a suffragan bishopric of the metropolitan see of Thrace, namely Heraclea. Leo refused to ratify the decision of the council and for the next six hundred years this grievance against Constantinople was never far from the minds of the popes.

Behind the matter of ecclesiastical precedence lay, however, a far deeper divergence of view concerning the role of the state, and the emperor as its representative, in the life of the Church. The Council of Chalcedon had been summoned by the emperor Marcian. He and his consort Pulcheria had been present at some of the more crucial of its deliberations. Through the lay commissioners who presided, he had been responsible for the terminology of the *Tome* of Leo being accepted in the Definition of Faith, and once he had given his views there was nothing left for the bishops but to applaud the 'new David' and 'new Constantine' and to obey.[12] Marcian was a professional soldier with none of the theological training of his predecessor Theodosius 11, or of Justinian, but he accepted automatically the theological view of kingship derived from Constantine. To him, as to his successors, his 'common oversight' over his realm involved concern for both the religious and material welfare of his people. He would have had little hesitation in agreeing with Theodosius 11 that 'the stability of the state depends on the religion by which we honour God', though he would have disagreed with him regarding his definition of right religion.[13] In any event, however, the initiative in matters of religion lay in his hands, and if any ecclesiastic disobeyed his edicts, then resignation and despatch into exile was all that he could hope for. It was in this tradition that Justinian built. His caesaro-papism was simply an explicit continuation of the ideas of Constantine and Constantius 11.

This view of the emperor's prerogatives also rested on a long tradition. Ultimately, it could be traced back to the ideal of the 'godly monarchy' propounded by Philo in the time of Augustus, and elaborated by generations of Greek Christian apologists from Melito of Sardis to Eusebius. The emperor was not only 'the friend of God', but also the reflection of the Divine Word, the ruler of the universe, the herald of God's command throughout the inhabited world, and hence the supreme authority in matters religious as well as political.[14] In the West, however, no such ideas were accepted. The Church remained a gathered community of the elect whether in suffering as under the pagan emperors, or in triumph as under Constantine and his successors, but however much the Church might benefit by the favour of the state, its goal remained distinct. The emperor, far from being arbiter over its affairs, was a layman, within the Church and not above it, and as an indication that this was no idle pretence Ambrose of Milan had humbled even Theodosius 1. 'Render unto Caesar . . .' was the touchstone of western ecclesiastical philosophy towards the Roman Empire. If the government of the world could be represented by the metaphor of the 'two swords', that wielded by the Church was the more effective, and that of the state could be better described as an executioner's axe.[15] These views were fully accepted by the popes. Though Leo accepted the emperor's right to summon a Church council, his views of the emperor's function in ecclesiastical affairs were well expressed in a letter to Marcian, namely that he must repress the disorders that emerged and in particular use his executive power against all heretics.[16] This was to be the role reserved for Justin and Justinian by Hormisdas.

If one looks back at the evidence, it would seem almost incredible that eastern and western Christendom remained in any degree united for as long as they did. The secret was that pope and emperor believed in the oneness of Christendom represented by Rome, whether symbolised by Old Rome or New Rome. The issue was where the power lay, in the hands of the descendant of the Fisherman, or in those of the descendants of Constantine. For the question to become a practical one required, however, an emperor at New Rome to be both determined and able to maintain his rule in both halves of the empire. Marcian, or rather, Pulcheria, did attempt this. His successor Leo 1 began as though he did, but gradually changed course, especially after the failure of the attempt in 468 to reconquer Vandal Africa. Zeno and Anastasius clearly saw the future of the empire as lying with the eastern provinces. It was Justin and Justinian who tried to turn back the tide and revert to the policies of Marcian.

Their accession on the death of Anastasius in July 518 found the religious differences between East and West already developed and hardened. The effective ending of the Roman empire in the West in 476 as well as the common ties of religion, culture and trade that bound the eastern provinces to Constantinople had concentrated the attention of the emperor and his advisers on the religious problems of the East. Though opposition to Chalcedon was strongest in Egypt, where the fall of Dioscorus and the slight on Cyril's Christology were never forgiven, it was lively in all the eastern provinces, but particularly wherever the monks were in evidence, for example in east Syria and Pamphylia.[17] There, congregations had turned on their bishops returning from Chalcedon with bitter reproaches of having betrayed the true doctrine.[18] Though ultimately the One-Nature Christology was to emerge as the religion of clearly defined territories, including most of Syriac-speaking Syria and Coptic Egypt and become the national religion of Armenia, Nubia and Ethiopia, it would be a great mistake to think of it originally as a movement of independence, or even one whose leaders thought in terms of provincial or regional particularism. An Egyptian in the fifth and sixth century regarded himself as a 'citizen of Jerusalem', that is of the capital of the whole 'race of Christians' and not as a Copt. His opposition to Chalcedon was not an eastern form of Donatism. Centuries after the ending of Byzantine rule in Syria, the Monophysite historian, the patriarch Michael of Antioch, was criticising Marcian because Chalcedon divided the empire in secular and religious matters alike and thereby contributed to its ruin.[19] One-Nature Christology implied the analogy of one Christendom and one empire, and the main objective of the successors of Dioscorus at Alexandria, Timothy the Cat, and Peter Mongus, had been not separation of Egypt from the rest of the empire but to secure the rejection of Chalcedon by the emperor himself. Their aim like that of Cyril and Dioscorus had been to vindicate the primacy of Alexandria as the 'city of the orthodox'.

In the twenty months' successful usurpation of Basiliscus, 475–6 the Alexandrians had nearly achieved their goal, for the Encyclical that Basiliscus promulgated had done just this, and upheld the doctrines of Cyril and the Egyptian Church as contained in Cyril's *Twelve Anathemas*. They failed, however, because Acacius, the patriarch of Constantinople, had realised that the outright rejection of Chalcedon would spell the end of the primatial jurisdiction of his own see. The alliance of primate, pillar-saints and populace of Constantinople, backed on this occasion by the papacy, had proved too much for Basiliscus and Timothy. The emperor Zeno after his return from exile in August 476 had solemnly reconfirmed Chalcedon and the rights of the see of Constantinople (17 Dec.) [20].

The matter, however, could not be left there. Acacius saw that the eastern provinces would not accept the *Tome* of Leo and Chalcedon as the basis of their religion, and Zeno himself came from a province, Isauria, where opinion was strongly anti-Chalcedonian. Above all, he was anxious not to go on his travels again. Using a formula that had originally been suggested by Martyrius, patriarch of Jerusalem, in 478, Acacius drafted a letter to the Church in Egypt setting out a compromise.[21] The *Henotikon* of Zeno, as it came to be called, of 28 July 482 did everything but condemn Leo and Chalcedon outright. It laid down as the basis of the faith of the empire the first three oecumenical councils together with Cyril's *Twelve Anathemas*. It proclaimed Jesus Christ as consubstantial with God and man, that he was in nature 'one and not two', and it condemned 'every person who has thought or thinks anything else either now or at any time, either in Chalcedon or in any synod whatsoever'. The effect of this was to demote Chalcedon to the level of a local and somewhat suspect synod whose condemnation both of Eutyches and Nestorius could, however, be accepted. It restored communion between the patriarchs of Alexandria and Constantinople on the latter's terms. It accepted by implication the emperor's right of pronouncing on doctrinal matters, and it had nothing to say to Rome or to western theology whatsoever.[22]

The *Henotikon* remained the official standpoint of the empire through the rest of the reign of Zeno and that of his successor Anastasius. Both these emperors regarded the eastern provinces as of greater moment than the West, including Italy, where both were prepared to accept a shadowy suzerainty first over Odoaker, and then Theodoric. Ecclesiastically the quasi-harmony of the four eastern patriarchates was more important than communion with Rome. Rome for its part had reacted with extreme anger against the *Henotikon*, hostility to its doctrinal provisions being reinforced by a belief in the personal duplicity of Acacius. In July 484 a

Roman synod solemnly excommunicated Acacius and all who were in communion with him. An ally of Rome in the person of one of the Sleepless Monks pinned the sentence to the pallium of Acacius as he was celebrating the eucharist in Sancta Sophia. For the next thirty-five years Rome and the eastern Roman provinces were not in communion with each other.

In the East, however, the *Henotikon* was regarded as a compromise.[23] On the one hand, there began to develop a school of theologians, predecessors of Leontius of Byzantium, who were prepared to accept Chalcedon, provided always that its definition of faith could be reconciled with the theology of Cyril.[24] On the other, the anti-Chalcedonians found two brilliant leaders in the person of Severus (patriarch of Antioch, 512–18) and Philoxenus of Maboug (Hierapolis). These men show how opposition to the council attracted individuals of entirely different background, outlook and race. Severus was the son of a rich landowning family in Pisidia in Asia Minor, whose grandfather had been at Ephesus in 431. He was a cosmopolitan, equally at home in the capital, Antioch or Alexandria, who admired the philosophy of Libanius almost as much as the Trinitarian theology of the Cappodocians, and accepted Cyril as providing in a manner of genius the only Christology compatible with the Creed of Nicaea and its development by the Cappodocian Fathers. His world was the world of Hellenistic philosophical theology with, as he says, every word of Cyril 'canonical'.[25]

Philoxenus, on the other hand, was a Persian by origin, a Syriac-speaker and writer, whose major theological contribution was a Syriac translation of the Bible.[26] He was a man of the people, harsh, uncompromising and turbulent, but who spoke for the monks of the province of Euphratesia, a vital province for the defence of the south-western approaches of Armenia on whose loyalty depended to a large extent the security of the whole of Rome's eastern frontier. No emperor could afford to ignore the opinion of the representatives of popular Christianity there, namely the monks.

Between them Severus and Philoxenus had brought about a revolution in the religious situation in the East in the first twenty years of the sixth century. The one by his great dialectical skill, and his insistence on 'accuracy' in doctrinal belief, meaning the exclusion of all thought of the Incarnate Christ existing in Two Natures, had gradually transformed the *Henotikon* from being a document of compromise to a means by which Chalcedon could be rejected, without calling into question the jurisdictional rights of Constantinople. The other, by his ability as an agitator, united the monks of Syria against the patriarch Flavian, himself loyal to the *Henotikon*, to drive him from office in November 512 and make way for Severus to become patriarch of Antioch. The emperor Anastasius was personally opposed to Chalcedon and in 510 he had denounced the council in a document known as the *Typos* drafted by Severus while in the capital. Next year, again at Severus's prompting, he had deposed the patriarch of Constantinople, Macedonius, for alleged 'Nestorianism', and had permitted the introduction of an addition to the Doxology, 'Holy God, Holy and mighty, holy and immortal have mercy upon us', the words 'who was crucified for us', which interpreted in the One-Nature sense meant that Christ as God suffered and died on the Cross.[27] Thus in 511 the east Roman world was to all intents and purposes Monophysite.

Anastasius had, however, forgotten that even the empire over which he ruled contained Latin-speaking provinces, and in proportion as the patriarchate of Antioch, comprising Syria and southern Asia Minor, swung towards Monophysitism, the Balkan provinces of Illyricum turned towards Rome. There the Acacian schism had brought three main developments, first, a hardening of doctrinal thinking towards the presentation of a Two-Nature Christology, in which the theology of Cyril played no part, secondly, the rejection of any participation in ecclesiastical affairs by the emperor, and thirdly a contempt for the Byzantine clergy as 'heretical Greeks', and above all for Acacius and his successors. All these tendencies were blatantly demonstrated in the correspondence between Pope Gelasius (492–6) and Anastasius, and the efforts by him and successive patriarchs of Constantinople to end the schism on terms which would not damn the memory of Acacius were rebuffed with contempt.[28]

In the final period of Anastasius's reign, the situation between East and West both in its religious and political aspects had become hopelessly confused. The middle way of the *Henotikon* had visibly failed to reconcile the conflicting parties. Alexandria and Antioch were Monophysite, while Constantinpole and Jerusalem were tending once more to accept the canonical status of Chalcedon. The Illyrian provinces and, significantly, the Greek cities of Syria Secunda had turned to Rome, and Roman and Chalcedonian orthodoxy was being forced on the reluctant court by the rebellion of the *Comes foederatorum*, Vitalian the Goth. This was the legacy to which Justin and Justinian succeeded on 9 July 518.

To all outward appearances the policy of the new rulers was a complete reversal of the old. Within a week of Anastasius's death, the crowd in Sancta Sophia were demanding the proclamation of the Council of Chalcedon, within a month a synod at Jerusalem had restored the council to the diptychs, on 7 September Justin and Justinian wrote to Pope Hormisdas informing him of their intention of restoring communion between Old and New Rome, and on 16 September Severus fled his patriarchal see of Antioch, never to return. Early in the new year, after some months of negotiation, the papal legates were making a triumphant progress through Illyricum to end the Acacian schism on their terms.[29] The scene on 28 March 519 when the patriarch Timothy signed the papal *libellus* and accepted the papal condemnation not only of Acacius, Timothy the Cat and Peter Mongus, but of his three predecessors, including the saintly Macedonius, and the emperors Zeno and Anastasius to boot, has been regarded as a great catastrophe for the Church in the East.[30] It certainly coloured the whole of the ecclesiastical policy of Justin and Justinian, and had a permanent effect on the relationship between the capital and the Monophysites in Syria and Egypt. A closer look, however, at what happened suggests that the papal triumph may be overstressed.

The initiative for the ending of the Acacian schism came from the emperor himself.[31] Justin's aim had been simply the restoration of unity between the two Romes, and in this he had been supported by his patriarch. The latter wrote to Pope Hormisdas on 28 March 'I accept that the two most holy Romes, that is to say, your Old Rome and our New Rome are one, and I admit that that see of St Peter and this see of the Imperial City are one'. He granted, as his predecessors had, precedence to Old Rome, and accepted the condemnation of Acacius and his successors, but the man who was the first patriarch of Constantinople to use the title 'ecumenical patriarch' shows no sign of humility or humiliation.[32] He wrote to Hormisdas as a colleague with whom he was glad to be in communion once more. The all-important 28th canon of Chalcedon had not been renounced. The view of the emperor and his nephew was still more significant. On 7 September 518 in the letter informing the pope of his intention to end the schism Justinian had written to Hormisdas telling him to come to Constantinople without delay; it was an order just as Vigilius was to be ordered a generation later.[33] Old Rome and its patriarch were to be brought once more into the orbit of the empire as a whole. The emperors had timed the move perfectly. People, as Procopius of Caesarea said, were tired with arguments about 'senseless doctrines', and if Christ was composed of Godhead and manhood as all agreed, was this not 'two natures'?[34] What was the difference between the essential union of the two making One, and the inseparable union of the two, making Two? Might not, in any event, Chalcedon be accepted as a disciplinary council condemning Eutyches and Nestorius? People were as bored with Severus and his 'accuracy' as they were with Philoxenus and his fighting monks.

The policy of Justin and Justinian was to ensure the religious unity of the Roman world under their aegis. The basic principle of their government was enunciated by Justinian in Novel 7, 'The priestly power and royal power are not widely separated, and sacred property is not far removed from that which all mankind hold in common, or from that which is owned by the state, because the churches are endowed with all their material resources and their status by the munificence of royal power . . .' In so many words this meant that Church and state were complementary aspects of one imperial rule; there might be *regnum* and *sacerdotium*, but no Two Swords. Moreover, if the exercise of right religion was necessary for the prosperity of the empire and its people, the decision of what that right religion was, and its enforcement, lay with the emperor. In this Justinian followed in the footsteps of Constantine, Theodosius I and II, Marcian, Zeno and Anastasius. The only difference with his two predecessors was that his concept of Roman unity entailed the acceptance of four oecumenical councils and not three; but the four were to be accepted in their totality including those canons that upheld the dignity of the see of Constantinople.

Very soon Justinian realised, like Zeno and Anastasius before him, that no unity could be built between East and West on the *Tome* of Leo. To the great majority of the Christian provincials this represented a vindication of Nestorius's 'two Christs', one before and one after incarnation, only one of whom was worthy of worship. If the *Henotikon* was to be abrogated it must be replaced by something very similar, and Justinian found his answer in the Theopaschite idea.

As with the preparation of the *Henotikon*, we find the patriarchate of Jerusalem playing a considerable role in preparing the Theopaschite formula.[35] Jerusalem was in a peculiar situation, the Holy Places being a centre of international pilgrimage, but with Christians only a bare majority of the total population, and the patriarchate ultimately dependent on the goodwill and power of the capital. These factors outweighed any leanings the monks may have had towards their Egyptian and Syrian counterparts, but though Chalcedonian in loyalty, the Palestinians were also Cyrillian in their theology and ready bridge-builders between the Monophysite and Chalcedonian positions. So, when the Scythian monks of the capital proposed a Christology which combined the Chalcedonian formula with the affirmation 'one of the Trinity suffered in the flesh' they could count on immediate support, including that of Justinian himself. This was Monophysite in its expression of piety, but lacked the associations of 'who was crucified for us'. The *Tome* plus Cyril was to become the orthodoxy of Justinian's age.

The papal legates, however, had come to the capital with no

wish to compromise with anyone; their loyalty was to the *Tome*, and to the *Tome* alone. If Justinian aimed at restoring unity between Old and New Rome, the pope was concerned only with the restoration of Petrine authority. That, and not the will of the emperor, represented orthodoxy. For Hormisdas as for Leo and Gelasius before him, the emperor was a son of the Church whose particular duty was to execute the Church's orders against heretics and schismatics.[36]

Between 519 and 521 first the legates and then Hormisdas himself insisted on the forceful repression of anti-Chalcedonian opinion in the East as the price of the restoration of communion. Though they found themselves politely thwarted in the capital, in the provinces no less than 55 bishops were deposed and, what was more fateful, there was a wholesale expulsion of Syrian monks from their monasteries. This act more than any other sowed the seed for the establishment of a Monophysite hierarchy in rivalry to that of Chalcedonian orthodoxy.

It is just possible that but for the 'ten years of exile' to which the monks and Monophysite clergy were subjected between 521 and 531, Justinian's theology might have succeeded at least as well as the *Henotikon*. Hormisdas (d.523) had more pliable successors and John 11 accepted it; in the West, the Severan Monophysites were regarded as 'Theopaschites' and Severus himself in exile, ageing and tormented by the growing division among his followers, between the Julianists and himself, might in time have accepted. The conferences with the orthodox leaders in 532 had shaken some of their arguments against Chalcedon, and their self-confidence.[37] For Justinian too, these four councils were no longer associated with the *Tome* of Leo but with the doctrine expounded in the patriarch Proclus' *Tome* to the Armenians of 435, which all parties in the East accepted as orthodox. If there was ever a chance of Justinian reconciling East and West in one religious and political realm under his own sway it was on the eve of Belisarius's expedition to Vandal Africa in 533.

The Acacian schism, however, had left too strong a legacy. Severus and his colleagues were still loyal to the person of the emperor, despite years of exile and hardship. Striking evidence for this may be seen in the letter which they sent to Justinian in the spring of 532 outlining once more their objections to Chalcedon while accepting an invitation to a conference in the capital. They prayed daily for the emperor's majesty, they declared, 'and for their own sins; and now they cried blessings of every sort on his name and on that of the empress for the destruction of all rebellion' – the reference was to the Nika riot – before expounding their faith.[38] Even so, trust was ebbing away. Before he himself left for the capital in the winter of 534–5 Severus let it be known that he had no real confidence in the outcome of any discussions there. 'Don't be deceived. In the lifetime of these emperors no means of peace will be found, but so that I do not appear to hinder or oppose it I will go through with heartsearchings. I will return without anything being accomplished'.[39] Meantime, he had authorised the first steps towards the creation of an independent Monophysite hierarchy through the ordination of presbyters by his lieutenant John of Tella.

Justinian for his part could not afford a complete break with Severus. The latter's supporters dominated not only Egypt, but the vital north-east frontier area with Persia, and the striking success of the first Monophysite ordinations, for which multitudes of candidates presented themselves, could not be denied. 'Hundreds of people' came to John of Tella 'like a flooded river that has burst its banks.'[40] This had contributed to the emperor's resolve to call the conference of 532. There was, too, the personality of Theodora. Whatever her origin and early life she was a powerful personality and a woman of the people, who shared the basic Monophysitism of the popular faith and she interpreted this accurately in her career as empress. Already in 523 she had interceded on behalf of the deposed bishop of Amida, and until her death in 548 she threw all her considerable influence on the Monophysite side. She was responsible for two events which ensured the perpetuation of the Monophysite movement. First, she ensured the election of the deacon Theodosius to the see of Alexandria after the death of Timothy IV in February 535, and secondly by giving him asylum in the palace of Hormisdas in the capital she enabled him to direct the entire Monophysite movement, including its missions and the consecration of a new hierarchy, for thirty years.[41] Justinian could never afford to ignore its existence.

Whatever may have been the emperor's own leanings, and his gradual move towards the Aphthartodocetism of the Julianist Monophysites suggests that at heart he may always have agreed with Severus's theology, politically there was no uncertainty. In the crisis caused by the patriarch Anthimus's conversion to Monophysitism in 535, as well as in the affair of the Origenist monks, and later in the Three Chapters controversy he never moved from the position that the religion of the empire must be based on the acceptance of the four councils and the union of the five patriarchates. He personally ordered the condemnation of Anthimus by the Home synod as a heretic. From 536 onwards, however, he was no more able to win the acceptance of the West to his ideas than he had been the Monophysites. Once again, the problems were those of the traditional theological positions combined with a lack of personal confidence between the principals.

Ostensibly, he could not have had a more favourable combination of political situations and personalities. Rome was under his direct authority, there was now a papal *apocrisarius* in the capital so that effective diplomatic contact could be maintained. In Vigilius, who became pope in December 537, he had an ecclesiastic who owed his position to his subservience to the emperor and Belisarius. Yet whatever the personal equation it was impossible for Old and New Rome to deviate one iota from previously fixed positions. Vigilius's pathetic intrigue in 538 in which he told Theodora that, 'we do not confess two natures in Christ, but that Christ was from two natures, one Son, one Christ and One Lord', was speedily withdrawn to limbo,[42] and by 547 Menas of New Rome and Vigilius were excommunicating each other.[43] Paradoxically, Theodora's last recorded public act before she died was to reconcile the warring prelates.

A similar pattern underlay the events surrounding the ten-year controversy (543–53) leading to the condemnation of the Three Chapters. The question was essentially one that affected the eastern patriarchates alone, how far could the Two-nature Christology defined by Chalcedon be watered down without denouncing Chalcedon itself, in order eventually to reconcile the Monophysites and the Origenist monks in Palestine. The latter, though loyal to Chalcedon by interest and emotion, were strongly opposed to the Two-nature Christology represented by the Antiochene theologians Theodore of Mopsuestia and Ibas of Edessa. The man behind the moves that culminated in the Fifth General Council and Vigilius's humiliation was Theodore Askidas, the *éminence grise* of the second half of Justinian's reign, who had ousted the papal representative at court at the moment when the latter looked like being able to regain for Rome its traditional influence in Alexandria.[44]

Vigilius himself seems to have had no great qualms about falling in with the emperor's views and condemning the Three Chapters. The sequel to the *Judicatum* of 548 showed, however, that theological traditions and language and cultural boundaries were stronger than the personal inclinations of pope and emperor. The long-term political effects of Justinian's military successes fifteen years before were becoming clearer. The restored Catholic Church in Africa felt little gratitude to Justinian, though many of its bishops may have owed their freedom and even their lives to the emperor's generals.[45] Looking back, it becomes clear how the African theology of Grace and the Augustinian doctrine of the Trinity which emphasised the factor of will and love as the union between the Persons of the Trinity and man's relation to God, would tend naturally towards the theology of Antioch and would not easily have reconciled itself to its outright condemnation. In addition, the Africans retained to a surprising degree the sense of independence and separation of Church-State relations that had characterised their outlook throughout the fourth century. After its restoration in 535 the Church had simply re-started where it left off with the onset of the Vandals a century before. In the archdeacon Liberatus, and Bishop Facundus of Hermiane it combined the theology of Theodore and Nestorius with the anti-imperialism of Donatus of Carthage. The Latin-speaking Illyrians proved trusty allies. In 550 their combined pressure forced Vigilius to withdraw the *Judicatum*. Three years later, though willing to attend the Fifth General Council, they disputed its findings hotly. Liberatus's *Breviarium* and Facundus's *Pro defensione trium Capitulorum* demonstrate western theological and political independence of the East, even at the apparently triumphant climax of Justinian's reign : in 553 not only Italy, but one third of Spain became his.

The Fifth General Council resulted, in effect, in the emergence of three different theologies in Christendom. The West, consolidated round the papacy, accepted Chalcedon and the *Tome* of Leo as the sole norm of orthodoxy : Vigilius was from time to time compelled to imitate at least the language of Leo. At Constantinople, however, it was Chalcedon, but craftily interpreted by Leontius and others so as to rid it of reliance on the *Tome* of Leo and replace this with the whole panoply of Cyrillian Christology. In Egypt and Syria, the latter only was accepted, and Chalcedon, because it also accepted the *Tome*, was instinctively rejected.

This triangle of incompatible interest was to persist in one form or another so long as the Byzantine empire existed. It is doubtful whether anything but total capitulation by one side or the other would have availed for a settlement. In 519 Justin and Justinian had made what appeared to them to be a supreme effort to achieve reunion with Old Rome and its patriarch, only to find that Hormisdas's terms were too steep even for them, while the 'Nestorianism' of the *Tome* of Leo and its representatives was intolerable to the Greek Christian populace. In its turn, the attempt to placate the papacy by persecuting the Monophysite monks led directly to the establishment of a rival Monophysite hierarchy whose existence then made reconciliation among eastern Christians impossible. Strong though Justinian's position was, and ably as he might manœuvre, he could never reconcile the conflicting interests of Constantinople, Rome and Alexandria. Chalcedon proved the stumbling block, and after Justinian had passed from the scene, there were never again men or conditions capable of removing it.

26   *Old and New Rome in the Age of Justinian*

NOTES

1   See Leo, *Ep.* 119.3, *PL* 54, and A. Michel, 'Die römische
     Angriffe auf Cerullarios wegen Antiocheia 1053/1054',
     BZ XLIV (1951) pp. 419–27.
2   Zacharias Rhetor, *HE*, ed. and tr. E. W. Brooks, *CSCO*,
     Scriptores Syri, Series III, VI (Louvain 1919–24) IX.17 and
     Procopius, *Wars*, III.10.19.
3   John Lydus, *De Magistratibus* III.39, ed. R. Wuensch, pp.
     126–7, and Cosmas Indicopleustes, *The Christian Topography*,
     ed. E. O. Windstedt (Cambridge 1909) p. 80. See W. E. Kaegi,
     Byzantium and the Decline of Rome (Princeton 1968) p. 143.
4   The best account of Justinian's religious policy is still that of
     E. Schwartz, 'Zur Kirchenpolitik Justinians', *Sitzber.
     Bayerisch. Akad. der Wiss.*, phil.-hist. Abt. (1940) pp. 32–81;
     also Ch. Diehl, *Justinien* (Paris 1901) ch. vii and B. Rubin, *Das
     Zeitalter Justinians* (Berlin 1960).
5   Procopius, *De Aedificiis*, 1.1. Compare Evagrius, *HE*, IV.3,
     ed. Bidez/Parmentier (London 1898).
6   See G. H. Armstrong, 'Fifth and Sixth Century Church-
     building in the Holy Land', *Greek Orthodox Theological Re-
     view*, XIV (1969) pp. 17–30, at p. 23. A useful survey also, of
     the veritable explosion of church-building in Justinian's
     reign and the reasons for it.
7   Zacharias Rhetor, *HE*, IX.15. For an account of one of the
     major confrontations written from a Chalcedonian stand-
     point, see the letter written by Innocentius of Maronia to
     Thomas, a presbyter in the Church of Thessalonica, *ACO*,
     IV, 2, pp. 169–84.
8   See R. V. Sellers, *The Council of Chalcedon* (London 1953)
     pp. 103ff.
9   At Chalcedon the bishops protested against any suggestion
     that they were being called upon to draw up an expression
     of the faith, see Mansi, VI, col. 953. In 457 Epiphanius,
     bishop of Perga, described the Definition as 'veluti scutum
     eam contra haereticos opponentes et non mathema fidei
     existentem', Codex Encyclius, *ACO*, II.5, p. 59.
10   For instance, in *Ep.* 145 of 11 July 457 to the emperor Leo I,
     'quia in illo concilio per sanctum spiritum congregato tam
     plenis et perfectis definitionibus cuncta firmata sunt, ut nihil
     ei regulae quae ex divina inspiratione prolata est, aut addi
     possit aut minui.'
11   Leo, *Epp.* 104, 105, 106 and 114–16. See, T. O. Martin, 'The
     Twenty-eighth Canon of Chalcedon, a background note,'
     Das Konzil von Chalkedon, ed. Grillmeier/Bacht (Würzburg
     1953), II, pp. 433–58, and E. Schwartz, 'Der sechste
     nicaëmschen Kanon auf der Synode von Chalkedon,' *Sitzber.
     Berliner Akad. der Wissenschaften* (1930) pp. 611–40.
12   Mansi, VII, col. 173; compare Zacharias Rhetor, *HE*, III.1.
13   Theodosius to the Council of Ephesus I, Mansi, IV, col.
     1112. Compare Zeno's statement of his motive in writing
     the *Henotikon* to the bishops and monks of Egypt in 482
     'cum sic igitur immaculata fides et nos et Romanam servet
     rempublicam.' Cited by Liberatus, *Breviarium*, XVII, *ACO*, II.5.
14   See E. Peterson's classic essay, *Der Monotheismus als politisches*

Problem (Leipzig 1935) and N.H.Baynes, 'Eusebius and the Christian Empire', *Mélanges Bidez*, 11 (1934) pp.13ff.

15 See S.L.Greenslade's summary of the western position in *Church and State from Constantine to Theodosius* (London 1954) pp.45ff.

16 Leo, *Ep.* 106.

17 For Pamphylia as Monophysite, see John of Ephesus, *HE*, ed. E.W.Brooks, *CSCO*, CV–CVI, *Script. Syri*, Ser.III, 3 (Louvain 1935–6) v, 6 and Severus of Antioch, *Select Letters*, ed. E.W.Brooks (London 1902) IV.3.

18 See the instances catalogued by John Rufus *circa* 500 under the title of *Plerophoria*, Ed. F.Nau, *PO*, VIII.

19 *Chronicon*, ed. J.B.Chabot (Paris 1901) 11, p. 122.

20 *Codex Justinianus*, 1.2.16. The best account of this period remains E.Schwartz, 'P[ublizistische] S[ammlungen zum Acacianischen Schisma]', *Abhandlungen der Bayerischen Akad. der Wiss.*, phil-hist. Kl. (1934) pp.170.

21 For this episode see, Zacharias, *HE*, v.6.

22 Complete text published by E.Schwartz, 'Codex Vaticanus, graecus 1431, Eine antichalkedonische Sammlung aus der Zeit Kaiser Zenos', *Abhandlungen Bayerisch. Akad. der Wiss.*, XXXII, Abhang VI (München 1927) pp.52ff. Eng. tr. in P.R.Coleman-Norton, *Roman State and Christian Church* (London 1966) III, pp.924–33.

23 Severus of Antioch, *Select Letters*. p.1. For the events see E.Schwartz, *PS* pp.202–10, and L.Duchesne, *The Early History of the Church*, 111, pp.346–59.

24 See Ch.Moeller, 'Un représentant de la christologie néo-chalcédonienne au début du VIe siècle en Orient, Nephalius d'Alexandrie,' *RHE*, XL, (1944/45) pp.110ff. and 'Le Chalcédonisme et le néo-chalcédonisme,' in Grillmeier/Bacht, *Chalkedon*, 1, pp.637–720.

25 *Select Letters* 1.9. See the *Life* of Severus by Zacharias Scholasticus, his contemporary, ed. H.Kugener, *PO* 11, and for his doctrine the studies of J.Lebon, 'La Christologie du monophysisme syrien,' in Grillmeier/Bacht, *Chalkedon* I, pp.425–580.

26 Compare Michael the Syrian, *Chronicon* IX.9 '[Philoxenus] was versed in everything contained in our writings and in our language.'

27 For this period see E.Honigmann, 'Évêques et évêchés monophysites d'Asie antérieure au VIe siècle,' *CSCO*, CXXVII, and E.Schwartz, *PS* pp.242–3 (on the addition to the Trishagion).

28 See in particular, Gelasius's *Epp.* 3, 10 and 12, ed. A.Thiel, *Epistolae romanorum pontificium genuinae* (Braunsberg 1868) and E.Caspar, *Geschichte des Papstums* (Tübingen 1933) 11, pp.65ff.

29 For the narrative of events, see [A.] Vasiliev, [*Justin the First*] (Dumbarton Oaks 1954) pp.136–60.

30 *Coll[ectio] Avell[ana]*, *Ep.* 216, ed. O. Guenther, *CSEL* XXXV and CCXXIII. For discussion, see Vasiliev, pp.174–8.

31 See for instance, *Coll. Avell. Ep.* 161, p.612, 'adunationem sanctissimis ecclesiis sapientissime comparavit (Iustinus).' Compare ibid. *Ep.* 147 (Justinian to Pope Hormisdas).

32   *Coll. Avell., Ep.* 159.

33   Ibid. *Ep.* 147.

34   Procopius, *Anecdota*, XI, 25.

35   On the role of the Palestinians in winning the court's accep-
      tance of the Theopaschite formula, see Philoxenus, *Letter
      to the Monks of Senoun*, ed. A. Halleux (1963) pp. 62, 66. For the
      Theopaschites, see L. Duchesne, *L'Eglise au VIᵉ siècle* (Paris
      1924) pp. 59–69, and the documentation, *ACO*, II.4, pp. 3ff.

36   Hormisdas to Justin, *Coll. Avell., Ep.* 168.3, of 9 July 519,
      'Haec prima sunt vestri fundamina principatus, deum placasse
      iustitia et asciusse vobis excellentissimae maiestatis auxilia,
      dum adversarios eius velut proprios comprimitis inimicos.'
      Compare ibid. *Ep.* 238 of 26 March 521.

37   One of their leaders, Philoxenus of Doliche in Syria, a friend
      of Severus, went over to the Chalcedonian side after the
      conferences. This, however, was to be cancelled out in 536 by
      the adhesion of Anthimus of Trebizond, who had been on the
      Orthodox side, to the Monophysite cause.

38   Zacharias, *HE*, IX.15.

39   Severus, recorded by John of Ephesus, *Lives of Five Patriarchs*,
      ed. E. W. Brooks, *PO*, XVIII, p. 687.

40   John of Ephesus, *Lives of Eastern Saints, PO*, XVIII, p. 518.

41   John of Ephesus describes her as 'desirous of furthering
      everything that would assist the opponents of the synod of
      Chalcedon,' and states that she was responsible for the con-
      secration of James Bar'adai and Theodore as bishops in 542,
      Life of James and Theodore, ed. E. W. Brooks, *PO*, XIX, p. 154.

42   The text of two letters allegedly written by Vigilius 538–40
      are preserved in Victor Tonnunnensis (*Chron.* ad ann. 542)
      and Liberatus, *Breviarium* XXII. Discussed by E. Schwartz,
      Zur Kirchenpolitik Justinians, p. 58. For Vigilius's confession
      of orthodoxy, see *Coll. Avell., Ep.* 92 of September 540 to
      Justinian, and *Ep.* 93 to Menas of Constantinople.

43   Theophanes, *Chron.*, A.M. 6039 (Bonn ed.) pp. 349–50.

44   On Askidas's motives, see Liberatus, *Breviarium*, XXIV, and on
      his influence over Justinian, see Evagrius, IV, 38. For the fifth
      general council, see the narrative in Hefele-Leclerq,
      III.1, pp. 1ff.

45   See R. A. Markus, 'Reflections on Religious Dissent in North
      Africa during the Byzantine period,' *Studies in Church History*,
      III (Leiden 1966) pp. 140–50.

XXI

NUBIA AS AN OUTPOST OF BYZANTINE
CULTURAL INFLUENCE*

Historians of the later Roman Empire have long been aware of the curious forms which the survival of Roman influence took among barbarian peoples long after the withdrawal of Roman political or economic control. The Moorish king, for instance, who in 476 put up an inscription in the fastnesses of the Aures mountains on which he described himself as "imperator" and "dux"[1] had his counterpart among the rulers of the Welsh Christians in the fifth and sixth centuries who sometimes claimed the titles of erstwhile officials such as "magistratus" and "protectors".[2] In western Mauretania it has long been observed that some of the most interesting Christian inscriptions from sites in the interior belong to the latter half of he sixth century when this area lay far beyond the Byzantine *limes*.[3] Byzantine survival can be equally surprising and significant: and the great international campaign organised by UNESCO to salvage the remains of the Nubian Christian culture in the Nile valley before its submersion under the waters of Lake Nasser, provided some interesting evidence for the long-continued survival of Byzantine influences in the Nubian kingdoms there.

Nubia was in direct contact with the Byzantine Empire for only a century, from 541—641, and the origins of that contact were mainly missionary. Unlike Armenia and other territories adjoining the Byzantine empire, Nubia does not provide much evidence for the penetration of Christian mission into the kingdoms before the final conversion took place, though it may be presumed that the Bishop of Philae below Aswan had some contact with the Nubians to the south of the Byzantine fron-

---

* This is the revised text of a communication read to the XIII International Congress of Byzantine Studies at Oxford, September 1966.

[1] The inscription was found at Arris in the Aures mountains. Described by J. Carcopino, *Un empereur maure inconnu, d'après une inscription latine récemment découverte dans l'Aures,* Rev. des Et. anciennes XLVI (1944) 94—120. Also Corp. Insc. Lat., VIII, 9835, "pro sal. et incol. reg(uli) Masunae gen(tium). Maur(orum) et Roman(orum)". Dated A. D. 508 from Altava in Mauretania Caesariensis.

[2] V. Nash-Williams, *The Early Christian Monuments of Wales.* Cardiff, 1950, № 138, Memoria (Voteporigis) Protectoris (*circa* 550), and № 103, p. 92—93 (*magistratus*).

[3] For instance, E. Diehl, *Inscriptiones Latinae Christianae Veteres* (ed. Moreau, Berlin, 1961), 3671, 3671 A and B, 3672, 3673, 3675 and 3675 A.

tier. The evangelisation of the three Nubian kingdoms that grew out of the ruins of the kingdom of Meroë from the end of the third century A. D., was largely the work of missions despatched by Justinian and Theodora. In 541 Justinian, alleging the expiry of the treaty which for nearly a century had allowed the Nubians to sacrifice to Isis on the island of Philae sent a general to destroy the temple and missionaries to convert them to Christianity. Meantime, however, Theodora despatched her own trusted emissary, the presbyter Julian to convert them to the Monophysite cause. Julian was supported by the Monophysite bishop of Philae and seems to have been initially the more successful.[4] By 543 Silka, the king of the Nobatae (the northernmost of the Nubian kingdoms) was converted, and within twenty years he had defeated his enemies, the Blemmyes who occupied stretches of the Nile valley as far south as Qasr Ibrim, 160 miles south of Aswan, and within a short time they too had become Christian.[5]

Meanwhile, Orthodoxy appears to have gained at least a temporary victory in Makuria,[6] the Nubian kingdom centred round Old Dongola, but in 580 the southern kingdom of Alwah with its capital at Soba near Khartoum was won for Monophysitism.[7] It is a measure of the religious problems that beset the emperors Maurice Tiberius and Maurice that by now the whole of the Nile valley from Alexandria to Lake Tamar with the single isolated exception of Makuria was Monophysite, and the Monophysite empire stretched over a greater area than Chalcedonian orthodoxy and Latin Christianity put together.

The Byzantines lost Egypt in 640—641 and there is no evidence for any subsequent direct contact between the court of Constantinople and Nubia. Yet Christianity, as is now known, was to last in Nubia for another eight centuries, and during that time the imprint of Byzantium was preserved and even extended. This is all the more remarkable, as the Nubians from first to last appear to have remained sincerely loyal to the Coptic Patriarch of Alexandria. The latter appointed and consecrated the Nubian bishops, and at Qasr Ibrim two richly illuminated scrolls commemorating his consecration at Old Cairo in 1372 as Bishop of Primis (Ibrim) and Pachoras (Faras) by the Patriarch Gabriel iv, were found with the body of Bishop Timotheos. This was found during the excavations in 1963—1964 half buried under the arch of the north crypt in his cathedral church at Qasr Ibrim. These scrolls were the

---

[4] The story is told by John of Ephesus (ed. E. W. Brooks) iv. 6—7. See, the brief, useful account of the Christianisation of Nubia in P. L. Shinnie, *Medieval Nubia,* Sudan Antiquities Service, Khartoum, 1954, 2—4.

[5] See W. B. Emery, *Egypt in Nubia.* London, 1965, 239.

[6] John of Ephesus, iv, 53 (Brooks, p. 182).

[7] John of Ephesus, *op. cit.,* iv, 50—53.

official letters written in Bohairic and Arabic respectively which the
Patriarch sent with Timotheos commending him to his people, and
ordering his enthronement.[8] Further south, writing of the kingdom of
Alwah, in the 13th century, the Arab writer Salim Aswani described
the inhabitants as Jacobite Christians whose "bishops are appointed
by the Patriarch of Alexandria, their books are in the Greek tongues
and are translated into the language of the country".[9] That this was
in all probability true of the northern kingdom also is indicated by
the large number of Greek and Nubian liturgical MSS, as well as Coptic
material that had once formed the cathedral library there.

The discovery of the Greek and Nubian MSS was a surprise for the
excavators of Qasr Ibrim, but it linked up with other evidence pointing
to the long-continued strength of the Byzantine cultural influence there.
Many years ago, Griffith discussing the meagre corpus of Christian
documents then known as coming from Nubia, concluded that initially
the influence of missionaries from Upper Egypt had brought about
the replacement of Greek by Coptic in the language of Nubian legal
and state documents. Coptic had prevailed up to *circa* 900 A. D., but
thereafter it had been replaced in its turn by Greek and Nubian.[10]
To prove his point Griffith cited the very latest Nubian document then
known, the graffito, in the monastery of St. Simeon near Aswan, mentioning King Kudanbes who reigned from 1322—1324, and was believed
to have been the last Christian king of Nubia. The graffito, however,
was written in debased Greek, but in a typical Nubian hand.[11] It was
a prayer for Kudanbes, largely theological, invoking the protection
of the archangel Michael and his power "to exclude false doctrines",
but it went on to extol the virtues of King Kudanbes himself, whom it
styled "President of the Caesars", and successor to a line of mighty
rulers.[12] At so late a date in the life of Christian Nubia the inscription
is remarkable as showing no signs of foreboding regarding the approaching destruction of the kingdom by the Moslems.

Even more remarkable are the high-sounding titles that occur on this)
strange inscription. "President of the Caesars", "sovereign" (βασιλεύς

---

[8] See the brief description of the find by J. Martin Plumley, *Qasr Ibrim, 1963—1964,*
Journ. of Egypt. Archaeol. 50 (1964) 3—4. A full publication of these splendid documents
is now being prepared by Professor Plumley on behalf of the Egypt Exploration Society
under whose auspices the excavation of Qasr Ibrim was carried out.

[9] Cited from E. W. Budge, *Nubian Texts* (British Museum, 1909), p. 5. For a similar
text see Abu Saleh, *Churches and Monasteries of Egypt and Some Neighbouring
Countries.* Oxford (ed. Evetts and Butler), 1895, 272.

[10] F. W. Griffith, *Christian Documents from Nubia.* British Academy Papers (1928)
17—18.

[11] Compare the writing of this document (Griffith, *loc. cit.,* Plate IV) with the Nubian
text published by E. W. Budge, *Nubian Texts* (British museum, 1909).

[12] F. W. Griffith, *op. cit.,* 18—30.

and "king worthy of three hundred years (of reign)" could be applied to the Byzantine emperors themselves. Below the supreme rank of Basileus, is that of *rex* (ϱ(ξ) the title probably of the sub-kings ruling the states into which Nubia had been divided.[13] These titles seem to have been traditional. We find in the middle of the eighth century King Kyriakos is recorded to have had thirteen kings under him when he invaded Egypt and compelled the emir Abd el-Melik 'bu Marwan to release the Coptic patriarch from prison and cease persecuting the Christians.[14] Kyriakos' father Merkurius under whom the northern and middle Nubian kingdoms were united under one crown and the Monophysite faith *circa* 700 was hailed, just as the Emperor Justin had been, as "the new Constantine".[15] Other texts, dating from the eighth to the eleventh century show that even in their Court and provincial administration the Nubians seem to have retained the strict hierarchy of Byzantine officialdom. A provincial governor was an *eparchos,* and palace officials caller "primicerius", "protodomesticus", "meizoteris" and "protomeizoteris" have been recorded.[16] The "meizoteris" or "mayor" suggests mediaeval Byzantium, and indeed the title may be related to the μείζων found among those listed by Constantine Porphyrogenitus.[17]

The terminology of the royal courts and administration does not stand alone as an example of the survival of Byzantine usages in the Nubian kingdoms. Even before the great salvage campaign on behalf of the Nubian monuments had been launched, Monneret de Villard had come to similar conclusions after a long study of the ecclesiastical monuments of Nubia. Christian art and architecture "was entirely independent of Christian art in Egypt"[18] he claimed, and though now the discovery of some of the wood-carving and other Christian symbolism found in Nubian churches must modify this statement, it remains broadly true. In particular, the Nubian basilican church (Monneret de Villard's *Hallenkirche*) seems to have affinities with basilican churches common in Syria, Asia Minor and North Africa in late-Roman and early-Byzantine times.[19] One finds in Nubia too, as one does in Byzantine North Africa, a few examples of cruciform martyria.[20] Many of the architectural features

---

[13] Griffith, *loc. cit.*

[14] *History of the Patriarchs* (ed. B. Evetts), Patrologia Orientalis V, 145.

[15] *Ibid.,* 115. For Justin, see A. A. Vasiliev, *Justin the First,* Harvard, 1950, 151. "Long live the new Constantine. Long live the orthodox father".

[16] Griffith, *loc. cit.* The title *eparchos* was clearly unfamiliar to the writer of the Life of the Patriarch Michael as he has to explain that the eparch was "one of the great men of the (Nubian) kingdom", *Lives of the Patriarchs*, p. 140.

[17] See Reiske's Commentary on Constantine Porphyrogenitus (ed. Bonn, II, 854—855).

[18] V. Monneret de Villard, *La Nubia medioevale.* Cairo, 1934—1957, I, p. iv.

[19] *Ibid.,* iii, p. 17.

[20] Ibid. A typical Byzantine cruciform martyrium was found at Tébessa-Khalia in Numidia. See A. Laout, Rev. Africaine (1937) 1—9.

too, such as the decoration of the stone capitals in Byzantine-Corinthian style or with elaborate interlaces ending with animal heads are reminiscent of Byzantine or Byzantineinspired copies of similar models.[21] Even the funerary formulae or tombs in Nubian cemeteries located near many of the churches appear to be Byzantine, and Coptic influence would seem to have been intrusive, partly due to persecutions in Egypt, rather than native.[22]

The great church at Qasr Ibrim with whose excavation the writer was associated with Rev. Professor J. M. Plumley had already been singled out by Monneret de Villard as comparable with some of the splendid Byzantine churches he had seen in Syria.[23] Indeed, from the outside, the walls, made of carefully hewn limestone blocks built on top of re-used blocks taken in all probability from a Meroitic temple near the site, were reminiscent of the fortress architecture of the African *limes* of the fourth century or of the Syrian stone-built village churches of two centuries later. Excavation revealed a magnificent stone-built cathedral, 100 feet X 70 feet, with five aisles, the outer pair defined by imposing stone arcades, and the inner by six granite columns ornamented by a cross reminiscent in form to Maltese crosses and surmounted by richly decorated capitals. The church with its stone paved floor, its ambo, the extensive rectangular *haikal* or sanctuary in front of the altar, the transepts each side of the apse, and the crypts below the transepts, could well have been a rather elaborate example of a large early Byzantine church almost anywhere in the Mediterranean. Only the semicircular tribunal ascended by the small, narrow steps shaped like a horse-shoe, and the baptismal (?) tank set in the (ecclesiastic) north wall of the transept are typically Nubian and find no obvious parallels in Byzantine church architecture. One draws attention too, to the Byzantine style of the capitals of the columns which flanked the nave of the church. On one, the central feature of the Maltese cross was surrounded by elaborate interlacing scroll-work, ending in two fine animal-head terminals   Such work is even reminiscent of the Byzantine-derived motifs from sculpture and illuminated MSS of western Europe in the Dark Ages. It is not easy to date this building, but judging from the amphorae found buried with two of the bodies in the crypt, if was probably built in the seventh century, a little earlier than the cathedral at Faras, and it may have remained in use at least until the end of the 14th century.

----

[21] Examples were noted by R. Michalowski at Faras, Kush XI (1963) 256.

[22] At Ibrim all the episcopal funerary inscriptions (10th and 11th century), were in Greek. But at Jovas some of the Bishops' funerary stelae wort in Greek in Coptic. I owe this information to my colleague J. M. Plumley.

[23] V. Monneret de Villard III, p. 3.

Qasr Ibrim must have possessed a fine ecclesiastical library. Scattered over the floor of the church, when this had already been covered by two inches of hard, compacted dust and debris, we found the remains of a great many manuscripts. These were prayers, biblical passages, homilies, and eucharistic sequences, and a significant proportion were written in Greek or Nubian. This confirms the statement made by the Armenian Abu Saleh who visited the northern kingdom of Nubia at the turn of the 13th century, that the bishops prayed in Greek.[24] Indeed, when one looks at some of the liturgical sequences with the pointing in red and black ink over individual letters one is perhaps justified in asking whether the notation was not Byzantine-inspired too.

Coptic MSS. were also found.[25] It suffices perhaps to mention four pages of the Homily of John Chrysostom on the Four Living Beasts, which the writer discovered beneath an upright stone in the debris of a house on the south side of the fortress, and some five New Testament fragments written in uncial (probably 11th century) which were recovered also from the debris of Christian houses and store-places in the same area. The Christians of Qasr Ibrim read and often possibly even wrote Coptic though they do not seem to have used it in the liturgy.[26]

One other find, also from the debris of a Christian house, however, corroborates Griffith's hypothesis that Greek and Nubian remained the official languages of the Nubian kingdoms. In a jar protected from damage by a fallen palm beam, and of a style such as we had already found in a 14th century environment during the excavation of the church, were recovered nine scrolls of soft leather probably gazelle-skin, roughly rectangular in shape. One of these scrolls seems to date to 15th century. These were evidently official documents, like that Griffith had published from Nauri.[27] The writing was in clear, thick black ink, and the language was Nubian. A Latin cross in the top left-hand corner indicated Christian date, and in the scroll which it was in fact possible to unroll on the spot, the royal name "Joel" could be deciphered.

No frescoes were found at Qasr Ibrim, and it would be out of place to comment on the magnificent series of more than a hundred paintings found by the Polish team of archaeologists at Faras—the ecclesiastical capital of northern Nubia. But relevant to our thesis are the conclusions of the finders. With the exception of the scene depicting the descent

[24] *Op. cit.*, 272. For a fragment of a Greek psalmody found at Faras, K. Michalowski, Kush xii (1964) 196.

[25] Four language seem to have been in use in Ibrim at one time, viz. Greek, Nubian, Coptic and Arabic.

[26] The writer found a letter written in Coptic on a piece of wood by an ecclesiastic, during the excavation of a building outside the church.

[27] *Op. cit.*, 12—13.

from the Cross on the east wall of the cathedral, which recalls Ethiopian pictorial art, the general cast of the features of the figures, and their arrangement and proportion is in keeping with the accompanying legends in Greek as well as Nubian. This and the range of colours, violet, orange, brown and vermilion have prompted the discoverers to ask whether these frescoes do not reflect a tradition inherited from Byzantium.[28] Writing of the representations of the Virgin and the Arch-angel Michael, they write "There is no doubt that here we have an example of Greek-Byzantine art, without trace of the typical style which marks Coptic art". One may perhaps add the same comments in respect of Dr. Claasen's discoveries of the frescoes in the walls of the small mud-walled church north of Abu Simbel.[29]

The aim of this short paper has been to raise questions rather than to answer them. It is however, evident that Byzantine influence survived in Nubia to an astonishing degree. Greek lasted for centuries as a language in official and ecclesiastical use in the Nubian kingdoms, and the Nubians when they came to write down their language chose Greek rather than Meroitic script as their model. In the northern kingdom they added three Coptic letters and some other signs which may be derived from Meroitic, though in the south the Coptic influence appears to have been less evident.[30] Finally, the latest Nubian churches, such as the little square buildings surmounted by a central cupola, of which Qasr Ibrim II (Plate) is typical, appear to reflect the change in the normal Byzantine style of church architecture from basilica to dome structure that took place in the Middle Ages.

The reasons for this development provides an obvious theme for future investigation. In conclusion, one might suggest, the continuance of trade links with the Byzantine world via the Red Sea where the Nubians had trading posts as late as the thirteenth century might account for some of the imitation of Syrian art and architectural forms. Added to this,

---

[28] K. Michalowski, *Polish Excavations at Faras, 1961*, Kush x (1962) 231. See also, Michalowski's subsequent reports in Kush, xi, xii and xiii. To date however, the best *coloured* representation of the frescoes will be found in the Colour Supplement of the *Sunday Times*, 14th July, 1963. * see p. 326

[29] To be published by their discoverer. I am grateful to Professor Claasen for permission to photograph the frescoes and to refer to his discovery. ** see p. 326

[30] Griffith himself was uncertain and puts two points of view. In his early work, "The Nubian Texts of the Christian Period", Berlin, 1913, p. 71: "The Old Nubian alphabet is essentially the Coptic re-inforced by a few extra letters (for the peculiar sounds of the language) which may of derived from the earlier pagan writing of Nubia, the so-called Meroitic." In his British Academy lecture however, he states concerning the southern kingdom, "The alphabet must have been formed independently to that of the northern kingdom; all the non-Greek letters are peculiar and there is no trace of letters borrowed from the Coptic" (*op. cit.*, p. 15). Further study of the now relatively numerous Nubian documents may cast light on this problem.

the progressive weakness of the Copts, coupled with the revival of Byzantine power in the tenth and eleventh centuries, may have encouraged the Nubians to continue to look to the distant *basileus* in Constantinople for support and to imitate things Byzantine. Similarly, when Byzantium declined irredemably in the fourteenth century, its influence gave way to that of Islam, and the conversion of the Nubians to Mohammedanism followed. The steps by which this took place are obscure, but one can detect on some late-Nubian sites a gradual penetration of Islam among the people.[31] In any event, the fifteenth century saw the end of Christian Nubia, and the Portugese mission under Alvarez reached Ethiopia in 1524 only to hear rumours of the death-throes of Christianity in the southermost kingdom of Soba (Alwah).[32]

* Later information and discussion, see K. Michalowski, *Faras*, Warsaw, 1974, 32-34
** See P. van Moorsel and colleagues, *The Central Church of Abdallah Nirqi*, Brill, Leiden, 1975.

[31] For instance, at *Meinarti*. See W. Y. Adams, *Sudan Antiquities Service Excavations in Nubia: Fourth Season*, Kush xii (1964) especially conclusions 240—241.

[32] Alvarez' account, edited by C. F. Beckingham and G. W. B. Huntingford, *Prester John of the Indies*. Hakluyt Society Publications, 2nd Ser. CXV, p. 129.

XXII

Coptic, Greek and Nubian at Q'asr Ibrim*

The position occupied by vernacular languages in business and administration as well as in the services of the Church is one of the most significant differences between the east and west Roman empires. In the west, neither Celtic in Gaul nor Punic or Berber in North Africa ever attained the status of an administrative or ecclesiastical language. Irenaeus might find himself compelled to preach in Celtic to the Gauls:[1] Augustine had to provide interpreters and Punic-speaking clergy for services in parts of rural North Africa,[2] but the Bible was never translated into either Celtic or Punic, and no trace of a liturgy in these languages has ever been discovered. Latin, representing the centralising ethos of both western empire and western Church exercised a monopoly in secular and ecclesiastical administration in the later Empire, and this remained so until the rise of the nation states at the end of the Middle Ages. Even in the missions Latin was the language of the Church and Christian inscriptions, thus spreading its influence in the fifth century beyond the northern and western borders of the empire, to Ireland and the Pictish kingdom of Strathclyde.

Meantime, fundamentally different developments had slowly been taking place in the east. Greek indeed was the normal language of the Church throughout those areas where Rome had succeeded the Hellenistic kings. But it was by no means exclusive. Even at the period of the greatest expansion of Greco-Roman civilisation the vernacular languages continued to be used by members of the literate classes. Thus, we find well-to-do families conversant with two or three languages and using them in correspondence. The family letters, for instance, abandoned in the "Cave of Letters" in the Wadi Murabbat during the revolt of Bar Kochba (132—35) contained items in Nabataean and Aramaic as well as in Greek.[3] Among Christian congregations in Syria Greek never attained a monopoly position. As early as the 260s when Sapor the Persian conqueror of Valerian deported a vast number of Syrians to his own dominions, the Christians among them are stated to have divided themselves up into Syriac-speaking and Greek-speaking congregations.[4] In Egypt, the turn of the fourth century saw already the production of a Sahidic New Testament,[5] and the language of the great majority of the monks was Coptic.

This situation may be associated with the autocephalous character of the eastern Churches, as well as the growth of self-identification among

---

* The revised text of a communication given at the XIV International Byzantine Congress at Bucharest in September 1971.

[1] Irenaeus, *Adversus Haereses*, Praefatio 3.

[2] Augustine, *Ep.* 108.5: compare *Ep.* 209.2.

[3] Israel Exploration Journ. xii (1962) 235 ff. and 258 ff.

[4] Chronicle of Séert, ed. A. Scher (= Patrologia Orientalis, iv), p. 222.

[5] See G. Steindorf, *Bemerkungen über die Anfänge der koptischen Sprache.* In: *Coptic Studies in Honour of W. E. Crum*, Boston 1950, p. 211.

the non-Greek peoples of the east. The patriarchs of Constantinople, Antioch and Alexandria might quarrel over precedence but made no claims to jurisdictional primacy over each other. Non-intervention in each other's territories laid down at the Second Ecumenical Council in 381[6] prevented the imposition of any single language in use for the liturgy and Church order, such as the Popes were able to impose in the west. If, for instance, those who used Syriac in services were occasionally regarded as "rustics" by Greek-speaking prelates, there was never any serious attempt to prevent it. Among the eastern missions too, we find attitudes towards the use of the vernacular in contrast with those prevailing in the west. Both in Armenia[7] and Ethiopia[8] the development of national languages with a characteristic script owes much to the work of missionaries from the east Roman Empire particularly from Syria. This pattern was repeated in the Christianisation of Nubia.

It can now be established that Christianity had been penetrating the northern Nubian kingdom a century before the arrival of Theodora's missionaries under the presbyter Julianus in 543. From that moment on, progress was rapid and in the course of the next generation all three Nubian kingdoms extending along the Nile valley from Aswan to below Khartoum had become Christian. At first the middle kingdom of Makkura with its capital at Old Dongola was Chalcedonian, but after its union with Nobatia under King Mercurios in *circa* 700 it too accepted the Monophysitism of its northern and southern neighbours.[9]

By this date Nubia had close relations with the Coptic patriarchate at Alexandria and depended on it for the consecration of its bishops. In addition, it received a steady influx of refugees resulting from the increasing persecution of Christians by the Egyptian emirs. The elaborate graffiti and inscriptions in Coptic found in an anchorite's cell at El-Wizz near Faras, and dating to A. D. 738 may have been the handiwork of one of these refugees.[10] In these circumstances Coptic could be expected to become the principal language of Court and Church in Nubia, and early researchers in this field concluded from the evidence to hand, which included legal documents dating to 750—850 that this indeed was the case down to *circa* A. D. 900.[11]

The inscriptions found at Faras and recorded by Michalowski and Jakobielski modify this assessment.[12] Foundation texts of buildings and official documents up to this date show a majority in Coptic closely followed by Greek. There are no such inscriptions in Old Nubian from the site. The legends on the murals, however, which provide a series

[6] Canon 2.

[7] For Syrian influence on the formation of the Armenian alphabet see K. Sarkissian, *The Council of Chalcedon and the Armenian Church.* London, S. P. C. K. 1965, p. 88—90.

[8] For Syrian influence on the translation of the Bible into Ge'ez see, E. Ullendorf, *Ethiopia and the Bible.* In: Schweich Lectures (1967), London 1968, p. 39.

[9] For a sketch of events see my *Christianity in the Middle East: a Survey to 1800*, Ch. vi of Vol. I of Ed. A. J. Arberry. In: Religion in the Middle East, Cambridge 1969, p. 275.

[10] Published by F. Ll. Griffith, Liverpool Annals of Archaeol. and Anthropol. 13 (1926) 56, and see also, G. R. Hughes, Q'asr el-Wizz, Orient. Instit. Reports, 1956, pp. 10—14.

[11] F. Ll. Griffith, *Christian Documents from Nubia*, Proceedings of the British Acad., xiv, 1928 (Coptic legal texts) and compare his earlier work, *The Nubian Texts of the Christian period*, Berlin 1913.

[12] In particular, see S. Jakobielski, *Some remarks on the Faras Inscriptions.* In: *Kunst und Geschichte Nubiens in Christlicher Zeit*, ed. E. Dinkler, Recklinghausen 1971, p. 29—38 and for detailed descriptions see K. Michalowski, *Faras*, Zurich 1967, p. 103—170.

of inscriptions from the mid-8th century onwards tell a different story. The discoverers point out that Greek "undisputably predominates" and that Coptic is only used in cases where the legend itself quoted the Bible text literally.[13] The same is true also of the tomb inscriptions found at Q'asr Ibrim. In one instance where the first verse of each of the four Gospels was found painted on the walls of an episcopal tomb outside the west of the Church, Coptic was used.[14] As languages in ordinary use, however, Greek and Old Nubian seem to prevail at both sites even in the early period of Christian Nubian history.

The predominance of these languages over Coptic is even more pronounced in the later period. Even before the publication of the magnificent Faras discoveries, J. F. Oates researching on a series of eighteen funerary texts found in northern Nubia between 1900—1960, and dating between A. D. 1006—1200 had concluded that Greek was a living language in Nubia at this period.[15] The monuments were not only written in reasonably good Greek and included the prayer for the dead in the Orthodox liturgy (the *Euchologion Mega*), but made good sense when the stone-mason was not merely copying liturgical formulae. The mistakes were mistakes in spelling due to mispronunciation of common words (τωπο for τόπῳ for instance) not to their complete unfamiliarity. Another piece of evidence pointing to the use of both Greek and Old Nubian as the languages of the Nubian court, is that the memorial inscription to King Georgios III in 1158 in the Church of the Virgin in the Wadi Natrun whither he had retired is in these two languages, and not in Coptic.[16] In this same period Coptic was a language that had to be learnt and used correctly, somewhat like Latin in the Britain of Gildas; each were essentially ecclesiastical languages used for formal purposes. The continuance of Greek follows therefore the continued use of the Byzantine system of administration and Byzantine influence in art and liturgy in Nubia. The presence of Nubian embassies at the court of Constantinople as late as 1204 illustrates the effort made to foster diplomatic and cultural links with this distant outpost of Byzantine culture.[17]

Let us now see how the discoveries made at Q'asr Ibrim some 70 miles north of Faras confirm the results from these sites and elsewhere in northern Nubia regarding the respective uses of Coptic, Greek and Nubian. At Q'asr Ibrim, excavations on behalf of the Egypt Exploration Society have been carried out in 1963—64, 1966 and 1969, with my colleague Professor J. M. Plumley as Director and myself as Associate Director 1963—64.[18] While no frescoes like those of Faras were uncovered, a very considerable amount of manuscript remains as well as memorial inscriptions were found. The majority came from the remains of what must have been the cathedral library. This had been pillaged at some period when the cathedral was falling into disuse, but before the site was

---

[13] S. Jakobielski, *op. cit.*, p. 30.
[14] To be published by J. M. Plumley and the writer.
[15] J. F. Oates, *A Christian Inscription from Armenia in Nubia*, Journ. of Egyptian Archaeol. 49 (1963) 161—171.
[16] F. Ll. Griffith, *Christian Documents in Nubia*, p. 2—12 of offprint.
[17] Robert of Clari, cited from K. Michalowski, *Faras*, p. 39.
[18] Briefly reported by J. M. Plumley in Journ. of Egyptian Archaeol. 50 (1964) 52 (1966) and 56 (1970), and by the writer in *Akten des VII. Internationale Kongresses für Christliche Archäologie, Roma 1968*, p. 531—538.

abandoned by its Christian inhabitants. The majority of manuscript fragments which were either parchment or paper were found in a layer of wind-blown sand about 2 cm. above the stone floor of the cathedral, i. e. silt was already beginning to form on the original floor suggesting squalour and neglect. The silt, however, lay below the level which contained the fallen columns of the church, indicating therefore that the deposit had been laid down before the building was destroyed. Other similar manuscripts were found outside the church; in one case the deposit was marked by an upright stone. A large number of others were found in the fill of episcopal tombs excavated in 1966 on the south flank of the church. It was noticeable that all these manuscripts had been torn or burnt, and the careful burial of the charred remains of a MS of a homily of John Chrysostom suggests something of a salvage operation following a catastrophe. In addition to the remains of the cathedral library were found what appear to be private letters dating to the Christian period. These were written in black ink on paper, now a light brown in colour but still comparatively tough, and carefully folded up into a small rectangular shape. Generally there would be a simple + in the left hand corner of the text. Also, in two places, first in the ruins of a house above the forecourt of the Meroitic temple and secondly, hidden in a recess in the walls of the late Nubian magazine which marked the final Christian occupation of the site, were found large storage pots containing leather scrolls of Christian date. In all probability these were legal documents. Finally, my colleague J. M. Plumley made a remarkable discovery of two magnificent manuscript scrolls attached to the thigh of Bishop Timotheos, Bishop of Ibrim and Faras (T i b y b e and P a c h o r a s) in the year 1372.

These written documents tell a similar story about the languages in use in northern Nubia to that of their counterparts from Faras and elsewhere. As the bishopric depended ecclesiastically on the Coptic patriarchate located at Old Cairo, formal ecclesiastical documents were as expected in Coptic. Thus the scrolls found on the body of the bishop, each of which was about 5 m. long and 0,35 m. wide, are written one in Bohairic Coptic and the other in Arabic. They are the consecration deeds of Bishop Timotheos and give the date of his consecration by the Coptic Patriarch, Gabriel IV in Old Cairo in 1372. An extract reads as follows: *"This commendatory letter for our father Aba Timotheos, your bishop (Gabriel) we have ratified with our own hands. We sent it with the most pious bishops who came with him to carry out his enthronement in the Church in which the bishops of his see (used to be enthroned)."*[19] While we are concerned here with these magnificent manuscripts as witnesses for the place of Coptic in the Nubian Church, their historical importance is not to be underrated. They show that Christianity was a living religion, sustained by an organised Church government half a century later than the overthrow of King Kudanbes in 1323, which was presumed to mark the end of Nubian Christianity.[20] Coptic was also used in translations of patristic works such as the four charred pages of John Chrysostom's *Homily on the Four Living Beasts,* mentioned previously, and there were New Testament fragments dating to the 11th century probably from the

---

[19] To be published by J. M. Plumley for the Egypt Exploration Society in 1973.
[20] Compare, K. Michalowski, *Faras,* p. 39.

handwriting, found on parchment in storage places dug into the floor of the forecourt of the temple by the occupants of Christian houses above. Coptic was used too, up to 1100 or so for other ecclesiastical purposes, as shown by a letter from a cleric written on wooden plaque found in a Christian house, complaining of the conduct of a colleague.

The majority of our Christian records, however, were either in Greek or Nubian. Of six complete tombstones found in the burial chapel outside the south side of the church five can be dated exactly from 1037 to 1132. All are inscribed in Greek containing extracts in varying lengths from the Byzantine *Euchologion,* and one contains a few mutilated lines of Old Nubian.[21] The comparatively barbarous character of the Greek sugests that all these monuments were manufactured locally, but it also shows, as Oates believed to be true of the Armenna monument, that Greek was in use as a living and not merely as a liturgical language throughout this period.

The manuscripts tell the same story. The dating of these is still obscure, though one is inclined to put them comparatively late in the Christian period, say 1100 +, on the grounds that the handwriting shows analogies with that found on other MS fragments in undeniably late horizons, such as the Old Nubian lectionary fragment from Sunnarti which could be 13th century.[22] The finest illuminated text so far found is in Old Nubian. The seated figure occupying the left hand top corner of the manuscript must represent a bishop exercising his office of preaching, and the text may be that of a sermon,[22a] Nearby, however, were found liturgical texts in Greek, including an *Anaphora* of Athanasius which had been illuminated in the same style as the illumination of the bishop's dedication scroll. There was also found part of the legendary Acts of St. George where the saint is shown challenging successfully a priest of Apollo. This was in Greek language but in a script which was markedly Nubian in character and similar to that inscribed on the leather scrolls found in the ruins of a Christian house over the forecourt of the temple. These were discovered in a large sealed pot which had been protected from damage by a palm beam probably fallen from the upper storey of one of these houses. The pot was of orange paste, burnished on the outside and decorated with geometric designs characteristic of the latest period of Christian Nubian pottery (a smaller but similar vessel was discovered behind a blocking wall built across the west crypt of the church and associated with a document dating to 1337 A.D.). Though the clay seals over the top of the pot were intact the neck had been cracked and hence it was desirable to investigate the contents on the spot. They were nine leather scrolls written in Old Nubian. They were roughly rectangular in shape measuring about 0.70 × 0.30 in. Their Christian character and date was indicated by a small Latin cross on the left hand top corner. The material was gazelle-skin, which perhaps to judge from traces of sutures round the edges had been used as garments. The hand-writing was on the soft inner side of the leather by means of a reed pen using black

---

[21] J. M. Plumley, *Some Examples of Christian Nubian Art from the Excavations at Q'asr Ibrim.* Kunst und Geschichte Nubiens, ed. E. Dinkler, 129—140, Abb. 131.

[22] C. Detlef—G. Müller, *Deutsche Textfunde in Nubien.* In: ed. E. Dinkler, op. cit., pp. 245—255.

[22a] A Photograph is published as Plate 13b in *Religion in the Middle East,* ed. A. J. Arberry, Vol. I (Cambridge 1969), p. 532.

ink, and the result was a hard, clear impress. They are probably legal documents, from the repetitions of words in the text, and one can distinguish a royal name "Joel", perhaps the same monarch whose name has been recovered on a graffito on the walls of a grotto at Djebel Adda about 25 miles to the south. Their great interest apart from the contents which still defies decipherment is the date. That at the top of the pot, and which had been inserted latest, bears the date in the Era of the Martyrs of 1137, i. e. 1421 A. D.[23] If this is confirmed there will be clear evidence for an organised Christian Nubian kingdom existing at least within a generation of the fall of Constantinople itself, with Old Nubian as the language of the Court.

Greek, however, had not been discarded entirely. Below Q'asr Ibrim, situated on a rocky promontory was a small square chapel surmounted by a dome corresponding to the latest period of Nubian churches. It had been visited and planned a generation ago by Monneret de Villard: the graffiti still survived; and these were in Greek, in a writing similar to that found on the latest plaster of the walls of Q'asr Ibrim itself. The invocation to the "Holy Trinity" (the word Τριάς is still decipherable) points to the continued use of Greek in the liturgy.[24]

The discoveries at Q'asr Ibrim help to confirm the evidence of the literary remains found on other sites, but they also carry the story down to a much later date. They leave the impression that the three languages of Coptic, Greek and Old Nubian remained in use in the eparchy of Nobatia throughout its history, but that their use and relation to each other tended to change. In the earlier centuries Greek and Coptic dominated the scene as official languages. They were the languages of the court and of the Church and this was reflected by the existence of bilingual Coptic and Greek monumental inscriptions. From about 1000 onwards, however, the use of Coptic for ordinary purposes declined, and by the 14th century it had become a school language and was confined to formal ecclesiastical documents, such as episcopal consecration diplomas. Whereas in Egypt itself Coptic had lost ground to Arabic, in Nubia the same process was going on in favour of Old Nubian. The remarkable feature however of the Q'asr Ibrim discoveries is that Greek continued to survive and perhaps even revive as a living language in the Nile valley. This seems to have been the case despite the continued Monophysitism of the Nubian Church. Thus the linguistic texts confirm the evidence of the frescoes and funerary monuments. Before its final collapse in face of attacks by Moslem Beduin tribes in the 15th century, Nubia was developing its own characteristic art, architecture and language, while retaining its thousand-year links with its cultural centre, Byzantium.[25]

---

[23] To be published in detail by the Egypt Exploration Society. Reported by the writer in Akten, p. 537—538.

[24] N. Monneret de Villard, *La Nubia Medioevale*, Cairo 1935—1957.

[25] See the writer's note, *Nubia as an Outpost of Nubian Cultural Influence*, ByzSlav XXIX (1968) 319—326; an important study on the Greek inscriptions at Faras is in preparation by Dr. Jadwiga Kubinska of the National Museum at Warsaw.

XXIII

Nomads and Christianity in the Middle Ages[1]

W hy did Christianity decline relatively to Islam in wide areas of the Mediterranean world during the European Middle Ages? The problem has deserved more attention than it has received from historians, for the pattern is not a consistent one and the decline where it took place, cannot be explained on the grounds of Moslem military superiority alone. The first generation of Moslem conquerors that so decisively defeated the Byzantine armies were plunderers who sought booty and revenge for past wrongs suffered at the hands of the Byzantine authorities or simply from the agricultural and urban populations of the east Roman frontier provinces. Confronted with undreamed of success, they had little idea of establishing either civil government or settling in the areas they had conquered. They had little desire also to convert their new Christian subjects, for that would diminish the flow of tribute exacted in exchange for protection. Yet as time went on, Christianity in the eastern Mediterranean showed none of the survival and recuperative power that characterised the Orthodox Church in the Balkans during the five centuries of Ottoman occupation from 1390–1912. Of the areas overrun by successive Moslem invaders down to 1400 only Spain, Sicily and Crete re-emerged as Christian territories. North Africa, Cyrenaica, the Nubian kingdoms in the Nile valley and the great majority of the population of eastern Syria, Egypt and Anatolia were lost to Christendom. Nubia is an interesting case, for here Christianity flourished for 800 years before perishing almost without trace during the fifteenth century. Is it possible to point to common factors that told in favour of Islam there and in North Africa and in Anatolia where Christianity also declined catastrophically? How was it that for two centuries between 1300 and 1500 Islam became the predominant religion of mankind?

The great changes that were to overtake Christendom, thanks to the emergence of Islam, can best be measured by a glance at the religious situation in the Mediterranean world about A.D. 600. The all-pervading influence was that of the Byzantine Church-State. Since the middle of Justinian's reign the last centres of traditional Mediterranean paganism that

[1] The revised text of a lecture given to a symposium on Nubian studies at Heidelberg University, May 1974.

had lingered in some of the Greek cities of Syria or in less accessible rural areas of Asia Minor had succumbed to a combination of imperial sanction and monastic missionary enterprise. The whole Mediterranean seaboard was Christian. Down the Nile successive missions between 542 and 569 under the patronage of the empress Theodora and Justin II had resulted in the Christianisation of the three Nubian kingdoms of Nobatia, Makurrah, and Alwah (Alodia). The Nile valley from Alexandria to Lake Tana was Christian, though the Christianity of its inhabitants was Monophysite and not Chalcedonian orthodoxy. To contemporaries of the emperor Maurice and pope Gregory the religious issues of the day revolved round which of the three major theological systems within the Christian tradition, that is, the Byzantine, Latin, or Alexandrian Monophysite would eventually prevail.[1]

Already, however, even before the onset of the Arab invasions in 634, one part of this vast Christian empire was showing signs of decay. The north African provinces had been reconquered from the Vandals by Belisarius in a single year 533-4. Catholic orthodoxy had been restored by edict on 1 August 535,[2] and the churches in many of the north African cities had been rebuilt on an even greater scale of magnificence than previously. The ease, however, of the initial restoration had masked the existence of unsuspected problems. The Vandals had not been the only contestants for North Africa in the first decades of the sixth century. In this period a new enemy to the patterns of urban and rural life established in North Africa since the second century A.D. began to make its presence felt.[3] What impelled the great confederation of nomadic Berber tribes, known as the Louata to move westwards along the edge of the Sahara from Cyrenaica in the early years of the sixth century is unknown. Their impact, however, on the Vandal kingdom was catastrophic. In many ways the Vandal occupation had been a continuation of that of Rome. The Vandals had occupied Carthage, and Constantine and Hippo Regius in Numidia and had settled in the fertile river valleys in the Roman Proconsular province. The remainder of the country, even within the boundaries of the Vandal kingdom, remained in the hands of Romano-African landowners and their tenants, the latter working under the same system of tenure and cultivation that had operated previously.[4] Beyond the borders of the Vandal kingdom had grown up Moorish principalities which still, however, retained some memory of Roman usages. Thus Mastimas, ruler of a

---

[1] See my, 'Old and New Rome in the Age of Justinian', in *Relations between East and West in the Middle Ages*, ed. D. Baker, Edinburgh, 1973, 25.

[2] Justinian, *Novella* 37, ed. Z. von Lingenthal, Teubner 1881-4, 207-11, 1 August 535 (addressed to Soloman).

[3] Ch. Courtois, *Les Vandales et l'Afrique*, Gouvernement Général de l'Algérie, Paris 1955, 343-352.

[4] See Ch. Courtois and colleagues, *Les Tablettes Albertini*, Gouvernement Général de l'Algérie, Paris 1950, 189 ff. Many of the documents speak of 'particelles agrorum ex culturis mancianis'. On the continuation of traditional Christian religious life in Numidia under the Vandals, see also my *The Donatist Church*, Oxford 1971, 306-7.

kingdom centred in the western part of the Aures mountains styled himself 'Res gentium romanorum et maurorum'[1] in the year 506 A.D.

The nomads, however, represented a complete break with the settled Romano-African civilisation that had survived both Vandal occupation and native Berber razzias. They moved over great areas with their camels, flocks and herds of goats, their axis being the chain of Sahara oases that link Egypt with north-west Africa along the twenty-ninth parallel, and their objectives were plunder and pasturage. From the time when their king Cabao met and defeated the Vandals near Leptis Magna in 520 to the end of the Byzantine occupation, they were a major threat to ordered life in North Africa, which they succeeded finally in overturning.[2] The pages of Procopius and Corippus show that while the Byzantine generals were usually successful against the Berber mountaineers, they could do little against the nomads. The Louata with their formidable camel mounted armies, and their barbaric pagan rites, including human sacrifice, form a permanent background to Byzantine rule.[3] The sites of the battles fought against them indicate that debatable land was no longer the river valleys of the granary of Rome fought over in the Vandal war. Conflict raged on the inland plains which provided the most cultivated areas of Roman and Vandal Africa, but for the nomads the exit from the inhospitable desert to more fertile areas to the north.[4] By the end of the seventh century Carthage itself had lost its political, strategic and religious importance.

The effect of the irruption of the Berber nomads on to the stage of North African history during the sixth century A.D. may be best considered in relation to the human geography of the Roman and Byzantine provinces. The area occupied by the Romans and Byzantines fell into two main parts, first, the well-watered coastal belt, extending about ninety miles inland, Mediterranean in climate, its people forming part and parcel of the Mediterranean world. In this area the Romano-Berber settlements such as Dougga, Mactar or Thuburbo Maius developed by the early third century A.D. into Roman cities whose ruins fill the tourist with wonder to-day.[5] South of this fertile area, sandwiched between it and the Aures mountains, or the great salt lakes to the west was another Africa, a high plateau sloping continuously towards the east from an elevation of 2,500 feet above sea level in the west, below Setif to sea level on the Tunisian

---

[1] See J. Carcopino, 'Un "empereur" maure inconnu d'après une inscription latine récemment découverte dans l'Aurès', *Rev. des Etudes anciens*, 46 (1944), 94–126. Also *The Donatist Church*, 304, for other examples.

[2] See Ch. Courtois, *Les Vandales et l'Afrique*, 349. The arrival of the 'grands nomades' as invaders of North Africa was 'un événement décisif dans l'histoire de la Berbérie'.

[3] Ibid., 344–5.

[4] See E. F. Gautier, *Le Passé de l'Afrique du Nord: les siècles obscurs*, Paris 1937, 264–280, for the geographical significance of the battle sites between Berber and Arab in the seventh century. In Numidia, as in Anatolia, the effect of the dominance of the nomad tribes was that the country reverted from settled agriculture to transhumance, ibid., 280.

[5] See G. Charles Picard, *La Civilisation de l'Afrique romaine*, Paris 1959, and Susan Raven, *Rome in Africa*, London 1969, for illustrations.

coast. When the Romans came this land was the home of semi-nomadic tribes, moving from plain to mountain with their meagre possessions according to season. Rome's administrators ended this way of life. The tribes were settled within closely defined limits and encouraged to farm. The key to the astonishing success that attended this policy was the introduction of the olive as the staple crop, which could thrust its roots deep into the subsoil and tap reserves of water below. The Berber farmers were given favourable terms of tenure (through the *Lex Mancia*) and by the middle of the second century A.D. a prosperous agriculture adapted to a dry climate had developed. By the time of the revolt of the Gordians against the emperor Maximin in 238, the abundance of the native population in what had previously been steppe and desert had become proverbial.[1]

The comments of Herodian are borne out completely by archaeological evidence. In the years before World War I when neither overpopulation nor pollution were the menaces they are to-day, a remarkable archaeological survey was carried out in Algeria. The results, published in 1911, showed that the High Plains then consisting of vast empty space, had been thickly peopled in Roman and Byzantine times with villages, some of which had been very large and not more than a few miles away from each other.[2] Further exploration of some of these sites brought out another interesting fact. The villages had been Christian.[3] None of those surveyed failed to yield at least one church and in some there were as many as four or five.[4] Next to the churches the remains of olive presses were the most prominent feature of the sites. Occupation had continued unbroken through Roman, Vandal and Byzantine times, but evidently not beyond. While some smaller towns in Numidia, such as Tiddis near Constantine, have yielded traces of Arab occupation down to the eleventh century, including the characteristic glass coins of the Abbasids, nothing similar has ever been reported from a Romano-Berber village.[5] Moreover, it is evident that before the end of the Byzantine occupation, churches were becoming smaller and more rudely constructed. Some were almost indistinguishable from native huts. The Latin of the seventh-century Christian Numidia was also almost unrecognisable. One text mentioning the exarch Peter who governed Byzantine Africa from circa 635–640, and several bishops found in the church at Telergma in Central Numidia defied the efforts of scholars to decipher it for nearly twenty years.[6] In 645, a wretched little building on a knoll outside Timgad was the last dated

[1] Herodian, *Historia*, ed. K. Stavenhagen, 1922, vii. 4. 14.
[2] See, for example, S. Gsell, *Atlas archéologique de l'Algérie*, Paris 1911, feuilles, Batna and Constantine.
[3] A. Berthier and colleagues *Les Vestiges du Christianisme antique dans la Numidie centrale*, Algiers 1942, 35.
[4] A. Berthier, op. cit., 48–75, (Oued Rizel).
[5] A. Berthier, *L'Algérie et son Passé*, Paris 1951, 149, referring to Tiddis.
[6] First published by J. Bosco and Mme J. Alquier in *Receuil de Constantine*, LV iii., 1927, 209–19. Its mysteries were finally solved by P. A. Février and Y. Duval in a long study, 'Inscription martyrologique sur plomb de la région de Telergma', *Mélanges de l'Ecole de Rome*, 81, 1969, 257–320.

church in Roman Africa. It was the work of the Patrician Gregorius. In this respect the story of the decline of Christianity resembles the terminal Christian phase in the Nile valley.[1]

What had happened? The insecurity of the High Plains from nomad attacks was probably largely responsible. As the Byzantines withdrew to the shelter of their massive forts built amid the wreckage of the Roman towns, the villagers were left to the mercy of plundering bands. Olives that take twenty years to mature were cut down. Livelihoods were lost overnight. Dams built to conserve the water from the wadis were neglected or destroyed. The Arab writer, Ibn Khaldoun, corroborates the Byzantine author's description of the Berber nomads: 'They live in tents and they breed camels', he says, 'They ride on horseback, transporting their dwellings from one place to another. They spend the summer in the coastal mountains (the Tell) and winter in the desert. They kidnap the inhabitants of the cultivated areas and they reject the rule of a just and regular government'.[2] Thanks to their attentions Numidia was already reverting to semi-nomadic economy whence it had emerged five centuries before, at the moment when the Arabs appeared on the scene.

In 647 the Arabs advanced across the desert of Sirte and entered the Byzantine province of Byzacena. They defeated and killed the Patrician Gregorius near his capital at Sbeitla. Byzantine power was not ended, however, and we hear of the Byzantines as allies of the Berbers against the Arabs for another thirty years. Henceforth, however, power passed from them to the Arab and Berber tribesmen. The fate of the cultivator was sealed. To quote another Arab historian whose theme was the Moslem conquest of Spain, we are told how the Louata split up and spread over the eastern part of Maghreb (north-west Africa) until they reached Sousse.[3] Another nomadic tribe, the Hawarra occupied Tripolitania.[4] The 'Afariq' (settled Berbers) previously subject to the Rum (Byzantines) were forced to pay tribute as was their wont to the occupiers of their country.[5]

Islands of cultivation retaining a degree of Romanisation survived until the great Hillalian invasions of the eleventh century which extinguished settled agriculture on the North African plains. They were, however, survivals only, and with the decline and abandonment of villages, Christianity also declined. The Arab chroniclers make a clear distinction between the settled farming population of 'Beranes' which was 'mostly Christian' and the nomads (Botr) who were not.[6] The situation had not changed since the time of Procopius and Corippus. The Louata who defeated the Vandals 'were ignorant of the Christian God',[7] and in many

---

[1] P. Monceaux, *Timgad chrétien*, Paris 1911, 22.

[2] Ibn Khaldoun, *Histoire des Berbères*, ed. G. de Slane, Paris 1858, iii. 179. See my 'North Africa and Europe in the Early Middle Ages', in *Trans-Royal Historical Society*, Ser. v, 5(1954), 74–5.

[3] Ibn abd al Hakam, *Conquête de l'Afrique du Nord et de l'Espagne*, ed. and trans. A. Gateau, Alger 1942, 31.

[4] Ibid.   [5] Ibid.   [6] Ibid., 77.

[7] Procopius, *De Bello Vandalico*, iii. 8. 18 and compare Corippus, *Iohannidos*, vii. 307–15, the Louata performing human sacrifices in the mid-sixth century.

cases were converted straight to Islam. Indeed of one large tribe, the Sanhadja, settled near Sousse, Ibn Khaldoun says they 'never had been Christian'.[1] Whether to avoid paying the *Kharaj* and to defend their womenfolk, or for other causes, the desert Berbers accepted Islam en masse.[2] In 710 they were among the foremost in the invading army that overthrew the Christian Visigoths in Spain. Though Christianity in North Africa never seems to have been proscribed by the Arabs and churches, whether in town or village show little, if any, sign of violent destruction, its extinction was final as the high plateaus became dominated by nomadic tribes. Not even a century of missionary-conscious occupation by the French had the slightest effect on the situation. Within fifty years of Gregorius's defeat, if not before, North Africa had for all practical purposes ceased to be Christian.

The battle of Sbeitla in 647 had much the same effect on the history of North Africa as the battle of Manzikert in 1071 had on the fortunes of the Byzantines in Anatolia. If anything, Christianity was even more strongly rooted in Asia Minor than it had been in North Africa. The province of Asia, occupying much of Western Asia Minor and including the cities of Ephesus, Pergamum, Smyrna and Sardis had been among the first areas to be Christianised. By the time of the Council of Nicaea in 325, Christianity was the predominant religion. The last pockets of rural paganism were converted by a combination of imperial pressure and monastic mission in the reign of Justinian. From then on, until the time of the disastrous battle of Manzikert, Anatolia was Greek in language and the great majority of its people adherents of Chalcedonian orthodoxy. Within a few years of 1071, however, the Seljuks had moved across the whole of the centre of Anatolia, and when the Crusaders entered the scene at the end of the century they had to fight their way across Asia Minor all the way from Nicaea to the Taurus mountains.

The Seljuk Turks presented the Byzantines with problems completely different from those with which the Moslem Arabs had confronted them in the previous four centuries. The Arabs had indeed broken in on the Byzantine dominions as a nomadic horde. The object of the first Arab armies had been plunder and the destruction of the settled life of villages and monasteries that they envied and hated. They had no interest in liberating anyone, Copts, Syrians or Armenian Monophysites from Byzantine rule. After their failure, however, to destroy the Byzantine empire in Asia Minor and to capture Constantinople in 717, an equilibrium had become established. The government of the Arab emirates had taken on the character of settled administrations and the razzias against the Byzantines became wars between evenly matched opponents with limited political objectives. In the reign of Basil 1 (d. 1025), it seemed as though a lasting frontier had been established between the two great faiths and systems of government.

[1] Ibn Khaldoun, op. cit, i. 212, referring to the situation circa 670.
[2] Ibn abd al Hakam, op. cit. 31–3, and Ibn Khaldoun i. 211 (duress).

NOMADS AND CHRISTIANITY IN THE MIDDLE AGES

The onset of the Seljuk Turks from central Asia brought about a new situation. The Turks were nomadic tribesmen led by a warrior aristocracy and remained such from the time they first threatened the Armenian principalities on Byzantium's eastern flank in 1015–1022, until the fateful clash with armies of Diogenes Romanus in 1071.[1] Only the previous year, bands of Seljuk tribesmen had raided over the 1200 miles that separated Armenia and the Lycos valley. In the decade that followed, the Anatolian plateau fell effectively under their control. First, the Cappadocian countryside was made untenable for the existing settled population and then the towns were isolated and captured. Churches were pillaged and desecrated and the population was scattered as refugees. In the reign of Michael VII, 1072–78, the chronicler Attaliotes records that 'the Turks were everywhere'. 'Asia was going up in flames'.[2]

The Crusaders undoubtedly saved the Byzantines from the first Turkish onrush. The campaign waged by the emperor Alexius I in 1097–98 in the wake of the Crusader victories was among the most effective undertaken by the Byzantines since the time of Basil. Once more an equilibrium was established with the Moslem invaders. Western Asia Minor reverted to Byzantine control. The Seljuks consolidated their hold on the Anatolian plateau and established their sultanate at Konya. In the twelfth century, war became formalised between armies that knew and respected each other's tactics. Even Manuel Comnenus's disaster at Myriokephalon in 1176 seemed to the Turks something of a Pyrrhic victory. Their own losses were very heavy and their effort to exploit their victory as far as Laodicea ended in defeat. They were glad to agree terms for a truce.[3]

Had the Turks of Konya been the only Islamic power established in Asia Minor, the frontier between Moslem and Christian territory could have consolidated, leaving western Asia Minor and the north and south coastal areas in Christian hands with the Turks controlling the Anatolian plateau. In addition, as had happened in the Arab occupied territories, there were also Christians in Asia Minor who preferred Turkish to Byzantine political rule. What made the situation for the Christians, however, far more unfavourable whether under Turkish rule or in the debatable land between Turk and Byzantium in Asia Minor, was the existence of the Turkomen nomads who accompanied the Turkish armies, but knew no law but that of the plunderer.[4]

These nomads were the greatest danger to the Byzantines and the

---

[1] The situation in Asia Minor in the three decades from the accession of Constantine IX in 1042 to the battle of Manzikert is excellently described by S. Vryonis, *The Decline of Mediaeval Hellenism in Asia Minor and the Process of Islamisation from the Eleventh through the Fifteenth Century*, University of California Press 1971, 85–96.

[2] Michael Attaliotes, ed. Niebuhr, Bonn, 213–4. Most of the damage at this stage was being done by Turcomen tribesmen and not by the victorious troops of Alp Arslan.

[3] Nicetas Choniates, *De Manuele Comneno*, vi.5, ed. I Bekker, Bonn, 245–6.

[4] For the activity of these tribesmen against the Byzantines during Manuel's campaign of 1175–6 and afterwards, see Nicetas Choniates vi. 6, 248–9 and 254–257.

Christian native population in western Asia Minor in the twelfth and thirteenth centuries.[1] Every contemporary writer comments on the destruction to settled civilisation and Christianity which they caused. Thus, at the end of the century, the Latin writer of the *Historia Peregrinorum* for instance, describes how these 'bandits' or 'Bedouin', whom Frederick Barbarossa encountered on his march across Asia Minor in 1189–90, lived in their tents and moved about with their herds from one pasture to another. They had no cities or even homes, and subject to no jurisdiction lived a life devoted to pillage. The same source tells of 'thousands' of these nomads who harassed the Crusaders near Philomelium in Phrygia.[2] For the previous fifty years, in fact, they had been steadily infiltrating Byzantine territory from the east and south-east. In the reign of Manuel Comnenus (1143–1180), they had occupied the upper Maeander and Lycos valleys and forced the Christian population to migrate.[3] When Manuel opened his great campaign against the Sultanate of Konya in 1175, he found far to the north of his line of advance that plains round the city of Dorylaeum were occupied by 2000 nomads and had been deserted by the farming population.[4] As he moved south he was harassed by swarms of Turkomen raiders. Already at this time the movement of population was leading to the change from Greek to Turkish place-names, and thus the permanent loss of the area both to Hellenism and to Christianity.[5]

Moreover, the Turkomen were actively hostile to Christianity. Both Byzantine and Moslem authorities agree that some of the bands were inspired by a sense of 'holy war' (*jihad*) against the Christians. Anna Comnena reports how circa 1150 a Seljuk general was reinforced against the Byzantines by Turkomen tribesmen from Asia (i.e. the inland Anatolian plateau).[6] Sometimes they operated also in close liaison with the sultanate of Konya.[7] As Vryonis has shown, 'the two most important religious shrines mentioned in Turkish epics located in the Turkomen country were those of Moslem martyrs who had fallen in battle against the Byzantines in the Arab-Byzantine wars'.[8] Quite naturally the Turkomen sided consistently with the Turks against the Christians.

[1] Thus, W. M. Ramsay (*Cities and Bishoprics of Phrygia*, Oxford 1897, 695) emphasises that the greatest danger to the Byzantines during the twelfth century came from the nomads who were constantly harrying the Christian settlements regardless whether there was a state of war or peace between the Turks and Byzantines.

[2] *Historia Peregrinorum*, ed. A. Chroust, *MGH*, N. S. v, Berlin 1928, 156: 'Hii sunt praedones qui soliti devastare terras finitimas ipsum eciam soldanum inquietere non verentur'. Compare also, Bar Hebraeus, *Chronicon*, ed. Abeloos and Lamy, Louvain 1872–77, i. 732. (Turcoman raids in Melitene circa 1250).

[3] *Historia Peregrinorum*, 155 referring to 'Turci sive Bedewini' nomads, 'Horum innumera multitudine . . .', in the area of Laodicea, then deserted by its inhabitants (A.D. 1190).

[4] John Cinnamus, *Historia*, ed. I. Bekker, Bonn, 190–1, and 198–9. See Vryonis, 188–9, and Ramsay, loc. cit.

[5] Thus, Ramsay's *Cities and Bishoprics*, ii. 373, referring to the area of Phrygia between Ushak to the north and Uluburlu and Chonae to the south, and ibid., 696.

[6] Nicetas Choniates, vi. 1, 227–8.

[7] Anna Comnena, *Alexias*, ed. A. Reifferscheid, xiv. 6, 284.

[8] Vryonis, op. cit., 192–3.

NOMADS AND CHRISTIANITY IN THE MIDDLE AGES

One can trace with some accuracy the progress of the decline of Christian populations in western Asia Minor in this period.[1] The first stage was characterised by the withdrawal of the Christian population from the countryside to the shelter of the towns. Then, towns situated in areas difficult to defend were themselves abandoned for strong points nearby. Thus, in the twelfth century, the inhabitants of Laodicea near Hierapolis moved from the remains of the city to the more defensible Denizli where the modern Turkish town stands to-day.[2] Alternatively, as at Sardis, the Christians withdrew from the city which had expanded in Greco-Roman times on to the plains, to the high ground to the south overlooking a ford. There the wretched building which served as the cathedral was built, and it was in use until the diocese collapsed soon after 1369. The survivors of the Christian population withdrew to the original acropolis, where a small chapel and cemetery were maintained until the sixteenth century.[3] The process of decline was slow but continuous as the nomads occupied the surrounding countryside and reduced the Christian communities to a series of disconnected and demoralised islands.

The significance of what was happening in Asia Minor may be assessed when measured against the situation resulting from the Turkish conquest of the Balkans in the fourteenth and fifteenth centuries. Here the Turkish armies were completely successful and within a century of their first appearance in Europe in 1358, the whole Balkan peninsula had been conquered. The Turkish empire lasted there until 1912. The Orthodox Church, however, survived. The only lasting penetration by Islam was among the heretical Christians, such as the Bogomils in Bosnia and in the fastnesses of Albania. This time the Moslems formed beleaguered islands amid a predominantly Christian population. One reason was that the Turkish armies were not accompanied by hordes of plundering nomads stirred to hatred of the Christian agricultural population by economic and religious interest. There were no herds of camels to be seen on the Athenian agora as one can see them to-day in the ruins of Ephesus or within a mile or two of Kairouan.

We may now apply these lessons to the question of the end of Christian civilisation in Nubia. The inhabitants of the three Nubian kingdoms that

[1] For instance, see W. C. Brice, 'The Turkish Colonisation of Anatolia'. *Bull. of John Rylands Library*, 38, 1955, 18–44, especially 26–7.

[2] W. M. Ramsay, op. cit., 16 ff. Philadelphia was described circa 1190 by the writer of the *Historia Peregrinorum*, 154, as being the only refuge of the Christian population in face of Turkish incursions. ('locus ille in illis partibus incursibus Turcorum christianis erat tutamen et refugium'.)

[3] Vryonis, op. cit., 298. Christianity was not immediately extinguished upon the Seljuk takeover in 1306. The cathedral was appropriated but the bishopric was not terminated, and the citadel of Sardis came back into its own as a Christian refuge. The American excavations at Sardis in 1972 established that a large cave on the acropolis had been used by the Christians. Frescos had once covered its walls and graves were found in the southern part of the rectangular major space. See G. M. A. Hanfmann, *Anatolian Studies*, (1972), 56–8. (I am grateful to Mr. G. J. Clement of Edinburgh University for the additional information.)

extended down the Nile valley from Aswan to Khartoum were agricul-
turists. In many cases the main settlements such as Senna, Q'asr Ibrim and
Faras succeeded settlements that had existed since Pharaonic times.
Christianity had gradually penetrated from Egypt during the fifth century
A.D.,[1] but it was not until the activity of emissaries of the empress Theodora
(d. 548) and the emperor Justin II (565–578) that Christianity became
their official religion. By the early eighth century Byzantine-style administrations prevailed, of which the best documented is that of the Eparch at
Faras.[2] The religion of the courts and people of Nubia was Monophysite
and they looked to the Coptic patriarch at Alexandria for spiritual
guidance and episcopal consecrations.[3] In addition, after the first clash
with the Moslem armies from Egypt in 652, a military equilibrium between
Christian Nubia and the emirs of Egypt became established.[4] This was
only rarely disturbed and then, as in the 960s when the Nubians were the
aggressors or in 1171–75 when Shams ed Doula led his famous expedition
against Qasr Ibrim and Faras for a limited time only.[5] Even at the end of
the thirteenth century the Nubians could mount quite a formidable
expedition, as shown by the attack on the Egyptian port of Aidhab on the
Red Sea by king David I in 1272. Only in 1288 did Nubia become an
Egyptian client-state. To that time Egyptian invasions seem to have
caused little permanent damage to the Nubian economy or religion. Nor
did the presence of Moslem merchant communities in some Nubian centres
such as Kalabsha, Derr, or Meinarti in the tenth and eleventh centuries
disturb the predominance of Christianity.

Yet Nubian Christianity like the Christianity of Anatolia was destined
to wither and die. It is difficult to put any evidence forward that points
incontrovertibly to Christianity surviving after the first half of the fifteenth
century. The leather scrolls found in a sealed jar in the ruins of a house
built above the Meroitic temple enclosure at Q'asr Ibrim cannot yet be
dated beyond argument. We know too little about the chronological
system, let alone the Nubian language in use at Ibrim at that time. The

---

[1] See, K. Michalowski, 'Open problems of Nubian Art and Culture in the Light of
Discoveries at Faras', (= *Kunst und Geschichte Nubiens in christlicher Zeit*, ed. E. Dinkler,
Rechlinghausen 1972, 12).

[2] U. Monneret de Villard, *Storia della Nubia cristiana*, Cairo 1934, 98 ff., and
S. Jakobielski. *Faras: A History of the Bishopric of Pachoras*, Warsaw 1972, 15–16.

[3] Thus, Eutychius, *Annales*, 387 (*P.G.* cxi. 1122–23,) and see M. Krause 'Zur
Kirchen-und Theologiegeschichte Nubiens' in *Kunst und Geschichte Nubiens in christlicher
Zeit*, ed. E. Dinkler, 71–87.

[4] The Arabic authors who write about Nubia record very few hostile incidents
between the Nubians and Egyptian rulers in the whole period 800–1200. There was a
Beja revolt in 855, the refusal of the Nubians to pay customary dues to Egypt which led to
Prince George's mission to Baghdad in 836, the Nubian raids into Egypt of 950–960 and
the Nubian-Egyptian war of 1171–75, but these are episodes in the otherwise peaceful
co-existence of the two kingdoms and religions.

[5] This seems to have been undertaken as a sort of re-insurance by the family of
Saladin to secure a base in the event of their expulsion from Egypt. An attack on the
Yemen for the same purpose was also considered. Thus, for instance, Ibn Khalkikan (d.
1281), Wafayat al ay ān, Section 127, ed. Ishan Abbas, Beirut, 1963- , i. 306–9.

date of the last scroll placed in the pot with a date on it apparently to the era of the martyrs 1137, i.e. 1421, still seems the most plausible.[1] On the other hand, the numerous sites which have been surveyed and worked upon show no signs of violent destruction. At Q'asr Ibrim the roof of the church had been burnt and formed a distinctive burnt layer overlying the floor of the church, but that building had already been in use for domestic purposes before this event occurred. Its conversion into a mosque was the last stage of occupation, perhaps as late as the eighteenth century. Similarly, the late Christian houses over the podium, though collapsed, showed no destruction by fire. No bodies lay among their ruins like those in the burnt ruins and hypocausts of Caistor-by-Norwich, pointing to the violent end of an urban population in Roman Britain.[2] In some places at Q'asr Ibrim the Moslem occupation seems to have succeeded the terminal Christian period without noticeable break. In others one finds a layer of windblown silt between the Christian and Moslem occupations. Even so, evidence of violence is absent. Other late Christian sites, such as Meinarti, Kulb and Kulubnarti, show similar trends. There was no evidence for a violent end of the Christian occupation, only decline and decay.[3]

The pattern, however, of occupation in Nubian sites between the late twelfth and fifteenth centuries has features in common. As Adams has pointed out, 'from the middle of the twelfth century we find an increasing concentration of the Christian population in a few protected settlements and the growth of defensive architecture.'[4] The late Christian communities show a preference for islands in the Nile such as Kulb and their defences such as the high watchtower at Q'asr Ibrim were designed to command as wide a view across the desert as possible. Even where the mainland settlement continued to be occupied, such as at Serra East, the defences were sited towards the landward rather than the riverward sides. These precautions were not directed at an enemy such as the Egyptian regular army advancing from the north and using river transport down the Nile. The enemy was awaited from the desert and the only enemy from that quarter was the nomadic marauder. Moreover, the late twelfth and thirteenth centuries saw a considerable inpouring of Arab tribes from Arabia into Egypt and the Sudan, which eventually resulted in the nomads actually outnumbering the settled Nubian population.[5] In addition, the position of the Nubian kingdoms, astride the pilgrim's way from the west

[1] See my, 'The Q'asr Ibrim expedition, 1963–4, *Acta*, vii *International Congress of Christian Archaeology*, Rome 1967, 537–8.
[2] Similarly at Colchester, see J. Morris, *The Age of Arthur; a history of the British Isles, from 350–650*, London 1973, 76.
[3] Thus, E. Dinkler, P. Grossmann and B. Diebner, 'Deutsche Nubien-Unternehumgen 1967', *Archäologischer Anzeiger*, 1968, 4, 720–38; W. Y. Adams, The University of Kentucky excavations at Kulubnarti, 1969 (=*Kunst und Geschichte Nubiens*, 141–55) and E. Dinkler, Die deutsche Ausgrabungen auf die Inseln Sunnarti, Tangur und in Kulb, 1968–69, ibid., 259–81.
[4] W. Y. Adams, 'Post-Pharaonic Nubia in the Light of Archaeology ii', *Journal of Egyptian Archaeology*, 51 (1965), 175–6.
[5] Ibid., iii, *JEA*, 52 (1966), 150.

African Moslem kingdoms to the Red Sea embarkation ports for Mecca, made their disappearance welcome to the latter. If the nomads needed any further spur for their depredations, the pilgrims would provide it.[1]

It is not known whether the Sahara and Arab nomads were as hostile to Christianity as their Turkomen counterparts in Anatolia. The damage they caused to the Nubians, however, was considerable. A Moslem Spanish writer of the thirteenth century, Ibn Said (d. 1285) spoke of one of these nomadic tribes, the Damadin as 'the Tartars of the Sudan', destructive enemies of the Nubians and Habasha (Ethiopians).[2] There is also an interesting statement from Ibn Khaldoun (1332–1406), this time writing nearly contemporary with the events he is describing, that in the fourteenth century 'the Juhayna Arabs (nomads), swept over the whole country (of Nubia) and settled down there and turned it into a land of plunder and anarchy'. He went on to say that the Arab chiefs had exploited the Nubian marriage and inheritance laws to seize power for themselves. As a result, ' no trace of royal power remained in this land, and the people reverted to nomadism. They followed the rains like the Arab nomads in Arabia'.[3] The whole country fell into disorder. Ibn Khaldoun hated nomadism and was not unprejudiced in what he wrote, but there was clearly an element of truth in his account.

Even before this destruction Christianity was evidently a declining religion. The churches were smaller and more poorly built. There are no more rich frescoes such as decorated the walls of Faras cathedral before its abandonment sometime after 1169.[4] Economic insecurity, the shift of trade routes from the Nile to the axis of the pilgrim route across the Sahara and the breakdown of ecclesiastical organisation each took their toll of Nubian Christianity.[5] The discovery of the consecration scrolls of bishop Timotheos at Q'asr Ibrim shows that episcopal organisation existed for Ibrim and Faras at the end of the fourteenth century.[6] This may have been the result of Ibrim and Do (Djebel Adda) forming part of a fief dependent on the Sultans of Egypt since the end of the thirteenth century. Even so, Christianity had become fragmented, and, as in Anatolia, the Christian communities at this period were becoming islands amidst an indifferent or hostile nomadic population. It may have been as the Portuguese Alvarez

[1] Adams, ibid., ii, 177.

[2] Ibn Said, published in *Monumenta Cartographica*, iii. 5, fols. 1080–1090, re Section iv of his *Kitab Jugrafiya*. He dates these events to 1224 A.D. In their war against the Nubians in 1287, the Egyptians employed nomads as allies. See *Baybars ad-Dawadan*, ed. Dr. Musad, Cairo 1965, 209.

[3] Ibn Khaldoun *Kitab al-Ibar*, ed. Maktaba, 3rd ed., Beirut 1960–7, referring to the immigration of the Juhayna Arab tribes across the Red Sea from Hejaz into the Eastern Desert and their overthrow of the Nubian kingdoms (ii. 516). Also Adams, *Post-Pharaonic Nubia*, iii. 150.

[4] See K. Michalowski, *Faras: die Kathedrale aus dem Wüstensand*, Zurich 1967, 38–9 and 96–102.

[5] Adams, loc. cit., iii, 153–6.

[6] See J. M. Plumley, *The Bishop's Scrolls from Q'asr Ibrim*, London (Egypt Exploration Society) 1974.

suggests, the simple fact that bishops could no longer reach them from Egypt that was the last straw, and thus, Christianity was abandoned.[1] Of all the factors leading to the decline and extinction of Nubian Christianity, the advent of the nomads both Arab immigrant and Saharan Berber would seem to have been the most important. Other challenges had been encountered in the 800-year history of the Nubian Christian kingdoms and these had been overcome.

That the nomadic peoples, by and large, preferred Islam to Christianity is a cardinal factor in the religious and cultural history of the Mediterranean world. The Nestorian missionaries were not without their successes among the Turkish tribes in central Asia, but these were isolated. The most significant fact was that in the autumn of 1295 the Mongol Khan Ghasan announced his conversion from Buddhism to Islam, and the vast confederation of tribes that looked to him as leader gradually followed suit.[2] Not until the Portuguese controlled the sea routes from western Europe to the East and showed that Islam could be defeated and relief brought to the hard-pressed Christian kingdom of Ethiopia did the tide turn. The nomad belonged to the heroic age of human history. He could not compete against the new-found economic and military power of the Europeans from the sixteenth century onwards. But in the centuries before this the damage he had done to the Christians in the eastern and southern Mediterranean had been enormous. The destruction of Nubian Christianity in the fourteenth and fifteenth centuries was the Moslem nomads' final triumph.

[1] Alvarez, 'A true relation of the lands of the Prester John', published as *The Prester John of the Indies*, ed. C. F. Beckingham and G. W. B. Huntingford, Cambridge 1961, 129 and 460-1.

[2] See B. Spuler, *The Moslems in History*, Eng. tr. G. Wheeler, London 1971, 44-8, and by the same author, *History of the Mongols*, Eng. tr. H. and S. Drummond, London 1972, 144-6.

XXIV

HERESY AND SCHISM AS SOCIAL AND NATIONAL MOVEMENTS

ON 6 July 1439 the delegates of the Greek and Latin Churches signed at Florence a decree of union that ostensibly ended the schism that had lasted for nearly four centuries. The Greeks had accepted the Latin views of purgatory, the eucharist, the Holy Spirit and the Roman primacy. The emperor John VIII received communion at the hands of pope Eugenius IV, and in a solemn mass the Greek and Latin bishops clad in resplendent robes exchanged the kiss of peace. There was dancing in the streets of Florence, and in the western European capitals, especially in the London of Henry VI, processions, festivals and Te Deums. In the next few years, Armenians, Jacobites and Copts trod the same path to Italy and signed similar formulae of union. By the end of 1445 the unity of Christendom appeared to have been restored for the first time since the crisis of the christological controversy almost precisely a thousand years before.[1]

The agreement, however, had been worked out by the leaders of the two communions under the dire pressure of the threat of a Turkish conquest of eastern Europe. The Greeks had submitted ultimately because they realised that the survival of the independence of a few square miles round the city of Constantinople and outposts in Greece and Asia Minor depended almost exclusively on Latin military aid. When that failed at the battle of Varna in November 1444 the flimsy façade of unity was torn down. Popular suspicions re-asserted themselves. The 'Greco-Latins' as those who accepted union were called, were hounded from public life. 'We have sold our faith', some were said to have admitted.[2] In Sancta Sophia the pope was not commemorated at the eucharist as an orthodox prelate. In the few years remaining before the final crisis of the siege of Constantinople Greek opinion

[1] The best account of the negotiations between the Greeks and the Latins at Florence is that by [Joseph] Gill, [*The Council of Florence*] (Cambridge 1959). For the celebrations in London see p 299.

[2] Ducas, *Historia byzantina*, ed I. Bekker (Bonn 1834) XXXII, p 216. See Gill, p 349.

rallied behind those who declared that they 'would rather see the sultan's turban than the Pope's mitre' in Constantinople.[1] They had their way. All that remained from the years of effort towards the restoration of a united Christendom were a few illustrious converts to the Latin view of which cardinal Bessarion was the most famous. In this instance, instinctive popular pressure had triumphed over theological formulae worked out by the leaders of the two communions with great conscientiousness. The forces of culture and civilisation which had found expression in the schism between the churches centuries before were not to be denied. In this paper we look more closely at the nature of some of these forces and their influence in fomenting and perpetuating divisions in the early centuries of the Church.

Divisions have contributed much to the history of the Church. One does not have to be an expert in New Testament criticism to realise that in the generation after the Crucifixion there were serious divisions between Jesus's adherents. Paul and James represented differing outlooks towards the status of Gentiles within the Church: at Antioch there was a breach between Peter and Paul on the same issue (Gal., 2:11), and in Corinth we hear of baptisms in the name of Apollos, Cephas and Christ and resulting divisions within the community (1 Cor., 1:12). Associated within these divergencies was the creation of differing types of church organisation. In Jerusalem the position of James delivering formal judgement at the apostolic council and directing the mission of the Church resembled that of the high priest to whom later generations compared him. His was the monarchical tradition of episcopacy with a focus of worship provided by the existence of the Temple.[2] Beyond the immediate influence of Jerusalem we find, however, prophets and teachers as the bearers of ministerial office, and the Pauline mission churches were ruled by individuals whom Paul addressed sometimes as 'presbyters' and sometimes as 'bishops'. What would have happened if James had had successors of comparable ability to himself or if Jerusalem had not fallen in 70, thus bringing the Palestinian Church to a virtual close, cannot be guessed at. It is evident, however, that even then the christian community was tending to divide along cultural lines, the Churches with the background of the Jewish dispersion adopting different forms of organisation with a less positive emphasis towards the Temple, its

---

[1] *Ibid* XXXVII, p 264, A statement attributed to Gennadius.
[2] On the cultural and geographical factors behind the various types of church government in the time of the apostles and their successors see A. A. T. Ehrhardt, *The Apostolic Succession* (London 1953) ch III.

Heresy and schism as social and national movements

cult and its hierarchical tradition from those favoured by the Jerusalem Christians. The difficulty of adapting a message of repentance and salvation preached to an Aramaic-speaking Palestinian countryside to the provincials of the remainder of the Greco-Roman world whose personal religion was often that of the mystery-cult was becoming evident even at this early stage.

So much may be judged from the events recorded in Acts and by St Paul in his letters, but one would be surprised if either Paul or his opponents had recognised these as among the underlying reasons for their quarrels. The tendencies which each represented only become plain gradually in the light of later events. This is a truism, but it is worth restating, since silence on the part of the participants concerning their non-theological motives has encouraged scholars sometimes to suppose that these did not exist. We must not ask too much of our evidence. We should be surprised to find a Montanist or a Donatist leader describing his opposition to the religion of the catholic clergy in terms of nineteenth-century nationalism. Yet when confronted by the emphasis on prophecy and martyrdom, and on the literal interpretation of the New Testament, especially its apocalyptic passages that characterised both these movements, the historian may be pardoned if he asks himself whether a pattern emerges that links the various rural Christianities in the early Church with each other; and distinguishes their outlook from that of the more conventional established communities in the cities.

This is as far as anyone would like to go, and for the purposes of demonstration I intend to move once again down the beaten trackways of Donatism and Monophysitism. Despite all that has been written in the last twenty years,[1] these seem to provide the best starting points for enquiring into the importance of the non-theological aspects of divisions in the Church in the patristic era in west and east respectively.

It must be sufficiently obvious that the storm that blew up in 311–12 over the election of the archdeacon, Caecilian, as bishop of Carthage, had a long history behind it. From the vantage points of time and distance one can see how the seeds of the controversy are to be found in developments that were present almost from the moment of the foundation of the Church in North Africa more than a century before. The christian mission there, whatever its source, had been confronted

[1] For a bibliography and discussion see my *The Donatist Church* (2nd ed, Oxford 1971) pp v–vi.

with problems different from those encountered in the Greek-speaking world. Roman Africa was ostensibly Latin, but beneath the outward form of latinisation, the population retained much of the religious and cultural heritage of Carthage. In addition, the Jews whose communities extended all the way from Carthage to Volubilis in Morocco [1] and formed a strong element in the background of the development of Christianity there, as elsewhere in the Mediterranean, seem to have been of a strict and legalistic type.[2] They differed considerably in outlook from the Jewish philosophers of Alexandria. For some years, too, the Christians were regarded by the Carthaginian Jews as 'Nazarenes', that is, schismatics from their own body.[3]

Theirs was an exclusive outlook and a harsh one also. Tertullian tells us as a matter of course how the Carthaginian Christians readily regarded themselves as a sect or school 'bound together by common religious purpose and unity of discipline',[4] whose sense of righteousness involved defiance against every manifestation of the existing order and a readiness to die for their convictions. The antitheses Athens versus Jerusalem, the Bible versus philosophy, Christ versus Belial, came readily to them.[5] Intense in their expectations of the approaching end of the world they believed in a judgement in which they would be revenged and would see their idolatrous foes committed to everlasting flames.[6] Believing in the continuous work of the Spirit among baptised Christians, their object was to keep the Church free from every form of defilement, particularly from contact with the pagan world, and they were merciless towards those of their number who appeared to make the slightest concession to the idolater. Their ideas, indeed, had much in common with those of Palestinian Jews in the Maccabaean period. There was the same sense of election, entailing the same rigorous attitude towards the outside world, the same emphasis on an uncompromising adherence to the prescriptions of their covenant and the same hope for the reversal of roles in one final day of reckoning. Indeed, consciousness of the legacy of the Maccabees was to be a factor in the immediate outbreak of the Donatist

---

[1] For Volubilis see P. Berger, *Bulletin Archéologique du Comité des Travaux Historiques* (Paris 1892) p 64, and R. Thouvenot, *Révue des Etudes Africaines* (Paris 1969) pp 352–9.
[2] See the comments of P. Monceaux in *Histoire littéraire de l'Afrique du Nord* (Paris 1901) ch I.
[3] Tertullian, *Adversus Marcionem*, III, 8.
[4] Tertullian, *Apologia*, XXXIX, 1 and *De Spectaculis*, II.
[5] For instance Tertullian, *De Praescriptione*, VII and *De Idololatria*, XIX.
[6] Tertullian, *De Spectaculis*, XXX.

Heresy and schism as social and national movements

crisis, and among the leaders of the Donatist Church during the fourth and early fifth centuries.[1]

The relatively full information about the African Church provided by Cyprian's correspondence half a century later and other writings of this time shows the same factors at work. Though the place of the confessor and prophet as the direct agents of the Spirit and guiding influences in the Church had now been taken by the bishop, the same ideals of apostolic purity and freedom from contagion with the secular world still predominated. 'No salvation outside the Church' rendered definition of the Church and its authority the most important doctrinal issues among the African Christians. The distinction between schism and misbelief tended to become blurred in a general condemnation of anything deemed to be 'outside the Church'. Breach of unity was regarded as the worst of sins, calling down on the heads of the culprits the penalty of Abiram, Dathan and Korah.[2] At the same time, the Church was the 'closed garden' and 'lily among thorns', its purity to be safeguarded at all costs. Even though backsliders among the laity might be tolerated as they had been in Israel there was no place for a cleric who had committed one of the traditional Jewish deadly sins, apostasy (including idolatry), bloodshed and adultery.[3] Not only that, but sacraments offered by such could turn to the detriment of those who partook of them. A congregation had the right and duty to separate itself from a cleric who had lapsed into deadly sin.[4] Final sanction of divine authority for these attitudes was seen in the death of Cyprian as a martyr on 14 September 258.

During Cyprian's episcopate African Christianity was still mainly an urban religion. Its adherents were usually small artisans some of whom, like Soliassus the mule-keeper and Paula a maker of mats, could win reputations for themselves by their wholehearted support of Cyprian's rivals.[5] The leadership, however, lay with a few strong-willed individuals who, like Cyprian himself, had accepted conversion as a radical alternative to the classical heritage and pagan society in which they had been reared. The scale of these conversions should not, however, be overestimated, for a generation later Lactantius a fellow

[1] As shown by the Numidian leader Secundus of Tigisis claiming how in contrast to the primate of Africa, Mensurius of Carthage, his stand during the persecution might be compared with that of Eleazer, the martyr priest in the saga of the Maccabees (2 *Macc.* 6:21). Augustine, *Brev[iculus] Coll[ationis cum Donatistis]*, III, 13, 25.

[2] Cyprian, *Epistolae*, ed W. Hartel, 3 vols, *CSEL*, III (1868–71), LXVII, 3, LXIX, 8.

[3] *Ibid ep* LXIX; *De Unitate Ecclesiae*, VI.

[4] Cyprian, *ep* LXVII, 3–6 (the case of the Spanish bishops).

[5] *Ibid ep* XLII, 1.

African tells us that he had few followers among the lettered classes and many thought him a crank.[1] Even in the beleaguered garrison that was the African Christian Church in the time of Decius and Valerian one can detect the emergence of incipient rifts along social lines. In time of crisis, the mass of the poorer Christians though open-handed when it came to rendering favours to relatives who had sacrificed to the gods tended to accept a rigorous doctrine of the Church with its hopes of recompense hereafter, whereas the wealthier members were often prepared to insure themselves with the authorities at least to the extent of accepting certificates of sacrifice.[2] Their breach with Roman civilisation was not total.

Fifty years later, the picture was essentially the same, though the relative strength and distribution of the different interests within the Church had modified considerably. Many of the urban communities were now, so far as the evidence goes, firmly in the hands of the moderates. These were people who accepted the state, and, unless told to do otherwise, the authorities accepted them. In return, some elements in Cyprianic rigorism including the emphasis placed on the requirement for baptism to be performed by a priest in every way in a state of grace was falling into desuetude.[3] In contrast to this, the artisan element had been reinforced powerfully by a fairly rapid spread of Christianity in the countryside and in particular in Numidia. There had also developed a growing sense of self-identification among the Numidian Christians, whose primate in the years between 260 and 300 acquired the right of consecrating the bishop of Carthage.

These new Christians brought to the Church much of the idealistic sectarianism that had characterised the African Church a century before. Denial of duties to the state, including military service, sense of brotherhood, acceptance of martyrdom, including voluntary martyrdom, a readiness to model conduct on the example of the Maccabees, and a fanaticism that could vent itself on more moderate attitudes were all apparent in Numidia and in the rural areas generally before the outbreak of the schism in 312.[4] So, at the very moment when Christianity among the citizens and wealthier people was becoming more conformist and more part of the general provincial scene, the masses

[1] Lactantius, *Divinae Institutiones*, ed S. Brandt, *CSEL*, XIX (1890) v, 1, 24.
[2] Thus Cyprian's comment in *De Lapsis* XI concerning wealthy *libellatici* 'Decepit multos patrimonii sui amor caecas', ed W. Hartel, *CSEL*, III, 1, p 244.
[3] This requirement was dropped with the agreement of the Caecilianists at the council of Arles in 314 (canon 9).
[4] See *The Donatist Church*, ch 1 and pp 141–4.

Heresy and schism as social and national movements

showed no tendencies towards abandoning the rigorist traditions of the African Church. The mention, too, of avoidance of the consequences of fiscal debt as one of the motives for voluntary martyrdom during the great persecution provides just a hint that some of the anti-pagan fanaticism of the countryside was shared by the poorer element among the Christians in Carthage.[1] Perhaps as Lactantius suggests, the economic reforms of the Tetrarchy, particularly the attempt to resuscitate the African cities after a generation of decay, and the multiplication of the bureaucracy following the provincial reforms had caused hardship and anger.[2] This found its outlet in violent protest against the edicts of persecution in 303 and 304.

Donatism was the heir to all this latent discontent. If one looks carefully at the events which led up to the schism one finds both in Numidia and in Carthage the Donatists being swept into office by popular acclaim regardless of their personal worthiness. At Cirta in 305 for instance, the capital of Numidia, the mob incarcerated the christian citizens in the cemetery of the martyrs, while a tumultuary election of the sub-deacon Silvanus as bishop was carried through by what was described as a crowd of peasants, quarry workers and women of the town.[3] Though their protest was supposed to be against the clergy, like the deceased bishop Paul who had handed over the scriptures to the authorities and thus become a *traditor*, the man they chose in his place had been almost equally guilty; he had handed over the church plate.[4] At Carthage in 312, the archdeacon Caecilian had the support of the citizens when he was elected as bishop but was unpopular with the people, and they accepted the leadership of the Numidians who saw their own interests threatened by Caecilian's election.[5] In addition to this, the Donatists represented the rigorist tradition of African theology true in every particular to the outlook and doctrine of the Church in the time of Cyprian. They were harsh towards backsliders, especially the *traditores* who were regarded as guilty of committing the word of God to the flames. They proclaimed the purity of the Church purged through the suffering of its martyrs. They

---

[1] Augustine, *Brev Coll*, III, 13, 25 'et fisci debitores, qui occasione persecutionis vel carere veilent onerosa multis debita vita...vel certe acquirere pecuniam'.

[2] Lactantius, *De Mortibus Persecutorum*, ed J. Moreau, 2 vols, S[ources] Ch[rétiens] XXXIX (Paris 1954) VII, XXIII.

[3] *Gesta apud Zenophilum*, ed C. Ziwsa, *CSEL*, XXVI (1893) p 196, 'Campenses et harenarii fecerunt illum [Silvanum] episcopum...Prostibulae illic fuerunt'.

[4] *Ibid* pp 188–9.

[5] Optatus, [*De Schismate Donatistorum*], ed C. Ziwsa, *CSEL*, XXVI (1893) I, 18.

had a vivid concept of divine wrath and judgement, and they rejected
with horror the possibility of an alliance with the Constantinian state.
The emperor to be sure, might be 'of God', and worthy to act as
umpire in a dispute with the Catholics, but his sphere of action was
a limited one. His duty was to secure earthly peace and liberty for the
Church, but not otherwise to intervene in its affairs, let alone coerce
its members. In all this the Donatists were by no means isolated from
the main stream of western thought as the writings of Victor of
Pettau or the schism of the Luciferians later in the century shows,[1]
but in Africa the strength of Christianity as the religion of town and
countryside alike had allowed parties to form representing irreconcil-
able interests reinforced by provincial divisions. Under the pressure of
the great persecution schism was the inevitable result.

The Donatist outlook remained consistent throughout the whole
period of the schism. Though in social terms they were strongest
among the populace of Carthage and in rural Numidia the background to their movement was always religious.[2] They claimed
strict adherence to the teaching of Cyprian regarding the nature of the
Church and the inviolability of its sacraments, the purity of its membership, and its complete separation from the world. A Donatist on being
baptised would be expected to renounce all connection with the
secular world and cleave to the Bible and its teaching only.[3] 'The
servants of God are those who are hated by the world', so ran the title
of a Donatist work which at the end of the fifth century Gennadius,
the presbyter of Marseilles, was to pronounce as irreproachable in its
orthodoxy.[4] This combat was always against the Devil and his allies;
the goal of christian life was the imitation of Christ through penance
and suffering leading to the martyr's death.

These objectives had, however, the effect of widening the scope of the
Donatist protest. It was not merely that the value to the Church of the
Constantinian revolution was denied. The Donatist saw the rulers of
the present age as permanently on the side of the Devil against the
servants of God. In a catena of denunciation which recalls 4 Maccabees
in its vituperative power, Petilian, bishop of Constantine (Cirta)

[1] On this theme, see my note on 'The Roman Empire in the Eyes of the Western Schismatics', *Miscellanea Historiae Ecclesiasticae*, II (Louvain 1961) pp 5–22.
[2] This aspect is brilliantly treated by [J. P.] Brisson, [*Autonomisme et Christianisme dans
l'Afrique romaine de Septime Sévère à l'invasion vandale*] (Paris 1958) ch I.
[3] As made clear in the case of bishop Marculus, *Passio Marculi*, PL 8 (1844) I, col 760.
[4] Gennadius, *De Scriptoribus Ecclesiasticis*, PL 59 (1862) IV, col 1059, concerning Vitellius
Afer, 'Si tacuisset de nostro velut persecutorum nomine egregiam doctrinam ediderat'.

Heresy and schism as social and national movements

writing c 400, recalled to his clergy how from creation to his own day, from the time of Abel's murder onwards, the righteous had received nothing but oppression from the world's rulers. 'But what have you to do with the kings of this world, in whom Christianity has never found anything save envy towards her? And to teach you shortly the truth of what I say: a king persecuted the brethren of the Maccabees. A king also condemned the three children to the sanctifying flames, being ignorant what he did, seeing that he himself was fighting against God. A king sought the life of the infant Saviour. A king exposed Daniel, as he thought, to be eaten by wild beasts. And the Lord Christ Himself was slain by a king's most wicked judge.'[1] Similarly, during the period of catholic ascendancy after the exile of Donatus in 347, the emperor Constans, good Nicene Christian though he was, found himself denounced as 'Anti-Christ' and his government as that of the Devil by Donatist pamphleteers in Carthage.[2]

These attitudes can be traced back to the period of the Maccabees when they reflected the religious attitudes of Jews striving for religious liberty against the Seleucids. The same outlook is reproduced almost exactly among the African Christians of the third century and continued by the Donatists. Indeed it is far from true to claim as some ancient historians have been tempted to do that 'it was only when the verdict of Constantine went against them that the Donatists evolved the doctrine that the Church should be independent of the state'.[3] Theirs was an attitude that belonged to the western tradition from its beginning, and behind that it looked back to some of the attitudes of Palestinian Judaism. The Donatist, like Tertullian two centuries before, was against 'the world'. His identification of the world with secular rule was not confined to the Roman empire and not to any individual emperor. After the empire's disappearance and replacement by the Vandals, Gaiseric was to be denounced with equal force by Donatist writers.[4] Nor does Donatist support for the African rebel leaders, Firmus and Gildo, necessarily suggest that they aimed at political separation from the Roman empire. The ultimate aim of both

---

[1] Augustine, *Contra Litteras Petiliani*, II, 92, 202.
[2] Especially in the *Passio Marculi* and *Passio Maximiani et Isaaci*, *PL* 8 (1844), cols 760–72.
[3] Thus A. H. M. Jones, 'Were ancient heresies national or social movements in disguise?', *JTS*, new series X, 2 (1959) pp 280–98 at p 282. Compare G. E. M. de Ste Croix, 'Christianity's encounter with the Roman government', *Crucible of Christianity* (London 1969) p 351.
[4] *Liber Genealogus*, ed T. Mommsen, *MGH, AA*, IX (Berlin 1892) p 195.

rebels is uncertain, but it is doubtful whether either saw themselves as independent rulers. Perhaps a 'kingdom of Africa' on the lines of Matsumas's 'kingdom of Moors and Romans' in the next century was the limit of their horizons.[1] To that extent, however, the Donatists may have been prepared to accept a change of political masters. Augustine's suggestion, albeit from the catholic standpoint, that small kingdoms living in harmony with each other were preferable to great empires,[2] may reflect a fragment of floating political tradition common to both parties in Africa at the end of the fourth century.

Mere change of secular masters was, however, not high on the Donatist list of priorities. Firmus's revolt in 372, however, seems to have been precipitated as a protest against overtaxation, in particular the tax which struck the rural population hardest, the *annona*.[3] It is on this level that the point of junction between the religious and non-religious factors in the Donatist schism may be found. A 'realised apocalyptic' designed to end all oppression provided a focus for the dual element in Donatist teaching. The idea of the end of the existing age presaging judgement associated with a massive reversal of fortunes struck the imagination of the people. It found a particularly ready acceptance in rural Numidia and Mauretania where extortionate taxation and perhaps over-population led to chronic indebtedness, and as a result, produced a restless rural proletariat fanatically christian, and ready to listen to preachers who promised the overthrow of the landowners and their bailiffs in the name of God. There is no evidence to show why the circumcellion movement should have come to notice in 340, except that 'extortionate exactions' seem to have been levied from imperial estates in Africa for a generation past, but in the three quarters of a century of its recorded existence it impressed its characteristics on contemporaries whether violently hostile or mildly admonishing, like Tyconius, in precisely the same way. Its leaders proclaimed themselves 'leaders of the saints' and combined the religious drive of men and women on perpetual pilgrimage among the shrines of the local martyrs with a revolutionary zeal aimed ultimately at winning the crown of martyrdom for themselves.[4]

The programme of social reform is unmistakable. Optatus of Milevis writing *c* 365 states that thanks to Fasir and Axeido, the

---

[1] See J. Carcofino, 'Un empereur maure inconnu', *Révue des Etudes anciennes*, XLVI (Paris 1944) pp 94–120.   [2] *De Civitate Dei*, IV, 3.
[3] Zosimus, *Historia Nova* ed L. Mendelssohn (Leipzig 1887) IV, 16.
[4] Optatus, III, 4. See *The Donatist Church*, pp 172–6; Brisson, chapter on 'L'Impatience populaire'; H. J. Diesner, *Kirche und Staat in spätromischen Reich* (Berlin 1963) pp 110 ff.

Heresy and schism as social and national movements

circumcellion leaders, 'no one could feel secure in his estates' and that the debtor's bond lost its force. No creditor possessed the liberty of exacting payment of a debt.[1] More than merely defending the unfortunate, the Circumcellions reversed earthly fortunes whenever chance arose. Rich men driving comfortable vehicles would be pitched out of them and made to run behind their carriages which were now occupied by their slaves.[2] This was not an isolated account. Seventy years later Augustine reports with lurid detail similar events.[3] His rival bishop of Hippo found himself in the position of leader of one of these bands operating against villas in the neighbourhood of the town.[4] There is the same catalogue of outrages, destruction of creditors' bonds, enforcement of slave labour on the possessing classes, compulsory freeing of slaves and threat of reprisal in case of disobedience. There is no reason to believe either, that the Circumcellions were other than religious fanatics. Augustine has much to say about their war cry 'Deo Laudes', their false pilgrimages and suicides under the pretext of seeking martyrdom, but makes no reference to any activities as day labourers using their clubs to knock down the olives ready for harvest.[5] It might be added too, that such evidence as exists, suggests that in the towns also the Donatists tended to represent the outlook of the serving and working rather than the privileged community.[6]

So far as Donatism is concerned the links between religious belief and popular discontent seem to be established. The clue however lies in the eschatology of the movement. Over all loomed the spectre of divine judgement. The battle against the Devil was unending. From resistance against Antichrist reflected in the persecuting authorities of the secular world in the third century,[7] the Christian moved towards overthrowing the Devil in the form of oppressive magistrates and extortionate landowners after the conversion of Constantine. In both the goal was victory not over 'flesh and blood' but over spiritual powers of wickedness, and if the weapon was usually the circumcellion's club, the ideal was self-immolation in the glory of martyrdom and assurance of vengeance at the Last Day.[8]

[1] Optatus, III, 4.
[2] *Ibid.*   [3] Augustine, *Epistolae*, CLXXXV, 4, 15 (written in 417).   [4] *Ibid* CVIII, 5, 14.
[5] As E. Tengström, *Donatisten und Katholiken* (Göteberg 1964) pp 51–2.
[6] Augustine, *Contra Litteras Petiliani*, II, 83, 184 (Donatist *inquilini* in Hippo).
[7] For the emperor Decius being regarded as the 'forerunner of Antichrist' in the popular view among African Christians see Cyprian, *Ep* LV, 9. Decius was 'ipsum anguem maiorem metatorem antichristi'.
[8] As defined by Petilian of Constantine, cited by Augustine, *Contra Litteras Petiliani*, II, 89, 196.

The equation of social revolutionary zeal coupled with eschatological hopes and the rejection of the established forms and organisation of religion was not a phenomenon confined to fourth-century North Africa. If one looks back to the past, one also finds it a recurring theme of late Jewish history; it is present as one of the themes in the second part of the Book of Daniel; in the great revolt against Rome in 66 we find the Zealots as hostile to the men of wealth among the Jews and the priestly caste, as they were bitter enemies of Rome.[1] Debtors' bonds were destroyed with their owners in best circumcellion style. Then as one looks ahead into the history of popular religious movements in medieval and reformation Europe the same phenomena are discernible. We have only to think of the Peasants' Revolt of 1381 and the jingle 'When Adam delved and Eve span, Who was then a gentleman', used as a text by John Ball, monk of St Albans, at the period of the rising, to see how biblical literalism could form a focus for political and social discontent. A generation later, in the 1420s, the Czech Adamites preached the approaching judgement and the duty of imitating Adam and Eve and wearing no clothes, but also not to pay any interest to anyone and to defy the authorities, including that of the Czech patriot Ziska.[2]

Ziska's Taborites were Millenarists, believing that all lords, nobles and knights would be cut down and exterminated in the forests like outlaws and the millennium established.[3] Their armed bands included a heterogeneous company of artisans, indentured servants, beggars and prostitutes, which could easily have been exchanged for the mobs that produced and sustained the Donatist leadership in fourth-century North Africa. In another part of central Europe, Thuringia, apocalyptic movements reflected peasant discontent for a century before the outbreak of the Peasants' Revolt in 1525. The militant Anabaptist, Thomas Müntzer (1485–1525) believed the uprising would herald the descent of New Jerusalem, and he believed too, like the circumcellion leaders, in an egalitarianism based on the Gospel, in which princes and lords would lose their traditional roles. In struggles against baronial and ecclesiastical oppression in Europe extending over a thousand years

[1] Josephus, *Wars*, IV, 3.2; IV, 6, 1. Zealots 'thirsting after the blood of valiant men and men of good families'. For zealot attitudes see M. Hengel, *Die Zeloten* (Leiden/Köln 1961) pp 266 ff.

[2] See T. Büttner and E. Werner, *Circumcellionen und Adamiten zwei Formen mittelalterlicher Haeresie* (Berlin 1959) pp 79–83

[3] See N. Cohn, *The Pursuit of the Millennium* (2nd ed, London 1970) pp 238 ff; G. Rupp, *Patterns of Reformation* (London 1969) pp 298–302.

Heresy and schism as social and national movements

we can point to the same features activating popular revolt. Prophecy and hope of martyrdom in expectation of future vindication motivated by the Book of Daniel and Revelation provided much of the inspiration for the peasant armies. In these movements the African Donatists paved the way for western Europe as a whole.

One turns now to the more complicated situation presented by the monophysite movement in the East. At first sight the Monophysites resembled the Donatists. They were schismatics, they drew their support from the masses of the people in Egypt and Syria, and even more than the Donatists their churches developed along national or territorial lines. By 600 they were dominant in a great band of territory extending from the Black Sea to the sources of the Nile embracing Armenia, much of Syria, many of the Arab tribes, Egypt, Nubia and Ethiopia. Theirs was a third religious force, territorially more extensive than Byzantine and Latin Christianity combined. The end product of an independent hierarchy based on national or territorial allegiances has tempted historians to see Monophysitism at its outset as an expression of popular will directed against the Byzantine emperor and the Chalcedonian faith that he represented. It is for the east, however, that the challenge contained in the article by my late mentor and friend A. H. M. Jones, 'Were the ancient heresies national and social movements in disguise?', has most validity.[1] At the same time, it has yet to be stated how and why the story of Monophysitism differs from that of the Donatists.

The first mistake that historians usually make is to place the emergence of a schismatic monophysite Church immediately after the council of Chalcedon in 451. It is then asserted that this Church reflected the hatred of the Coptic and Syrian peasantry for their Byzantine overlords, and that this hostility made what to all intents and purposes was simply a difference over words impossible to settle.[2] A study of the available evidence suggests that this interpretation of events, even if it were related to the period immediately before the Arab invasions in the 630s is an over-simplification, and that the monophysite movement cannot be interpreted by the same categories that are valid for Donatism and its successors in the west.

The acceptance in the Chalcedonian definition of the Two-Nature formula (Christ was to be acknowledged 'in two natures inseparably

[1] *JTS*, new series x, 2 (1959) pp 280–98.
[2] For the 'nationalist' thesis as applied to Monophysitism see E. L. Woodward, *Christianity and Nationalism in the Later Roman Empire* (London 1916) ch II.

united') indeed caused a spontaneous outbreak of popular anger unparalleled in the history of the east Roman provinces.[1] Most Christians had come to accept the arguments of Cyril of Alexandria (died 444) and his turbulent successor Dioscorus (died 454) that in order to safeguard the full deity of Christ and his saving work for humanity, He must be confessed as being formed 'out of the two natures of God and Man, one incarnate nature', that of the Divine Logos assuming flesh from the Virgin. Chalcedon was regarded as a betrayal and violent hostility awaited many of the bishops who signed the definition on their return to their sees. In Egypt the presbyter Proterius who accepted consecration as patriarch in Dioscorus's stead was shunned and on Maundy Thursday 457 lynched by the Alexandrian mob, while in Palestine the powerful and ambitious Juvenal of Jerusalem had to flee for his life.[2] Despite the depth of hostility, however, no formal schism developed. No 'altar was set up against altar' in western style. Even in Egypt, the constant objective of the anti-Chalcedonian line of patriarchs was to get the emperor to renounce the Two-Nature christology and Chalcedon and make Cyril's theology in its entirety the theology of the empire as a whole. On the first point they had some success, for the letter which the emperor Zeno sent to the Egyptian clergy, monks and laity in July 482, known to history as the *Henotikon*, expressly declared that Christ must be acknowledged as 'one and not two', and that any other opinion expressed whether at Chalcedon or elsewhere was anathema.[3] On the other hand, no emperor could renounce Chalcedon as a whole, because the title deeds of the see of Constantinople accepting its ecclesiastical preeminence next to that of Old Rome rested on the 28th canon of the council. Leo's *Tome* might be expendable but not the council itself.

Hence the stalemate that developed between Alexandria and the other important sees of the east. For many years, however, there was no thought in Alexandria of establishing a separate Church in Egypt whose orthodoxy alone could be guaranteed, and even the idea that at any time during the fifth century the Monophysites represented the

---

[1] See, for instance, the catalogue of incidents recorded in John Rufus, *Plerophoria*, PO 8, 1 (1911) and in Michael the Syrian, [*Chronicle*], ed J. B. Chabot (Paris 1901) VIII, 11–12.

[2] Zacharius Rhetor, *HE*, ed E. W. Brooks, *CSCO*, Series III, *Syriaci Scriptores*, V–VI (1919–24) bk III, 3, p 107.

[3] For the text see E. Schwartz, 'Eine antichalkedonische Sammlung aus der Zeit Kaiser Zenos', *Abhandlung en der bayerischen Akademie der Wissenschaften*, Philologische-Historische Klasse, VI (Munich 1927) p 52. For an English translation and notes see R. M. Coleman Norton, *Roman Empire and Church* (London 1966) pp 924–33.

Heresy and schism as social and national movements

Copts while the Chalcedonians represented the Greeks in Egypt is fallacious. As far back as 346 when Athanasius had been welcomed home from exile by the Greek-speaking magistrates of Alexandria who went out 100 miles from the city to meet him (ten miles was a more normal mark of respect for a visiting dignitary) and joined hands with the Coptic monks from the deserts, the patriarch of Alexandria had been the leader of the Egyptian people as a whole. Athanasius and Donatus represented analogous situations in Egypt and North Africa. At the heart of the monophysite position as with the Donatist, lay loyalty to a theological tradition personified in a single great leader, Cyril on the one hand, Cyprian on the other.

Cyril had united Egypt around his doctrine and his personality. His successor Dioscorus, however, had endangered this unity through his abominable conduct against, among others, Cyril's relatives.[1] The Chalcedonian party that formed in Egypt after 451, while including imperial officials also numbered a considerable force of Pachomian monks and laity who considered that Dioscorus had deserved the condemnation passed on him at Chalcedon. Similarly, Alexandrians of all classes and monks accepted his monophysite successor, Timothy the Cat. Contemporary sources indicate that the rift between the parties divided families and not racial communities.[2] In 455 the emperor Marcian wrote to the prefect of Egypt, Palladius, to the effect that both Alexandria and the rest of Egypt was a prey to Apollinarian heresy.[3] This pattern was to persist until the sixth century at least. Indeed, only in the time of Heraclius do we find Coptic monks equating the fact of their being Egyptian with their opposition to the emperor's Chalcedonian creed.[4] Even in the Arab invasion one looks in vain for evidence of a Coptic rising against Byzantine landlords.

Another point. We have seen how separation of church from state was a cardinal point in Donatist and indeed all western schismatic thinking. Among the Monophysites, however, the opposite was true. For many, the One Nature of Christ implied also the unity of the Roman empire under one ruler who was God's vice-regent on earth. In a letter to the emperor Justin I, James of Saroug, one of the monophysite leaders, asked why the emperor wore a cross on his crown if he

[1] Outlined in the letter of the presbyter Athanasius to the council of Chalcedon, Mansi VI, col 1029.
[2] *Plerophoria*, LXI, no greetings exchanged in the streets between the families of rival allegiances.
[3] Text in *ACO*, II, ii, 2, pp 24–6.
[4] *History of the Patriarchs*, ed B. Evetts, PO I (1907) I, ch XIV, p 498.

did not believe in the unity of Christ and the unity of the empire.[1] Among the torrent of abuse which the Monophysites heaped upon the emperor Marcian for his furtherance of Chalcedon was that he had divided the empire just as the definition accepted by the council divided Christ and divided the Church.[2] Far from uttering defiance at the emperor and his representatives as Donatus of Carthage had done, the monophysite leaders lost no opportunity of asserting their loyalty to the emperor, while their chroniclers such as John of Ephesus seem to go out of the way to record the 'God-loving' character of the rulers. The Egyptian monks too, arrogant and rumbustuous though their spokesmen were, reserved any miraculous powers of destruction for the benefit of pagan landowners. They felt a sense of identity against the stranger, but until the seventh century this did not imply a national hostility towards the creed of the capital. Indeed, down to the time of Heraclius their relationship with the emperor and his officials was almost always one of mutual respect. Like their leaders in Alexandria their prime object was to secure the renunciation of Chalcedon by the emperor as the only means of preserving for humanity divine favour and ultimate salvation.

Against this background it is not easy to speak in terms of nationalism or social revolution when one considers the formation of the mono-physite kingdoms. The Byzantine Church always tended to the development of autocephalous patriarchates and metropolitans, and in Armenia, Nubia and Abyssinia these came early in course of time to be identified with a national religion which was Monophysitism. It took eighty years from the time of the council of Chalcedon before any move was made to establish an anti-Chalcedonian hierarchy in the empire, and then Severus of Antioch and his associates in exile at Alexandria acted with great reluctance. In 530 after ten years of persecution by Justin and Justinian the numbers of clergy loyal to them was waning. Their concern became the maintenance of an 'orthodox' hierarchy who could dispense the sacraments to the faithful. Any idea that they were serving the cause of permanent religious separation would have been laughed to scorn. At the same time, the great volume of public support, not only in Egypt and Syria but also in Asia Minor, to the mono-physite ideal made itself clear. 'Thousands', we are told, 'offered themselves for ordination'.[3] A new Church came into being despite itself.

---

[1] Cited from A. Vasiliev, *Justin the First* (Harvard 1950) p 234.
[2] Michael the Syrian, VIII, 14, p 122.
[3] See John of Ephesus, *Lives of the Eastern Saints; John of Tella*, ed E. W. Brooks, *PO* XVIII, 4 (1924) pp 518–19.

Heresy and schism as social and national movements

At this point, however, other factors contributing to the establishment of Monophysitism on a territorial basis began to assert themselves. From sources as disparate as Schenute of Atripe and Theodoret of Cyrrhus one gathers that in parts of Egypt and Syria social and economic conditions were as bad as they were in North Africa.[1] Taxation bore heavily on the cultivator, there were merciless landowners and degrading conditions were imposed on the debtor. These territories had, however, produced monks and not circumcellions, and by the latter half of the fifth century, fed by bequests and donations, as well as the fruits of their own husbandry, the monks were beginning to become a power economically as well as spiritually. In northern Syria it seems that the regime of the secular landowner often gave way to that of the monastery, and the same appears to have been happening in parts of Egypt.[2] The influence which the monks exerted on the villagers among whom they settled was thus consolidated. As the monks were in the vast majority anti-Chalcedonian, Monophysitism gradually began to take on a territorial aspect, which except in Egypt it had previously lacked. Even so, to speak of this development as one representing a native Syrian movement hostile to the continuance of imperial authority can hardly be sustained.

As one searches for the reasons for the differing attitudes of the eastern and western schismatics towards the Roman empire two factors suggest themselves. The first concerns public relations and the second theology. Anyone looking at the history of the Roman empire in the fourth and fifth centuries must be impressed by the enormous difference in approach which marked the relations between the emperor and his subjects, especially his christian subjects in the two halves of the empire. Constantine's embrace at the council of Nicaea of the confessor, Paphnutius, cruelly maimed in the great persecution, was a masterpiece of tact, and ensured that hatred of the slayers of the martyrs among the Copts was confined strictly to his pagan predecessors.[3] Sixty years later, in 387, Theodosius I was prepared to lend a kindly ear to the solicitations of Macedonius, the Barley-eater, and spare the city of Antioch whose punishment he had intended.[4] No such mercy was granted to Thessalonica four years later. Ambrose could only excommunicate the emperor when the deed was done. Indeed the

---

[1] Besa, *Life of Schenute*, ed J. Leipoldt, *CSCO*, Series II, *Scriptores Coptici*, II; IV, 3; V, 4 (1906–13) latin translation H. Wiesmann (1931–6) LXXXI. Theoderet, *Letters*, ed Y. Azéma, *SC* XL, XCVIII, CXI (1955–65) no 42.
[2] G. Tchalenko, *Villages, antiques de la Syrie du Nord* (Paris/Beyrouth 1953) I, p 178.
[3] Socrates, *HE*, I, 11   [4] Theodoret, *HE*, v, 20

monks formed an essential link in a chain of relationships which brought the emperor into direct touch with his eastern subjects, and the reward was their loyalty against Hun and Persian alike.

The mutual respect of emperor and monks might not have been so deep-seated if the east had shared the theological assumptions of the west. Ever since Justin Martyr and Melito of Sardes had stressed the harmony of church and empire theologians had striven to provide this concept with divine sanction. As in so much else in Greek theology, Platonism contributed largely to the answer. All the world was ultimately God's world, the Church and its liturgy was a reflection of the celestial hierarchy and its service to God. Through the right training of body and mind individuals moved along the road towards communion with God. The monks were the true philosophers challenging the demons, confronting the forces of unreason and obstruction to human progress towards God with their feats of asceticism and prayer. To the emperor was due the obedience of all humanity, not merely because this was commanded in scripture but because the emperor reflected the image of Christ and controlled all the affairs, civil and ecclesiastical of the civilised world.[1] Judgement and divine anger that played so great a part in western theology received less consideration. Original sin was conceived as loss of the image of God to be made good by human effort, not as a fatal disease passed down from Adam to his descendants. There was no opposition of interest between emperor and his subjects, and no 'two swords' relationship with the Church. However bitter the christological debate, none would deny that the emperor as well as his theological opponents belonged to the same christian *oikoumene*. 'Long live the emperor', 'Long live the Roman empire', echoing in the streets of monophysite Edessa in 449,[2] was not a cry often heard in the west.

The contrast with the Latins remained in this and other respects. The Greek Christians could never understand why the Latins insisted that the definition of Chalcedon and the council's canons (except the 28th, which they refused to accept) were not subject to the slightest modification or negotiation, whereas they took their own stand on Nicaea alone. The definition of Chalcedon was a valuable bulwark against Nestorian or Eutychian heresy, but the only symbol of faith which they recognised was that of Nicaea supplemented by Constan-

---

[1] Thus Eusebius, Tricennial Oration I, 6; see N. H. Baynes, 'The Byzantine State', in *Byzantine Studies and Other Essays* (London 1955) pp 53–8.
[2] Ed J. Flemming, *Nachrichten der Gesellschaft der Wissenschaften zu Göttingen*, new series xv (1917) p 33.

Heresy and schism as social and national movements

tinople in 381 and confirmed at the first council of Ephesus. What to Rome was simply the assertion of the paternal care of all churches entrusted by Christ to Peter and his heirs was to the Greek churches innovation and arrogance: for them the Church was governed by autocephalous patriarchs, with the emperor as descendant of Constantine, the 'friend of God' and 'thirteenth apostle' speaking for them all. Between these views nothing that happened in the next thousand years succeeded in providing a compromise. When at Florence in 1439 the theological arguments between the two sides appeared to be settled, the people of Constantinople remembered as they had after the council of Lyons in 1274 the successive humiliations they had received at the hands of the Latins, and even with the Turk at their gates preferred the turban to the mitre as ruler of New Rome.

The question therefore how far schisms in the early Church may be regarded as reflections of social and political dissent may be answered more positively than sometimes has been the case. The religious issue indeed is always primary. The Donatists would not have existed without Cyprian any more than the Monophysites would without Cyril, but in both cases the teaching represented by these leaders struck a responsive chord among the humbler Christians who had no training or interest in the subtleties of ecclesiastical debate. In the West, however, the links between the Donatists and the aspirations of the poor and downtrodden are clearer cut and easier to understand than in the case of the Monophysites. They put into a practical form the hopes that Christianity involved some sort of great revolution and reversal of roles that one finds in the verses of the poet Commodian. Moreover, as one follows their legacy through the Middle Ages to better documented periods nearer our own day, the association of biblical-inspired religion and political nonconformity becomes more evident. In western Europe anabaptist-inspired peasants in Germany, Covenanters in Highland crofts, and first-generation Methodists in northern industrial towns continue to represent similar patterns of thought and action. In the East, however, such equations are less easy to establish. There, the ideal was of the christian *oikoumene* guided by the emperor, and of the individual's communion with God. Both aspirations led to a more optimistic and universalist view of human salvation which blurred the edges of religious controversy and delayed the formation of separatist religious communities along hard and fast lines. At no time before the Arab invasions did the monophysite leaders abandon hope of ultimate reunion with the emperor's Church. Only as decade succeeded decade and no formula could be found which would vindicate both Cyril and the Chalcedonian definition did the mono-physite churches consolidate into national and regional areas. In addition, in Armenia, Syria, Nubia and Abyssinia, Monophysitism came to reflect national consciousness through a vernacular liturgy and script that no other force has since been able to achieve. Like the Byzantines themselves they conceived national independence in terms of religious allegiance. Such are some of the factors that have moved humanity through the ages down almost to our own day. It has been said not untruly that the real history of man is the history of religion. Throughout the period we have been dealing with, religion was what made men 'tick'. Those who would seek to unify the Churches will have little success if they fail to realise the strength of this legacy from a time when religion included man's experience in its entirety.

XXV

LIBERTY AND UNITY

THE QUESTION YOU HAVE ASKED ME to discuss is both timely and important. Quite suddenly, within a single generation the world has become a very small and crowded place. Many of of us can remember when flights from London to Johannesburg or to Darwin were hazardous affairs, and when a journey to the Cape would be measured in weeks rather than days. Now all this has changed, and the social, religious and political implications of the Jet-age are enormous. It is not merely the fact that London to Johannesburg is now an overnight journey, or that one can comfortably give one lecture in a course at Cambridge on a Monday and the next at Grahamstown 6000 miles distant on the Wednesday, but a completely new perspective is being given to a whole range of human relationships. It is not possible for communities to remain self-sufficient in their own separate territories and thought-world. Oceans and deserts no longer divide and what happens in one part of the world is known within seconds everywhere else. Problems therefore, which might have been left to work themselves out over decades now demand a solution within months. Mankind is not faced with a dream of future unification, but with the fact of unity. The only question is the form that unity will take.

The Christian Church cannot stand aside from these universal trends. The irrelevance of many of the differences that divide group from group have become increasingly clear. The pressure among Christians for an outward expression of their hope of unity has become a major factor in the world to-day. If I plead for forethought and caution it is not because I am an admirer of the court of King Canute, but because I believe it essential to be clear why religious divisions exist before one tries to decide what the general direction of Christian unity should be. Are we to think of Christian division as heresies, and schisms the result of human misunderstanding, blindness and sin, or do we regard them in a positive light as the expression of far-reaching social, economic and cultural distinctions, the stuff of human existence, which claim our respect to-day ? Do we speak of "heresy" or of "religious tradition" ?

My predecessor in these lectures, Professor Owen Chadwick, made the point how divisions between Churches could be perpetuated by apparently trivial incidents. These, however, had come to symbolise deep human emotions which no neat formulas could bridge. He mentioned the events which took place in Constantinople in 1054, in which the highlight was the act of the Papal legate in pinning a formula of excommunication on the back of the Patriarch of Constantinople as he processed under the great dome of Ayia Sophia. He explained how in recent conversations between Anglicans and Orthodox held in Moscow, Orthodox rejection of the *filioque* was still a question not so much of reasoned dogma but of passionately held conviction. This attitude still symbolised the independence of the Russian Orthodox Church and summed up the great historical divide between Eastern and Western Christendom.

This evening I want to probe further along the same line of inquiry, and see what historical factors lie behind the division between East and West, and between some aspects of the divisions within Western Christendom. An understanding of the origins of these movements may give us some insights into their situation to-day. To draw attention to a passage in Rev. Professor P. B. Hinchliff's inaugural lecture in this University in 1960, "the theologians have come to realise that a resolution of doctrinal differences cannot be achieved without a study of the historical origins of those differences." [1] In one of his famous lectures before the Berlin Academy just prior to the outbreak of the First World War, [2] Adolf von Harnack pointed out how it was no accident that a European crisis had arisen over Bosnia and Herzegovina, nor that the Italians were disputing with the Serbs and Montenegrins for control of Albania. The collapse of the Turkish Empire had opened the way for two great conflicts of interest in the Balkans: first, that between Slav and non-Slav, whether German or Italian, but secondly and even more important, between the adherents of the Greek Orthodox and the Latin Churches.

The age-old boundary between the Greek and Latin worlds and between the Greek and Latin communions had passed through the province of Bosnia. This had been in Roman and Byzantine times a cultural, religious and linguistic frontier; Eastern Illyrium had been debatable land between the Eastern and Western empires in the fifth century; it had re-emerged in a similar rôle in Harnack's own day. It was on this frontier that the First World War opened a few days more than 50 years ago.

The detailed comparison which Harnack went on to make between the Greek and Latin forms of Christianity, between Greek Christian-Platonism and Latin legalism and the ramifications in art, liturgy and architecture does not concern us here. Important however, to him as for us, was that the Balkans provided a classic example of age-long interaction of religion and culture, and that behind seemingly pedantic differences of rite and belief lay profound historical traditions.

Let us look at these historical traditions a little more carefully. We think of 1054 as marking the final breach between Greek Orthodoxy and Rome. It is a valuable symbolic date, though perhaps it might be argued that the final barriers between the two communions were not set up before the sack of Constantinople by the Latins in 1204. But the die had been cast centuries previously, and a Church historian might be forgiven if he points to the Council of Serdica in 343 as the decisive moment in the lives of the Eastern and Western Churches.

What had been happening? The Creed of Nicaea with its statement that Jesus Christ was "of one substance with the Father" had been accepted in 325 only with reluctance by the great majority of the bishops of the Eastern provinces of the Roman Empire. It had in fact been imposed by Constantine, and was obeyed as the order of the Emperor. They believed that the assertion was unScriptural and opened the way to both Judaism and the heretical religion of the Manichees. In their view, God the Father transcended all things, including the Son, and He only was not subject to any form of generation, origin or change. The Son, though God's agent of creation and the exact image of God through whom man might recapture his own lost image of God and be saved, was in some sense distinct from and subordinate to God, and therefore not of the same essence as He. Athanasius of Alexandria and his Western supporters, however, believed that salvation consisted more of salvation from physical torment hereafter rather than of the soul moving positively towards communion with God. They therefore stressed that for man to be saved from the consequences of his sin the full essence of God must have been present in Jesus Christ and in His Eucharist. Thus, Christ must be "of one substance with the Father". In the West too, there was a tendency actually to identify God the Father and God the Son without specifying essential distinctions between them.

Already one can see that behind the single letter involved in the difference between the Nicene *homoousios* (of the same substance) and the Eastern *homoiousios* (of like substance) lay considerable differences of belief in particular, differences in eschatology.

But this was not all. From the start, religious and political divergencies were connected. In the twelve years between the Council of Nicaea and the death of Constantine in 337, the Eastern bishops gradually regained the ground they had lost at the Council itself. On one pretext or another, their major opponents had been silenced, removed from their bishoprics and sent into exile by the Imperial court. Even Athanasius had been banished. Then, on 22nd May 337 Constantine had died, and there was a reaction. In the ensuing division of the Empire Constantine's elder sons who were pro-Nicene took over the West. This gave the West seniority over the East where Constantius II the youngest of the three brothers was anti-Nicene. At the same time, Athanasius' presence in the West even though as an exile transformed support for his cause there from something nominal to one to which the West was from now on dedicated.

The council of Serdica was convened in 343 to break the deadlock. It was a complete fiasco. The site, modern Sofia, was just inside the Western half of the Empire, and the Westerns led by Constantine's old adviser, Hosius of Cordoba had a majority of 97 bishops to the Easterners' 76. This was enough for the western Bishops to rule that Athanasius should be re-admitted forthwith to communion and his main accusers excommunicated in their turn. At this, the Eastern clergy set a precedent for other dissident minorities. They walked out, and held a rival synod at Philippopolis over the frontier in the Eastern half of the Empire. Each side anathematised the other and though divisions were often apparently patched up the ecclesiastical historian Socrates, writing in Constantinople a century later summed up the situation : "From that time therefore, the Western church was severed from the Eastern, and the boundary of communion between the two was the mountain called Soucis which divides the Illyrians from the Thracians." (*Eccl. Hist.*, ii, 22).

The geographical factor in the division of the churches on what appears on the surface to be a matter purely of metaphysics was plain enough to contemporaries. What did this involve ? First, of course, were the misunderstandings caused by language barriers. By the early part of the fourth century, the Roman Empire had fallen into its Greek and Latin halves, with the language boundary running through the Balkans in exactly the way Harnack had described, and with little cultural contact between the two halves. A Greek-speaking bishop in the West, like St. Augustine's predecessor Valerius, in Hippo Regius in North Africa was an obvious misfit who had little contact with his flock. Augustine's own dislike of the Greek classics is well known ("Not one word did I understand", says he of Homer).[3] On the whole, Greek representatives in the West, such as Syrian merchants were useful but unpopular. Thus, Salvian of Marseille writing in 440 asks, "Is the life of the Syrian merchants who have seized the greater part of all our towns anything else but plotting, trickery and falsehood ?"[4] Augustine comments that one might as well look for a crow in Achaea as Greek-speakers in North Africa.[5] The two halves of the Roman Empire corresponded to political and cultural realities.

Moreover, this isolation affected mutual understanding between the theologians. Thus while the Westerners were devoted to the Creed of Nicaea, few of them had read it. Hilary of Poitiers one of the Western leaders, for instance, a man who regarded the emperor Constantius II as a persecutor in direct line of descent from Nero and Diocletian confessed that he never read that document until he was enjoying the enforced leisure of a comfortable exile in Phrygia in 357.[6] He was nonetheless determined to resist the imposition of an eastern religious formula on the West, just as the easterners had resisted a western formula only fourteen years before.

Language, however, was not the only barrier in preventing agreement between East and West. Two other factors are worth noting. First, in the two halves of the Empire Roman power stood for quite different things. In the east the Roman

Empire was the direct heir to the former Hellenistic Kingdoms, where the concept of the monarchy as in some way or other the reflection of a Divine Monarchy from whom flowed all creative activity, was deeply rooted in the popular consciousness. Constantine was in a large measure the successor of the Seleucid and Ptolemaic kings. Thus his own claim to be "bishop" [7] and that made on his behalf, that "in direct imitation of his (divine) superior he directs the helm of all the affairs of the world",[8] were both intelligible and acceptable to the great mass of Eastern Christians and their leaders. What came to be called in the West "Caesaro-Papism" was not the dream of a megalomaniac but the way in which ordinary people had always regarded the relationship of their ruler to God. The Eastern, or Semi-Arian creed gave theological expression to this political ideal. The second factor was equally deep-rooted in the way of thought of the East, and like the status of the Christian emperor, originated in the pre-Christian period. In contrast to their Palestinian contemporaries the Jews dispersed among the Greek cities of the Roman-Hellenistic world spoke, wrote, and thought in Greek. Though they believed that the law of Moses was the perfect philosophy they were sufficiently realistic to respect the philosophy of their contemporaries and to accept that it too was the product of the Divine Wisdom. It needed, however, completing and purifying by the law. The conflict then between Hellenistic Judaism and Greek philosophy could never be absolute, and when Christianity took over the mantle of Judaism in the East, its representatives maintained the same tradition.

In the third century A. D. Clement and Origen of Alexandria were maintaining the value of reason and Greek philosophy as adjuncts towards understanding the Bible, and were upholding a basically optimistic view of human progress and the aspiration of unity between Church and Empire. Just as the world had been federated into a single whole by Augustus at the very time of Jesus' birth, so the next great step forward for humanity would be its government by a monarch truly devoted to God, namely a Christian emperor.[9] No wonder the conversion of Constantine caused an outburst of joy in Eastern Christendom. Eusebius' tenth book of his *Ecclesiastical history*, written after Constantine's defeat of Licinius, is one tremendous hymn of praise and confidence in the future. Moreover, on the level of individual salvation, this optimism

was translated into belief in a gradual advance towards knowledge of, and communion of the soul with God. Jesus Christ
was portrayed as the guide, teacher and healer of mankind
manifesting the fullness of God's image on earth.[10] Those
aspects of Biblical teaching connected with witness, confession, and martyrdom, to which Western Christians gave so
large a place and attributed to the power of the Holy Spirit,
fell into the background compared with the ideal of gradual
education and perfection of the rational soul. Eastern theology
tended to be Binitarian, that is, the theology of God and His
Divine Word, while Western theology was Trinitarian. The
Easterner placed little if any emphasis on physical judgement,
material hell, or ultimate damnation. In the last resort, most
clergy and educated Christians would have agreed with Origen's view that all would ultimately be saved, and God once
more would be all in all.[11]

So we see that the Easterners came to Serdica to defend, not
a single letter in a metaphysical formula, but a theology based
on religious and cultural traditions whose origins could be
found before the Christian era itself. All the facts of human
life, geography, politics, language and culture combined to
forge the distinctive Eastern Orthodox tradition.

When one turns to their Western opponents one finds
theology equally firmly based on non-theological factors. That
the West lacked a Plato, or a Jewish philosopher such as Philo
of Alexandria to interpret him, need hardly be stressed. Neither
Rome nor Carthage produced an equivalent of the Christian
Platonists of Alexandria. In addition, however, the Roman
Empire in the West fulfilled an entirely different function
from its role in the East. The provinces of the Western Empire
were conquered provinces, either "barbarous tribes" as
Irenaeus of Lyons described the Gauls whom he sought to
evangelise, or the hostile Semitic culture of Carthage which
Rome had overthrown by force of arms. Roman civilization
was not the continuation of a deep-rooted past, but the imposition of a new and not always welcome Latin way of life. To
some extent then, Christianity was accepted as a religion of
protest against the Roman emperor and his servants. It is
perhaps no accident that the first wave of religious conversion
in Carthage coincided wth a determined effort by the Roman
authorities towards the end of the 2nd century A.D. to
humanise and romanise traditional Carthaginian religion.[12]

11

Moreover, for reasons which are not entirely clear, Christianity in Rome and North Africa seem to have been influenced, not by Hellenistic Judaism, but by the Judaism of Palestine and the non-Greek world. As the Dead Sea Scrolls show, this was an uncompromising, apocalyptic outlook in which the world of humanism, philosophy and the Greco-Roman state were condemned to utter destruction in one vast majestic or brutal Armageddon holocaust. This was the tradition which the early Fathers of the West such as Hermas, Hippolytus of Rome and Tertullian of Carthage were to continue. It was a theology which portrayed Christianity in terms of God's elect, as a gathered community inspired by the Holy Spirit to witness against the world, to defy the pagan authorities and their false worship, and to aspire to the martyr's crown.[13] This alone washed away the guilt of sins committed after baptism and assured the Christian the bliss of material paradise hereafter. Christ was not educator and healer but judge. The Christian hope was not immortality of the soul but resurrection of the body. The pagan world, far from being gradually purified and educated to higher things was unreservedly condemned. The persecutions of the Roman emperors were a continuance of the persecution of the saints told in the Old and New Testaments. In this thought-world the conversion of Constantine was merely the Devil using guile instead of open warfare against the Christian Elect.[14] Grace and predestination determined who belonged to this community, and the Holy Spirit rather than the Divine Word was the inspirer of Christian life and conduct. No wonder Eastern and Western theologians failed to agree at Serdica. The wonder is that they ever reached the council chamber at all.

The broad picture is then of Eastern and Western Christianity dividing along geographical and cultural lines in the fourth century, never again effectively to re-unite. To prevent existing hopes of ultimate unity and uniformity between the two halves of Christendom soaring too high, it is worth remembering that in 1439 Greek and Latin theologians attending the Council of Florence, did agree on formulae of reunion, only for the Greeks to find themselves repudiated by their congregations on their return home.[15] If one reads "Communist menace" for "Turkish menace", and Pope Paul VI for Eugenius IV one could set the stage for a similar failure to-day.

When we consider the divisions within the Latin Church

and the influence of history and culture upon them we are on more familiar ground. The Rhine-Main line in Germany which in 1648 divided Protestants from Catholics, or the more local division between Presbytery in Scotland and Episcopacy in England which emerged a little later are examples of this situation in the Reformation period. The Latin world of post-1789 is a world of Catholicism or anti-clerical revolution which remains, along with the racial issue one of the latent explosive situations in the world to-day. We should be warned by the Spanish Civil War. But once again, it is useful to go back to the origins of the two different types of theory concerning the nature of the Church for light on the real factors which contribute to their continuance to-day. Tertullian's "Church of the spiritual man" contrasted with "Church of the number of bishops" remains one of the great divides in Western Christianity.[16]

I don't intend to repeat here what I have already written about the North African Church and the Donatist Controversy.[17] In the Donatist movement of the fourth and early fifth centuries A.D., one is confronted with the clearest example of how religious, social, and geographical factors can combine to produce an explosion of regional religious sentiment. In the outbreak of the Donatist controversy in 312 we find the same combination of trivial pretexts and clashes of personalities with deep underlying theological and social differences that existed in the early stages of Arian controversy in the East. For more than a century North African Christianity had harboured its puritan and less-puritan wings and kept them together through successive crises. Tertullian's controversy with Callistus of Rome on the right of the Church to forgive grievous sinners, Cyprian's dispute with Stephen over Rebaptism in 255–56 are milestones along that road. Rome and Carthage were on different sides ecclesiastically as they had been centuries before politically. Then, under the shock of the Great Persecution of 303–305 the cracks could no longer be papered over. Underlying, however, contrasting views on the subject of the nature of the Church, the role of the prophet and martyr as against that of the cleric, and the meaning of the sacrament of baptism, two different ways of life confronted each other representing two distinct geographical areas. If one looks at a map of Roman North Africa one is struck by the contrasts between the provinces of Proconsular Africa and Numidia, corresponding very roughly to modern Tunisia and Algeria. The one lay open to European influences, had abundant rainfall and was the granary of Rome. It was the site of a great number of latinised cities and of a true Romano-African culture whose language had some points in common with the Latin spoken in Spain. Numidia, on the other hand, was a harsh, dry, salty high plain on an average 2500 ft. above sea level, enclosed by mountains to the north and south. Its main product was olive oil, a crop ideally suited to semi-desert conditions; its people lived in small communities rather than in cities. They were tenaciously conservative in their language, dress and customs; the greatness of the Latin Church meant to them not so much its expansion along the length and breadth of the civilised world, as the size and grandeur of their local cathedrals. A distribution map of known orthodox and Donatist sees and inscriptions leaves no doubt that here too, the geographical boundary between the two Roman provinces was also the boundary between the predominance of the two African Christian communions.

There was an additional factor that made the schism unbridgeable. As I said, in the West adoption of Christianity was often a symbol of protest. In the last part of the third century the Mediterranean world was stricken by a combination of ills due to incessant wars on the frontiers, the expansion of the imperial administrative machine, and the collapse of urban economics due to massive inflation of the currency. Much of the additional burden fell on the peasants, and the North African peasant replied in a startling manner. The old gods whom he had worshipped for thousands of years had deserted him. He would desert them. Within a generation Numidia had become Christian, but it was a Christianity dominated by apocalyptic in which the Roman authorities played the part of the Satanic powers.[18] Gradually, however, the struggle against the authorities became extended to a struggle against the great landowners.[19] The Donatist Church was the first and only Church in the ancient world which was prepared to challenge the established social and economic order in the name of social justice. The peasant uprisings of the African Circumcellions foreshadow the similar peasant risings of the Peasants' Revolt in England in 1381 and the Peasants' War in Germany in 1523, both cases where religious and social aspirations are inseparably interwoven. For Augustine these Donatist extremists provided a striking example of the equation of human free-will and human corruption, for the social order which the Catholic Church represented was the "ordo naturalis" decreed by God.

So, in 422 he writes, "Among the Donatists herds of abandoned men were disturbing the peace of the innocent for one reason or another in the spirit of the most reckless madness. What master was not compelled to live in dread of his own servant if he had put himself under the guardianship of the Donatists? Who dared even threaten one who had sought his own with punishment? Who dared to exact payment of a debt from one who had consumed his stores or from any debtor whatsoever that sought their assistance and protection? Under the threat of beating and burning all documents compromising the worst of slaves were destroyed, that they might depart in freedom."

And there is much more, Augustine paints a picture of religious fanaticism and terrorism with which we are all familiar to-day. Once more, adherence to two types of Church government concealed a whole range of contrasting social and cultural ideals founded on distinct geographical conditions.

The fact of theological differences coinciding with geographical divisions in one part of Africa brings us to the situation in this part of the continent in the last fifty years. Isolation has been the curse of all southern Africa. The gradual drying-up of the Sahara associated with the movement of atmospheric depressions northward, condemned a considerable portion of the human race to wander about in one part of a continent in unhealthy and inhospitable climatic conditions. The resulting backwardness of the African has made him a difficult neighbour for the European settler. Added to this fact, has been the isolation of South Africa, which during an entire half century from 1900–1950 lay off the main sea and air routes alike. This has meant that intellectual and religious tendencies which might have been overlaid by the bold and optimistic provisions of the Union in 1910 have for the time being been thwarted. The religion of the Transvaal has tended to become more Calvinist and isolationist than the reverse, while its wealth has swung the political balance away from the Cape in its favour. When on 16 December 1903, Ds. J. D. du Toit claimed that the religious strength of the Afrikanerdom and its power as a cause lay in "the isolation of our principle", few people took

15

much notice.[21] But there on the High Veld was being born a Donatism in embryo, with the mystique of a chosen people and an apocalyptic view of its destiny and history. Cape and Transvaal have reproduced in our own age something of the religious situation of fourth-century North Africa.

From the three situations which we have been discussing it is obvious that religious divisions are very often the outward expression of strong non-theological divisions separating community from community. Since the Resurrection the Christian Church has seldom been organically united. The contrasts between Greek-speaking and Aramaic Christianity in the first century were followed by those between prophetic and ecclesiastical in the second century, and between Latin and Greek in the third. The Wars of Religion should show the futility of attempting to impose a uniform religious obedience on mankind. And even on the less ambitious plane, in considering questions such as episcopacy versus presbytery, celibate versus married clergy, or Biblical versus ecclesiastical authority, it is doubtful whether solutions can be reached through text and precedent alone. Differences of rite and tradition have always stood for cultural and political identities. Quite rightly, the Thirty-Nine Articles may be regarded as an English declaration of independence against both Rome and Geneva in the context of Reformation and Counter-Reformation, as well as a formulation of precise statements of theological belief. Similarly, the Savoy conference of 1604 and the Synod of Dort in 1619 are great political as well as ecclesiastical landmarks.

On the other hand, out of the torment and agony of the last fifty years has sprung the unification of mankind. Nothing can alter that, for in this case an ideal born of common suffering is sustained by the revolutionising of communications by the Telstar and the Jet-age. Arguments which favour separate development in matters of Church and State might have been relevant even in the age of Franz Josef (1848–1916), but they do not seem to provide an answer to our problems to-day.[22]

If, however, we reject uniformity as an aim which has been tried and found wanting, and separate development as an impossibility, we must face the implications of unity in diversity. How large is the multitude of sins that charity can cover ? Can a World Council of Churches which contains Greek Orthodox and Chilean Pentecostalists be made to signify anything ? This sort of syncretism has failed in the past; are the prospects more favourable to-day ? We trust so, for we are only beginning to explore and to use the rich varieties of human experience and consider them as tradition rather than aberration from an organic Truth. "In my Father's house are many abiding-places". The great mystery cannot be approached by one road only. What the pagan leader, Quintus Aurelius Symmachus stated in the Altar of Victory controversy with St. Ambrose in 384, remains true to-day.[23]

We must therefore accept the fact of our differences. We must recognise that the whole people of God, clergy and laity, black and white have their own parts to play in building Christ's kingdom on earth – that is in the dimension which we can deal with now. No Church or institution on earth is perfect and none can do without the fellowship of others. Thus, Cardinal Suenens, the Roman Catholic Primate of Belgium, put the matter on 5 May 1964 "We must never identify the Universal Church with the Latin Church". The whole Church was on a journey. "She has not yet come to realise her full nature as a Church".[24] This is a welcome admission opening up possibilities of understanding and cooperation between the Latin Church and the rest of Christendom. Meantime, we must be true to our own traditions, we must aim at fellowship between our Churches, not seeking to absorb one Church into another, nor striving to convert individuals by taking advantage of their fears or their idealism. We must avoid exaggerations of dogma and Church law, we must oppose restrictions on religious liberty and conflicts in the mission field. We must tackle fearlessly those areas where conflict and latent bitterness lie deepest, in mixed marriages and denominational education. We must say without fear or favour where each of us stands. Let us remember that much of our destiny lies in our own hands and our own wills. "God does not give eternal life", wrote Origen, "He sets it before us. 'Behold I have set life before thy face' (Deut. 30 : 15). It is in our power to stretch out our hand, to do good works, and to lay hold on life and deposit it in our soul. This life is the Christ who said: 'I am the life' (John 11 : 25."[25] What was true in the 230s is equally true to-day.

REFERENCES

[1] P. B. Hinchliff, *Ecclesiastical History, its Nature and Purpose*, Grahamstown, Rhodes University, 1960, p. 22.

[2] A. von Harnack, "Der Geist der morgenländischen Kirche", *Sitzungsberichte der Kgl. Preussischen Akademie der Wissenschaften zu Berlin*, 1913.

[3] *Confessions*, 1.13.20, "But why did I hate so much the Greek which I studied as a boy ? For the Latin I loved".

[4] Salvian, *On the Government of God*, iv. 14.

[5] Augustine, *Letter* 118.9 (ed. A. Goldbacher, p. 674): "Facilius quippe corniculas in Africa audieris quam in illis partibus hoc genus vocis" (i.e. Greek).

[6] Hilary, *De Synodis*, 91.

[7] Socrates, *Hist. Eccl.*, 1.9

[8] Eusebius, *Tricennial Oration*, 1.6

[9] Origen, *Contra Celsum*, ii.30

[10] For instance, Origen, *Contra Celsum*, ii.24

[11] Origen, *De Principiis*, 1.6.3

[12] See the excellent article by G. Charles-Picard, "Pertinax et les prophètes de Caelestis". *Revue de l'Histoire des Religions*, 155, 1959, p.41–62.

[13] See for instance Tertullian's definition of Christian society in his *Apology*, 39.1.–6, his assertion of the duty and blessings of martyrdom, *ibid.* 50.14–16, his panorama of the "Day of Judgement', *De Spectaculis*, 30, and his encouragement of instransigence in the face of authorities, *To Scapula*, 5.

[14] The view expressed by a pamphleteer writing about A.D. 320, whose work has survived in the *Passio Donati*, (Migne, *Patrologia Latina*, 8, 752.

[15] See J. Gill, *The Council of Florence*, Cambridge 1959, ch. 10. The Chronicler Ducas' comment, "We have sold our faith", was typical. (Ducas, *Historia Byzantina*, ed. Bekker, 1834, p. 216).

[16] Tertullian, *On Chastity*, ch. 22.

[17] W. H. C. Frend, *The Donatist Church, a Movement of Protest in Roman North Africa*, Oxford, 1952.

[18] See my article, "The Failure of the Persecutions", *Past and Present*, 16, 1959, p. 10–30.

[19] See Optatus of Mileuis' account of the early days of the Circumcellion movement *circa* 340, *De Schismate Donatistarum*, iii. 4.

[20] Augustine, *Letter* 185.4.15.

[21] Cited from L.M. Thompson, *Unification of South Africa*, 1902–1910, Oxford, 1960, p. 18.

[22] The last great Indian reserve in the United States, that comprising a large part of the State of Oklahoma, was created in 1907.

[23] Symmachus, *Relatio* 3. See T. R. Glover, Life and Letters in the *Fourth Century*, Cambridge, 1901, p. 154.

[24] As reported in *Grocott's Daily Mail*, Grahamstown, 6th May 1964.

[25] Origen, Dialogue with Heraclides, in *Alexandrian Christianity*, ed. by J.E.L. Oulton and H. Chadwick, p. 454 (Library of Christian Classics, vol. 2).

INDEX

Abdallah Nirqi: XXI 325

Abel: X 16;XXIV 45

Abraham: III 139,142,143

Abram, hermit: VIII 15

Acacius, Patriarch of
Constantinople: XVIII 19;
XX 17,19-20

Acacian Schism: XIX 263,269;
XXII 19-20,22

Acta Martyrum: VI 141;IX 21;X 16

Acts of the Pagan Martyrs: I 147

Adam: IX 20,21,23;XXIV 48

Adamites: XXIV 48

Adams, W.Y.: XXIII 219

Adimantius, Manichee: XII 20

Aelianus, Proconsul of Africa:
V 346

Aelius Aristides, Philosopher:
II 34

Afrikanerdom: XXV 15-16

Agapetus, Pope: XVIII 21

Ain Zoui: XI 491

Akiba, Rabbi: I 143,155;III 141

Alaric: XV 114,127

Alexander, Bishop of Alexandria:
XVI 30

Alexander Severus, emperor:
II 27;V 347-351

Alexander, Bishop of Jerusalem:
V 337

Alexander of Lycopolis: XII 18

Alexandria: II 31;III 133,147;
V 334,336,341;VI 142;VII 309;
VIII 11,23;X 18;XVI 21-22,36;
XVII 19,21,23;XVIII 16;
XIX 264,265;XX 23;XXI 320;
XXIII 218;XXIV 50-52;
Judaism in: XVI 25;
"city of the orthodox":
XX 16-17

Algeria: XXIII 212-214

Alwah, Nubian kingdom:
XXI 320-321,326;XXIII 210

Alvarez, Portuguese explorer
and missionary:
XXI 326;XXIII 220-221

Alypius, friend of Augustine:
XII 22,24;XIII 865;XIV 190;
XV 103,112,115,119

Amanda, friend of Paulinus:
XV 114,117

Amandus, presbyter: XV 103,104,
106,109

Amandus, missionary: VIII 20

Ambrose, Bishop of Milan:
VIII 13;XV 100-101,106,113,124;
XVI 20;XVIII 7,16;XX 15

Ambrosiaster, Christian author:
X 12

Amelekites: III 138,143

Anastasius, emperor: XVIII 8,20;
XIX 266,269;XXII 16,18-19,20

Anastasius, Pope: XV 121

Anatolia: XXIII 214-217

Annius Anulinus, Proconsul
of Africa: VI 142

Anthimus, Patriarch of
Constantinople: XVIII 21;
XIX 274;XX 23

Anti-Christ: XVI 34-35;XVIII 42;
XXIV 45

Anti-Encyclical: XVIII 19

Antioch: I 145;III 147;V 337,
342-343;VIII 4,15;XVII 21,
27-28;XVIII 5,13,16;XIX 266,
268,270;XX 11,24

Antiochus IV, Seleucid ruler:
I 143;IX 21,23;X 16,19

Antipas, martyr: II 28

Antony, monk: XVI 26-27,32,37;
XVIII 10-11

Aper, friend of Paulinus:
XV 103,114,126

Apologists: III 129ff.

Apollo: XVI 22;XVII 27

Apollinaris of Laodicea: XV 114;
XVI 36;XVII 22,27;XXIV 51

Apollonius, martyr: V 335

Apollonius of Tyana: VII 308

Aquileia: VIII 7

Arabs: XVIII 13;XXIII 219-221

Arcadius, emperor: XVIII 7

Ariminum, Council of: XVI 35-36

Aristeas, Letter of: III 140

Aristides, Apologist: II 34

Arius, Arianism: VIII 12-13;X 18;
XIII 859;XV 112;XVI 23,28,30;
XVII 20;XVIII 18

Arles, Councils of: VI 142;X 20

Armenia: XIX 273;XX 16;
XXII 225;XXIII 214

Armorica: XVIII 19

Arnobius, Christian writer:
XII 14,19,20

Arrius Antoninus, Proconsul
of Asia: II 33

Arsenius, Bishop: XVI 24,32

Asclepiades, Bishop of Antioch: V 337

DATE DUE

JUN 2 '78			
DEC 31 '78			
GAYLORD			PRINTED IN U.S.A.